LECTURES ON
RUSSIAN LITERATURE

It is difficult to refrain from the relief of irony, from the luxury of contempt, when surveying the mess that meek hands, obedient tentacles guided by the bloated octopus of the state, have managed to make out of that fiery, fanciful free thing—literature. Even more: I have learned to treasure my disgust, because I know that by feeling so strongly about it I am saving what I can of the spirit of Russian literature. Next to the right to create, the right to criticize is the richest gift that liberty of thought and speech can offer. Living as you do in freedom, in that spiritual open where you were born and bred, you may be apt to regard stories of prison life coming from remote lands as exaggerated accounts spread by panting fugitives. That a country exists where for almost a quarter of a century literature has been limited to illustrating the advertisements of a firm of slave-traders is hardly credible to people for whom writing and reading books is synonymous with having and voicing individual opinions. But if you do not believe in the existence of such conditions, you may at least imagine them, and once you have imagined them you will realize with new purity and pride the value of real books written by free men for free men to read.*

---

*This is a single untitled leaf, numbered 18, that appears to represent all that survives of an introductory survey of Soviet literature that VN prefixed to his lectures on the great Russian writers. Ed.

Vladimir Nabokov

LECTURES ON RUSSIAN LITERATURE

EDITED AND WITH AN INTRODUCTION
BY **Fredson Bowers**

A HARVEST BOOK

HARCOURT BRACE & COMPANY

BRUCCOLI CLARK LAYMAN

San Diego   New York   London

Library of Congress Cataloging-in-Publication Data
Nabokov, Vladimir Vladimirovich, 1899–1977.
Lectures on Russian literature.
1. Russian literature — 19th century — History and criticism — Addresses, essays, lecturers.
I. Bowers, Fredson Thayer. II. Title.
PG3012.N3   1980   891.7'09'003   81-47315
ISBN 0-15-649591-0 (Harvest: pbk.)   AACR2

Printed in the United States of America

J I H G F

Contents

Editor's Introduction   vii

Russian Writers, Censors, and Readers   1

NIKOLAY GOGOL   15
Dead Souls   15
"The Overcoat"   54

IVAN TURGENEV   63
Fathers and Sons   71

FYODOR DOSTOEVSKI   97
Crime and Punishment   109
Memoirs from a Mousehole   115
The Idiot   125
The Possessed   128

LEO TOLSTOY   137
Anna Karenin   137
The Death of Ivan Ilych   236

ANTON CHEKHOV   245
"The Lady with the Little Dog"   255
"In the Gully"   263
Notes on *The Seagull*   282

MAXIM GORKI   297
"On the Rafts"   304

Philistines and Philistinism   309

The Art of Translation   315

L'Envoi   323

Appendix   325

The editor and publisher are indebted to Simon Karlinsky, Professor of Slavic Languages at the University of California, Berkeley, for his careful checking of the lectures and his advice on transliterations. Professor Karlinsky's assistance has been crucial to this volume.

Introduction
by Fredson Bowers

According to his own account, in 1940 before launching on his academic career in America, Vladimir Nabokov "fortunately took the trouble of writing one hundred lectures—about 2,000 pages—on Russian literature. . . . This kept me happy at Wellesley and Cornell for twenty academic years."* It would seem that these lectures (each carefully timed to the usual fifty-minute American academic limit) were written between his arrival in the United States in May 1940 and his first teaching experience, a course in Russian literature in the 1941 Stanford University Summer School. In the autumn semester of 1941, Nabokov started a regular appointment at Wellesley College where he was the Russian Department in his own person and initially taught courses in language and grammar, but he soon branched out with Russian 201, a survey of Russian literature in translation. In 1948 he transferred to Cornell University as Associate Professor of Slavic Literature where he taught Literature 311-312, Masters of European Fiction, and Literature 325-326, Russian Literature in Translation.

The Russian writers represented in the present volume seem to have formed part of an occasionally shifting schedule in the Masters of European Fiction and Russian Literature in Translation courses. In the Masters course Nabokov usually taught Jane Austen, Gogol, Flaubert, Dickens, and—irregularly—Turgenev; in the second semester he assigned Tolstoy, Stevenson, Kafka, Proust, and Joyce.** The Dostoevski, Chekhov, and Gorki sections in this volume are from Russian Literature in Translation, which, according to

---

Strong Opinions (New York: McGraw-Hill, 1973), p. 5.
**Nabokov's lectures on the non-Russian European writers have been published in *Lectures on Literature* (New York: Harcourt Brace Jovanovich/Bruccoli Clark, 1980; London: Weidenfeld & Nicolson, 1981).

Nabokov's son Dmitri, also included minor Russian writers for whom the lecture notes are not preserved.*

After the success of *Lolita* enabled him to leave teaching in 1958, Nabokov planned to publish a book based on his various lectures on Russian and European literature. He never began the project, although fourteen years earlier his short book on *Nikolai Gogol* incorporated in revised form his classroom lectures on *Dead Souls* and "The Overcoat." At one time he planned a textbook edition of *Anna Karenin*, but after some work abandoned it. The present volume preserves all that has come down to us from his own manuscripts of the lectures on Russian authors.

Some differences mark Nabokov's presentation of the material from that he adopted for the European authors treated in the first volume, *Lectures on Literature*. In the lectures on European authors Nabokov paid no attention to biography, and he made no attempt, even in a cursory manner, to sketch in for his students an account of the authors' works that were not to be read for class. The concentration was exclusively on a single book assigned for each writer. In contrast, for the Russian lectures the usual formula is to present a capsule biography followed by a summary account of the author's other works, and then to shift to a close examination of the major work to be studied. One may surmise that this standard academic approach represents Nabokov's first teaching attempts at Stanford and Wellesley. From some scattered comments he appears to have felt that the students he was to address were innocent of any knowledge of Russian literature. Hence the teaching formula customary in academia at the time may have seemed to him best suited to introduce students to strange writers and an unfamiliar civilization. By the time he gave the Masters of European Fiction course at Cornell he had developed the more individual and sophisticated approach illustrated by such lectures as those on Flaubert or Dickens or Joyce, but seems never to have altered materially his written-out Wellesley lectures for delivery at Cornell. However, since the Russian lectures covered such familiar ground for him, it is possible that at Cornell he modified his discourse with more extemporaneous comment and was less rigid in his delivery, described thus in *Strong Opinions*: "Although, at the lectern, I evolved a subtle up and down movement of my eyes, there was never any doubt in the minds of alert students that I was reading, not speak-

---

*Among the authors that Dmitri Nabokov lists as having been taught during the Cornell years are Pushkin, Zhukovski, Karamazin, Griboedov, Krylov, Lermontov, Tyutchev, Derzhavin, Avvakum, Batyushkov, Gnedich, Fonvizin, Fet, Leskov, Blok, and Goncharov. If these had all been included in one course, it must have been a rapid survey. In the spring of 1952 while a visiting lecturer at Harvard, Nabokov gave a seminar in Pushkin alone, presumably from material he was collecting for his edition of *Eugene Onegin*.

ing." Indeed, for some of his lectures on Chekhov, and especially for the lecture on Tolstoy's "Ivan Ilyich," reading from manuscript would have been quite impossible since no finished script exists.

One may also detect a more subtle difference than that of structure. In lecturing on the great nineteenth-century Russian writers of fiction Nabokov was completely in his element. Not only did these writers represent to him the absolute height of Russian literature (with Pushkin, of course) but they also flourished counter to the utilitarianism that he despised both in the social critics of the time and, more bitingly, in its later Soviet development. In this respect the public lecture "Russian Writers, Censors, and Readers" mirrors the attitude one finds in his approach. In the classroom lectures the social element in Turgenev is deplored, that in Dostoevski is ridiculed, but Gorki's works are savaged. Just as in *Lectures on Literature* Nabokov had emphasized that students must not read *Madame Bovary* as a history of bourgeois life in nineteenth-century provincial France, so his highest admiration is reserved for Chekhov's refusal to allow social commentary to interfere with his exact observation of people as he saw them. "In the Gully" represents, artistically, life as it is, and people as they are, without the distortion that would have followed on a concern with the social system that could produce such characters. Correspondingly, in the Tolstoy series he regrets, half smiling, that Tolstoy did not see that the beauty of the curls of dark hair on Anna's tender neck was artistically more important than Lyovin's (Tolstoy's) views on agriculture. The emphasis on artistry in *Lectures on Literature* was broad and constant; nevertheless, in this Russian group it may seem to be more intense since in Nabokov's mind the principle of artistry combats not merely the prepossessions of the 1950s reader, as one feels he is arguing in the earlier volume, but also—more important for the writers—the antagonistic and eventually triumphant utilitarian attitude of the contemporary nineteenth-century Russian critics later hardened into the dogma of statecraft by the Soviet Union.

Tolstoy's world perfectly imaged Nabokov's lost homeland. The nostalgia he felt at the disappearance of this world and its people (he had met Tolstoy as a child) strengthens his typical emphasis on the artistic presentation of life in the fiction of Russia's golden age, especially in the works of Gogol, Tolstoy, and Chekhov. In aesthetics, artistic is, of course, not far from aristocratic, and it is not too much to suggest that both of these powerful strains in Nabokov may lie in back of his repugnance at what he regarded as Dostoevski's false sentimentalism. They certainly feed his contempt for Gorki. Because he was lecturing on Russian literature in translation Nabokov could not discuss the importance of style in any precise detail; but it seems clear that his dislike of Gorki (apart from political considerations) was based as much on his proletarian style as on what Nabokov regarded as the ineptness of his presentation of character and situation. His lack of admiration for Dostoevski's style may also have influenced in part his generally unfavorable judgment of this writer. Wonderfully effective are the several occasions when Nabokov quotes Tolstoy's Russian in the original to illustrate to his hearers the extraordinary effects from sound joined to sense.

The pedagogical stance that Nabokov adopts in these lectures does not differ materially from that found in *Lectures on Literature*. He knew that he was lecturing to students on what was an unfamiliar subject. He knew that he had to entice his hearers to join him in savoring the rich life and the complex people of a vanished world in literature that he hailed as Russia's Renaissance. Thus he relied heavily on quotation and interpretive narrative selected to make intelligible the feelings his students should have as they read, the reactions that should follow the course of the feeling that he was attempting to direct, and the creation of an understanding of great literature based on alert and intelligent appreciation instead of on what he regarded as sterile critical theory. His whole method was to draw his students in to share his own excitement at great writing, to envelop them in a different world of reality that is all the more real for being an artistic semblance. These are, then, very personal lectures emphasizing shared experience. And, of course, because of their Russian subject they are somehow more personally felt than his hearty appreciation of Dickens, his penetration of Joyce, or even his writer's empathy for Flaubert.

This is not to say, however, that critical analysis is in any way wanting in these lectures. He may make plain important hidden themes as when he points out in *Anna Karenin* the motifs of the double-nightmare. That Anna's dream foreshadows her death is not its only significance: in one moment of awful illumination Nabokov suddenly links it with the emotions that follow Vronski's conquest of Anna in their first adulterous union. And the implications of the horse race in which Vronski kills his mount Frou-Frou are not neglected. It is a special insight that despite the richly sensual love of Anna and Vronski their spiritually sterile and egotistic emotions doom them, whereas Kitty's marriage to Lyovin brings the Tolstoyan ideal of harmony, responsibility, tenderness, truth, and family joys.

Nabokov is fascinated by Tolstoy's time schemes. The how of the feeling that the reader's and the author's time-sense completely coincide in a manner that produces ultimate reality he gives up as an unsolved secret. But Tolstoy's juggling of the time-scheme between the Anna-Vronski and the Kitty-Lyovin actions is worked out in most interesting detail. He can point out how Tolstoy's presentation of Anna's thoughts in her drive through Moscow on the day of her death anticipates the stream-of-consciousness technique of James Joyce. He has an eye for the oddity, also, as that two officers in Vronski's regiment represent the first portrayal of homosexuality in modern literature. He is tireless in illustrating how Chekhov made the ordinary seem of supreme value to the reader. If he criticizes the banality of Turgenev's character biographies interrupting the narrative and the relation of what happens to everyone after the ending of the story proper, Nabokov can yet appreciate the delicacy of Turgenev's cameo descriptions and of his modulated sinuous style, which he compares to "a lizard sun-charmed on a wall." If the mark of Dostoevski's sentimentality offends him, as in his outraged description of Raskolnikov and the prostitute in *Crime and Punishment* bent together over the Bible, he is appreciative of Dostoevksi's wild humor; and his conclusion that in *The Brothers Karamazov* a writer who could have been a great dramatist is struggling unsuccessfully within the novel form is a unique perception.

It is the mark of a great teacher as well as critic that he can rise to the author's level in a masterpiece. Particularly in the Tolstoy lectures, which provide the most exhilarating reading and are the heart of this volume, Nabokov from time to time joins Tolstoy at a dizzy level of imaginative experience. The interpretive description with which he guides the reader through the story of *Anna Karenin* is itself a work of art.

Perhaps the most valuable contribution that Nabokov made to his students was not merely his emphasis on shared experience but on shared *informed* experience. As a creative writer himself he could meet the authors he treated on their own ground and make their stories and characters come alive by his own understanding of what constitutes the art of writing. In his persistent emphasis on intelligent reading he found that nothing equalled the reader's command of detail as the key to unlock the secret of how masterpieces work. His commentary notes on *Anna Karenin* are a treasure of information that enhances the reader's awareness of the inner life of the novel. This scientific yet artistic appreciation of detail, characteristic of Nabokov himself as a writer, constitutes ultimately the heart of his teaching method. He summed up his feeling as follows: "In my academic days I endeavored to provide students of literature with exact information about details, about such combinations of details as yield the sensual spark without which a book is dead.* In that respect, general

*On this passage John Simon remarks: "But Nabokov does demand, for all his rejection of crude reality—'those farcical and fraudulent characters called Facts'—a powerful semblance of reality, which, as he himself might have put it, is not the same as a *re*semblance. As he said in an interview, unless you know the streets of Joyce's Dublin and what the semi-sleeping

ideas are of no importance. Any ass can assimilate the main points of Tolstoy's attitude toward adultery but in order to enjoy Tolstoy's art the good reader must wish to visualize, for instance, the arrangement of a railway carriage on the Moscow-Petersburg night train as it was a hundred years ago." And he continued, "Here diagrams are most helpful."* So we have his blackboard diagram of the crisscross journeys made by Bazarov and Arkadi in *Fathers and Sons*, and his drawing of the layout of the sleeping car in which Anna journeyed from Moscow to Petersburg on the same train as Vronski. The dress that Kitty would have worn skating is reproduced from a contemporary fashion illustration. We have discourses on how tennis was played, what Russians had for breakfast, luncheon, and dinner, and at what times. This scientist's respect for fact combined with the writer's own understanding of the intricate trails of passion that inform a great work of imagination is quintessentially Nabokovian and is one of the particular virtues of these lectures.

This is the teaching method, but the result is a warm sense of shared experience between Nabokov and the hearer-reader. One reacts with joy to his communication of understanding through feeling, a gift given particularly to critics who are themselves great literary artists. That the magic he felt so keenly in literature should be aimed at pleasure we learn from these lectures and from the anecdote that at the first meeting of Literature 311 in September 1953, at Cornell, Vladimir Nabokov asked the students to explain in writing why they had enrolled in the course. At the next class he approvingly reported that one student had answered, "Because I like stories."

Editorial Method

The fact cannot and need not be disguised that the texts for these essays represent Vladimir Nabokov's written-out notes for delivery as classroom lectures and that they cannot be regarded as a finished literary product such as he produced when he revised his classroom lectures on Gogol for publication as a book. (The Gogol essay published here is excerpted from *Nikolai Gogol* [New York: New Directions, 1944].) The lectures exist in very different states

---

car on the Petersburg-Moscow express looked like in 1870, you cannot make sense of *Ulysses* and *Anna Karenin[a]*. In other words, the writer makes use of some specific realities, but only as bait with which to trap the readers into the greater unreality — or greater reality — of his fiction." ("The Novelist at the Blackboard," *The Times Literary Supplement* [April 24, 1981], 458.) Of course, if the reader does not understand and assimilate this detail, he remains outside the imaginative reality of the fiction. It is quite true that without Nabokov's explanation of the conditions under which Anna traveled on that fateful journey to Petersburg certain of the motifs in her nightmare cannot be understood.

Strong Opinions, pp. 156-157.

of preparation and polish, and even of completed structure. Most are in his own handwriting, with only occasional sections (usually the biographical introductions) typed by his wife Vèra as an aid to delivery. The degree of preparation ranges from the handwritten rough notes for the Gorki lecture to a considerable amount of typed material for Tolstoy that seems to have been planned as part of an extended general introduction to the lectures on *Anna Karenin* reworked as a textbook. (The appendices to the *Anna Karenin* essay consist of material prepared for Nabokov's edition.) When typing exists the text was usually further modified by Nabokov, who might add fresh comments by hand or revise phrases for felicity. Thus the typed pages are likely to run a little more smoothly than the handwritten. The holograph pages on a few occasions appear to be fair copies, but normally they give every indication of initial composition, and they are often much worked over both during the writing-out and on review.

Some separate sections in the lecture folders clearly represent simple background notes made in the initial stages of preparation and either not utilized or else considerably revised and incorporated subsequently into the lectures themselves. Other independent sections are more ambiguous, and it is not always demonstrable whether they reflect stages of amplification during the course of repeated delivery in different years and in different places from the basic Wellesley series (seemingly not much modified, except for Tolstoy, when delivered later at Cornell) or else jottings for possible incorporation in a future revision. Whenever possible all such material not manifestly background and preparatory memoranda has been salvaged and worked into the texture of the discourse at appropriate places.

The problem of making a reading edition from these manuscripts falls into two main parts: structural and stylistic. Structurally, the main order of delivery, or the organization of the lectures on any one of the authors, is not ordinarily in question, but problems do arise, especially in the Tolstoy lectures, which are composed of a series of discrete sections. The evidence appears to be quite contradictory, for example, whether Nabokov intended Anna's story to be finished before he took up in any major way the Lyovin narrative with which he proposed to conclude, or else whether the plot line of Anna and Vronski was to begin and to end the series, as presented here. It is not entirely clear, also, whether *Notes from Underground* (i.e., *Memoirs from a Mousehole*) was intended to end the series of lectures on Dostoevski or to follow *Crime and Punishment*. Thus even in an essay like that on *Anna Karenin* in which at least some preliminary preparations looking toward publication can be encountered, the proposed organization is in some legitimate doubt. The problem is intensified in the lecture on "The Death of Ivan Ilyich," which exists only in the form of a few fragmented notes. Between these two extremes comes a series like that on Chekhov, which is only partly organized. The section devoted to "The Lady with the Little Dog" is fully worked out, but "In the Gully" is represented only by rough notes with directions to read certain pages from the story. *The Seagull* handwritten manuscript was discovered apart from the rest but appears to belong to the series. It is rather elementary in its form, but it seems to have received Nabokov's approval since its beginning has been typed and then a note in Russian refers to the continuation in the rest of the manuscript.

In some lectures a small rearrangement has been necessary in cases of doubt about the progression. In a few of the folders isolated pages of Nabokov's remarks are interspersed—sometimes little independent essays but sometimes only notes or trials—which have been editorially integrated in the discourse in an effort to preserve the maximum discussion that Nabokov made of the authors, their works, and the art of literature in general.

Quotation bulked large in Nabokov's teaching methods as an aid in transmitting to students his ideas of literary artistry. In the construction of the present reading edition from the lectures, Nabokov's method has been followed with very little cutting except of the most extended quoted illustrations, for the quotations are most helpful in recalling a book to the reader's memory or else in introducing it to a fresh reader under Nabokov's expert guidance. Quotations, therefore, ordinarily follow Nabokov's specific instructions to read certain passages (usually marked also in his own classroom copy) with the effect that the reader may participate in the talk as if he were present as a listener. To further this flow-in of quotation with discussion, the convention of quotation marks at every indentation has been set aside, and except for opening and closing marks and the usual marks about dialogue, the distinction between quotation and text has been deliberately blurred. When a useful purpose might be served, the editor has occasionally added quotations to illustrate Nabokov's discussion or description, especially when his teaching copies of the books are not available and one does not have the guidance of passages marked for quotation in addition to those specified in the body of the lecture as to be read.

Only the teaching copies for *Anna Karenin* and for certain of the Chekhov works have been preserved. These are marked for quotation and contain notes about the context, most of these comments also being present in the written-out lectures but other notes clue Nabokov in on some oral remark to make about the style or the content of passages to be emphasized by quotation or verbal reference. Whenever possible, comments in the annotated copies have been worked into the texture of the lectures as appropriate occasion arose. Nabokov highly disapproved of Constance Garnett's translations from the Russian. Thus the passages marked for quotation in his teaching copy of *Anna Karenin* are interlined heavily with his own corrections of errors of translation or his own versions of the authorial expression. Quotation in the present volume follows, of course, Nabokov's own alterations in the basic translation as he would have read them, but usually omits his bitter sidenotes about the translator's incompetency, directed at Constance Garnett's blunders. The Tolstoy lectures, perhaps because of their partial reworking for a proposed book, are unique in presenting many of the quotations typed out in full within the text instead of relying on Nabokov's usual practice of noting passages to read from his teaching copy. (This teaching copy differs from that of *Madame Bovary* where the entire text was freely annotated in that after part one only selected passages in *Anna Karenin* have been revised.) The typing-out of quotations poses something of a problem because changes made in the Garnett text in these typescripts do not always agree with the alterations made in the text of the teaching copy and these passages are frequently abridged. There is also a separate section, presumably intended for publication but not here reproduced, labeled as corrections to the Garnett edition for the first part of *Anna Karenin* which, when referring to the quoted passages, does not always agree either with the manuscript or the marked book. A choice of one of these three as the exclusive copy for the text of the quotations in the present volume would be partly unsatisfactory since each series of revisions seems to have been made without reference to the others. Under these conditions, where chronological priority has little or no significance, it has seemed most useful to provide the reader with the maximum number of changes that Nabokov made in the Garnett version by using the abridged manuscript copy as the norm but freely inserting in its text whatever further alterations he made either in the teaching copy or the typed-out list.

Nabokov was acutely conscious of the need to shape the separate lectures to the allotted classroom hour, and it is not unusual to find noted in the margin the time at which that particular point should have been reached. Within the lecture text a number of passages and even separate sentences or phrases are enclosed in square brackets. Some of these brackets seem to indicate matter that could be omitted if time were pressing. Others may represent matter that he queried for omission more for reasons of content or expression than for time restrictions; and indeed some of these bracketed queries were subsequently deleted, just as some, alternatively, have been removed from the status of queries by the substitution for them of parentheses. All such undeleted brack-eted material has been faithfully reproduced but without sign of the bracket-ing, which would have been intrusive for the reader. Deletions are observed, of course, except for a handful of cases when it has seemed to the editor possible that the matter was excised for considerations of time or, sometimes, of position, in which latter case the deleted matter has been transferred to a more appropriate context. On the other hand, some of Nabokov's comments di-rected exclusively to his students and often on pedagogical subjects have been omitted as inconsistent with the aims of a reading edition, although one that otherwise retains much of the flavor of Nabokov's lecture delivery. Among such omissions one may mention remarks like "you all remember who *she* was" when he compares Anna Karenin to Athena, or his adjuration to the undergraduates that they should enjoy the pathetic scene of Anna's visit to her son on his tenth birthday, or his spelling out Tyutchev's name with a long "u" (which sounds, he remarks, like "a kind of caged twitter," a comment worth preserving), or observations for an unsophisticated audience in his analysis of Tolstoy's structure: "I realize that synchronization is a big word, a five syllable word—but we can console ourselves by the thought that it would have had six syllables several centuries ago. By the way it does not come from sin—s, i, n—but s, y, n—and it means arranging events in such a way as to indicate coexistence." However, some of these classroom asides have been retained when not inappropriate for a more sophisticated reading audience, as well as most of Nabokov's imperatives.

Stylistically the most part of these texts by no means represents what would have been Nabokov's language and syntax if he had himself worked them up in book form, for a marked difference exists between the general style of these classroom lectures and the polished workmanship of several of his public lectures. Since publication without reworking had not been contemplated when Nabokov wrote out these lectures and their notes for delivery, it would be pedantic in the extreme to try to transcribe the texts *literatum* in every detail from the sometimes rough form found in the manuscripts. The editor of a reading edition may be permitted to deal more freely with inconsistencies, inadvertent mistakes, and incomplete inscription, including the need some-times to add bridge passages in connection with quotation. On the other hand, no reader would want a manipulated text that endeavored to "improve" Nabokov's writing in any intrusive way even in some of its unpolished sections. Thus a synthetic approach has been firmly rejected, and Nabokov's language has been reproduced with fidelity save for words missing by accident and inadvertent repetitions often the result of incomplete revision.

Corrections and modifications have been performed silently. Thus the only footnotes are Nabokov's own or else occasional editorial comments on points of interest such as the application of some isolated jotting, whether among the manuscripts or in the annotated copy of the teaching book, to the text of the lecture at hand. The mechanics of the lectures, such as Nabokov's notes to himself, often in Russian, have been omitted, as have been his markings for correct delivery of the vowel quantities in pronunciation and the accenting of syllables in certain names and unusual words. Nor do footnotes interrupt what one hopes is the flow of the discourse to indicate to the reader that an unassigned section has been editorially inserted at a particular point.

The transliteration of Russian names to their English equivalents has posed a slight problem since Nabokov was not always consistent in his own usage; and even when he made up a list of the forms of names in *Anna Karenin*, part one, presumably for the planned publication of the Tolstoy lectures, the transliterated spellings do not always agree with the forms in his own manuscripts, or even internally in their system. Quotations from the texts of the translators of other authors introduce a variety of different systems, also. Under these conditions it has seemed best to make a thorough revised transliteration of the Russian names in all these lectures according to a consistent system that has been agreed upon and performed by the joint efforts of Professor Simon Karlinsky and Mrs. Vladimir Nabokov, to whom special thanks are due.

"L'Envoi" is drawn from Nabokov's final remarks to his class before he went on to discuss in detail the nature and requirements of the final examination. In these remarks he states that he has described at the beginning of the course the period of Russian literature between 1917 and 1957. This opening lecture has not been preserved among the manuscripts except perhaps for one leaf, which appears as the epigraph to this volume.

The editions of the books that Nabokov used as teaching copies for his lectures were selected for their cheapness and general availability. Nabokov admired the translations from the Russian of Bernard Guilbert Guerney, but of few others. The texts from which Nabokov taught are as follows: Tolstoy, *Anna Karenina* (New York: Modern Library, 1930); *The Portable Chekhov*, ed. Avrahm Yarmolinsky (New York: Viking Press, 1947); *A Treasury of Russian Literature*, edited and translated by Bernard Guilbert Guerney (New York: Vanguard Press, 1943).

LECTURES ON
RUSSIAN LITERATURE

Russian Writers, Censors and Readers

(read at Festival of Arts, Cornell, 10 April 1958)

No wenapaps No zache

The notion: "Russian literature" -- "Russian literature" as
an immediate idea, this notion in the minds of non-Russians is
generally limited to the awareness of Russia's having produced
half a dozen great masters of prose between the middle of the
Nineteenth century and the first decade of the Twentieth. This
notion is ampler in the minds of Russian readers since it comprises
in addition to the novelists -- some of them unknown here -- a
number of untranslatable poets; but even so, the native
mind remains focussed on the resplendent of the Nineteenth
century. In other words "Russian literature" is a recent event. It
is also a limited event, and the foreigner's mind tends to regard
it as something complete, once for all. This is mainly due to
the bleakness of the typically regional literature produced
during the last four decades under the Soviet rule.

I calculated once that the acknowledged best in the way of
Russian fiction and poetry produced since the beginning of last
century runs to about 23,000 pages of ordinary print. It is evident
that neither French nor English literature can be so compactly
handled. They sprawl over many more centuries, the number of
masterpieces is formidable -- and this brings me to my first
point. If we exclude one medieval masterpiece, the beautifully

Russian Writers, Censors, and Readers*

Russian Literature" as a notion, an immediate idea, this notion
in the minds of non-Russians is generally limited to the awareness of Russia's
having produced half a dozen great masters of prose between the middle of the
nineteenth century and the first decade of the twentieth. This notion is ampler
in the minds of Russian readers since it comprises, in addition to the novelists,
a number of untranslatable poets; but even so, the native mind remains focused
on the resplendent orb of the nineteenth century. In other words, "Russian
literature" is a recent event. It is also a limited event, and the foreigner's mind
tends to regard it as something complete, something finished once and for all.
This is mainly due to the bleakness of the typically regional literature produced
during the last four decades under the Soviet rule.

I calculated once that the acknowledged best in the way of Russian fiction
and poetry which had been produced since the beginning of the last century
runs to about 23,000 pages of ordinary print. It is evident that neither French
nor English literature can be so compactly handled. They sprawl over many
more centuries; the number of masterpieces is formidable. This brings me to
my first point. If we exclude one medieval masterpiece, the beautifully com-
modious thing about Russian prose is that it is all contained in the amphora of

*Read at the Festival of the Arts, Cornell University, April 10, 1958.

Opening page of Nabokov's lecture on "Russian Writers, Censors, and Readers."   1 one round century—with an additional little cream jug provided for whatever surplus may have accumulated since. One century, the nineteenth, had been sufficient for a country with practically no literary tradition of its own to create a literature which in artistic worth, in wide-spread influence, in everything except bulk, equals the glorious output of England or France, although their production of permanent masterpieces had begun so much earlier. This miraculous flow of esthetic values in so young a civilization could not have taken place unless in all other ramifications of spiritual growth nineteenth-century Russia had not attained with the same abnormal speed a degree of culture which again matched that of the oldest Western countries. I am aware that the recognition of this past culture of Russia is not an integral part of a foreigner's notion of Russian history. The question of the evolution of liberal thought in Russia before the Revolution has been completely obscured and distorted abroad by astute Communist propaganda in the twenties and thirties of this century. They usurped the honor of having civilized Russia. But it is also true that in the days of Pushkin or Gogol a large majority of the Russian nation was left out in the cold in a veil of slow snow beyond the amber-bright windows, and this was a tragic result of the fact that a most refined European culture had arrived too fast in a country famous for its misfortunes, famous for the misery of its numberless humble lives—but that is another story.

Or perhaps it is not. In the process of sketching a picture of the history of recent Russian literature, or more precisely in the process of defining the forces which struggled for the possession of the artist's soul, I may, if I am lucky, tap the deep pathos that pertains to all authentic art because of the breach between its eternal values and the sufferings of a muddled world—this world, indeed, can hardly be blamed for regarding literature as a luxury or a toy unless it can be used as an up-to-date guidebook.

For an artist one consolation is that in a free country he is not actually forced to produce guidebooks. Now, from this limited point of view, nineteenth-century Russia was oddly enough a free country: books and writers might be banned and banished, censors might be rogues and fools, be-whiskered Tsars might stamp and storm; but that wonderful discovery of Soviet times, the method of making the entire literary corporation write what the state deems fit—this method was unknown in old Russia, although no doubt many a reactionary statesman hoped to find such a tool. A staunch determinist might argue that between a magazine in a democratic country applying financial pressure to its contributors to make them exude what is required by the so-called reading public—between this and the more direct pressure which a police state brings to bear in order to make the author round out his novel with a suitable political message, it may be argued that between the two pressures there is only a difference of degree; but this is not so for the simple reason that there are many different periodicals and philosophies in a free country but only one government in a dictatorship. It is a difference in quality. If I, an American writer, decide to write an unconventional novel about, say, a happy atheist, an independent Bostonian, who marries a beautiful Negro girl, also an atheist, has lots of children, cute little agnostics, and lives a happy, good, and gentle life to the age of 106, when he blissfully dies in his sleep—it is quite possible that despite your brilliant talent, Mr. Nabokov, we feel [in such cases we don't *think*, we *feel*] that no American publisher could risk bringing out such a book simply because no bookseller would want to handle it. This is a publisher's opinion, and everybody has the right to have an opinion. Nobody would exile me to the wilds of Alaska for having my happy atheist published after all by some shady experimental firm; and on the other hand, authors in America are never ordered by the government to produce magnificent novels about the joys of free enterprise and of morning prayers. In Russia before the Soviet rule there did exist restrictions, but no orders were given to artists. They were—those nineteenth-century writers, composers, and painters—quite certain that they lived in a country of oppression and slavery, but they had something that one can appreciate only now, namely, the immense advantage over their grandsons in modern Russia of not being compelled to say that there was no oppression and no slavery.

Of the two forces that simultaneously struggled for the possession of the artist's soul, of the two critics who judged his work, the first was the government. Throughout the last century the government remained aware that anything outstanding and original in the way of creative thought was a jarring note and a stride toward Revolution. The government's vigilance in its purest form was perfectly expressed by Tsar Nicholas I in the thirties and forties. His chilly personality pervaded the scene much more thoroughly than did the philistinism of the next sovereigns, and his attachment to literature would have been touching had it really come from the heart. With striking perseverance he tried to be everything in relation to Russian writers of his time—a father, a godfather, a nurse, a wetnurse, a prison warden, and a literary critic all rolled up in one. Whatever qualities he may have shown in his own kingly profession, it must be admitted that in his dealing with the Russian Muse he was at the worst a vicious bully, at the best a clown. The system of censorship that he evolved lasted till the 1860s, was eased by the great reforms of the sixties, stiffened again in the last decades of the century, broke down for a short spell in the first decade of this century, and then had a most sensational and formidable comeback after the Revolution under the Soviets.

In the first half of the last century, meddlesome officials, heads of police who thought that Byron was an Italian revolutionary, smug old censors, certain journalists in the government's pay, the quiet but touchy and wary church, this combination of monarchism, bigotry, and cringing administration hampered the author to a considerable degree but also afforded him the keen pleasure of pin-pricking and deriding the government in a thousand subtle, delightfully subversive ways with which governmental stupidity was quite unable to cope. A fool may be a dangerous customer, but the fact of his having such a vulnerable top-end turns danger into a first-rate sport; and whatever defects the old administration in Russia had, it must be conceded that it possessed one outstanding virtue—a lack of brains. In a certain sense, the censor's task was made more difficult by his having to disentangle abstruse political allusions instead of simply cracking down upon obvious obscenity. True, under Tsar Nicholas I a Russian poet had to be careful, and Pushkin's imitations of naughty French models, of Parny, of Voltaire, were easily crushed by censorship. But prose was virtuous. Russian literature had no Renaissance tradition of vigorous outspokenness as other literatures had, and up to this day the Russian novel remains on the whole the most chaste of all novels. And, of course, Russian literature of the Soviet period is purity itself. One cannot imagine a Russian writing, for example, *Lady Chatterley's Lover*.

So the first force fighting the artist was the government. The second force tackling the nineteenth-century Russian author was the anti-governmental, social-minded utilitarian criticism, the political, civic, radical thinkers of the day. It must be stressed that these men in general culture, honesty, aspirations, mental activity, and human virtue were immeasurably superior to the rogues in the government's pay or to the muddled old reactionaries that clustered around the shivering throne. The radical critic was concerned exclusively with the welfare of the people and regarded everything—literature, science, philosophy—as only a means to improve the social and economic situation of the underdog and to alter the political structure of his country. He was incorruptible, heroic, indifferent to the privations of exile, but also indifferent to the niceties of art. These men who fought despotism—the fiery Belinski of the forties, the stubborn Chernyshevski and Dobrolyubov of the fifties and sixties, Mihaylovski, the well-meaning bore, and dozens of other honest obstinate men—all may be grouped under one heading: political radicalism affiliated to the old French social thinkers and to German materialists, foreshadowing the revolutionary socialism and stolid communism of recent years, and not to be confused with Russian Liberalism in its true sense, which was absolutely the same as cultured democracy elsewhere in Western Europe and America. In looking through old periodicals of the sixties and seventies,

VLADIMIR NABOKOV

one is astounded to find what violent ideas these men were able to express in a country ruled by an absolute monarch. But with all their virtues, these radical critics were as great a nuisance in regard to art as was the government. Government and revolution, the Tsar and the Radicals, were both philistines in art. The radical critics fought despotism, but they evolved a despotism of their own. The claims, the promptings, the theories that they tried to enforce were in themselves just as irrelevant to art as was the conventionalism of the administration. What they demanded of an author was a social message and no nonsense, and from their point of view a book was good only insofar as it was of practical use to the welfare of the people. There was a disastrous flaw in their fervor. Sincerely and boldly they advocated freedom and equality but they contradicted their own creed by wishing to subjugate the arts to current politics. If in the opinion of the Tsars authors were to be the servants of the state, in the opinion of the radical critics writers were to be the servants of the masses. The two lines of thought were bound to meet and join forces when at last, in our times, a new kind of regime, the synthesis of a Hegelian triad, combined the idea of the masses with the idea of the state.

One of the best examples of the clash between the artist and his critics in the twenties and thirties of the nineteenth century is the case of Pushkin, Russia's first great writer. Officialdom headed by Tsar Nicholas himself was madly irritated by this man who instead of being a good servant of the state in the rank and file of the administration and extolling conventional virtues in his vocational writings (if write he must), composed extremely arrogant and extremely independent and extremely wicked verse in which a dangerous freedom of thought was evident in the novelty of his versification, in the audacity of his sensual fancy, and in his propensity for making fun of major and minor tyrants. The church deplored his levity. Police officers, high officials, critics in the pay of the government dubbed him a shallow versificator; and because he emphatically refused to use his pen for copying humdrum acts in a governmental office, Pushkin, one of the best educated Europeans of his day, was called an ignoramus by Count Thingamabob and a dunce by General Donnerwetter. The methods which the state employed in its attempts to throttle Pushkin's genius were banishment, fierce censorship, constant pestering, fatherly admonishment, and finally a favorable attitude toward the local scoundrels who eventually drove Pushkin to fight his fatal duel with a wretched adventurer from royalist France.

Now, on the other hand, the immensely influential radical critics, who in spite of absolute monarchy managed to voice their revolutionary opinions and hopes in widely read periodicals — these radical critics who blossomed forth in the last years of Pushkin's short life, were also madly irritated by this man who instead of being a good servant of the people and of social endeavor wrote extremely subtle and extremely independent and extremely imaginative verse about all things on earth, the very variety of his interests somehow lessening the value of revolutionary intention that might be discerned in his casual, too casual, pokes at minor or major tyrants. The audacity of his versification was deplored as being an aristocratic adornment; his artistic aloofness was pronounced a social crime; mediocre writers but sound political thinkers dubbed Pushkin a shallow versificator. In the sixties and seventies famous critics, the idols of public opinion, called Pushkin a dunce, and emphatically proclaimed that a good pair of boots was far more important for the Russian people than all the Pushkins and Shakespeares in the world. In comparing the exact epithets used by the extreme radicals with those used by the extreme monarchists in regard to Russia's greatest poet, one is struck by their awful similarity.

Gogol's case in the late thirties and forties was somewhat different. First let me say that his play *The Government Inspector* and his novel *Dead Souls* are products of Gogol's own fancy, his private nightmares peopled with his own incomparable goblins. They are not and could not be a picture of the Russia of his time since, apart from other reasons, he hardly knew Russia; and indeed his failure to write a continuation of *Dead Souls* was due to his not possessing sufficient data and to the impossibility of using the little people of his fancy for a realistic work that would improve the morals of his country. But the radical critics perceived in the play and in the novel an indictment of bribery, of coarse living, of governmental iniquity, of slavery. A revolutionary intention was read into Gogol's works and he, a timorous law-abiding citizen with many influential friends in the conservative party, was so appalled at the things that had been found in his works that in his subsequent writings he endeavored to prove that the play and the novel, far from being revolutionary, had really conformed to religious tradition and to the mysticism which he later evolved. Dostoevski was banished and almost executed by the government in his youth for some indulgence in juvenile politics; but when afterwards he extolled in his writings the virtues of humility, submission, and suffering, he was murdered in print by the radical critics. And these same critics fiercely attacked Tolstoy for depicting what they called the romantic romps of titled ladies and gentlemen, while the church excommunicated him for his daring to evolve a faith of his own making.

These examples will I think suffice. It can be said without much exaggeration that almost all the great Russian writers of the nineteenth century went through this strange double purgatory.

Then the marvelous nineteenth century came to a close. Chekhov died in 1904, Tolstoy in 1910. There arose a new generation of writers, a final sunburst, a hectic flurry of talent. In these two decades just before the Revolution, modernism in prose, poetry, and painting flourished brilliantly. Andrey Bely, a precursor of James Joyce, Aleksandr Blok, the symbolist, and several other avant-garde poets appeared on the lighted stage. When, less than a year after the Liberal Revolution, the Bolshevik leaders overturned the Democratic regime of Kerenski and inaugurated their reign of terror, most Russian writers went abroad; some, as for example the futurist poet Mayakovski, remained. Foreign observers confused advanced literature with advanced politics, and this confusion was eagerly pounced upon, and promoted, and kept alive by Soviet propaganda abroad. Actually Lenin was in art a philistine, a bourgeois, and from the very start the Soviet government was laying the grounds for a primitive, regional, political, police-controlled, utterly conservative and conventional literature. The Soviet government, with admirable frankness very different from the sheepish, half-hearted, muddled attempts of the old administration, proclaimed that literature was a tool of the state; and for the last forty years this happy agreement between the poet and the policeman has been carried on most intelligently. Its result is the so-called Soviet literature, a literature conventionally bourgeois in its style and hopelessly monotonous in its meek interpretation of this or that governmental idea.

It is interesting to ponder the fact that there is no real difference between what the Western Fascists wanted of literature and what the Bolsheviks want. Let me quote: "The personality of the artist should develop freely and without restraint. One thing, however, we demand: acknowledgement of our creed." Thus spoke one of the big Nazis, Dr. Rosenberg, Minister of Culture in Hitler's Germany. Another quotation: "Every artist has the right to create freely; but we, Communists, must guide him according to plan." Thus spoke Lenin. Both of these are textual quotations, and their similitude would have been highly diverting had not the whole thing been so very sad.

"We guide your pens"—this, then, was the fundamental law laid down by the Communist party, and this was expected to produce "vital" literature. The round body of the law had delicate dialectical tentacles: the next step was to plan the writer's work as thoroughly as the economic system of the country, and this promised the writer what Communist officials called with a simper "an endless variety of themes" because every turn of the economic and political path implied a turn in literature: one day the lesson would be "factories"; the next, "farms"; then, "sabotage"; then, "the Red Army," and so on (what variety!); with the Soviet novelist puffing and panting and dashing about from model hospital to model mine or dam, always in mortal fear that if he were not nimble enough he might praise a Soviet decree or a Soviet hero that would both be abolished on the publication day of his book.

In the course of forty years of absolute domination the Soviet government has never once lost control of the arts. Every now and then the screw is eased for a moment, to see what will happen, and some mild concession toward individual self-expression is accorded; and foreign optimists acclaim the new book as a political protest, no matter how mediocre it is. We all know those bulky best-sellers *All Quiet on the Don*, *Not by Bread Possessed*, and *Zed's Cabin* — mountains of triteness, plateaus of platitudes, which are called "powerful" and "compelling" by foreign reviewers. But, alas, even if the Soviet writer does reach a level of literary art worthy of, say, an Upton Lewis — not to name any names — even so the dreary fact remains that the Soviet government, the most philistine organization on earth, cannot permit the individual quest, the creative courage, the new, the original, the difficult, the strange, to exist. And let us not be fooled by the natural extinction of elderly dictators. Not a jot changed in the philosophy of the state when Lenin was replaced by Stalin, and not a jot has changed now, with the rise of Krushchev, or Hrushchyov, or whatever his name is. Let me quote Hrushchyov on literature at a recent party reunion (June 1957). This is what he said: "Creative activity in the domain of literature and art must be penetrated with the spirit of struggle for communism, must imbue hearts with buoyancy, with the strength of convictions, must develop socialistic consciousness and group discipline." I love this group style, these rhetorical intonations, these didactic clauses, this snowballing journalese.

Since a definite limit is set to an author's imagination and to free will, every proletarian novel must end happily, with the Soviets triumphing, and thus the author is faced with the dreadul task of having to weave an interesting plot when the outcome is in advance officially known to the reader. In an Anglo-Saxon thriller, the villain is generally punished, and the strong silent man generally wins the weak babbling girl, but there is no governmental law in Western countries to ban a story that does not comply with a fond tradition, so that we always hope that the wicked but romantic fellow will escape scot-free and the good but dull chap will be finally snubbed by the moody heroine.

But in the case of the Soviet author there is no such freedom. His epilogue is fixed by law, and the reader knows it as well as the writer does. How, then, can he manage to keep his audience in suspense? Well, a few ways have been found. First of all, since the idea of a happy end really refers not to the characters but to the police state, and since it is the Soviet state that is the real protagonist of every Soviet novel, we can have a few minor characters—fairly good Bolsheviks though they be—die a violent death provided the idea of the Perfect State triumphs in the end; in fact, some cunning authors have been known to arrange things in such a way that on the very last page the death of the Communist hero *is* the triumph of the happy Communist idea: I die so that the Soviet Union may live. This is one way—but it is a dangerous way, for the author may be accused of killing the symbol together with the man, the boy on the burning deck together with the whole Navy. If he is cautious and shrewd, he will endow the Communist who comes to grief with some little weakness, some slight—oh, so slight!—political deviation or streak of bourgeois eclecticism, which, without affecting the pathos of his deeds and death, will lawfully suffice to justify his personal disaster.

An able Soviet author proceeds to collect a number of characters involved in the creation of this factory or that farm much in the same way as a mystery story writer collects a number of people in a country house or a railway train where a murder is about to occur. In the Soviet story the crime idea will take the form of some secret enemy tampering with the work and plans of the Soviet undertaking in question. And just as in an ordinary mystery story, the various characters will be shown in such a way that the reader is not quite sure whether the harsh and gloomy fellow is really bad, and whether the smooth-tongued, cheerful mixer is really good. Our detective is represented there by the elderly worker who lost one eye in the Russian Civil War, or a splendidly healthy young woman who has been sent from Headquarters to investigate why the production of some stuff is falling in such an alarming way. The characters— say, the factory workers—are so selected as to show all the shades of state-consciousness, some being staunch and honest realists, others nursing romantic memories of the first years of the Revolution, others again with no learning or experience but with a lot of sound Bolshevik intuition. The reader notes the action and dialogue, notes also this or that hint, and tries to discover who among them is sincere, and who has a dark secret to hide. The plot thickens and when the climax is reached and the villain is unmasked by the strong silent girl, we find out what we had perhaps suspected—that the man who was wrecking the factory is not the ugly little old workman with a trick of mispronouncing Marxist definitions, bless his little well-meaning soul, but the slick, easygoing fellow well versed in Marxian lore; and his dark secret is that his stepmother's cousin was the nephew of a capitalist. I have seen Nazi novels doing the same thing on racial lines. Apart from this structural resemblance to the tritest kind of crime-thriller, we must note here the "pseudo-religious" side. The little old workman who proves to be the better man is a kind of obscene parody of the poor-in-wits but strong in spirit and faith, inheriting the Kingdom of Heaven, while the brilliant pharisee goes to the other place. Especially amusing in these circumstances is the romantic theme in Soviet novels. I have here two examples culled at random. First, a passage from *The Big Heart*, a novel by Antonov, published serially in 1957:

> Olga was silent.
> "Ah," cried Vladimir, "Why can't you love me as I love you."
> "I love my country," she said.
> "So do I," he exclaimed.
> "And there is something I love even more strongly," Olga continued, disengaging herself from the young man's embrace.
> "And that is?" he queried.
> Olga let her limpid blue eyes rest on him, and answered quickly: "It is the Party."

My other example is from a novel by Gladkov, *Energiya*:

> The young worker Ivan grasped the drill. As soon as he felt the surface of metal, he became agitated, and an excited shiver ran through his body. The deafening roar of the drill hurled Sonia away from him. Then she placed her hand on his shoulder and tickled the hair on his ear. . . .
> Then she looked at him, and the little cap perched on her curls mocked and provoked him. It was as though an electric discharge had pierced both the young people at one and the same moment. He gave a deep sigh and clutched the apparatus more firmly.

I have now described with less sorrow I hope than contempt, the forces that fought for the artist's soul in the nineteenth century and the final oppression which art underwent in the Soviet police state. In the nineteenth century genius not only survived, but flourished, because public opinion was stronger than any Tsar and because, on the other hand, the good reader refused to be controlled by the utilitarian ideas of progressive critics. In the present era when public opinion in Russia is completely crushed by the government, the good reader may perhaps still exist there, somewhere in Tomsk or Atomsk, but his voice is not heard, his diet is supervised, his mind divorced from the minds of his brothers abroad. His brothers—that is the point: for just as the universal family of gifted writers transcends national barriers, so is the gifted reader a universal figure, not subject to spatial or temporal laws. It is he—the good, the excellent reader—who has saved the artist again and again from being destroyed by emperors, dictators, priests, puritans, philistines, political moralists, policemen, postmasters, and prigs. Let me define this admirable reader. He does not belong to any specific nation or class. No director of conscience and no book club can manage his soul. His approach to a work of fiction is not governed by those juvenile emotions that make the mediocre reader identify himself with this or that character and "skip descriptions." The good, the admirable reader identifies himself not with the boy or the girl in the book, but with the mind that conceived and composed that book. The admirable reader does not seek information about Russia in a Russian novel, for he knows that the Russia of Tolstoy or Chekhov is not the average Russia of history but a specific world imagined and created by individual genius. The admirable reader is not concerned with general ideas: he is interested in the particular vision. He likes the novel not because it helps him to get along with the group (to use a diabolical progressive-school cliche); he likes the novel because he imbibes and understands every detail of the text, enjoys what the author meant to be enjoyed, beams inwardly and all over, is thrilled by the magic imageries of the master-forger, the fancy-forger, the conjuror, the artist. Indeed, of all the characters that a great artist creates, his readers are the best.

In sentimental retrospect, the Russian reader of the past seems to me to be as much of a model for readers as Russian writers were models for writers in other tongues. He would start on his charmed career at a most tender age and lose his heart to Tolstoy or Chekhov when still in the nursery and nurse would try to take away *Anna Karenin* and would say: Oh, come, let me tell it to you in my own words (*Day-ka, ya tebe rasskazhu svoimi slovami* [*slovo-word*]). That is how the good reader learned to beware of translators of condensed masterpieces, of idiotic movies about the brothers Karenins, and of all other ways of toadying to the lazy and of quartering the great.

And to sum up, I would like to stress once more, Let us not look for the soul of Russia in the Russian novel: let us look for the individual genius. Look at the masterpiece, and not at the frame—and not at the faces of other people looking at the frame.

The Russian reader in old cultured Russia was certainly proud of Pushkin and of Gogol, but he was just as proud of Shakespeare or Dante, of Baudelaire or of Edgar Allan Poe, of Flaubert or of Homer, and this was the Russian reader's strength. I have a certain personal interest in the question, for if my fathers had not been good readers, I would hardly be here today, speaking of these matters in this tongue. I am aware of many things being quite as important as good writing and good reading; but in all things it is wiser to go directly to the quiddity, to the text, to the source, to the essence—and only then evolve whatever theories may tempt the philosopher, or the historian, or merely please the spirit of the day. Readers are born free and ought to remain free; and the following little poem by Pushkin, with which I shall close my talk, applies not only to poets, but also to those who love the poets.

I value little those much vaunted rights
that have for some the lure of dizzy heights;
I do not fret because the gods refuse
to let me wrangle over revenues,
or thwart the wars of kings; and 'tis to me
of no concern whether the press be free
to dupe poor oafs or whether censors cramp
the current fancies of some scribbling scamp.
These things are words, words, words. My spirit fights
for deeper Liberty, for better rights.
Whom shall we serve—the people or the State?
The poet does not care—so let them wait.
To give account to none, to be one's own
vassal and lord, to please oneself alone,
to bend neither one's neck, nor inner schemes,
nor conscience to obtain some thing that seems
power but is a flunkey's coat; to stroll
in one's own wake, admiring the divine
beauties of Nature and to feel one's soul
melt in the glow of man's inspired design
—that is the blessing, those are the rights!

[Translated by V. Nabokov]

From Pushkin

I value little those much vaunted rights
that have for some the lure of dizzy heights;
I do not fret because the gods refuse
to let me wrangle over revenues,
or thwart the wars of kings; and 'tis to me
of no concern whether the press be free
to dupe poor oafs or whether censors cramp
the current fancies of some scribbling scamp.
These things are words, words, words. My spirit fights
for deeper Liberty, for better rights.
Whom shall we serve--the people or the State?
The poet does not care,--so let them wait.
To give account to none, to be one's own
vassal and lord, to please oneself alone,
to bend neither one's neck, nor inner schemes,
nor conscience to obtain some thing that seems
power but is a flunkey's coat; to stroll
in one's own wake, admiring the divine
beauties of Nature and to feel one's soul
melt in the glow of man's inspired design
--that is the blessing, those are rights!

(transl. by V. Nabokov)

In order to ... [our talking] ... I propose to give a short account of Gogol's greatest work "Dead Souls" then ponder all things that magic which I shall try to show is the magic here. With the book Gogol ... in ... did his ... I am by ... to ... something never ... so ... but had not been done before: painting the the motion ... mass of an author's life-work and ... of the book the author's face appear through the transparent picture ...

The hero is the chubby glossy-cheeked cheat, Chichikov — not Chichikov, but Chee-chikov [(the correct pronunciation is given on the right side — with a circle around the accented part.)]

⊗

The five landowners whom Mr ~~Chichikov~~ Chichikov visits are: ~~Manilov~~. Man(eel)ov — a mannered ... somewhat eel-like man — maneelov the man-eel ... Then the miser ?(lew)shkin spelt Plushkin but the a moth has made a hole in that "plush" making it plewsh. There is the bear-like or ~~shaggy dog~~ like Sob(akay)vich — not Sobakevich as a football coach ~~would~~ say, but Sob(akay)vich. Sobáka means dog ... in Russian and the name ... means son of a doggie ...

Then we have Nozd(you)v ... the Why-O ... as in "yonder". If you like, you may call him Mr Nostril which is the foundation of his nasd ... Gogol was very nose-conscious and had a very long bone nose himself. Finally there is one female landowner — Mrs Korobochka — Dame Korobochka — Dame Smallbox — this is the meaning of her name. We had Smallpox and Smallweed in Bleak House and this is not Smallpox but Small box.]

Well that takes care of the main characters ...

NIKOLAY GOGOL (1809-1852)

Dead Souls (1842)

Socially minded Russian critics saw in *Dead Souls* and in *The Government Inspector* a condemnation of the social *poshlust* emanating from serf-owning bureaucratic provincial Russia and thus missed the true point. Gogol's heroes merely happen to be Russian squires and officials; their imagined surroundings and social conditions are perfectly unimportant factors—just as Monsieur Homais might be a business man in Chicago or Mrs. Bloom the wife of a schoolmaster in Vyshni-Volochok. Moreover, their surroundings and conditions, whatever they might have been in "real life," underwent such a thorough permutation and reconstruction in the laboratory of Gogol's peculiar genius that (as has been observed already in connection with *The Government Inspector*) it is as useless to look in *Dead Souls* for an authentic Russian background as it would be to try and form a conception of Denmark on the basis of that little affair in cloudy Elsinore. And if you want "facts," then let us inquire what experience had Gogol of provincial Russia. Eight hours in a Podolsk inn, a week in Kursk, the rest he had seen from the window of his traveling carriage, and to this he had added the memories of his essentially Ukrainian youth spent in Mirgorod, Nezhin, Poltava—all of which towns lay far outside Chichikov's itinerary. What seems true however is that

Dead Souls provides an attentive reader with a collection of bloated dead souls belonging to *poshlyaki* (males) and *poshlyachki* (females) described with that Gogolian gusto and wealth of weird detail which lift the whole thing to the level of a tremendous epic poem; and "poem" is in fact the subtle subtitle appended by Gogol to *Dead Souls*. There is something sleek and plump about *poshlust*, and this gloss, these smooth curves, attracted the artist in Gogol. The immense spherical *poshlyak* (singular of the word) Pavel Chichikov eating the fig at the bottom of the milk which he drinks to mellow his throat, or dancing in his nightgown in the middle of the room while things on shelves rock in response to his Lacedaemonian jig (ending in his ecstatically hitting his chubby behind—his real face—with the pink heel of his bare foot, thus propelling himself into the true paradise of dead souls) these are visions which transcend the lesser varieties of *poshlust* discernible in humdrum provincial surroundings or in the petty iniquities of petty officials. But a *poshlyak* even of Chichikov's colossal dimensions inevitably has somewhere in him a hole, a chink through which you see the worm, the little shriveled fool that lies all huddled up in the depth of the *poshlust*-painted vacuum. There was something faintly silly from the very start about that idea of buying up dead souls, —souls of serfs who had died since the last census and for whom their owners continued to pay the poll-tax, thus endowing them with a kind of abstract existence which however was quite concretely felt by the squire's pocket and could be just as "concretely" exploited by Chichikov, the buyer of such phantasma. This faint but rather sickening silliness was for a certain time concealed by the maze of complex machinations. *Morally* Chichikov was hardly guilty of any special crime in attempting to buy up dead men in a country where live men were lawfully purchased and pawned. If I paint my face with home made Prussian Blue instead of applying the Prussian Blue which is sold by the state and cannot be manufactured by private persons, my crime will be hardly worth a passing smile and no writer will make of it a Prussian Tragedy. But if I have surrounded the whole business with a good deal of mystery and flaunted a cleverness that presupposed most intricate difficulties in perpetrating a crime of that kind, and if owing to my letting a garrulous neighbor peep at my pots of home-brewn paint I get arrested and am roughly handled by men with authentic blue faces, then the laugh for what it is worth is on me. In spite of Chichikov's fundamental irreality in a fundamentally unreal world, the fool in him is apparent because from the very start he commits blunder upon blunder. It was silly to try to buy dead souls from an old woman who was afraid of ghosts; it was an incredible lapse of acumen to suggest such a Queer Street deal to the braggard and bully Nozdryov. I repeat however for the benefit of those who like books to provide them with "real people" and "real crime" and a "message" (that horror of horrors borrowed from the jargon of quack reformers) that *Dead Souls* will get them nowhere. Chichikov's guilt being a purely conventional matter, his destiny can hardly provoke any emotional reaction on our part. This is an additional reason why the view taken by Russian readers and critics, who saw in *Dead Souls* a matter-of-fact description of existing conditions, seems so utterly and ludicrously wrong. But when the legendary *poshlyak* Chichikov is considered as he ought to be, i.e., as a creature of Gogol's special brand moving in a special kind of Gogolian coil, the abstract notion of swindling in this serf-pawning business takes on strange flesh and begins to mean much more than it did when we considered it in the light of social conditions peculiar to Russia a hundred years ago. The dead souls he is buying are not merely names on a slip of paper. They are the dead souls that fill the air of Gogol's world with their leathery flutter, the clumsy animula of Manilov or of Korobochka, of the housewives of the town of N., of countless other little people bobbing throughout the book. Chichikov himself is merely the ill-paid representative of the Devil, a traveling salesman from Hades, "our Mr. Chichikov" as the Satan & Co. firm may be imagined calling their easy-going, healthy-looking but inwardly shivering and rotting agent. The *poshlust* which Chichikov personifies is one of the main attributes of the Devil, in whose existence, let it be added, Gogol believed far more seriously than he did in that of God. The chink in Chichikov's armor, that rusty chink emitting a faint but dreadful smell (a punctured can of conserved lobster tampered with and forgotten by some meddling fool in the pantry) is the organic aperture in the devil's armor. It is the essential stupidity of universal *poshlust*.

Chichikov is doomed from the start and he rolls to that doom with a slight wobble in his gait which only the *poshlyaki* and *poshlyachki* of the town of N. are capable of finding genteel and pleasant. At important moments when he launches upon one of those sententious speeches (with a slight break in his juicy voice—the tremolo of "dear brethren"), that are meant to drown his real intentions in a treacle of pathos, he applies to himself the words "despicable worm" and, curiously enough, a real worm is gnawing at his vitals and becomes suddenly visible if we squint a little when peering at his rotundity. I am reminded of a certain poster in old Europe that advertised automobile tires and featured something like a human being entirely made of concentric rings of rubber; and likewise, rotund Chichikov may be said to be formed of the tight folds of a huge flesh-colored worm.

If the special gruesome character attending the main theme of the book has been conveyed and if the different aspects of *poshlust* which I have noted at random have become connected in such a way as to form an artistic phenomenon (its Gogolian leitmotiv being the "roundness" of *poshlust*), then *Dead Souls* will cease to mimic a humorous tale or a social indictment and henceforth may be adequately discussed. So let us look at the pattern a little more closely.

———

"The gates of the hostelry in the governmental town of N. [so the book begins] admitted a smallish fairly elegant *britzka* on springs, of the sort used by bachelors such as retired colonels, staff-captains, country squires who own about a hundred souls of peasants—in short by all those who are dubbed 'gentlemen of medium quality.' Sitting in the *britzka* was a gentleman whose countenance could not be termed handsome, yet neither was he ill-favored: he was not too stout, nor was he too thin; you could not call him old, just as you could not say that he was still youthful. His arrival produced no stir whatever in the town and was not accompanied by anything unusual; alone two Russian *muzhiks* who were standing at the door of a dram-shop opposite the inn made certain remarks which however referred more to the carriage than to the person seated therein. 'Look at that wheel there,' said one. 'Now what do you think—would that wheel hold out as far as Moscow if need be, or would it not?' 'It would,' answered the other. 'And what about Kazan—I think it would not last that far?' 'It would not,'—answered the other. Upon this the conversation came to a close. And moreover, as the carriage drove up to the inn, a young man chanced to pass wearing white twill trousers that were very tight and short and a swallow-tail coat with claims to fashion from under which a shirtfront was visible fastened with a Tula bronze pin in the shape of a pistol. The young man turned his head, looked back at the carriage, caught hold of his cap, which the wind was about to blow off, and then went his way."

The conversation of the two "Russian *muzhiks*" (a typical Gogolian pleonasm) is purely speculative—a point which the abominable Fisher Unwin and Thomas Y. Crowell translations of course miss. It is a kind of to-be-or-not-to-be meditation in a primitive form. The speakers do not know whether the *britzka* is going to Moscow or not, just as Hamlet did not trouble to look whether, perhaps, he had not mislaid his bodkin. The *muzhiks* are not interested in the question of the precise itinerary that the *britzka* will follow; what fascinates them is solely the ideal problem of fixing the imaginary instability of a wheel in terms of imaginary distances; and this problem is raised to the level of sublime abstraction by their not knowing the exact distance from N. (an imaginary point) to Moscow, Kazan or Timbuctoo—and caring less. They impersonate the remarkable creative faculty of Russians, so beautifully disclosed by Gogol's own inspiration, of working in a void. Fancy is fertile only when it is futile. The speculation of the two *muzhiks* is based on nothing tangible and leads to no material results; but philosophy and poetry are born that way; meddlesome critics looking for a moral might conjecture that the rotundity of Chichikov is bound to come to grief, being symbolized by the rotundity of that doubtful wheel. Andrey Bely, who was a meddler of genius, saw in fact the whole first volume of *Dead Souls* as a closed circle whirling on its axle and blurring the spokes, with the theme of the wheel cropping up at each new revolution on round Chichikov's part. Another special touch is exemplified by the chance passer-by—that young man portrayed with a sudden and wholly irrelevant wealth of detail: he comes there as if he was going to stay in the book (as so many of Gogol's homunculi seem intent to do—and do not). With any other writer of his day the next paragraph would have been bound to begin: "Ivan, for that was the young man's name" . . . But no: a gust of wind interrupts his stare and he passes, never to be mentioned again. The faceless saloon-walker in the next passage (whose movements are so quick as he welcomes the newcomers that you cannot discern his features) is again seen a minute later coming down from Chichikov's room and spelling out the name on a slip of paper as he walks down the steps. "Pa-vel I-va-no-vich Chi-chi-kov"; and these syllables have a toxonomic value for the identification of that particular staircase.

In such works by Gogol as *The Government Inspector* I find pleasure in rounding up those peripheral characters that enliven the texture of its background. Such characters in *Dead Souls* as the inn-servant or Chichikov's valet (who had a special smell of his own which he imparted at once to his variable lodgings) do not quite belong to that class of Little People. With Chichikov himself and the country squires he meets they share the front stage of the book although they speak little and have no visible influence upon the course of Chichikov's adventures. Technically speaking, the creation of peripheral personages in the play was mainly dependent upon this or that character alluding to people who never emerged from the wings. In a novel the lack of action or speech on the part of secondary characters would not have been sufficient to endow them with that kind of backstage existence, there being no footlights to stress their actual absence from the front place. Gogol however had another trick up his sleeve. The peripheral characters of his novel are engendered by the subordinate clauses of its various metaphors, comparisons and lyrical outbursts. We are faced by the remarkable phenomenon of mere forms of speech directly giving rise to live creatures. This is perhaps the most typical example of how this happens.

"Even the weather had obligingly accommodated itself to the setting: the day was neither bright nor gloomy but of a kind of bluey-grey tint such as is found only upon the worn-out uniforms of garrison soldiers, for the rest a peaceful class of warriors except for their being somewhat inebriate on Sundays."

It is not easy to render the curves of this life-generating syntax in plain English so as to bridge the logical, or rather biological, hiatus between a dim landscape under a dull sky and a groggy old soldier accosting the reader with a rich hiccup on the festive outskirts of the very same sentence. Gogol's trick consists in using as a link the word *"vprochem"* ("for the rest," "otherwise," *"d'ailleurs"*) which is a connection only in the grammatical sense but mimics a logical link, the word "soldiers" alone affording a faint pretext for the juxtaposition of "peaceful"; and as soon as this false bridge of *"vprochem"* has accomplished its magical work these mild warriors cross over, staggering and singing themselves into that peripheral existence with which we are already familiar.

When Chichikov comes to a party at the Governor's house, the chance mention of black-coated gentlemen crowding around the powdered ladies in a brilliant light leads to a fairly innocent looking comparison with buzzing flies—and the very next instant another life breaks through:

"The black tailcoats flickered and fluttered, separately and in clusters, this way and that, just as flies flutter over dazzling white chunks of sugar on a hot July day when the old housekeeper [here we are] hacks and divides it into sparkling lumps in front of the open window: all the children [second generation now!] look on as they gather about her, watching with curiosity the movements of her rough hands while the *airy* squadrons of flies that the light *air* [one of those repetitions so innate in Gogol's style that years of work over every passage could not eradicate them] has raised, fly boldly in, complete mistresses of the premises [or literally: 'full mistresses,' *'polnya khozyaiki,'* which Isabel F. Hapgood in the Crowell edition mistranslates as 'fat housewives'] and, taking advantage of the old woman's purblindness and of the sun troubling her eyes, spread all over the dainty morsels, here separately, there in dense clusters."

It will be noticed that whereas the dull weather plus drunken trooper image comes to an end somewhere in the dusty suburban distance (where Ukhovyortov, the Ear-Twister, reigns) here, in the simile of the flies, which is a parody of the Homeric rambling comparison, a complete circle is described, and after his complicated and dangerous somersault, with no net spread under him, as other acrobatic authors have, Gogol manages to twist back to the initial "separately and in clusters." Several years ago during a Rugby game in England I saw the wonderful Obolensky kick the ball away on the run and then changing his mind, plunge forward and catch it back with his hands . . .

something of this kind of feat is performed by Nikolay Vasyilievich. Needless to say that all these things (in fact whole paragraphs and pages) were left out by Mr. T. Fisher Unwin who to the "considerable joy" of Mr. Stephen Graham (see preface, edition of 1915, London) consented to re-publish *Dead Souls*. Incidentally, Graham thought that "*Dead Souls* is Russia herself" and that Gogol "became a rich man and could winter at Rome and Baden-Baden."

The lusty barking of dogs which met Chichikov as he drove up to Madame Korobochka's house proves equally fertile:

"Meanwhile the dogs were lustily barking in all possible tones: one of them, with his head thrown back, indulged in such conscientious ululations as if he were receiving some prodigious pay for his labors; another hammered it out cursorily like your village sexton; in between rang out, similar to the bell of a mailcoach, the persistent treble of what was probably a young whelp; and all this was capped by a basso voice belonging presumably to some old fellow endowed with a tough canine disposition, for his voice was as hoarse as that of a basso profundo in a church choir, when the concerto is in full swing with the tenors straining on tiptoe in their eagerness to produce a high note and all the rest, too, throwing their heads back and striving upwards—while he alone with his bristly chin thrust into his neckerchief, turns his knees out, sinks down almost to the ground and issues thence that note of his which makes the window-panes quake and rattle."

Thus the bark of a dog breeds a church chorister. In yet another passage (where Pavel arrives at Sobakevich's house) a musician is born in a more complicated way remindful of the "dull sky drunken trooper" simile.

"As he drove up to the porch he noticed two faces which almost simultaneously appeared at the window: one belonged to a woman in a ribboned cap and it was as narrow and long as a cucumber; the other was a man's face and round and broad it was, like those Moldavian pumpkins, called *gorlyanki* from which in our good country *balalaikas* are made, two-stringed light *balalaikas*, the adornment and delight of a nimble young rustic just out of his teens, the cock of his walk and a great one at whistling through his teeth and winking his eye at the white-bosomed and white-necked country-lasses who cluster around in order to listen to the delicate twanging of his strings." (This young yokel was transformed by Isabel Hapgood in her translation into "the susceptible youth of twenty who walks blinking along in his dandified way.")

The complicated maneuver executed by the sentence in order to have a village musician emerge from burly Sobakevich's head consists of three stages: the comparison of that head to a special kind of pumpkin, the transformation of that pumpkin into a special kind of *balalaika*, and finally the placing of that *balalaika* in the hands of a young villager who forthwith starts softly playing as he sits on a log with crossed legs (in brand new high boots) surrounded by sunset midgets and country girls. Especially remarkable is the fact that this lyrical digression is prompted by the appearance of what may seem to the casual reader to be the most matter-of-fact and stolid character of the book.

Sometimes the comparison-generated character is in such a hurry to join in the life of the book that the metaphor ends in delightful bathos:

"A drowning man, it is said, will catch at the smallest chip of wood because at the moment he has not the presence of mind to reflect that hardly even a fly could hope to ride astride that chip, whereas he weighs almost a hundred and fifty pounds if not a good two hundred."

Who is that unfortunate bather, steadily and uncannily growing, adding weight, fattening himself on the marrow of a metaphor? We never shall know—but he almost managed to gain a footing.

The simplest method such peripheral characters employ to assert their existence is to take advantage of the author's way of stressing this or that circumstance or condition by illustrating it with some striking detail. The picture starts living a life of its own—rather like that leering organ-grinder with whom the artist in H. G. Wells' story *The Portrait* struggled, by means of jabs and splashes of green paint when the portrait he was making became alive and disorderly. Observe for instance the ending of chapter 7, where the intention is to convey the impressions of night falling upon a peaceful provincial town. Chichikov after successfully clinching his ghostly deal with the landowners has been entertained by the worthies of the town and goes to bed very drunk; his coachman and his valet quietly depart on a private spree of their own, then stumble back to the inn, most courteously propping up each other, and soon go to sleep too.

". . . emitting snores of incredible density of sound, echoed from the neighboring room by their master's thin nasal wheeze. Soon after this everything quieted down and deep slumber enveloped the hostelry; one light alone remained burning and that was in the small window of a certain lieutenant who had arrived from Ryazan and who was apparently a keen amateur of boots inasmuch as he had already acquired four pairs and was persistently trying on a fifth one. Every now and again he would go up to his bed as though he intended to take them off and lie down; but he simply could not; in truth those boots were well made; and for a long while still he kept revolving his foot and inspecting the dashing cut of an admirably finished heel."

Thus the chapter ends—and that lieutenant is still trying on his immortal jackboot, and the leather glistens, and the candle burns straight and bright in the only lighted window of a dead town in the depth of a star-dusted night. I know of no more lyrical description of nocturnal quiet than this Rhapsody of the Boots.

The same kind of spontaneous generation occurs in chapter 9, when the author wishes to convey with special strength the bracing turmoil which the rumors surrounding the acquisition of dead souls provoked throughout the province. Country squires who for years had been lying curled up in their holes like so many dormice all of a sudden blinked and crawled out:

"There appeared a certain Sysoy Pafnutievich, and a certain Macdonald Carlovich [a singular name to say the least but necessary here to underline utter remoteness from life and the consequent irreality of that person, a dream in a dream, so to speak], about whom nobody had heard before; and a long lean impossibly tall fellow [literally: 'a certain long long one, of such tall stature as had never been even seen'] with a bullet wound in his hand . . ."

In the same chapter, after explaining at length that he will name no names because "whatever name be invented there is quite sure to crop up in some corner of our empire—which is big enough for all purposes—some person who bears it, and who is sure to be mortally offended and to declare that the author sneaked in with the express intention of nosing out every detail," Gogol cannot stop the two voluble ladies whom he sets chattering about the Chichikov mystery from divulging their names as if his characters actually escaped his control and blurted out what he wished to conceal. Incidentally, one of those passages which fairly burst with little people tumbling out and scattering all over the page (or straddling Gogol's pen like a witch riding a broomstick) reminds one in a curious anachronistic fashion of a certain intonation and trick of style used by Joyce in *Ulysses* (but then Sterne too used the abrupt question and circumstantial answer method).

"Our hero however was utterly unconscious of this [i.e., that he was boring with his sententious patter a certain young lady in a ballroom] as he went on telling her all kinds of pleasant things which he had happened to utter on similar occasions in various places. [Where?] In the Government of Simbirsk, at the house of Sofron Ivanovich Bespechnoy, where the latter's daughter, Adelaida Sofronovna, was also present with her three sisters-in-law, Maria Gavrilovna, Alexandra Gavrilovna and Adelheida Gavrilovna; at the house of Frol Vasilievich Pobedonosnoy, in the Government of Penza; and at that of the latter's brother, where the following were present: his wife's sister Katerina Mikhailovna and her cousins, Roza Feodorovna and Emilia Feodorovna; in the Government of Viatka, at the house of Pyotr Varsonofievich, where his daughter-in-law's sister Pelageya Egorovna was present, together with a niece, Sophia Rostislavna and two step-sisters: Sophia Alexandrovna and Maklatura Alexandrovna."

Through some of these names runs that curious foreign strain (quasi-German in this case) which Gogol generally employs to convey a sense of remoteness and optical distortion due to the haze; queer hybrid names fit for difform or not yet quite formed people; and while squire Bespechnoy and squire Pobedonosnoy are, so to speak, only slightly *drunken* names (meaning as they do "Unconcerned" and "Victorious") the last one of the list is an apotheosis of nightmare nonsense faintly echoed by the Russian Scotsman whom we have already admired. It is inconceivable what type of mind one must have to see in Gogol a forerunner of the "naturalistic school" and a "realistic painter of life in Russia."

Not only people, but things too indulge in these nomenclatorial orgies. Notice the pet names that the officials of the town of N. give to their playing cards. *Chervi* means "hearts"; but it also sounds very much like "worms," and with the linguistic inclination of Russians to pull out a word to its utmost length for the sake of emotional emphasis, it becomes *chervotochina*, which means worm-eaten core. *Piki* — "spades" — French *piques* — turn into *pikentia*, that is, assume a jocular dog-Latin ending; or they produce such variations as *pikendras* (false Greek ending) or *pichura* (a faint ornithological shade), sometimes magnified into *pichurishchuk* (the bird turning as it were into an antediluvian lizard, thus reversing the order of natural evolution). The utter vulgarity and automatism of these grotesque nicknames, most of which Gogol invented himself, attracted him as a remarkable means to disclose the mentality of those who used them.

The difference between human vision and the image perceived by the faceted eye of an insect may be compared with the difference between a half-tone block made with the very finest screen and the corresponding picture as represented by the very coarse screening used in common newspaper pictorial reproduction. The same comparison holds good between the way Gogol saw things and the way average readers and average writers see things. Before his and Pushkin's advent Russian literature was purblind. What form it perceived was an outline directed by reason: it did not see color for itself but merely used the hackneyed combinations of blind noun and dog-like adjective that Europe had inherited from the ancients. The sky was blue, the dawn red, the foliage green, the eyes of beauty black, the clouds grey, and so on. It was Gogol (and after him Lermontov and Tolstoy) who first saw yellow and violet at all. That the sky could be pale green at sunrise, or the snow a rich blue on a cloudless day, would have sounded like heretical nonsense to your so-called "classical" writer, accustomed as he was to the rigid conventional color-schemes of the Eighteenth Century French school of literature. Thus the development of the art of description throughout the centuries may be profitably treated in terms of vision, the faceted eye becoming a unified and prodigiously complex organ and the dead dim "accepted colors" (in the sense of "idées reçues") yielding gradually their subtle shades and allowing new wonders of application. I doubt whether any writer, and certainly not in Russia, had ever noticed before, to give the most striking instance, the moving pattern of light and shade on the ground under trees or the tricks of color played by sunlight with leaves. The following description of Plyushkin's garden in *Dead Souls* shocked Russian readers in much the same way as Manet did the bewhiskered philistines of his day.

"An extensive old garden which stretched behind the house and beyond the estate to lose itself in the fields, alone seemed, rank and rugged as it was, to lend a certain freshness to these extensive grounds and alone was completely picturesque in its vivid wildness. The united tops of trees that had grown wide in liberty spread above the skyline in masses of green clouds and irregular domes of tremulous leafage. The colossal white trunk of a birchtree deprived of its top, which had been broken off by some gale or thunderbolt, rose out of these dense green masses and disclosed its rotund smoothness in midair, like a well proportioned column of sparkling marble; the oblique, sharply pointed fracture in which, instead of a capital, it terminated above, showed black against its snowy whiteness like some kind of headpiece or a dark bird. Strands of hop, after strangling the bushes of elder, mountain ash and hazel below, had meandered all over the ridge of the fence whence they ran up at last to twist around that truncate birchtree halfway up its length. Having reached its middle, they hung down from there and were already beginning to catch at the tops of other trees, or had suspended in the air their intertwined loops and thin clinging hooks which were gently oscillated by the air. Here and there the green thicket broke asunder in a blaze of sunshine and showed a deep unlighted recess in between, similar to dark gaping jaws; this vista was all shrouded in shadow and all one could discern in its black depth was: the course of a narrow footpath, a crumbling balustrade, a toppling summer-house, the hollow trunk of a decrepit willow, a thick growth of hoary sedge bristling out from behind it, an intercrossment and tangle of twigs and leaves that had lost their sap in this impenetrable wildwood, and lastly, a young branch of maple which had projected sideways the green paws of its leaves, under one of which a gleam of sunlight had somehow managed to creep in after all, unexpectedly making of that leaf a translucid and resplendent marvel burning in the dense darkness.

"On the very edge of the garden several great aspens stood apart, lording it over the rest, with the huge nests of crows propped up by their tremulous summits. On some of these trees dislocated boughs that were not quite detached from the trunks hung down together with their shriveled foliage. In a word all was beautiful as neither nature nor art can contrive, beautiful as it only is when these two come together, with nature giving the final touch of her chisel to the work of man (that more often than not he has piled up anyhow), alleviating its bulky agglomeration and suppressing both its crudely obvious regularity and the miserable gaps through which its stark background clearly showed and casting a wonderful warmth over all that had been evolved in the bleakness of measured neatness and propriety."

I do not wish to contend that my translation is especially good or that its clumsiness corresponds to Gogol's disheveled grammar, but at least it is exact in regard to sense. It is entertaining to glance at the mess which my predecessors have made of this wonderful passage. Isabel Hapgood (1885) for instance, who at least attempted to translate it in toto, heaps blunder upon blunder, turning the Russian "birch" into the non-endemic "beech," the "aspen" into an "ashtree," the "elder" into "lilac," the "dark bird" into a "blackbird," the "gaping" (*ziyavshaya*) into "shining" (which would have been *siyavshaya*), etc. etc.

The various attributes of the characters help to expand them in a kind of spherical way to the remotest regions of the book. Chichikov's aura is continued and symbolized by his snuffbox and his traveling case; by that "silver and enamel snuffbox"which he offered generously to everybody and on the bottom of which people could notice a couple of violets delicately placed there for the sake of their additional perfume (just as he would rub on Sunday mornings his sub-human, obscene body, as white and as plump as that of some fat woodboring larva, with eau de cologne—the last sickly sweet whiff of the smuggling business of his hidden past); for Chichikov is a fake and a phantom clothed in a pseudo-Pickwickian rotundity of flesh, and trying to smother the miserable reek of inferno (something far worse than the "natural smell" of his moody valet) permeating him, by means of maudlin perfumes pleasing to the grotesque noses of the inhabitants of that nightmare town. And the traveling chest:

"The author feels sure that among his readers there are some curious enough to be desirous of knowing the plan and inner arrangement of that chest. Being anxious to please he sees no reason to deny them their satisfaction. Here it is, this inner arrangement."

And without having warned the reader that what follows is not a box at all but a circle in hell and the exact counterpart of Chichikov's horribly rotund soul (and that what he, the author, is about to undertake is the disclosure of

Chichikov's innards under a bright lamp in a vivisector's laboratory), he continues thus:

"In the center was a soap-container [Chichikov being a soap bubble blown by the devil]; beyond the soap-container were six or seven narrow little interspaces for razors [Chichikov's chubby cheeks were always silky-smooth: a fake cherub], then two square niches for sand-box and inkstand, with little troughs for pens, sealing wax and all things that were longish in shape [the scribe's instruments for collecting dead souls]; then all sorts of compartments with and without lids, for shortish things; these were full of visiting cards, funeral notices, theatre tickets and such like slips which were stored up as souvenirs [Chichikov's social flutters]. All this upper tray with its various compartments could be taken out, and beneath it was a space occupied by piles of paper in sheets [paper being the devil's main medium of intercourse]; then followed a small secret drawer for money. This could be slipped out inconspicuously from the side of the chest [Chichikov's heart]. It would always be drawn out and pushed back so quickly by its owner [systole and diastole] that it is impossible to say exactly how much money it contained [even the author does not know]."

Andrey Bely, following up one of those strange subconscious clues which are discoverable only in the works of authentic genius, noted that this box was the *wife* of Chichikov (who otherwise was as impotent as all Gogol's sub-human heroes) in the same way as the cloak was Akaky's mistress in *The Overcoat* or the belfry Shponka's mother-in-law in *Ivan Shponka and his Aunt*. It may be further observed that the name of the only female landowner in the book, "Squiress" Korobochka means "little box"—in fact, Chichikov's "little box" (reminding one of Harpagon's ejaculation: "Ma cassette!" in Molière's *L'Avare*); and Korobochka's arrival in the town at the crucial moment is described in buxological terms, subtly in keeping with those used for the above quoted anatomic preparation of Chichikov's soul. Incidentally the reader ought to be warned that for the true appreciation of these passages he must quite forget any kind of Freudian nonsense that may have been falsely suggested to him by these chance references to connubial relations. Andrey Bely has a grand time making fun of solemn psychoanalysts.

We shall first note that in the beginning of the following remarkable passage (perhaps the greatest one in the whole book) a reference to the night breeds a peripheral character in the same way as it did the Amateur of Boots.

"But in the meantime, while he [Chichikov] sat in his uncomfortable armchair, a prey to troublesome thoughts and insomnia, vigorously cursing Nozdryov [who had been the first to disturb the inhabitants' peace of mind by bragging about Chichikov's strange commerce] and all Nozdryov's relatives [the 'family tree' which grows out spontaneously from our national kind of oath], in the faint glow of a tallow candle which threatened to go out at any moment under the black cap that had formed long ago all over its wick, and while the dark night blindly stared into his windows ready to shade into blue as dawn approached, and distant cocks whistled to one another in the distance [note the repetition of 'distant' and the monstrous 'whistled': Chichikov, emitting a thin nasal whistling snore, is dozing off, and the world becomes blurred and strange, the snore mingling with the doubly-distant crowing of cocks, while the sentence itself writhes as it gives birth to a quasi-human being], and somewhere in the sleeping town there stumbled on perchance a freize overcoat—some poor devil wearing that overcoat [here we are], of unknown standing or rank, and who knew only one thing [in the text the verb stands in the feminine gender in accordance with the feminine gender of 'freize overcoat' which, as it were, has usurped the place of man]—that trail [to the pub] which, alas, the devil-may-care Russian nation has burnt so thoroughly,—in the meantime [the "meantime" of the beginning of this sentence] at the other end of town. . . ."

Let us pause here for a moment to admire the lone passer-by with his blue unshaven chin and red nose, so different in his sorry condition (corresponding to Chichikov's troubled mind) from the passionate dreamer who had delighted in a boot when Chichikov's sleep was so lusty. Gogol continues as follows:

". . . at the other end of the town there was happening something that was to make our hero's plight even worse. To wit: through remote streets and by-alleys of the town rumbled a most queer vehicle which it is doubtful anybody could have named more exactly. It looked neither like a *tarantas* [simplest kind of traveling carriage], nor like a calash, nor like a *britzka*, being in sooth more like a fat-cheeked very round watermelon set upon wheels [now comes a certain subtle correspondence to the description of round Chichikov's box]. The cheeks of this melon, that is, the carriage doors, that bore remnants of their former yellow varnish, closed very poorly owing to the bad state of the handles and locks which had been perfunctorily fixed up by means of string. The melon was filled with chintz cushions, small ones, long ones, and ordinary ones, and stuffed with bags containing loaves of bread and such eatables as *kalachi* [purse-shaped rolls], *kokoorki* [buns with egg or cheese stuffing], *skorodoomki* [skoro-dumplings] and *krendels* [a sort of magnified *kalach* in the form of a capital B, richly flavored and decorated]. A chicken-pie and a *rassolnik* [a sophisticated giblet-pie] were visible even on the top of the carriage. The rear board was occupied by an individual that might have been originally a footman, dressed in a short coat of speckled homespun stuff, with a slightly hoary stubble on his chin, the kind of individual known by the appellation of 'boy' (though he might be over fifty). The rattle and screech of the iron clamps and rusty screws awakened a police sentry at the other end of the town [another character is born here in the best Gogolian manner], who, raising his halberd, shocked himself out of his slumber with a mighty roar of 'Who goes there?', but upon becoming aware that nobody was passing and that only a faint rumble was coming from afar [the dream melon had passed into the dream town], he captured a beast of sorts right upon his collar and walking up to a lantern slew it on his thumbnail [i.e., by squashing it with the nail of the curved index of the same hand, the adopted system of Russians for dealing with hefty national fleas], after which he put his halberd aside and went to sleep again according to the rules of his particular knighthood [here Gogol catches up with the coach which he had let go by while busy with the sentry]. The horses every now and then fell on their foreknees not only because they were not shod but also because they were little used to comfortable town pavements. The rickety coach after turning this way and that down several streets, turned at last into a dark lane leading past the little parish church called Nikola-na-Nedotychkakh and stopped at the gate of the *protopopsha's* [priest's wife or widow] house. A kerchiefed and warmly clothed servant girl climbed out of the *britzka* [typical of Gogol: now that the nondescript vehicle has arrived at its destination, in a comparatively tangible world, it has become one of the definite species of carriages which he had been careful to say it was not] and using both her fists banged upon the gate with a vigor a man might have envied; the 'boy' in the speckled coat was dragged down somewhat later for he was sleeping the sleep of the dead. There was a barking of dogs, and at last the gates, gaping wide, swallowed, although not without difficulty, that clumsy traveling contrivance. The coach rolled into a narrow yard which was crammed with logs of wood, chicken coops and all sorts of cages; out of the carriage a lady emerged; this lady was a collegiate secretary's widow and a landowner herself: Madame Korobochka.''

Madame Korobochka is as much like Cinderella as Pavel Chichikov is like Pickwick. The melon she emerges from can hardly be said to be related to the fairy pumpkin. It becomes a *britzka* just before her emergence, probably for the same reason that the crowing of the cock became a whistling snore. One may assume that her arrival is seen through Chichikov's dream (as he dozes off in his uncomfortable armchair). She does come, in reality, but the appearance of her coach is slightly distorted by his dream (all his dreams being governed by the memory of the secret drawers of his box) and if this vehicle turns out to be a *britzka* it is merely because Chichikov had arrived in one too. Apart from these transformations the coach is round, because plump Chichikov is himself a sphere and all his dreams revolve round a constant center; and at the same time her coach is also his roundish traveling case. The plan and inner arrangement of the coach is revealed with the same devilish graduation as those of the box had been. The elongated cushions are the "long things" of the box; the fancy pastries correspond to the frivolous mementoes Pavel preserved; the papers for jotting down the dead serfs acquired are weirdly symbolized by the drowsy serf in the speckled jacket; and the secret compartment, Chichikov's heart, yields Korobochka herself.

———————

I have already alluded, in discussing comparison-born characters, to the lyrical gust which follows immediately upon the appearance of stolid Sobakevich's huge face, from which face, as from some great ugly cocoon, emerges a bright delicate moth. The fact is that, curiously enough, Sobakevich, in spite of his solemnity and bulk, is the most poetical character in the book, and this may require a certain amount of explanation. First of all here are the emblems and attributes of his being (he is visualized in terms of furniture).

"As he took a seat, Chichikov glanced around at the walls and at the pictures that hung upon them. All the figures in these pictures were those of brawny fellows—full length lithographic portraits of Greek generals: Mavrocordato resplendent in his red-trousered uniform, with spectacles on his nose, Miaoulis, Kanaris. All these heroes had such stout thighs and such prodigious mustachios that it fairly gave one the creeps. In the midst of these robust Greeks a place had been given, for no earthly reason or purpose, to the portrait of a thin wispy little Bagration [famous Russian general] who stood there above his little banners and cannons in a miserably narrow frame. Thereupon a Greek personage followed again, namely the heroine Bobelina, whose mere leg seemed bigger than the whole body of any of the fops that swarm in our modern drawing rooms. The owner being himself a hardy and hefty man apparently wished his room to be adorned with hardy and hefty people too."

But was this the only reason? Is there not something singular in this leaning toward romantic Greece on Sobakevich's part? Was there not a "thin wispy little" poet concealed in that burly breast? For nothing in those days provoked a greater emotion in poetically inclined Russians than Byron's quest.

"Chichikov glanced again around the room: everything in it was both solid and unwieldy to the utmost degree and bore a kind of resemblance to the owner of the house himself. In one corner a writing desk of walnut wood bulged out on its four most ridiculous legs—a regular bear. Table, chair, armchair—everything was of the most heavy and uncomfortable sort; in a word, every article, every chair seemed to be saying: 'and I also am Sobakevich!' or 'and I also am very much like Sobakevich!' "

The food he eats is fare fit for some uncouth giant. If there is pork he must have the whole pig served at table, if it is mutton then the whole sheep must be brought in; if it is goose, then the whole bird must be there. His dealings with food are marked by a kind of primeval poetry and if there can be said to exist a gastronomical rhythm, his prandial meter is the Homeric one. The half of the saddle of mutton that he dispatches in a few crunching and susurrous instants, the dishes that he engulfs next—pastries whose size exceeds that of one's plate and a turkey as big as a calf, stuffed with eggs, rice, liver and other rich ingredients—all these are the emblems, the outer crust and natural ornaments of the man and proclaim his existence with that kind of hoarse eloquence that Flaubert used to put into his pet epithet "Hénorme." Sobakevich works in the food line with great slabs and mighty hacks, and the fancy jams served by his wife after supper are ignored by him as Rodin would not condescend to notice the rococo baubles in a fashionable boudoir.

"No soul whatever seemed to be present in that body, or if he did have a soul it was not where it ought to be, but, as in the case of Kashchey the Deathless [a ghoulish character in Russian folklore] it dwelled somewhere beyond the mountains and was hidden under such a thick crust, that anything that might have stirred in its depths could produce no tremor whatever on the surface."

The "dead souls" are revived twice: first through the medium of Sobakevich (who endows them with his own bulky attributes), then by Chichikov (with the author's lyrical assistance). Here is the first method—Sobakevich is boosting his wares:

" 'You just consider: what about the carriage-maker Mikheyev, for instance? Consider, every single carriage he used to make was complete with springs! And mind you, not the Moscow kind of work that gets undone in an hour, but solid, I tell you, and then he would upholster it, and varnish it too!' Chichikov opened his mouth to observe that however good Mikheyev might have been he had long ceased to exist; but Sobakevich was warming up to his subject, as they say; hence this rush and command of words.

" 'Or take Stepan Probka, the carpenter. I can wager my head that you will not find his like anywhere. Goodness, what strength that man had! Had he served in the Guards he would have got every blessed thing he wanted: the fellow was over seven feet high!'

"Again Chichikov was about to remark that Probka too was no more; but

Sobakevich seemed to have burst his dam: such torrents of speech followed that all one could do was to listen.

" 'Or Milyushkin, the bricklayer, he that could build a stove in almost any house! Or Maxim Telyatnikov, the shoemaker: with his awl he would prick a thing just once and there was a pair of boots for you; and what boots—they made you feel mighty grateful; and with all that, never swallowing a drop of liquor. Or Yeremey Sorokoplekhin—ah, that man could have stood his own against all the others: went to trade in Moscow and the tax alone he paid me was five hundred roubles every time.' "

Chichikov tries to remonstrate with this strange booster of non-existent wares, and the latter cools down somewhat, agreeing that the "souls" are dead, but then flares up again.

" 'Sure enough they are dead. . . . But on the other hand, what good are the live peasants of today? What sort of men are *they*? Mere flies—not men!'

" 'Yes, but anyway they can be said to exist, while those others are only figments.'

" 'Figments indeed! If only you had seen Mikheyev. . . . Ah, well, you are not likely to set eyes on anybody of that sort again. A great hulky mass that could hardly have squeezed into this room. In those great big shoulders of his there was more strength than in a horse. I should very much like to know where you could find another such figment!' "

Speaking thus Sobakevich turns to the portrait of Bagration as if asking the latter's advice; and some time later when, after a good deal of haggling the two are about to come to terms and there is a solemn pause, "eagle-nosed Bagration from his vantage point on the wall watched very attentively the clinching of the deal." This is the nearest we get to Sobakevich's soul while he is about, but a wonderful echo of the lyrical strain in his boorish nature may be discerned further on when Chichikov peruses the list of dead souls that the burly squire had sold him.

"And presently, when he glanced at these lists of names belonging to peasants who had really been peasants once, had labored and caroused, had been ploughmen and carriers, had cheated their owners, or perhaps had simply been good *muzhiks*, he was seized with a queer feeling which he could not explain to himself. Every list seemed to have a special character of its own, and consequently the peasants themselves seemed to acquire a special character. Almost all those that had belonged to Korobochka possessed various append-ages and nicknames. Brevity distinguished Plyushkin's list, where many of the peasants were merely defined by the initial syllables of their Christian names and patronymics followed by a couple of dots. Sobakevich's list struck one by its extraordinary completeness and wealth of detail. . . . 'Dear me,' said Chichikov to himself with a sudden gust of emotion peculiar to sentimental scoundrels, 'how many of you have been crowded in here! What sort of lives did you lead, my friends?' [He imagines these lives, and one by one the dead *muzhiks* leap into existence shoving chubby Chichikov aside and asserting themselves.] 'Ah, here he is, Stepan Probka, the giant who would have graced the Guards. I guess you have tramped across many provinces with your axe hanging from your belt and your boots slung over your shoulder [a Russian peasant's way of economizing on footgear], living upon a pennyworth of bread and some dry fish for the double of that, and bringing in every time, I guess, [to your master] at the bottom of your money bag, a hundred silver roubles or so, or perhaps a couple of banknotes sewed up in your canvas trousers or thrust deep into your boot. What manner of death was yours? Had you climbed right up to the domed roof of a church in trying to make more money [in wages for repairs] or had you perhaps hoisted yourself up to the very cross on that church, and did you slip from a beam thereon to dash your brains out on the ground whereat [some elderly comrade of yours] standing nearby only scratched the back of his head and said with a sigh: 'Well, my lad, you sure did have a fall'—and then tied a rope round his waist and climbed up to take your place. . . .'

" '. . . And what about you, Grigori Doyezhäi-ne-doye-desh [Drive-to-where-you-won't-get]? Did you ply a carrier's trade and having acquired a *tröika* [three horses] and a bast-covered *kibitka*, did you forsake forever your home, your native den, in order to trundle merchants to the fair? Did you surrender your soul to God on the road? Were you dispatched by your own comrades in a quarrel for the favors of some plump and ruddy beauty whose soldier husband was away? Or did those leathern gauntlets you wore and your three short-legged but sturdy steeds tempt a robber on some forest road? Or perhaps, after a good bit of desultory thinking as you lay in your bunk, you suddenly made for the pothouse, just like that, and then plunged straight into a hole in the ice of the river, never to be seen again?' "

The very name of one "Neoovazhäi-Koryto" (a weird combination of "disrespect" and "pigtrough") suggests by its uncouth straggling length the kind of death that had befallen this man: "A clumsy van drove over you as you were lying asleep in the middle of the road." The mention of a certain Popov, domestic serf in Plyushkin's list, engenders a whole dialogue after it has been assumed that the man had probably received some education and so had been guilty (note this superlogical move) not of vulgar murder, but of genteel theft.

" 'Very soon however some Rural Police Officer comes and arrests you for having no passport. You remain unconcerned during the confrontation. 'Who is your owner?' asks the Rural Police Officer, seasoning his question with a bit of strong language as befits the occasion. 'Squire So-and-so,' you reply briskly. 'Then what are you doing here [miles away],' asks the Rural Police Officer. 'I have been released on *obrok* [meaning that he had been permitted to work on his own or for some other party under the condition that he paid a percentage of his earnings to the squire who owned him], you reply without a moment's hesitation. 'Where is your passport?' 'My present boss, the merchant Pimenov, has it.' 'Let Pimenov be called! . . . You are Pimenov?' 'I am Pimenov.' 'Did he give you his passport?' 'No, he did nothing of the sort,' 'Why have you been lying?' asks the Rural Police Officer with the addition of a bit of strong language. 'That's right,' you answer briskly, 'I did not give it him because I came home late—so I left it with Antip Prokhorov, the bellringer.' 'Let the bellringer be called!' 'Did he give you his passport?' 'No, I did not receive any passport from him.' 'Lying again,' says the Rural Police Officer, spicing his speech with a bit of strong language. "Come now, where is that passport of yours?' 'I had it,' you answer promptly, 'but with one thing and another it is very likely I dropped it on the way.' 'And what about that army coat?' says the Rural Police Officer, again treating you to a bit of strong language. 'Why did you steal it? And why did you steal a trunk full of coppers from the priest?' "

It goes on like that for some time and then Popov is followed to the various prisons of which our great land has always been so prolific. But although these "dead souls" are brought back to life only to be led to misfortune and death, their resurrection is of course far more satisfactory and complete than the false "moral resurrection" which Gogol intended to stage in the projected second or third volumes for the benefit of pious and law-abiding citizens. His art through a whim of his own revived the dead in these passages. Ethical and religious considerations could only destroy the soft, warm, fat creatures of his fancy.

The emblems of rosy-lipped, blond, sentimental, vapid and slatternly Manilov (there is a suggestion of "mannerism" in his name and of *tuman* which means mist, besides the word *manil*, a verb expressing the idea of dreamy attraction) are: that greasy green scum on the pond among the maudlin charms of an "English garden" with its trimmed shrubs and blue pillared pavilion ("Temple of Solitary Meditation"); the pseudo-classical names which he gives to his children; that book permanently lying in his study, and opened permanently at the fourteenth page (not fifteenth, which might have implied some kind of decimal method in reading and not thirteenth which would have been the devil's dozen of pages, but *fourteenth*, an insipid pinkish-blond numeral with as little personality as Manilov himself); those careless gaps in the furniture of his house, where the armchairs had been upholstered with silk of which, however, there had not been enough for all, so that two of them were simply covered with coarse matting; those two candlesticks, one of which was very elegantly wrought of dark bronze with a trio of Grecian Graces and a mother-of-pearl shade, while the other was simply "a brass invalid," lame, crooked and besmeared with tallow; but perhaps the most appropriate emblem is the neat row of hillocks formed by the ashes that Manilov used to shake out of his pipe and arrange in symmetrical piles on the window-sill—the only artistic pleasure he knew.

"Happy is the writer who omits these dull and repulsive characters that disturb one by being so painfully real; who comes close to such that disclose the lofty virtue of man; who from the great turmoil of images that whirl daily around him selects but a few exceptions; who has been always faithful to the sublime harmony of his lyre, has never come down from those heights to visit his poor insignificant kinsmen and remained aloof, out of touch with the earth, wholly immersed in remote magnificent fancies. Ay, doubly enviable is his admirable lot: those visions are a home and a family to him: and at the same time the thunder of his fame rolls far and wide. The delicious mist of the incense he burns dims human eyes; the miracle of his flattery masks all the sorrows of life and depicts only the goodness of man. Applauding crowds come streaming in his wake to rush behind his triumphal chariot. He is called a great universal poet, soaring high above all other geniuses of the world even as an eagle soars above other high flying creatures. The mere sound of his name sends a thrill through ardent young hearts; all eyes greet him with the radiance of responsive tears. He has no equal in might; he is God.

"But a different lot and another fate await the writer who has dared to evoke all such things that are constantly before one's eyes but which idle eyes do not see—the shocking morass of trifles that has tied up our lives, and the essence of cold, crumbling, humdrum characters with whom our earthly way, now bitter, now dull, fairly swarms; has dared to make them prominently and brightly visible to the eyes of all men by means of the vigorous strength of his pitiless chisel. Not for him will be the applause, no grateful tears will he see, no souls will he excite with unanimous admiration; not to him will a girl of sixteen come flying, her head all awhirl with heroic fervor. Not for him will be that sweet enchantment when a poet hears nothing but the harmonies he has engendered himself; and finally, he will not escape the judgment of his time, the judgment of hypocritical and unfeeling contemporaries who will accuse the creatures his mind has bred of being base and worthless, will allot a contemptible nook for him in the gallery of those authors who insult mankind, will ascribe to him the morals of his own characters and will deny him everything, heart, soul and the divine flame of talent. For the judgment of his time does not admit that the lenses through which suns may be surveyed are as marvellous as those that disclose the movement of otherwise imperceptible insects; for the judgment of his time does not admit that a man requires a good deal of spiritual depth in order to be able to throw light upon an image supplied by base life and to turn it into an exquisite masterpiece; nor does the judgment of his time admit that lofty ecstatic laughter is quite worthy of taking its place beside the loftiest lyrical gust and that it has nothing in common with the faces a mountebank makes. The judgment of his time does not admit this and will twist everything into reproof and abuse directed against the unrecognized writer; deprived of assistance, response and sympathy, he will remain, like some homeless traveler alone on the road. Grim will be his career and bitterly will he realize his utter loneliness. . . .

"And for a long time yet, led by some wondrous power, I am fated to journey hand in hand with my strange heroes and to survey the surging immensity of life, to survey it through the laughter that all can see and through unknown invisible tears. And still far away is that time when with a gushing force of a different origin the formidable blizzard of inspiration will rise from my austere and blazing brow and, in a sacred tremor, humans will harken to the sublime thunder of a different speech."

Immediately after this extravagant eloquence, which is like a blaze of light revealing a glimpse of what at the time Gogol expected to be able to do in the second volume of his work, there follows the diabolically grotesque scene of fat Chichikov, half naked, dancing a jig in his bedroom—which is not quite the right kind of example to prove that "ecstatic laughter" and "lyrical gusts" are good companions in Gogol's book. In fact Gogol deceived himself if he thought he could laugh that way. Nor are the lyrical outbursts really parts of the solid pattern of the book; they are rather those natural interspaces without which the pattern would not be what it is. Gogol indulges in the pleasure of being blown off his feet by the gale that comes from some other clime of his world, (the Alpine-Italianate part), just as in *The Government Inspector* the modulated cry of the invisible reinsman ("Heigh, my winged ones!") brought in a whiff of summer night air, a sense of remoteness and romance, an *invitation au voyage*.

The main lyrical note of *Dead Souls* bursts into existence when the idea of Russia as Gogol saw Russia (a peculiar landscape, a special atmosphere, a symbol, a long, long road) looms in all its strange loveliness through the tremendous dream of the book. It is important to note that the following passage is sandwiched between Chichikov's final departure, or rather escape, from the town (which had been set upside down by the rumors of his deal) and the description of his early years.

"Meanwhile the *britzka* had turned into emptier streets; soon, only fences [a Russian fence is a blind grey affair more or less evenly serrated on top and resembling in this the distant line of a Russian firwood] stretched their wooden lengths and foretold the end of the town [in space, not in time]. See, the pavement comes to an end and here is the town barrier ["Schlagbaum": a movable pole painted with white and black stripes] and the town is left behind, and there is nothing around, and we are again travelers on the road. And again on both sides of the highway there comes an endless succession of mileposts, post station officials, wells, burdened carts, drab hamlets with samovars, peasant women and some bearded innkeeper who briskly pops out with a helping of oats in his hand; a tramp in worn shoes made of bast trudging a distance of eight hundred *versts* [note this constant fooling with figures—not five hundred and not a hundred but eight hundred, for numbers themselves tend toward an individuality of sorts in Gogol's creative atmosphere]; miserable little towns built anyhow with shabby shops knocked together by means of a few boards, selling barrels of flour, bast shoes [for the tramp who has just passed], fancy breads and other trifles; striped barriers, bridges under repair [i.e., *eternally* under repair—one of the features of Gogol's straggling, drowsy, ramshackle Russia]; a limitless expanse of grassland on both sides of the road, the traveling coaches of country squires, a soldier on horseback dragging a green case with its load of leaden peas and the legend: 'Battery such-and-such'; green, yellow and black bands [Gogol finds just the necessary space allowed by Russian syntax to insert "freshly upturned" before "black," meaning stripes of newly plowed earth] variegating the plains; a voice singing afar; crests of pines in the mist; the tolling of church bells dying away in the distance; crows like flies and the limitless horizon. . . . Rus! Rus! [ancient and poetic name for Russia] I see you, from my lovely enchanted remoteness I see you: a country of dinginess and bleakness and dispersal; no arrogant wonders of nature crowned by the arrogant wonders of art appear within you to delight or terrify the eyes: no cities with many-windowed tall palaces that have grown out of cliffs, no showy trees, no ivy that has grown out of walls amid the roar and eternal spray of waterfalls; one does not have to throw back one's head in order to contemplate some heavenly agglomeration of great rocks towering above the land [this is Gogol's private Russia, not the Russia of the Urals, the Altai, the Caucasus]. There are none of those dark archways with that tangle of vine, ivy and incalculable millions of roses, successive vistas through which one can suddenly glimpse afar the immortal outline of radiant mountains that leap into limpid silvery skies; all within you is open wilderness and level ground; your stunted towns that stick up among the plains are no more discernible than dots and signs [i.e., on a map]: nothing in you can charm and seduce the eye. So what is the incomprehensible secret force driving me towards you? Why do I constantly hear the echo of your mournful song as it is carried from sea to sea throughout your entire expanse? Tell me the secret of your song. What is this, calling and sobbing and plucking at my heart? What are these sounds that are both a stab and a kiss, why do they come rushing into my soul and fluttering about my heart? Rus! Tell me what do you want of me! What is the strange bond secretly uniting us? Why do you look at me thus, and why has everything you contain turned upon me eyes full of expectancy? And while I stand thus, sorely perplexed and quite still, lo, a threatening cloud heavy with future rains comes over my head and my mind is mute before the greatness of your expanse. What does this unlimited space portend? And since you are without end yourself, is it not within you that a boundless thought will be born? And if a giant comes will it not happen there where there is room enough for the mightiest limbs and the mightiest stride? Your gigantic expanse grimly surrounds me and with a dreadful vividness is reflected in my depths; a supernatural power makes my eyes bright. . . . Oh, what a shining, splendid remoteness unknown to the world! Rus! . . .

" 'Stop, stop, you fool,' Chichikov was shouting at Selifan [which stresses the fact of this lyrical outburst's not being Chichikov's own meditation]. 'Wait till I give you a slap with my scabbard,' shouted a State Courier with yard long moustaches, . . . 'Damn your soul, don't you see that this is a governmental carriage?' And like a phantom the *troika* vanished with a thunder of wheels and a whirl of dust."

The remoteness of the poet from his country is transformed into the remoteness of Russia's future which Gogol somehow identifies with the future of his work, with the second part of *Dead Souls*, the book that everybody in Russia was expecting from him and that he was trying to make himself believe he would write. For me *Dead Souls* ends with Chichikov's departure from the town of N. I hardly know what to admire most when considering the following remarkable spurt of eloquence which brings the first part to its close: the magic of its poetry—or magic of quite a different kind; for Gogol was faced by the double task of somehow having Chichikov escape just retribution by flight and of diverting the reader's attention from the still more uncomfortable fact that no retribution in terms of human law could overtake Satan's home-bound, hell-bound agent.

". . . Selifan added in a special singsong treble key something that sounded like 'Come, boys.' The horses perked up and had the light *britzka* speeding as if it were made of fluff. Selifan contented himself with waving his whip and emitting low guttural cries as he gently bounced up and down on his box while the *troika* either flew up a hillock or skimmed downhill again all along the undulating and slightly sloping highway. Chichikov did nothing but smile every time he was slightly thrown up on his leathern cushions, for he was a great lover of fast driving. And pray, find me the Russian who does not care for fast driving? Inclined as he is to let himself go, to whirl his life away and send it to the devil, his soul cannot but love speed. For is there not a kind of lofty and magic melody in fast driving? You seem to feel some unknown power lifting you up and placing you upon its wing, and then you are flying yourself and everything is flying by: the mileposts fly, merchants fly by on the boxes of their carriages, forests fly by on both sides of the road in a dark succession of firs and pines together with the sound of hacking axes and the cries of crows; the entire highway is flying none knows whither away into the dissolving distance; and there is something frightening in this rapid shimmer amid which passing and vanishing things do not have time to have their outlines fixed and only the sky above with fleecy clouds and a prying moon appears motionless. Oh *troika*, winged *troika*, tell me who invented you? Surely, nowhere but among a nimble nation could you have been born: in a country which has taken itself in earnest and has evenly spread far and wide over one half of the globe, so that once you start counting the milestones you may count on till a speckled haze dances before your eyes. And, methinks, there is nothing very tricky about a Russian carriage. No iron screws hold it together; its parts have been fitted and knocked into shape anyhow by means of an axe and a gauge and the acumen of a Yaroslav peasant; its driver does not wear any of your foreign jackboots; he consists of a beard and a pair of mittens, and he sits on a nondescript seat; but as soon as he strains up and throws back his whip-hand, and plunges into a wailing song, ah then—the steeds speed like the summer wind, the blurred wheelspokes form a circular void, the road gives a shiver, a passer-by stops short with an exclamation of fright—and lo, the *troika* has wings, wings, wings. . . . And now all you can see afar is a whirl of dust boring a hole in the air.

"Rus, are you not similar in your headlong motion to one of those nimble *troikas* that none can overtake? The flying road turns into smoke under you, bridges thunder and pass, all falls back and is left behind! The witness of your course stops as if struck by some divine miracle: is this not lightning that has dropped from the sky? And what does this awesome motion mean? What is the passing strange force contained in these passing strange steeds? Steeds, steeds—what steeds! Has the whirlwind a home in your manes? Is every sinew in you aglow with a new sense of hearing? For as soon as the song you know reaches you from above, you three, bronze-breasted, strain as one, and then your hoofs hardly touch the ground, and you are drawn out like three taut lines that rip the air, and all is transfigured by the divine inspiration of speed! . . . Rus, whither are you speeding so? Answer me. No answer. The middle bell trills out in a dream its liquid soliloquy; the roaring air is torn to pieces and becomes Wind; all things on earth fly by and other nations and states gaze askance as they step aside and give her the right of way."

Beautiful as all this final crescendo sounds, it is from the stylistic point of view merely a conjuror's patter enabling an object to disappear, the particular object being—Chichikov.

———

Leaving Russia again in May 1842 Gogol resumed his weird wanderings abroad. Rolling wheels had spun for him the yarn of the first part of *Dead Souls*; the circles he had described himself on his first series of journeys through a blurred Europe had resulted in round Chichikov becoming a revolving top, a dim rainbow; physical gyration had assisted the author in hypnotizing himself and his heroes into that kaleidoscopic nightmare which for years to come simple souls were to accept as a "panorama of Russia" (or "Homelife in Russia"). It was time now to go into training for the second part.

One wonders whether at the back of his mind which was so fantastically humped, Gogol did not assume that rolling wheels, long roads unwinding themselves like sympathetic serpents and the vaguely intoxicating quality of smooth steady motion which had proved so satisfactory in the writing of the first part would automatically produce a second book which would form a clear luminous ring round the whirling colors of the first one. That it must be a halo, of this he was convinced; otherwise the first part might be deemed the magic of the Devil. In accordance with his system of laying the foundation for a book after he had published it he managed to convince himself that the (as yet unwritten) second part had actually given birth to the first and that the first would fatally remain merely an illustration bereft of its legend if the parent volume was not presented to a slow-witted public. In reality, he was to be hopelessly hampered by the autocratic form of the first part. When he attempted to compose the second, he was bound to act in much the same way as that murderer in one of Chesterton's stories who was forced to make all the note paper in his victim's house conform to the insolite shape of a fake suicide message.

Morbid wariness may have added certain other considerations. Passionately eager as he was to learn in detail what people thought of his work—any kind of person or critic, from the knave in the Government's pay to the fool fawning on public opinion—he had a hard time trying to explain to his correspondents that what merely interested him in critical reviews was a more extensive and objective view that they were giving him of his own self. It greatly bothered him to learn that earnest people were seeing in *Dead Souls*, with satisfaction or disgust, a spirited condemnation of slavery, just as they had seen an attack on corruption in *The Government Inspector*. For in the civic reader's mind *Dead Souls* was gently turning into *Uncle Tom's Cabin*. One doubts whether this bothered him less than the attitude of those critics— blackcoated worthies of the old school, pious spinsters and Greek Orthodox puritans—who deplored the "sensuousness" of his images. He was also acutely aware of the power his artistic genius had over man and of the— loathsome to him—responsibility that went with such power. Something in him wanted a still greater sway (without the responsibility) like the fisherman's wife in Pushkin's tale who wanted a still bigger castle. Gogol became a preacher because he needed a pulpit to explain the ethics of his books and because a direct contact with readers seemed to him to be the natural development of his own magnetic force. Religion gave him the necessary intonation and method. It is doubtful whether it gave him anything else.

A unique rolling stone, gathering—or thinking he would gather—a unique kind of moss, he spent many summers wandering from spa to spa. His complaint was difficult to cure because it was both vague and variable: attacks of melancholy when his mind would be benumbed with unspeakable forebodings and nothing except an abrupt change of surroundings could bring relief; or else a recurrent state of physical distress marked by shiverings when no abundance of clothing could warm his limbs and when the only thing that helped, if persistently repeated, was a brisk walk—the longer the better. The paradox was that while needing constant movement to prompt inspiration, this movement physically prevented him from writing. Still, the winters spent in Italy, in comparative comfort, were even less productive than those fitful stage coach periods. Dresden, Bad Gastein, Salzburg, Munich, Venice, Florence, Rome, Florence, Mantua, Verona, Innsbruck, Salzburg, Karlsbad, Prague, Greifenberg, Berlin, Bad Gastein, Prague, Salzburg, Venice, Bologna, Florence, Rome, Nice, Paris, Frankfurt, Dresden,—and all over again, this series with its repetitions of names of grand tour towns is not really the itinerary of a man seeking health—or collecting hotel labels to show in Moscow, Idaho, or Moscow, Russia—but merely the dotted line of a vicious circle with no geographical meaning. Gogol's spas were not really spatial. Central Europe for him was but an optical phenomenon—and the only thing that really mattered, the only real obsession, the only real tragedy was that his creative power kept steadily and hopelessly ebbing away. When Tolstoy surrendered the writing of novels to the ethical, mystical and educational urge, his genius was ripe and ruddy, and the fragments of his imaginative work posthumously published show that his art was still developing after Anna Karenina's death. But Gogol was a man of few books and the plans he had made to write the book of his life happened to coincide with the beginning of his decline as a writer—after he had reached the summits of *The Government Inspector*, *The Overcoat*, and the first volume of *Dead Souls*.

———

The period of preaching begins with certain last touches that he put to *Dead Souls*—those strange hints at a prodigious apotheosis in the future. A peculiar biblical accent swells the contours of his sentences in the numerous letters he writes to his friends from abroad. "Woe to those who do not heed my word! Leave all things for a while, leave all such pleasures that tickle your fancy at idle moments. Obey me: during one year, one year only, attend to the affairs of your country estate." Sending landowners back to face the problems of country life (with all the contemporary implications of the business—unsatisfactory crops, disreputable overseers, unmanageable slaves, idleness, theft, poverty, lack of economic and "spiritual" organization) becomes his main theme and command—a command couched in the tones of a prophet ordering men to discard all earthly riches. But, despite the tone, Gogol was ordering landowners to do exactly the opposite (although it did sound like some great sacrifice that he was demanding from his bleak hilltop, in the name of God): leave the great town where you are frittering away your precarious income and return to the lands that God gave you for the express purpose that you might grow as rich as the black earth itself, with robust and cheerful peasants gratefully toiling under your fatherly supervision. "The landowners' business is divine"—this was the gist of Gogol's sermon.

One cannot help noting how eager, how overeager he was not only to have those sulky landowners and disgruntled officials return to their provincial offices, to their lands and crops, but also to have them give him a minute account of their impressions. One almost might suppose that there was something else at the back of Gogol's mind, that Pandora's box mind, something more important to him than the ethical and economic conditions of life in rural Russia; namely—a pathetic attempt to obtain "authentic" first-hand material for his book; because he was in the worst plight that a writer can be in: he had lost the gift of imagining facts and believed that facts may exist by themselves.

The trouble is that bare facts do not exist in a state of nature, for they are never really quite bare: the white trace of a wrist watch, a curled piece of sticking plaster on a bruised heel, these cannot be discarded by the most ardent nudist. A mere string of figures will disclose the identity of the stringer as neatly as tame ciphers yielded their treasure to Poe. The crudest *curriculum vitae* crows and flaps its wings in a style peculiar to the undersigner. I doubt whether you can even give your telephone number without giving something of yourself. But Gogol in spite of all the things he said about wishing to know mankind because he loved mankind, was really not much interested in the personality of the giver. He wanted his facts absolutely bare—and at the same time he demanded not mere strings of figures but a complete set of minute observations. When some of his more indulgent friends yielded reluctantly to his requests and then warmed up to the business and sent him accounts of provincial and rural affairs—they would get from him a howl of disappointment and dismay instead of thanks; for his correspondents were not Gogols. They had been ordered by him to describe things—just describe them. They did so with a vengeance. Gogol was balked of his material because his friends were not writers whereas he could not address himself to those friends of his who were writers, because then the facts supplied would be anything but bare. The whole business is indeed one of the best illustrations of the utter stupidity of such terms as "bare facts" and "realism." Gogol—a "realist"! There are text books that say so. And very possibly Gogol himself in his pathetic and futile efforts to get the bits that would form the mosaic of his book from his readers themselves, surmised that he was acting in a thoroughly rational way. It is so simple, he kept on peevishly repeating to various ladies and gentlemen, just sit down for an hour every day and jot down all you see and hear. He might as well have told them to mail him the moon—no matter in what quarter. And never mind if a star or two and a streak of mist get mixed up with it in your hastily tied blue paper parcel. And if a horn gets broken, I will replace it.

His biographers have been rather puzzled by the irritation he showed at not getting what he wanted. They were puzzled by the singular fact that a writer of genius was surprised at other people not being able to write as well as he did. In reality what made Gogol so cross was that the subtle method he had devised of getting material, which he could no longer create himself, did not work. The growing conscience of his impotence became a kind of disease which he concealed from himself and from others. He welcomed interruptions and obstacles ("obstacles are our wings" as he put it) because they could be held responsible for the delay. The whole philosophy of his later years with such basic notions as "the darker your heavens the more radiant tomorrow's blessing will be" was prompted by the constant feeling that this morrow would never come.

On the other hand, he would fly into a terrific passion if anybody suggested that the coming of the blessing might be hastened—I am not a hack, not a journeyman, not a journalist—he could write. And while he did all he could to make himself and others believe that he was going to produce a book of the utmost importance to Russia (and "Russia" was now synonymous with "humanity" in his very Russian mind) he refused to tolerate rumors which he engendered himself by his mystical innuendoes. The period of his life following upon the first part of *Dead Souls* may be entitled "Great Expectations"—from the reader's point of view at least. Some were expecting a still more definite and vigorous indictment of corruption and social injustice, others were looking forward to a rollicking yarn with a good laugh on every page. While Gogol was shivering in one of those stone cold rooms that you find only in the extreme South of Europe, and was assuring his friends that henceforth his life was sacred, that his bodily form must be handled with care and loved and nursed as the cracked earthen jar containing that wine of wisdom, (i.e., the second part of *Dead Souls*), the glad news was spread at home that Gogol was completing a book dealing with the adventures of a Russian general in Rome—the funniest book he had ever written. The tragical part of the business was that as a matter of fact the best thing in the remnants of the second volume that have reached us happens to be the passages relating to that farcical automaton, General Betrishchev.

———

Rome and Russia formed a combination of a deeper kind in Gogol's unreal world. Rome was to him a place where he had spells of physical fitness that the North denied him. The flowers of Italy (of which flowers he said: "I *respect* flowers that have grown by themselves on a grave") filled him with a fierce desire to be changed into a Nose: to lack everything else such as eyes, arms, legs, and to be nothing but one huge Nose, "with nostrils the size of two goodly pails so that I might inhale all possible vernal perfumes." He was especially nose-conscious when living in Italy. There was also that special Italian sky "all silvery and shot with a satiny gloss but disclosing the deepest tone of blue when viewed through the arches of the Coliseum." Seeking a kind of relaxation from his own distorted and dreadful and devilish image of the world he pathetically endeavored to cling to the normality of a second rate painter's conception of Rome as an essentially "picturesque" place: "I like the donkeys too—the donkeys that amble or jog at full speed with half closed eyes and picturesquely carry upon their back strong stately Italian women whose white caps remain brightly visible as they recede; or when these donkeys drag along, in a less picturesque way, with difficulty and many a stumble, some lank stiff Englishman who sports a greenish brown waterproof mackintosh [literal translation] and screws up his legs so as to avoid scraping the ground; or when a bloused painter rides by complete with Vandyke beard and wooden paintbox" etc. He could not keep up this kind of style for long and the conventional novel about the adventures of an Italian gentleman that at one time he contemplated writing happily remained limited to a few lurid generalizations "Everything in her from her shoulders to her *antique breathing* leg and to the *last toe* of her foot is the crown of creation"—no, enough of that, or the hemmings and hawings of a wistful provincial clerk musing his misery away in the depths of Gogolian Russia will get hopelessly mixed up with classical eloquence.

Then there was Ivanov in Rome, the great Russian painter. For more than twenty years he worked at his picture "The Appearance of the Messiah to the People." His destiny was in many respects similar to that of Gogol with the difference that at last Ivanov *did* finish his masterpiece: the story is told that when it was finally exhibited (in 1858) he calmly sat there putting a few final touches to it—this after twenty years of work!—quite unconcerned by the crowd in the exhibition hall. Both Ivanov and Gogol lived in permanent poverty because neither could tear himself away from his life work in order to earn a living; both were constantly pestered by impatient people rebuking them for their slowness; both were highstrung, ill-tempered, uneducated, and ridiculously clumsy in all worldly matters. In his capital description of Ivanov's work Gogol stresses this relationship, and one cannot help feeling that when he spoke of the chief figure in the picture ("And He, in heavenly peace and divine remoteness, is already nearing with quick firm steps" . . .), Ivanov's picture got somehow mixed in his thoughts with the religious element of his own still unwritten book which he saw steadily approaching from the silvery Italian heights.

The letters he wrote to his friends while working on *Selected Passages from Correspondence with Friends* did not include these passages (if they had, Gogol would not have been Gogol), but they much resemble them both in matter and tone. He thought some of them so inspired from above that he requested their being read "daily during the week of Fast"; it is doubtful however whether any of his correspondents were sufficiently meek to do this—to summon the members of their household and selfconsciously clear their throats—rather like the Mayor about to read the all-important letter in act one of *The Government Inspector*. The language of these epistles is almost a parody of sanctimonious intonation but there are some beautiful interruptions, as when, for instance, Gogol uses some very strong and worldly language in regard to a printing house which had swindled him. The pious actions which he plans out for his friends come to coincide with more or less bothersome commissions. He developed a most extraordinary system of laying penance on "sinners" by making them slave for him—running errands, buying and packing the books he needed, copying out critical reviews, haggling with printers, etc. In compensation he would send a copy of, say, *The Imitation of Jesus Christ* with detailed instructions telling how to use it—and quite similar instructions occur in passages concerning hydrotherapy and digestive troubles—"Two glasses of cold water before breakfast" is the tip he gives a fellow sufferer.

"Set aside all your affairs and busy yourself with my own"—this is the general trend—which of course would have been quite logical had his correspondents been disciples firmly believing that "he who helps Gogol helps God." But the real people who got these letters from Rome, Dresden or Baden-Baden decided that Gogol was either going mad or that he was deliberately playing the fool. Perhaps he was not too scrupulous in using his divine rights. He put his comfortable situation as God's representative to very personal ends as, for instance, when giving a piece of his mind to persons who had offended him in the past. When the critic Pogodin's wife died and the man was frantic with grief, this is what Gogol wrote him: "Jesus Christ will help you to become a gentleman, which you are neither by education or inclination—she is speaking through me."—a letter absolutely unique in the correspondence of compassion. Aksakov was one of the few people who decided at last to let Gogol know his reaction to certain admonishments. "Dear Friend," he wrote, "I never doubt the sincerity of your beliefs or your good will in respect to your friends; but I frankly confess being annoyed by the form your beliefs take. Even more—they frighten me. I am 53 years old. I read Thomas à Kempis before you were born. I am as far from condemning the beliefs of others as I am from accepting them—whereas you come and tell me as if I were a schoolboy—and without having the vaguest notion of what my own ideas are—to read the *Imitation*—and moreover, to do so at certain fixed hours after my morning coffee, a chapter a day, like a lesson. . . . This is both ridiculous and aggravating. . . ."

But Gogol persisted in his newly found *genre*. He maintained that whatever he said or did was inspired by the same spirit that would presently disclose its mysterious essence in the second and third volumes of *Dead Souls*. He also maintained that the volume of *Selected Passages* was meant as a test, as a means of putting the reader into a suitable frame of mind for the reception of the sequel to *Dead Souls*. One is forced to assume that he utterly failed to realize the exact nature of the stepping stone he was so kindly providing.

The main body of the *Passages* consists of Gogol's advice to Russian landowners, provincial officials and, generally, Christians. County squires are regarded as the agents of God, hard working agents holding shares in paradise and getting more or less substantial commissions in earthly currency. "Gather all your *mouzhiks* and tell them that you make them labor because this is what God intended them to do—not at all because you need money for your pleasures; and at this point take out a banknote and in visual proof of your words burn it before their eyes. . . ." The image is pleasing: the squire standing on his porch and demonstrating a crisp, delicately tinted banknote with the deliberate gestures of a professional magician; a Bible is prepared on an innocent-looking table; a boy holds a lighted candle; the audience of bearded peasants gapes in respectful suspense; there is a murmur of awe as the banknote turns into a butterfly of fire; the conjuror lightly and briskly rubs his hands—just the inside of the fingers; then after some patter he opens the Bible and lo, Phoenix-like, the treasure is there.

The censor rather generously left out this passage in the first edition as implying a certain disrespect for the Government by the wanton destruction of state money—much in the same way as the worthies in *The Government Inspector* condemned the breaking of state property (namely chairs) at the hands of violent professors of ancient history. One is tempted to continue this simile and say that in a sense Gogol in those *Selected Passages* seemed to be impersonating one of his own delightfully grotesque characters. No schools, no books, just you and the village priest—this is the educational system he suggests to the squire. "The peasant must not even *know* that there exist other books besides the Bible." "Take the village priest with you everywhere . . . . Make him your estate manager." Samples of robust curses to be employed whenever a lazy serf is to be pricked to the quick are supplied in another astounding passage. There are also some grand bursts of irrelevant rhetoric— and a vicious thrust at the unlucky Pogodin. We find such things as "every man has become a rotten rag" or "compatriots, I am frightened"—the "compatriots" ("saw-are-tea-chesstven-nikee") pronounced with the intonation of "comrades" or "brethren"—only more so.

The book provoked a tremendous row. Public opinion in Russia was essentially democratic—and, incidentally, deeply admired America. No Tsar could break this backbone (it was snapped only much later by the Soviet regime). There were several schools of civic thought in the middle of the last century; and though the most radical one was to degenerate later into the atrocious dullness of Populism, Marxism, Internationalism and what not (then to spin on and complete its inevitable circle with State Serfdom and Reactionary Nationalism), there can be no doubt whatever that in Gogol's time the "Westerners" formed a cultural power vastly exceeding in scope and quality anything that reactionary fogeys could think up. Thus it would not be quite fair to view the critic Belinski, for instance, as merely a forerunner (which phylogenetically he of course was) of those writers of the 1860s and 1870s who virulently enforced the supremacy of civic values over artistic ones; what they meant by "artistic" is another question: Chernyshevski or Pisarev would solemnly accumulate reasons to prove that writing textbooks for the people was more important than painting "marble pillars and nymphs"—which they thought was "pure art." Incidentally this outdated method of bringing all esthetic possibilities to the level of one's own little conceptions and capacites in the water color line when criticizing "art for art" from a national, political or generally philistine point of view, is very amusing in the argumentation of some modern American critics. Whatever his naive shortcomings as an appraiser of artistic values, Belinski had as a citizen and as a thinker that wonderful instinct for truth and freedom which only party politics can destroy—and party politics were still in their infancy. At the time his cup still contained a pure liquid; with the help of Dobrolyubov and Pisarev and Mikhaylovski it was doomed to turn into a breeding fluid for most sinister germs. On the other hand Gogol was obviously stuck in the mud and had mistaken the oily glaze on a filthy puddle for a mystic rainbow of sorts. Belinski's famous letter, ripping up as it does the *Selected Passages* ("this inflated and sluttish hullaballoo of words and phrases") is a noble document. It contained too a spirited attack on Tsardom so that distribution of copies of the "Belinski letter" soon became punishable by Hard Labor in Siberia. Gogol, it seems, was mainly upset by Belinski's hints at his fawning upon aristocrats for the sake of financial assistance. Belinski, of course, belonged to the "poor and proud" school; Gogol as a Christian condemned "pride."

In spite of the torrents of abuse, complaints and sarcasm that flooded his book from most quarters, Gogol kept a rather brave countenance. Although admitting that the book had been written "in a morbid and constrained state of mind" and that "inexperience in the art of such writing had, with the Devil's help, transformed the humility I actually felt into an arrogant display of self-sufficiency" (or, as he puts it elsewhere, "I let myself go like a regular Khlestakov"), he maintained with the solemnity of a staunch martyr that his book was necessary, and this for three reasons: it had made people show him what he was; it had shown him and themselves what *they* were; and it had cleansed the general atmosphere as efficiently as a thunderstorm. This was about equal to saying that he had done what he had intended to do: prepare public opinion for the reception of the second part of *Dead Souls*.

During his long years abroad and hectic visits to Russia Gogol kept jotting down on scraps of paper (in his carriage, at some inn, in a friend's house, anywhere) odds and ends relating to the supreme masterpiece. At times he would have quite a series of chapters which he would read to his most intimate friends in great secret; at others he would have nothing; sometimes a friend would be copying pages and pages of it and sometimes Gogol insisted that not a word had been penned yet—everything was in his brain. Apparently there were several minor holocausts preceding the main one just before his death.

At a certain point of his tragic efforts he did something which, in view of his physical frailty, was rather in the nature of a feat: he journeyed to Jerusalem with the object of obtaining what he needed for the writing of his book—divine advice, strength and creative fancy—much in the same fashion as a sterile woman might beg the Virgin for a child in the painted darkness of a medieval church. For several years, however, he kept postponing this pilgrimage: his spirit, he said, was not ready; God did not wish it yet; "mark the obstacles he puts in my way"; a certain state of mind (vaguely resembling the Catholic "grace") had to come into being so as to ensure a maximum probability of success in his (absolutely pagan) enterprise; moreover, he needed a reliable traveling companion who would not be a bore; would be silent or talkative at moments exactly synchronizing with the pilgrim's prismatic mood; and who, when required, would tuck in the traveling rug with a soothing hand. When at last in January, 1848, he launched upon his hazardous enterprise, there was just as little reason for its not turning into a dismal flop as there ever had been.

A sweet old lady, Nadezhda Nikolayevna Sheremetev, one of Gogol's truest and dullest correspondents, with whom he had exchanged many a prayer for the welfare of his soul saw him to the town barrier beyond Moscow. Gogol's papers were probably in perfect order but somehow or other he disliked the idea of their being examined, and the holy pilgrimage began with one of those morbid mystifications which he was wont to practice on policemen. Unfortunately, it involved the old lady too. At the barrier she embraced the pilgrim, broke into tears and made the sign of the cross over Gogol who responded effusively. At this moment papers were asked for: an official wanted to know who exactly was leaving. "This little old lady," cried Gogol, and rolled away in his carriage, leaving Madame Sheremetev in a very awkward position.

To his mother he sent a special prayer to be read in church by the local priest. In this prayer he begged the Lord to save him from robbers in the East and to spare him seasickness during the crossing. The Lord ignored the second request: between Naples and Malta, on the capricious ship "Capri," Gogol vomited so horribly that "the passengers marveled greatly." The rest of the pilgrimage was singularly dim so that had there not been some official proof of its actual occurrence one might easily suppose that he invented the whole journey as he had formerly invented an excursion to Spain. When for years on end you have been telling people that you are going to do something and when you are sick of not being able to make up your mind, it saves a good deal of trouble to have them believe one fine day that you have done it already—and what a relief to be able to drop the matter.

"What can my dreamlike impressions convey to you? I saw the Holy Land through the mist of a dream." (From a letter to Zhukovski). We have a glimpse of him quarreling in the desert with Bazsili, his traveling companion. Some-where in Samaria he plucked an asphodel, somewhere in Galilee a poppy (having a vague inclination for botany as Rousseau had). It rained at Nazareth, and he sought shelter, and was stranded there for a couple of hours "hardly realizing that I was in Nazareth as I sat there" (on a bench under which a hen had taken refuge) "just as I would have been sitting at some stage-coach station somewhere in Russia." The sanctuaries he visited failed to fuse with their mystic reality in his soul. In result, the Holy Land did as little for his soul (and his book) as German sanatoriums had done for his body.

———

During the last ten years of his life, Gogol kept stubbornly brooding over the sequel to *Dead Souls*. He had lost the magic capacity of creating life out of nothing; his imagination needed some ready material to work upon for he still had the strength of repeating himself; although unable to produce a brand new world as he had done in the first part, he thought he could use the same texture and recombine its designs in another fashion, namely: in conformity with a definite purpose which had been absent from the first part, but which was now supposed not only to provide a new driving force, but also to endow the first part with a retrospective meaning.

Apart from the special character of Gogol's case, the general delusion into which he had lapsed was of course disastrous. A writer is lost when he grows interested in such questions as "what is art?" and "what is an artist's duty?" Gogol decided that the purpose of literary art was to cure ailing souls by producing in them a sense of harmony and peace. The treatment was also to include a strong dose of didactic medicine. He proposed to portray national defects and national virtues in such a manner as to help readers to persever in the latter and rid themselves of the former. At the beginning of his work on the sequel his intention was to make his characters not "wholly virtuous," but "more important" than those of Part One. To use the pretty slang of publishers and reviewers he wished to invest them with more "human appeal." Writing novels were merely a sinful game if the author's "sympathetic attitude" towards some of his characters and a "critical attitude" towards others, was not disclosed with perfect clarity. So clearly, in fact, that even the humblest reader (who likes books in dialogue form with a minimum of "descriptions"—because conversations are "life") would know whose side to take. What Gogol promised to give the reader—or rather the readers he imagined—were facts. He would, he said, represent Russians not by the "petty traits" of individual freaks, not by "smug vulgarities and oddities," not through the sacrilegious medium of a lone artist's private vision, but in such a manner that "the Russian would appear in the fullness of his national nature, in all the rich variety of the inner forces contained in him." In other words the "dead souls" would become "live souls."

It is evident that what Gogol (or any other writer having similar unfortunate intentions) is saying here can be reduced to much simpler terms "I have imagined one kind of world in my first part, but now I am going to imagine another kind which will conform better to what I imagine are the concepts of Right and Wrong more or less consciously shared by my imaginary readers." Success in such cases (with popular magazine novelists, etc.) is directly dependent on how closely the author's vision of "readers" corresponds to the traditional, i.e. imaginary, notions that readers have of their own selves, notions carefully bred and sustained by a regular supply of mental chewing gum provided by the corresponding publishers. But Gogol's position was of course not so simple, first because what he proposed to write was to be on the lines of a religious revelation, and second, because the imaginary reader was supposed not merely to enjoy sundry details of the revelation but to be morally helped, improved or even totally regenerated by the general effect of the book. The main difficulty lay in having to combine the material of the first part, which from a philistine's viewpoint dealt with "oddities" (but which Gogol *had to* use since he could no longer create a new texture), with the kind of solemn sermon, staggering samples of which he had given in the *Selected*

Passages. Although his first intention was to have his characters not "wholly virtuous" but "important" in the sense of their fully representing a rich mixture of Russian passions, moods and ideals, he gradually discovered that these "important" characters coming from under his pen were being adulterated by the inevitable oddities that they borrowed from their natural medium and from their inner affinity with the nightmare squires of the initial set. Consequently the only way out was to have another alien group of characters which would be quite obviously and quite narrowly "good" because any attempt at rich characterization in their case would be bound to lead to the same weird forms which the not "wholly virtuous" ones kept assuming owing to their unfortunate ancestry.

When in 1847 Father Matthew, a fanatical Russian priest who combined the eloquence of John Chrysostom with the murkiest fads of the Dark Ages, begged Gogol to give up literature altogether and busy himself with devotional duties, such as preparing his soul for the Other World as mapped by Father Matthew and such like Fathers—Gogol did his best to make his correspondent see how very good the good characters of *Dead Souls* would be if only he was allowed by the Church to yield to that urge for writing which God had instilled in him behind Father Matthew's back: "Cannot an author present, in the frame of an attractive story, vivid examples of human beings that are better men than those presented by other writers? Examples are stronger than argumentations; before giving such examples all a writer needs is to become a good man himself and lead the kind of life that would please God. I would never have dreamt of writing at all had there not been nowadays such a widespread reading of various novels and short stories, most of which are immoral and sinfully alluring, but which are read because they hold one's interest and are not devoid of talent. I too have talent—the knack of making nature and men live in my tales; and since this is so, must I not present in the same attractive fashion righteous and pious people living according to the Divine Law? I want to tell you frankly that this, and not money or fame, is my main incentive for writing."

It would be of course ridiculous to suppose that Gogol spent ten years merely in trying to write something that would please the Church. What he was really trying to do was to write something that would please both Gogol the artist and Gogol the monk. He was obsessed by the thought that great Italian painters had done this again and again: a cool cloister, roses climbing a wall, a gaunt man wearing a skull-cap, the radiant fresh colors of the fresco he is working upon—these formed the professional setting which Gogol craved. Transmuted into literature, the completed *Dead Souls* was to form three connected images: Crime, Punishment, and Redemption. The attainment of this object was absolutely impossible not only because Gogol's unique genius was sure to play havoc with any conventional scheme if given a free hand, but because he had forced the main role, that of the sinner, upon a person—if Chichikov can be called a person—who was most ridiculously unfit for that part and who moreover moved in a world where such things as saving one's soul simply did not happen. A sympathetically pictured priest in the midst of the Gogolian characters of the first volume would have been as utterly impossible as a *gauloiserie* in Pascal or a quotation from Thoreau in Stalin's latest speech.

In the few chapters of the second part that have been preserved, Gogol's magic glasses become blurred. Chichikov though remaining (with a vengeance) in the center of the field somehow departs from the focal plane. There are several splendid passages in these chapters, but they are mere echoes of the first part. And when the "good" characters appear—the thrifty landowner, the saintly merchant, the God-like Prince, one has the impression of perfect strangers crowding in to take possession of a draughty house where familiar things stand in dismal disorder. As I have already mentioned, Chichikov's swindles are but the phantoms and parodies of crime, so that no "real" retribution is possible without a distortion of the whole idea. The "good people" are false because they do not belong to Gogol's world and thus every contact between them and Chichikov is jarring and depressing. If Gogol did write the redemption part with a "good priest" (of a slightly Catholic type) saving Chichikov's soul in the depths of Siberia (there exist some scraps of information that Gogol studied Pallas' *Siberian Flora* in order to get the right background), and if Chichikov was fated to end his days as an emaciated monk in a remote monastery, then no wonder that the artist, in a last blinding flash of artistic truth, burnt the end of *Dead Souls*. Father Matthew could be satisfied that Gogol shortly before dying had renounced literature; but the brief blaze that might be deemed a proof and symbol of this renunciation happened to be exactly the opposite thing: as he crouched and sobbed in front of that stove ("Where?" queries my publisher. In Moscow.), an artist was destroying the labor of long years because he finally realized that the completed book was untrue to his genius; so Chichikov, instead of piously petering out in a wooden chapel among ascetic fir trees on the shore of a legendary lake, was restored to his native element; the little blue flames of a humble hell.

". . . a certain man who was, I daresay, not very remarkable: short he was and somewhat poxmarked and somewhat on the carroty side, and somewhat even blear-eyed and a little bald in front, with symmetrically wrinkled cheeks and the kind of complexion termed hemorrhoidal . . .

". . . His name was Bashmachkin. Already the name itself clearly shows that it had formerly come from *bashmak* — a shoe. But when, and at what time it had come from "shoe," this is totally unknown. All of them — the father and the grandfather, and even the brother-in-law — absolutely all the Bashmachkins — used to wear boots which they resoled not more often than three times a year."

"The Overcoat" (1842)

Gogol was a strange creature, but genius is always strange; it is only your healthy second-rater who seems to the grateful reader to be a wise old friend, nicely developing the reader's own notions of life. Great literature skirts the irrational. *Hamlet* is the wild dream of a neurotic scholar. Gogol's *The Overcoat* is a grotesque and grim nightmare making black holes in the dim pattern of life. The superficial reader of that story will merely see in it the heavy frolics of an extravagant buffoon; the solemn reader will take for granted that Gogol's prime intention was to denounce the horrors of Russian bureaucracy. But neither the person who wants a good laugh, nor the person who craves for books "that make one think" will understand what *The Overcoat* is really about. Give me the creative reader; this is a tale for him.

Steady Pushkin, matter-of-fact Tolstoy, restrained Chekhov have all had their moments of irrational insight which simultaneously blurred the sentence and disclosed a secret meaning worth the sudden focal shift. But with Gogol this shifting is the very basis of his art, so that whenever he tried to write in the round hand of literary tradition and to treat rational ideas in a logical way, he lost all trace of talent. When, as in his immortal *The Overcoat*, he really let himself go and pottered happily on the brink of his private abyss, he became the greatest artist that Russia has yet produced.

The sudden slanting of the rational plane of life may be accomplished of course in many ways, and every great writer has his own method. With Gogol it was a combination of two movements: a jerk and a glide. Imagine a trap-door that opens under your feet with absurd suddenness, and a lyrical gust that

---

A page from Nabokov's lecture on "The Overcoat" with his drawing of a furred carrick.

From places? gate?

picture overcoat with cape

Gogol 1809-1852   Kroowin

Comparisons in The overcoat

bottom of p 133

collar - neck - plaster ... cotton - german peddlars

Only one Gogeiramp !
approaction Gogeimamp

Shinel   from chenille
The Furred carrick   a kind of fabric

Who has read the stars
Read it at next time

p. 136   even
          the brother in law
          - despite a squint ... and pockmarks   } the irrelevant "even" or "despite"

p. 134 bottom to 135   The wonderful rambling description, following
                        the simple statement " Even at those hours when

the eloquent crescendo 142-143 ... of this life had become fuller ...
... p. 160 he even leaves ...

What was The name of the "important person was"?   De Stepan Varlaamovich
                                                      for name p.153.

sweeps you up and then lets you fall with a bump into the next traphole. The absurd was Gogol's favorite muse—but when I say "the absurd," I do not mean the quaint or the comic. The absurd has as many shades and degrees as the tragic has, and moreover, in Gogol's case, it borders upon the latter. It would be wrong to assert that Gogol placed his characters in absurd situations. You cannot place a man in an absurd situation if the whole world he lives in is absurd; you cannot do this if you mean by "absurd" something provoking a chuckle or a shrug. But if you mean the pathetic, the human condition, if you mean all such things that in less weird worlds are linked up with the loftiest aspirations, the deepest sufferings, the strongest passions—then of course the necessary breach is there, and a pathetic human, lost in the midst of Gogol's nightmarish, irresponsible world would be "absurd," by a kind of secondary contrast.

On the lid of the tailor's snuff-box there was "the portrait of a General; I do not know what general because the tailor's thumb had made a hole in the general's face and a square of paper had been gummed over the hole." Thus with the absurdity of Akaki Akakievich Bashmachkin. We did not expect that, amid the whirling masks, one mask would turn out to be a real face, or at least the place where that face ought to be. The essence of mankind is irrationally derived from the chaos of fakes which form Gogol's world. Akaki Akakievich, the hero of *The Overcoat*, is absurd *because* he is pathetic, *because* he is human and *because* he has been engendered by those very forces which seem to be in such contrast to him.

He is not merely human and pathetic. He is something more, just as the background is not mere burlesque. Somewhere behind the obvious contrast there is a subtle genetic link. His being discloses the same quiver and shimmer as does the dream world to which he belongs. The allusions to something else behind the crudely painted screens, are so artistically combined with the superficial texture of the narration that civic-minded Russians have missed them completely. But a creative reading of Gogol's story reveals that here and there in the most innocent descriptive passage, this or that word, sometimes a mere adverb or a preposition, for instance the word "even" or "almost," is inserted in such a way as to make the harmless sentence explode in a wild display of nightmare fireworks; or else the passage that had started in a rambling colloquial manner all of a sudden leaves the tracks and swerves into the irrational where it really belongs; or again, quite as suddenly, a door bursts open and a mighty wave of foaming poetry rushes in only to dissolve in bathos, or to turn into its own parody, or to be checked by the sentence breaking and reverting to a conjuror's patter, that patter which is such a feature of Gogol's style. It gives one the sensation of something ludicrous and at the same time stellar, lurking constantly around the corner—and one likes to recall that the difference between the comic side of things, and their cosmic side, depends upon one sibilant.

So what is that queer world, glimpses of which we keep catching through the gaps of the harmless looking sentences? It is in a way the *real* one but it looks wildly absurd to us, accustomed as we are to the stage setting that screens it. It is from these glimpses that the main character of *The Overcoat*, the meek little clerk, is formed, so that he embodies the spirit of that secret but real world which breaks through Gogol's style. He is, that meek little clerk, a ghost, a visitor from some tragic depths who by chance happened to assume the disguise of a petty official. Russian progressive critics sensed in him the image of the underdog and the whole story impressed them as a social protest. But it is something much more than that. The gaps and black holes in the texture of Gogol's style imply flaws in the texture of life itself. Something is very wrong and all men are mild lunatics engaged in pursuits that seem to them very important while an absurdly logical force keeps them at their futile jobs—this is the real "message" of the story. In this world of utter futility, of futile humility and futile domination, the highest degree that passion, desire, creative urge can attain is a new cloak which both tailors and customers adore on their knees. I am not speaking of the moral point or the moral lesson. There can be no moral lesson in such a world because there are no pupils and no teachers: this world *is* and it excludes everything that might destroy it, so that any improvement, any struggle, any moral purpose or endeavor, are as utterly impossible as changing the course of a star. It is Gogol's world and as such wholly different from Tolstoy's world, or Pushkin's, or Chekhov's or my own. But after reading Gogol one's eyes may become gogolized and one is apt to see bits of his world in the most unexpected places. I have visited many countries, and something like Akaki Akakievich's overcoat has been the passionate dream of this or that chance acquaintance who never had heard about Gogol.

The plot of *The Overcoat** is very simple. A poor little clerk makes a great decision and orders a new overcoat. The coat while in the making becomes the

*The *shinel* (from chenille) of the Russian title is a deep-caped, ample-sleeved furred carrick.

dream of his life. On the very first night that he wears it he is robbed of it on a dark street. He dies of grief and his ghost haunts the city. This is all in the way of plot, but of course the *real* plot (as always with Gogol) lies in the style, in the inner structure of this transcendental anecdote. In order to appreciate it at its true worth one must perform a kind of mental somersault so as to get rid of conventional values in literature and follow the author along the dream road of his superhuman imagination. Gogol's world is somewhat related to such conceptions of modern physics as the "Concertina Universe" or the "Explosion Universe"; it is far removed from the comfortably revolving clockwork worlds of the last century. There is a curvature in literary style as there is curvature in space,—but few are the Russian readers who do care to plunge into Gogol's magic chaos head first, with no restraint or regret. The Russian who thinks Turgenev was a great writer, and bases his notion of Pushkin upon Chaykovski's vile libretti, will merely paddle into the gentlest wavelets of Gogol's mysterious sea and limit his reaction to an enjoyment of what he takes to be whimsical humor and colorful quips. But the diver, the seeker for black pearls, the man who prefers the monsters of the deep to the sunshades on the beach, will find in *The Overcoat* shadows linking our state of existence to those other states and modes which we dimly apprehend in our rare moments of irrational perception. The prose of Pushkin is three-dimensional; that of Gogol is four-dimensional, at least. He may be compared to his contemporary, the mathematician Lobachevski, who blasted Euclid and discovered a century ago many of the theories which Einstein later developed. If parallel lines do not meet it is not because meet they cannot, but because they have other things to do. Gogol's art as disclosed in *The Overcoat* suggests that parallel lines not only may meet, but that they can wriggle and get most extravagantly entangled, just as two pillars reflected in water indulge in the most wobbly contortions if the necessary ripple is there. Gogol's genius is exactly that ripple—two and two make five, if not the square root of five, and it all happens quite naturally in Gogol's world, where neither rational mathematics nor indeed any of our pseudophysical agreements with ourselves can be seriously said to exist.

————

The clothing process indulged in by Akaki Akakievich, the making and the putting on of the cloak, is really his *disrobing* and his gradual reversion to the stark nakedness of his own ghost. From the very beginning of the story he is in training for his supernaturally high jump—and such harmless looking details as his tiptoeing in the streets to spare his shoes or his not quite knowing whether he is in the middle of the street or in the middle of the sentence, these details gradually dissolve the clerk Akaki Akakievich so that towards the end of the story his ghost seems to be the most tangible, the most real part of his being. The account of his ghost haunting the streets of St. Petersburg in search of the cloak of which he had been robbed and finally appropriating that of a high official who had refused to help him in his misfortune—this account, which to the unsophisticated may look like an ordinary ghost story, is transformed towards the end into something for which I can find no precise epithet. It is both an apotheosis and a *degringolade*. Here it is:

"The Important Person almost died of fright. In his office and generally in the presence of subordinates he was a man of strong character, and whoever glanced at his manly appearance and shape used to imagine his kind of temper with something of a shudder; at the present moment however he (as happens in the case of many people of prodigiously powerful appearance) experienced such terror that, not without reason, he *even* expected to have a fit of some sort. He *even* threw off his cloak of his own accord and then exhorted the coachman in a wild voice to take him home and drive like mad. Upon hearing tones which were generally used at critical moments and were *even* [notice the recurrent use of this word] accompanied by something far more effective, the coachman thought it wiser to draw his head in; he lashed at the horses, and the carriage sped like an arrow. Six minutes later, or a little more, [according to Gogol's special timepiece] the Important Person was already at the porch of his house. Pale, frightened and cloakless, instead of arriving at Caroline Ivanovna's [a woman he kept] he had thus come home; he staggered to his bedroom and spent an exceedingly troubled night, so that next morning, at breakfast, his daughter said to him straightaway: 'You are quite pale today, papa.' But papa kept silent and [now comes the parody of a Bible parable!] he told none of what had befallen him, nor where he had been, nor whither he had wished to go. The whole occurrence made a very strong impression on him [here begins the downhill slide, that spectacular bathos which Gogol uses for his particular needs]. Much more seldom *even* did he address to his subordinates the words 'How dare you?—Do you know to whom you are speaking?'—or at least if he did talk that way it was not till he had first listened to what they had to tell. But still more remarkable was the fact that from that time on the ghostly clerk quite ceased to appear: evidently the Important Person's overcoat fitted him well; at least no more did one hear of overcoats being snatched from people's shoulders. However, many active and vigilant persons refused to be appeased and kept asserting that in remote parts of the city the ghostly clerk still showed himself. And indeed a suburban policeman saw with his own eyes [the downward slide from the moralistic note to the grotesque is now a tumble] a ghost appear from behind a house. But being by nature somewhat of a weakling (so that once, an ordinary full-grown young pig which had rushed out of some private house knocked him off his feet to the great merriment of a group of cab drivers from whom he demanded, and obtained, as a penalty for this derision, ten coppers from each to buy himself snuff), he did not venture to stop the ghost but just kept on walking behind it in the darkness, until the ghost suddenly turned, stopped and inquired: 'What d'you want, you?'—and showed a fist of a size rarely met with *even* among the living. 'Nothing,' answered the sentinel and proceeded to go back at once. That ghost, however, was a much taller one and had a huge moustache. It was heading apparently towards Obukhov Bridge and presently disappeared completely in the darkness of the night.

The torrent of "irrelevant" details (such as the bland assumption that "full-grown young pigs" commonly occur in private houses) produces such a hypnotic effect that one almost fails to realize one simple thing (and that is the beauty of the final stroke). A piece of most important information, the main structural idea of the story is here deliberately masked by Gogol (because all reality is a mask). The man taken for Akaki Akakievich's cloakless ghost is actually the man who stole his cloak. But Akaki Akakievich's ghost existed solely on the strength of his lacking a cloak, whereas now the policeman, lapsing into the queerest paradox of the story, mistakes for this ghost just the very person who was its antithesis, the man who had stolen the cloak. Thus the story describes a full circle: a vicious circle as all circles are, despite their posing as apples, or planets, or human faces.

So to sum up: the story goes this way: mumble, mumble, lyrical wave, mumble, lyrical wave, mumble, lyrical wave, mumble, fantastic climax, mumble, mumble, and back into the chaos from which they all had derived. At this superhigh level of art, literature is of course not concerned with pitying the underdog or cursing the upperdog. It appeals to that secret depth of the human soul where the shadows of other worlds pass like the shadows of nameless and soundless ships.

As one or two patient readers may have gathered by now, this is really the only appeal that interests me. My purpose in jotting these notes on Gogol has, I hope, become perfectly clear. Bluntly speaking it amounts to the following; if you expect to find out something about Russia, if you are eager to know why the blistered Germans bungled their blitz, if you are interested in "ideas" and

VLADIMIR NABOKOV

"facts" and "messages," keep away from Gogol. The awful trouble of learning Russian in order to read him will not be repaid in your kind of hard cash. Keep away, keep away. He has nothing to tell you. Keep off the tracks. High tension. Closed for the duration. Avoid, refrain, don't. I would like to have here a full list of all possible interdictions, vetoes and threats. Hardly necessary of course—as the wrong sort of reader will certainly never get as far as this. But I do welcome the right sort—my brothers, my doubles. My brother is playing the organ. My sister is reading. She is my aunt. You will first learn the alphabet, the labials, the linguals, the dentals, the letters that buzz, the drone and the bumblebee, and the Tse-tse Fly. One of the vowels will make you say "Ugh!" You will feel mentally stiff and bruised after your first declension of personal pronouns. I see however no other way of getting to Gogol (or to any other Russian writer for that matter). His work, as all great literary achievements, is a phenomenon of language and not one of ideas. "Gaw-gol," not "Go-gall." The final "l" is a soft dissolving "l" which does not exist in English. One cannot hope to understand an author if one cannot even pronounce his name. My translations of various passages are the best my poor vocabulary could afford, but even had they been as perfect as those which I hear with my innermost ear, without being able to render their intonation, they still would not replace Gogol. While trying to convey my attitude towards his art I have not produced any tangible proofs of its peculiar existence. I can only place my hand on my heart and affirm that I have not imagined Gogol. He really wrote, he really lived.

Gogol was born on the 1st of April, 1809. According to his mother (who, of course, made up the following dismal anecdote) a poem he had written at the age of five was seen by Kapnist, a well-known writer of sorts. Kapnist embraced the solemn urchin and said to the glad parents: "He will become a writer of genius if only destiny gives him a good Christian for teacher and guide." But the other thing—his having been born on the 1st of April—is true.

(thus the patronymic is
pronounced instead
of the full ending:
—gay<u>e</u>vitch

The difference
between
"соха" and
"плугъ"

сравнить
соха
плугъ

1876   <u>Hole</u>. Virgin soil, fresh land
which should be turned up not
by the superficially gliding "соха"
                        turns up?
but by the deeply "забирающий плугъ"

from the note-book of a farmer

The typical beginning of a novel: the stating
of a date, as here:

on a springday in 1868
a little after noon
часу въ первомъ дня

Дверь отворилась скромно и плавно, и медленно
снимая вылощенную шляпу съ благообразной,
коротко остриженной головы, въ комнату
вошелъ мужчина лѣтъ подъ сорокъ, высокаго
роста, сухощавый и величавый [сюжетный]

                          perfectly modulated
a typical example of his smooth [well oiled
prose especially when picturing slow movement
The phrase grows still, like a lizard
basking on a sunlit wall with ....

IVAN TURGENEV (1818-1883)

I van Sergeievich Turgenev was born in 1818 in Orel, Central Russia, in the family of a wealthy squire. His early youth was spent on a country estate where he was able to observe the life of the serfs and the relations between master and serf at their worst: his mother was possessed of a tyrannical nature and led her peasants and also her immediate family a miserable life. Though she adored her son, she persecuted him and had him flogged for the least childish disobedience or misdemeanor. In later life, when Turgenev tried to intercede for the serfs, she cut his allowance, obliging him to live in misery in spite of the rich inheritance that awaited him. Turgenev never forgot the painful impressions of his childhood. After his mother's death he did much to improve the peasants' circumstances, freed all his domestic servants, and went out of his way to cooperate with the government when the peasants were emancipated in 1861.

Turgenev's early education was patchy. Among his numerous tutors, indiscriminately engaged by his mother, there were all sorts of odd people, including at least one professional saddler. One year at the Moscow University and three at the Petersburg University, whence he was graduated in 1837, did not give him a feeling of having obtained a well-balanced education, and from 1838 to 1841 he attended the university in Berlin, filling out its gaps. During his life in Berlin he became intimate with a group of young Russians similarly en-

The opening page of Nabokov's Turgenev notebook.

gaged, who later formed the nucleus of a Russian philosophic movement highly colored by Hegelianism, the German "idealist" philosophy.

In his early youth Turgenev produced some half-baked poems mostly imitative of Mikhail Lermontov. Only in 1847, when he turned to prose and published a short story, the first of his series of *A Sportsman's Sketches*, did he come into his own as a writer. The story produced a tremendous impression and when later together with a number of others it was published as a volume, the impression only grew stronger. Turgenev's plastic musical flowing prose was but one of the reasons that brought him immediate fame, for at least as much interest was contributed by the special subject of these stories. They were all written about serfs and not only present a detailed psychological study, but go even further to idealize these serfs as superior in their human quality to their heartless masters.

From these stories some purple patches:

"Fedya, not without pleasure, lifted the forcedly smiling dog up into the air and placed it into the bottom of the cart." ("Khor' and Kalinych")

". . . a dog, all his body a-quiver, his eyes half-closed, was gnawing a bone on the lawn." ("My Neighbor Radilov")

"Vyacheslav Illarionovich is a tremendous admirer of the gentle sex, and as soon as he sees a pretty little person on the boulevard of his country-town, he there and then starts to follow her, but—and this is the peculiar point—he at once begins to limp." ("Two Country Squires")

At sunset on a country-road:
"Masha (the hero's gypsy mistress who left him) stopped and turned her face to him. She stood with her back to the light—and thus appeared to be of a dusky black all over, as if carved in dark wood. The whites of her eyes alone stood out like silver almonds, whereas the iris had grown still darker." ("Chertopkhanov's End")

"Evening had come, the sun had hid behind a small aspen grove . . . its shadow spread endlessly across the still fields. A peasant could be seen riding at a trot on white horse along a dark narrow path skirting that distant grove; he could be seen quite clearly, every detail of him, even the patch on his shoulder—although he was moving in the shade; the legs of his horse flickered with a kind of pleasing distinctness. The setting sun flushed the trunks of the

aspen-trees with such a warm glow that they seemed the color of pine-trunks."
(*Fathers and Sons*)

These are Turgenev at his very best. It is these mellow colored little paintings—rather watercolors than the Flemish glory of Gogol's art gallery—inserted here and there into his prose, that we still admire to-day. These plums are especially numerous in *A Sportsman's Sketches*.

Turgenev's presentation in the *Sketches* of his gallery of idealistic and touchingly human serfs stressed the obvious odiousness of serfdom, an emphasis that irritated many influential people. The censor who had passed the manuscript was retired and the government seized the first opportunity to punish the author. After Gogol's death Turgenev wrote a short article which was suppressed by the Petersburg censorship; but when he sent it to Moscow the censor passed it and it was published. Turgenev was put in prison for a month for insubordination and then was exiled to his estate where he remained for more than two years. Upon his return he published his first novel *Rudin*, followed by *A Nest of Gentlefolk* and *On the Eve*.

Rudin, written in 1855, depicts the generation of the 1840s, the idealistic idealistic Russian intelligentsia bred in German universities.

There is some very good writing in *Rudin*, such as ". . . many an old lime-tree-alley, gold-dark and sweet-smelling, with a glimpse of emerald light at its end," where we have Turgenev's favorite vista. Rudin's sudden appearance in Lasunski's house is fairly well done, based as it is on Turgenev's pet method of having a convenient fight at a party or dinner between the cool, bland, clever hero and some quick-tempered vulgarian or pretentious fool. We may note the following typical sample of the whims and ways of Turgenev's characters: "Meanwhile Rudin went up to Natalia. She rose, her face expressed confusion. Volyntsev, who was sitting next to her, rose too. '—Ah, I see a pianoforte,'—Rudin began softly and caressingly, as if he were a travelling prince.' " Then somebody else plays Schubert's *Erlkönig*. " '—This music and this night' [a starry summer night which "seemed to nestle and to let one's soul nestle too"—a great exponent of the "music and night" theme was Turgenev], said Rudin,—'reminds me of my student years in Germany.' " He is asked how students dress. "—Well, at Heidelberg I used to wear riding boots with spurs and a Hungarian jacket with braidings; I had let my hair grow, so that it almost reached down to my shoulders." Rudin is a rather pompous young man.

Russia in those days was one huge dream: the masses slept—figuratively; the intellectuals spent sleepless nights—literally—sitting up and talking about things, or just meditating until five in the morning and then going out for a walk. There was a lot of the flinging-oneself-down-on-one's-bed-without-undressing-and-sinking-into-a-heavy-slumber stuff, or jumping into one's clothes. Turgenev's maidens are generally good get-uppers, jumping into their crinolines, sprinkling their faces with cold water, and running out, as fresh as roses, into the garden, where the inevitable meeting takes place in a bower.

Before going to Germany, Rudin had been a student at Moscow University. A friend of his thus tells us of their youth: "Half-a-dozen youths, a single tallow candle burning . . . the cheapest brand of tea, dry old biscuits . . . but our eyes glow, our cheeks are flushed, our hearts beat . . . and the subjects of our talk are God, Truth, the Future of Mankind, Poetry—we talk nonsense sometimes, but what is the harm?"

As a character, Rudin, the progressive idealist of the 1840s, can be summed up by Hamlet's answer "words, words, words." He is quite ineffectual in spite of his being wholly wrapped up in progressive ideas. His whole energy spends itself in passionate streams of idealistic babble. A cold heart and a hot head. An enthusiast lacking in staying power, a busybody incapable of action. When the girl who loves him, and whom, he thinks, he loves too, tells him there is no hope of her mother consenting to their marriage, he at once gives her up, although she was ready to follow him anywhere. He departs and roams all over Russia; all his enterprises fizzle out. But the bad luck that haunts him and which at the outset was the inability to express the energy of his brain otherwise than by a flow of eloquent words finally shapes him, hardens the outline of his personality, and leads him to a useless but heroic death on the barricades of 1848 in remote Paris.

In *A Nest of Gentlefolk* (1858) Turgenev glorified all that was noble in the orthodox ideals of the old gentry. Liza, the heroine of this novel, is the most consummate incarnation of the pure and proud "Turgenev maiden."

On the Eve (1860) is the story of another Turgenev girl, Elena, who leaves her family and country in order to follow her lover Insarov, a Bulgarian hero whose sole object in life is the emancipation of his country (then under Turkish domination). Elena prefers Insarov, who is a man of action, to the ineffectual young men who surround her in her Russian youth. Insarov dies of consumption and Elena continues bravely in his path.

On the Eve, in spite of its good intentions, is artistically the least successful of Turgenev's novels. Nevertheless, it was the most popular one. Elena, though a female character, was the type of heroic personality that society wanted: a person ready to sacrifice everything to love and duty, bravely surmounting every difficulty fate put in her path, faithful to the ideal of freedom—emancipation of the oppressed, freedom of the woman to choose her way in life, freedom of love. After showing the moral defeat of the idealists of the 1840s, after making his only male active hero a Bulgarian, Turgenev was reproached for not having created a single positive active type of a Russian male. This he tried to do in *Fathers and Sons* (1862). In it Turgenev pictures the moral conflict between the good-meaning, ineffectual and weak people of the 1840s and the new strong revolutionary generation of the "nihilistic" youth. Bazarov, the representative of this younger generation, is aggressively materialistic; for him exists neither religion nor any esthetic or moral values. He believes in nothing but "frogs," meaning nothing but the results of his own practical scientific experience. He knows neither pity nor shame. And he is, par excellence, the active man. Though Turgenev rather admired Bazarov, the radicals whom he thought he was flattering in the face of this strong active young man were indignant at the portrait and saw in Bazarov only a caricature drawn to please their opponents. Turgenev, it was declared, was a finished man who had expended all his talent. Turgenev was dumbfounded. From the darling of the progressive society he suddenly saw himself transformed into a sort of detestable bogey. Turgenev was a very vain man; not only fame, but the outward marks of fame, meant a lot to him. He was deeply offended and disappointed. He was abroad at the time and remained abroad for the rest of his life, making but rare short visits to Russia.

His next piece of writing was a fragment, "Enough," in which he declared his decision to give up literature. In spite of this he wrote two more novels and continued writing to the end of his life. Of these last two novels, in *Smoke* he expressed his bitterness against all classes of Russian society, and in *Virgin Soil* (Nov') he tried to show different types of Russians confronted with the social movement of their time (the 1870s). On one hand we have the revolutionaries trying hard to get in touch with the people: (1) The Hamlet-like hesitations of the hero of the novel, Nezhdanov, cultured, refined, with a secret yearning for poetry and romance, but devoid of all sense of humor, like most of Turgenev's positive types—moreover, weak and hampered in everything by a morbid sense of inferiority and his own uselessness; (2) Marianna, the pure, true, austerely-naive girl, ready to die there and then for the "cause"; (3) Solomin, the strong silent man; (4) Markelov, the honest blockhead. On the other side we find the sham liberals and frank reactionaries, such as Sipyagin and Kallomeytsev. It is a very tame affair, this novel, with the author's fine talent struggling, and just failing, to keep alive the characters and the plot he had selected not so much because his art urged him, but rather because he was eager to air his own views upon the political problems of his day.

Incidentally, Turgenev, as most writers of his time, is far too explicit, leaving nothing to the reader's intuition; suggesting and then ponderously explaining what the suggestion was. The labored epilogues of his novels and long short stories are painfully artificial, the author doing his best to satisfy fully the reader's curiosity regarding the respective destinies of the characters in a manner that can hardly be called artistic.

He is not a great writer, though a pleasant one. He never achieved anything comparable to *Madame Bovary*, and to say that he and Flaubert belonged to the same literary school is a complete misconception. Neither Turgenev's readiness to tackle any social problem that happened to be a là mode, nor the banal handling of plots (always taking the easiest way) can be likened to Flaubert's severe art.

Turgenev, Gorki, and Chekhov are particularly well known outside of Russia. But there is no natural way of linking them. However, it may be noticed perhaps that the worst of Turgenev was thoroughly expressed in Gorki's works, and Turgenev's best (in the way of Russian landscape) was beautifully developed by Chekhov.

Besides *A Sportsman's Sketches* and the novels, Turgenev wrote numerous short stories and long short stories or nouvelles. The early ones are devoid of any special originality or literary quality; some of the later are quite remarkable. Among the latter "A Quiet Backwater" and "First Love" deserve particular mention.

Turgenev's personal life was not very happy. The great, the only true love of his life, was for the famous singer Mme. Pauline Viardot-Garcia. She was happily married, Turgenev was on friendly terms with her family, he had no hope of personal happiness, but nevertheless he devoted all his life to her, lived whenever possible in their vicinity, gave a dower to her two daughters when they got married.

In general he was much happier living abroad than in Russia. There no radical critics gnawed the life out of him with their vigorous attacks. He was on friendly terms with Merimée and Flaubert. His books were translated into French and German. Since he was the only Russian writer of some stature known to the Western literary circles, he was inevitably considered not only the greatest but in fact *the* Russian writer, and Turgenev basked in the sun and felt happy. He impressed foreigners with his charm and graceful manners, but in his encounters with Russian writers and critics he at once felt self-conscious and arrogant. He had had quarrels with Tolstoy, Dostoevski, Nekrasov. Of Tolstoy he was jealous though at the same time he greatly admired his genius.

In 1871 the Viardots settled down in Paris and so did Turgenev. In spite of his faithful passion for Mme. Viardot he felt lonely and lacked the comforts of a family of his own. He complained in letters to friends of lonesomeness, his "cold old age," his spiritual frustration. Sometimes Turgenev longed to be back in Russia but he lacked the will power to make such a drastic change in his life routine: a lack of will power had always been his weak point. He never had the stamina to stand up under the attacks of Russian critics who, after the publication of *Fathers and Sons*, never ceased being prejudiced against his new publications. However, in spite of the hostility of the critics, Turgenev was extremely popular with the Russian reading public. The readers liked his books—his novels were popular even as late as the beginning of this century; and the humane liberal feelings he professed attracted the public to him, especially the younger part of it. In 1883 he died at Bougival, near Paris, but his body was brought to Petersburg. Thousands of people followed his coffin to the cemetery. Delegations had been sent by numerous societies, towns, universities, etc. Countless wreaths had been received. The funeral procession was almost two miles long. Thus the Russian reading public gave a final demonstration of the love it bore Turgenev during his life.

Besides being good at painting nature, Turgenev was likewise excellent at painting little colored cartoons which remind one of those seen in British country clubs: consider, for instance, the cartoons Turgenev loved to make of the fops and lions of the Russian sixties and seventies: ". . . he was dressed in the very best English manner: the colored tip of a white silk handkerchief protruded in the form of a small triangle from the flat side-pocket of his variegated jacket; his monocle dangled on a rather broad black ribbon; the dead tint of his suede gloves matched the pale gray of his check trousers." Then, too, Turgenev was the first Russian writer to notice the effect of broken sunlight or the special combination of shade and light upon the appearance of people. Remember that gypsy girl who, with the sun behind her, "appeared to be of a dusky black all over as if carved in dark wood" and those "whites of her eyes" standing out "like silver almonds."

These quotations are good examples of his perfectly modulated well-oiled prose which is so nicely adapted to the picturing of slow movement. This or that phrase of his reminds one of a lizard sun-charmed on a wall—and the two or three final words of the sentence curve like the lizard's tail. But generally speaking his style produces a queer effect of patchiness, just because certain passages, the artist's favorites, have been pampered much more than the others and, in consequence, stand out, supple and strong, magnified, as it were, by the author's predilection among the general flow of good, clear, but undistinguished prose. Honey and oil—this comparison may be well applied to those perfectly rounded graceful sentences of his, when he settles down to the task of writing beautifully. As a story-teller, he is artificial and even lame; indeed, when following his characters, he begins to limp as that hero of his did in "Two Country Squires." His literary genius falls short on the score of literary imagination, that is, of naturally discovering ways of telling the story which would equal the originality of his descriptive art. Being perhaps aware of this fundamental flaw, or else being led by that instinct of artistic self-preservation that keeps an author from lingering there where he is most likely to flop, he shuns action or, more exactly, does not expose action in terms of sustained narration. His novels and stories consist mainly of conversations in diverse settings charmingly described—good long talks interrupted by delightful short biographies and dainty pictures of the countryside. When, however, he goes out of his way to look for beauty outside the old gardens of Russia, he wallows in abject sweetness. His mysticism is of the plastic picturesque sort with perfumes, floating mists, old portraits that may come alive any moment, marble pillars, and the rest. His ghosts do not make the flesh creep, or rather they make it creep the wrong way. In describing beauty he goes the whole hog: his idea of luxury turns out to be ". . . gold, crystal, silk, diamonds, flowers, fountains"; and maidens bedecked with flowers but otherwise scantily dressed sing hymns in boats, while other maidens, with the tiger skins and golden cups of their profession, romp on the banks.

The volume of *Poems in Prose* (1883) is his work that dates most of all. Their melody is all wrong; their luster looks cheap and their philosophy is not deep enough to justify pearl-diving. Still they remain good examples of pure well-balanced Russian prose. But the author's imagination never rises above perfectly commonplace symbols (such as fairies and skeletons); and if, at its best, his prose reminds one of rich milk, these prose poems may be compared to fudge.

It is perhaps *A Sportsman's Sketches* that contains some of his best writing. In spite of a certain idealization of the peasants, the book presents Turgenev's most unaffected, most genuine characters, and some extremely satisfying descriptions of scenes, people, and, of course, nature.

Of all Turgenev's characters, the "Turgenev maiden" has probably achieved the greatest fame. Masha ("A Quiet Backwater"), Natalia (*Rudin*), Liza (*A Nest of Gentlefolk*) vary but little among themselves and are undoubtedly contained in Pushkin's Tatiana. But with their different stories they are given more scope for the use of their common moral strength, gentleness, and not only their capacity but, I would say, their thirst to sacrifice all worldly considerations to what they consider their duty, be it complete resignation of personal happiness to higher moral considerations (Liza) or complete sacrifice of all worldly considerations to their pure passion (Natalia). Turgenev envelops his heroines in a kind of gentle poetical beauty which has a special appeal for the reader and has done much to create the general high concept of Russian womanhood.

Fathers and Sons (1862)

Fathers and Sons is not only the best of Turgenev's novels, it is one of the most brilliant novels of the nineteenth century. Turgenev managed to do what he intended to do, to create a male character, a young Russian, who would affirm his—that character's—absence of introspection and at the same time would not be a journalist's dummy of a socialistic type. Bazarov is a strong man, no doubt—and very possibly had he lived beyond his twenties (he is a graduate student when we meet him), he might have become, beyond the horizon of the novel, a great social thinker, a prominent physician, or an active revolutionary. But there was a common debility about Turgenev's nature and art; he was incapable of making his masculine characters triumph within the existence he invents for them. Moreover, in Bazarov's character there is behind the brashness and the will-power, and the violence of cold thought, a stream of natural youthful ardency which Bazarov finds difficult to blend with the harshness of a would-be nihilist. This nihilism sets out to denounce and deny everything, but it fails to dismiss passionate love—or to reconcile this love with his opinions regarding the simple animal character of love. Love turns out to be something more than man's biological pastime. The romantic fire that suddenly envelops his soul shocks him; but it satisfies the requirements of true art, since it stresses in Bazarov the logic of universal youth which transcends the logic of a local system of thought—of, in the present case, nihilism.

Turgenev, as it were, takes his creature out of a self-imposed pattern and places him in the normal world of chance. He lets Bazarov die not from any peculiar inner development of Bazarov's nature, but by the blind decree of fate. He dies with silent courage, as he would have died on the battlefield, but there is an element of resignation about his decay that goes well with the general trend of mild submission to fate which colors Turgenev's whole art.

The reader will notice—I will direct his attention to those passages in a moment—that the two fathers and the uncle in the book are not only very

Itineraries on Platen at Sitka

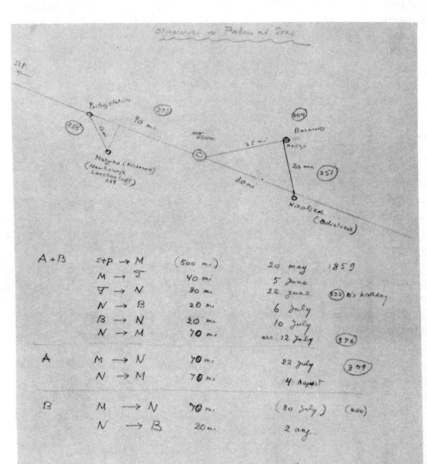

A + B	S+P → M	(500 mi)	20 may	1859
	M → J	40 mi	5 June	
	J → N	80 mi	22 June	(322) B's birthday
	N → B	20 mi	6 July	
	B → N	20 mi	10 July	
	N → M	70 mi	arr. 12 July	(376)
A	M → N	70 mi	22 July	(379)
	N → M	70 mi	4 August	
B	M → N	70 mi	(30 July)	(400)
	N → B	20 mi	2 aug.	

Between May 20 and aug. 4   My travel about 300 miles

different from Arkadi and Bazarov, but also different from each other. One will also note that Arkadi, the son, is of a much gentler and simpler and more routine and normal nature than Bazarov. I shall look through a number of passages that are especially vivid and significant. One will mark, for instance, the following situation. Old Kirsanov, Arkadi's father, has that quiet, tender, altogether charming mistress, Fenichka, a girl of the people. She is one of the passive types of Turgenev's young women, and around this passive center three men revolve: Nikolay Kirsanov, and also Pavel, his brother, who by some twist of memory and imagination sees in her a resemblance to a former flame of his, a flame that colored his entire life. And moreover there is Bazarov, who is shown flirting with Fenichka, a casual flirtation that brings on a duel. However, not Fenichka but typhus will be the cause of Bazarov's death.

———

One will observe a queer feature of Turgenev's structure. He takes tremendous trouble to introduce his characters properly, endowing them with pedigrees and recognizable traits, but when he has finally assembled them all, lo and behold the tale is finished and the curtain has gone down whilst a ponderous epilogue takes care of whatever is supposed to happen to his invented creatures beyond the horizon of his novel. I do not mean there are no events in this story. On the contrary, this novel is replete with action; there are quarrels and other clashes, there is even a duel—and a good deal of rich drama attends Bazarov's death. But one will notice that all the time throughout the development of the action, and in the margin of the changing events, the past lives of the characters are being pruned and improved by the author, and all the time he is terribly concerned with bringing out their souls and minds and temperaments by means of functional illustrations, for instance the way simple folks are attached to Bazarov or the way Arkadi tries to live up to his friend's new-found wisdom.

The art of translation from theme to theme is for an author the most difficult technique to master, and even a first-rate artist, as Turgenev is at his best, will be tempted (because of the kind of reader he imagines, a matter-of-fact reader accustomed to certain methods) to follow traditional devices in this passing from one scene to another. Turgenev's transitions are very simple, and indeed even trite. As we go through the story, and stop at various points of style and structure, we shall gradually accumulate a small collection of these simple devices.

There is first of all the introductional intonation: "Well, anything in sight . . . was the question asked on May 20, 1859, by a gentleman of a little over forty"—et cetera, et cetera. Then Arkadi arrives; then Bazarov is introduced:

"Nikolay Petrovich turned around quickly and, going up to a tall man in a long, loose, rough coat with tassels, who had only just got out of the carriage, he warmly pressed the ungloved rough hand, which the latter did not at once hold out to him.

" 'I am heartily glad,' he began, 'and very grateful for your kind intention of visiting us. . . . May I ask your name, and your father's?'

" 'Eugene Vasilievich,' answered Bazarov in a lazy but manly voice; and as he turned down the collar of his rough coat Nikolay Petrovich could see his whole face. Long and lean, with a broad forehead, a nose flat at the bridge but pointed at the tip, large greenish eyes, and sandy drooping side whiskers, it was lighted by a tranquil smile and showed self-confidence and intelligence.

" 'I hope, dear Eugene Vasilievich, you won't be bored at our place,' continued Nikolay Petrovich.

"Bazarov's thin lips moved just perceptibly, though he made no reply, merely taking off his cap. His long thick dark blond hair did not hide the prominent bumps on his head."

Uncle Pavel is introduced in the beginning of chapter 4:

". . . at that instant a man of medium height, dressed in a dark English suit, a fashionable low cravat, and kid shoes, entered the drawing room. This was Pavel Petrovich Kirsanov. He looked about forty-five: his close-cropped gray hair shone with a dark luster, like new silver; his face, yellow but free from wrinkles, was exceptionally regular and pure in line, as though carved by a light and delicate chisel, and showed traces of remarkable good looks; especially fine were his clear, black, almond-shaped eyes. The whole mien of Arkadi's uncle, exquisite and thoroughbred, had preserved the gracefulness of youth and that air of striving upward, of spurning the earth, which for the most part is lost after the twenties are past.

"Pavel Petrovich took out of his trousers pocket his exquisite hand with its long tapering pink nails, a hand which seemed still more beautiful because of the snowy whiteness of the cuff, buttoned with a single big opal, and gave it to his nephew. After a preliminary handshake in the European style, he kissed him thrice after the Russian fashion, that is to say, he touched his cheek three times with his fragrant mustache, and said, 'Welcome.' "

He and Bazarov dislike each other at sight, and Turgenev's device here is the comedy technique of each confiding his feelings separately and symmetrically to a friend. Thus Uncle Pavel, talking to his brother, criticizes the unkempt appearance of Bazarov, and a little later, after supper, Bazarov in talking to Arkadi criticizes Pavel's beautifully groomed fingernails. A simple symmetrical device, which is especially obvious because the ornamentation of the conventional structure is artistically superior to the convention. The first meal together, the supper, passes quietly. Uncle Pavel has been confronted by Bazarov but we have to wait for their first clash. Another person is introduced into Uncle Pavel's orbit at the very end of this chapter 4: Pavel Petrovich "sat in his study until long past midnight, in a beautifully made, roomy armchair before the fireplace, on which the coals were smoldering into faintly glowing embers. . . . His expression was concentrated and grim, which is not the case when a man is absorbed solely in recollections. And in a small back room [of the house], a young woman in a blue, warm, sleeveless jacket, with a white kerchief thrown over her dark hair, was sitting on a large trunk. This was Fenichka. She was now listening, now dozing, now glancing at the open door through which one could see a child's crib and hear the regular breathing of a sleeping baby."

It is important for Turgenev's purpose to tie up in the reader's mind Uncle Pavel with the mistress of Nikolay. Arkadi finds he has a baby brother, Mitya, a little later than the reader does.

The next meal, breakfast, begins without Bazarov. The ground has not yet been prepared, and Turgenev sends Bazarov away to collect frogs while he has Arkadi explain to Uncle Pavel about Bazarov's ideas:

" 'What is Bazarov?' Arkadi smiled. 'Would you like me, Uncle, to tell you precisely what he is?'

" 'If you will be so obliging, Nephew.'

" 'He's a nihilist. . . .'

" 'A nihilist,' Nikolay Petrovich managed to say. 'That's from the Latin, *nihil*, *nothing*, as far as I can judge; the word must mean a man who—who recognizes nothing.'

" 'Say, "who respects nothing," ' put in his brother, and he set to work on the butter again.

" 'Who regards everything from the critical point of view,' observed Arkadi.

" 'Isn't that the same thing?' inquired the uncle.

" 'No, it isn't. A nihilist is a man who does not bow down before any authority, who does not accept any principle on faith no matter what an aura of reverence may surround that principle.'. . .

" 'So that's it. Well, I see it's not in our line. . . . There used to be Hegelists, but now you have nihilists. We shall see how you will exist in a void, in a vacuum. And now please ring, brother Nikolay Petrovich—it's time I had my cocoa.' "

Immediately after this Fenichka appears. Note her admirable description: "She was a young woman of about three-and-twenty, all dainty whiteness and softness, with dark hair and eyes, red, childishly plump small lips, and delicate little hands. She wore a neat print dress; a new blue kerchief lay lightly on her soft shoulders. She was carrying a large cup of cocoa and, having set it down before Pavel Petrovich, she was overwhelmed with confusion; the hot blood rushed in a wave of crimson over the delicate skin of her endearing face. She dropped her eyes and stood at the table, leaning a little on the very tips of her fingers. Apparently ashamed of having come in, she at the same time felt she had a right to come."

Bazarov, the frog hunter, returns at the end of the chapter, and in the next one the breakfast table is the arena of the first round between Uncle Pavel and the young nihilist, both men scoring heavily:

" 'Arkadi was telling us just now that you do not acknowledge any authorities whatsoever—that you do not believe in them?'

" 'But why should I acknowledge them? And what should I believe in? When anyone talks sense, I agree, and that's all.'

" 'And all the Germans [scientists] talk sense?' asked Pavel Petrovich, and his face assumed an expression as impassive, as remote, as if he had withdrawn to some empyrean height.

" 'Not all,' replied Bazarov with a short yawn. He obviously did not care to continue the debate. . . .

" 'For my own part,' Pavel Petrovich began again, not without some effort, 'I am so unregenerate as not to like Germans. . . . My brother, for instance, is very favorably inclined toward them. . . . But now they've all turned chemists and materialists—'

" 'A chemist who knows his business is twenty times as useful as any poet,' broke in Bazarov."

On a collecting expedition Bazarov has found what he and Turgenev call a rare specimen of beetle. The term of course, is not specimen, but species, and that particular water-beetle is not a rare species. Only people who know nothing about natural history confuse specimen with species. In general Turgenev's descriptions of Bazarov's collecting are rather lame.

One will notice that despite Turgenev having prepared the first clash rather carefully, Uncle Pavel's rudeness strikes the reader as not very realistic. By "realism," of course, I merely indicate what an average reader in an average state of civilization feels as conforming to an average reality of life. Now in the reader's mind Uncle Pavel has already been imprinted as an image of a very fashionable, very experienced, very well groomed gentleman who would hardly take the trouble to heckle so viciously a chance boy, his nephew's friend and his brother's guest.

I have mentioned that a curious feature of Turgenev's structure is the spreading of antecedents over the action part of the story. An illustration comes at the end of chapter 6, "And Arkadi told Bazarov the story of Uncle Pavel." The story is passed on to the reader in chapter 7 and conspicuously interrupts the flow of the story which has already started. We read here about Uncel Pavel's love affair with the fascinating and fateful Princess R. back in the 1830s. This romantic lady, a sphinx with a riddle who finally found its solution in organized mysticism, around 1838 leaves Pavel Kirsanov and in 1848 she dies. Since then, till now, 1859, Pavel Kirsanov has retired to his brother's country seat.

Now further on we discover that Fenichka has not only replaced his [dead] wife Mary in the affections of Nikolay Kirsanov but has also replaced Princess R. in the affections of Uncle Pavel, another case of simple structural symmetry. We are shown Fenichka's room through Uncle Pavel's eyes:

"The small low-ceiled room in which he found himself was very clean and cozy. It smelt of the freshly painted floor, of camomile and melissa. Along the walls were ranged chairs with lyre-shaped backs, bought by the late general [as far back as the campaign of 1812]; in one corner was a high, small bedstead under a muslin canopy, near an ironbound chest with a rounded lid. In the opposite corner a little image-lamp was burning before a big dark icon of St. Nikolay the Wonder-Worker, a tiny porcelain egg hung by a red ribbon from the protruding gold halo down the saint's breast; on the window sills stood greenish glass jars of last year's jam, carefully tied and with the light green showing through them; on their paper tops Fenichka herself had written in big letters *Gooseberry* —Nikolay Petrovich was particularly fond of this jam. Near the ceiling, on a long cord, hung a cage with a bobtailed siskin; it was constantly chirping and hopping about, and the cage was constantly shaking and swinging, while hempseeds fell with a light tap on the floor. On the wall, just above a small chest of drawers, hung some rather poor photographs of Nikolay Petrovich in various poses, taken by some itinerant photographer; there, too, hung a photograph of Fenichka herself, which was an absolute failure: an eyeless face wearing a forced smile, in a dingy frame—one could make out nothing more. And above Fenichka, General Yermolov, in a Circassian felt cloak, scowled menacingly upon the Caucasian mountains in the distance, from beneath a little pincushion in the form of a shoe, which came down right over his eyebrows."

Now look at the way the story pauses again to allow the author to describe Fenichka's past:

"Nikolay Petrovich had made Fenichka's acquaintance three years before when he happened to stay overnight at an inn in a remote district town. He was agreeably struck by the cleanness of the room assigned to him, by the freshness of the bed linen. . . . Nikolay Kirsanov had at that time just moved into his new home and not wishing to keep serfs in the house, was on the lookout for hired servants; the landlady for her part complained of the small number of transients in the town, and the hard times; he proposed to her to come into his house in the capacity of housekeeper; she consented. Her husband had long been dead, leaving her an only daughter—Fenichka . . . who was at that time seventeen . . . she lived ever so quietly, ever so unassumingly, and only on Sundays did Nikolay Petrovich notice in the parish church, somewhere off on the side, the delicate profile of her small white face. More than a year passed thus."

Nikolay treats her for an inflamed eye, which was soon well again, "but the impression she had made on Nikolay did not pass away so soon. He was forever haunted by that pure, delicate, timorously lifted face; he felt on his palms that soft hair, and saw those innocent, slightly parted lips, through which pearly teeth gleamed moistly in the sun. He began to watch her with great attention in church, he tried to get into conversation with her. . . .

"By degrees she began to get used to him, but was still shy in his presence, when suddenly Arina, her mother, died of cholera. Which way was Fenichka to turn? She inherited from her mother a love for order, common sense, and sedateness; but she was so young, so lonely. Nikolay Petrovich was himself so good and modest. There is no need to relate the rest."

The details are admirable, that inflamed eye is a work of art, but the structure is lame and the paragraph concluding the account is lame and coy. "There is no need to relate the rest." A strange and silly remark implying that some things are so well known to readers that they are not worth describing. Actually the gentle reader should not find it very difficult to imagine precisely the event which Turgenev so prudently and prudishly masks.

Bazarov meets Fenichka—and no wonder her baby falls for him. We know already about that way Bazarov has with simple little souls—bearded peasants, urchins, maid-servants. We also hear, with Bazarov, old Kirsanov playing Schubert.

The beginning of chapter 10 well illustrates another typical Turgenev device—an intonation that we hear in the epilogues of his short novels, or, as here, when the author finds it necessary to pause and survey the arrangement and distribution of his characters. Here is how it goes—it is really a pause for station identification. Bazarov is classified through the reactions of other people toward him:

"Everyone in the house had grown used to him, to his careless manners and his monosyllabic and abrupt speech. Fenichka in particular had become so used to him that one night she sent to wake him up. Mitya had had convulsions. And Bazarov had come and, half joking, half yawning after his wont, had stayed two hours with her and relieved the child. On the other hand Pavel Kirsanov had grown to detest Bazarov with all the strength of his soul; he regarded him as proud, impudent, cynical, and plebian. He suspected that Bazarov had no respect for him—him, Pavel Kirsanov. Nikolay Petrovich was rather afraid of the young "nihilist," and entertained doubts whether his influence over Arkadi was for the good, but he willingly listened to him and was willingly present at his scientific and chemical experiments. Bazarov had brought his microscope with him and busied himself with it for hours on end. The servants, too, took to him, though he poked fun at them; they felt that, after all, he was one with them under the skin, that he was not a master. . . . The boys on the farm simply ran after the 'doctor' like puppies. The old man Prokofyich was the only one who did not like him; he handed him the dishes at table with a surly face. . . . Prokofyich in his own way was quite as much of an aristocrat as Pavel Kirsanov."

Now for the first time in the novel we have the tedious Eavesdropping Device, which has been so well described in regard to Lermontov:

"One day they had lingered rather late before returning home; Nikolay Petrovich went to meet them in the garden, and as he reached the arbor he suddenly heard the quick steps and the voices of the two young men. They were walking on the other side of the arbor and could not see him.

" 'You don't know my father well enough,' Arkadi was saying.

" 'Your father's a good fellow,' Bazarov pronounced, 'but he's a back number; his act is finished.'

"Nikolay Petrovich strained his ears. Arkadi made no answer.

"The 'back number' remained standing motionless for a couple of minutes and then slowly shuffled off home.

" 'The day before yesterday I saw him reading Pushkin,' Bazarov went on in the meantime. 'Explain to him, please, that it's of no earthly use. For he isn't a little boy, after all; it's time to drop all such rubbish. The very idea of being romantic at this time of day! Give him something useful to read.'

' 'Such as what?' asked Arkadi.

" 'Oh, I think Büchner's *Stoff und Kraft* for a start.'

" 'That's what I think,' Arkadi observed approvingly, '*Stoff und Kraft* is written in popular language.' "

It would seem that Turgenev is casting around for some artificial structures to enliven his story: "Stoff und Kraft" (Matter and Force) provides a little comic relief. Then a new puppet is produced in Matthew Kolyazin, the cousin of the Kirsanovs, who had been brought up by Uncle Kolyazin. This Matthew Kolyazin, who happens to be a governmental inspector, checking on the activities of the local town mayor, will be instrumental in permitting Turgenev to arrange matters in such a way that Arkadi and Bazarov will take a trip to town, which trip in its turn will provide Bazarov with his meeting with a fascinating lady, not unrelated to Uncle Pavel's Princess R.

In the second round of the fight between Uncle Pavel and Bazarov they come to grips at evening tea two weeks after their first fight. (The intervening meals, of which there have been perhaps as many as fifty—three per day multiplied by fourteen—are only vaguely imagined by this reader.) But the ground must be cleared first:

"The conversation turned to one of the neighboring landowners. 'Trash; just a miserable little aristocrat,' indifferently remarked Bazarov, who had met the fellow in Petersburg.

" 'Allow me to ask you,' began Pavel Petrovich, and his lips began to tremble, 'according to your conceptions the words "trash" and "aristocrat" signify one and the same thing.'

" 'I said "just a miserable little aristocrat," ' replied Bazarov, lazily swallowing a sip of tea. . . .

"Pavel Petrovich turned white.

" 'That's an entirely different matter. I'm under no compulsion whatever to explain to you now why I sit twiddling my thumbs, as you are pleased to put it. I wish to tell you merely that aristocracy is a principle, and in our time none but immoral or frivolous people can live without principles.' . . .

"Pavel Petrovich puckered up his eyes a little. 'So that's it!' he observed in a strangely composed voice. 'Nihilism is to cure all our woes, and you, you are our heroes and saviors. So. But why do you berate others—even those same denunciators, say? Don't you do as much chattering as all the others?' . . .

" 'Our argument has gone too far; it's better to cut it short, I think. But I'll be quite ready to agree with you,' Bazarov added, getting up, 'when you bring forward a single institution in our present mode of life, either domestic or social, which does not call forth complete and merciless repudiation. . . .

" 'Take my advice, Pavel Petrovich, give yourself a couple of days to think about it; you're not likely to find anything right off. Go through all our classes and think rather carefully over each one, and in the meantime Arkadi and I will—'

" 'Go on scoffing over everything,' Pavel Petrovich broke in.

" 'No, we will go on dissecting frogs. Come Arkadi. Good-by for the present, gentlemen.' "

Curiously enough, Turgenev is still engaged in describing the minds of his characters, in setting up his scenes rather than in having the protagonists act. This is especially clear in chapter 11 where the two brothers Pavel and Nikolay are compared, and where occurs incidentally that charming little landscape ("Evening had come, the sun had hid behind a small aspen grove which lay a quarter of a mile from the garden; its shadow spread endlessly across the still fields. . . .")

The next chapters are devoted to Arkadi's and Bazarov's visit to town. The town appears now as a middle point and a structural link between the Kirsanov country seat and the Bazarov country place, which is twenty-five miles from the town in another direction.

Some rather obvious grotesque personages are shown. Mme. Odintsov is first mentioned in a conversation at the house of a feminist progressive lady:

" 'Are there any pretty women here?' inquired Bazarov, as he drank up a third glass of wine.

" 'Yes, there are,' answered Eudoxia, 'but then they're all such empty-headed creatures. *Mon amie* Odintsov, for instance, isn't at all bad-looking. It's a pity that her reputation is sort of . . .' " Bazarov sees Mme. Odintsov for the first time at the Governor's ball.

"Arkadi turned and saw a tall woman in a black dress standing at the door of the room. He was struck by the dignity of her carriage. Her bare arms lay gracefully along her slender waist; gracefully some light sprays of fuchsia drooped from her gleaming hair on to her sloping shoulders; her clear eyes looked out from under a somewhat overhanging white brow, with a tranquil and intelligent expression—tranquil, precisely, and not pensive—and a scarcely perceptible smile hovered on her lips. Her face radiated a gracious and gentle force. . . .

"Bazarov's attention, too, was directed to Mme. Odintsov.

" 'Who in the world is she?' he remarked. 'She's different from the rest of the females here.' "

Arkadi is presented to her and asks her for the next mazurka.

"Arkadi made up his mind that he had never before met such an attractive woman. He could not get the sound of her voice out of his ears; the very folds of her dress seemed to hang upon her differently from all other women—more gracefully and amply—and her movements were peculiarly smooth and natural."

Instead of dancing (he was a bad dancer) Arkadi chats with her during the mazurka, "permeated by the happiness of being near her, talking to her, looking at her eyes, her lovely brow, all her endearing dignified, clever face. She said little, but from some of her observations Arkadi concluded that this young woman had already contrived to feel and think a great many things.

" 'Who was that you were standing with,' she asked him, 'when M'sieu' Sitnikov brought you to me?'

" 'Oh, so you noticed him?' Arkadi asked in his turn. 'He has a splendid face, hasn't he? He's a certain Bazarov, a friend of mine.'

Arkadi fell to talking about this "friend" of his. He spoke of him in such detail, and with such enthusiasm, that Mme. Odintsov turned toward him and gave him an attentive look. . . .

"The Governor came up to Mme. Odintsov, announced that supper was ready, and, with a careworn face, offered her his arm. As she went away, she turned to give a last smile and nod to Arkadi. He bowed low, followed her with his eyes (how graceful her waist seemed to him, the grayish luster of black silk apparently poured over it!). . . .

" 'Well?' Bazarov questioned him as soon as Arkadi had rejoined him in the corner. 'Have a good time? A gentleman has been telling me just now that this lady is—my, my, my! But then the gentleman himself strikes me as very much of a fool. Well, now, according to you, is she really—my, my, my?'

" 'I don't quite understand that definition,' answered Arkadi.

" 'Oh, now! What innocence!'

" 'In that case, I don't understand the gentleman you quote. Mme. Odintsov is indisputably most endearing, but she behaves so coldly and austerely, that—'

" 'Still waters—you know!' Bazarov put in quickly. 'She's cold, you say. That's just where the taste comes in. For you like ice cream, don't you?'

" 'Perhaps,' Arkadi muttered. 'I can't judge about that. She wishes to make your acquaintance and asked me to bring you to see her.'

" 'I can imagine how you've painted me! However, you did the right thing. Take me along. Whatever she may be—whether she's simply a provincial lioness, or an "emancipated woman," à la Kukshina [Eudoxia], the fact remains that she's got a pair of shoulders whose like I've not set eyes on for a long while.' "

This is Turgenev at his best, the delicate and vivid paintbrush (that gray gloss is great), a marvelous sense of color and light, and shade. The my-my-my is the famous Russian exclamation *oy-oy-oy*—still preserved in New York City among Armenian, Jewish, and Greek groups stemming from Russia. Note the first revelation when the following day he is presented to her that Bazarov, the strong man, may lose his confidence. "Arkadi presented Bazarov, and noticed with secret wonder that he seemed embarrassed, while Mme. Odintsov remained perfectly tranquil, as she had been the night before. Bazarov himself was conscious of his embarrassment and was irritated by it. 'Of all things! Frightened of a petticoat!' he thought, and, sprawled out in an armchair just like Sitnikov, began talking with an exaggerated unrestraint, while Mme. Odintsov kept her clear eyes fixed on him." Bazarov, the confirmed plebian, is going to fall madly in love with the aristocratic Anna.

Turgenev now uses the device which is beginning to pall—the pause for a biographical sketch where the past of the young widow Anna Odintsov is described. (Her marriage to Odintsov had lasted six years until his death.) She sees the charm of Bazarov through the rough exterior. An important observation on Turgenev's part is: Vulgarity alone repelled her, and no one could have accused Bazarov of vulgarity.

With Bazarov and Arkadi we now visit Anna's charming country seat. They will spend a fortnight there. The estate, Nikolskoe, is situated a few miles from the city, and from there Bazarov intends to travel on to his father's country place. It will be noted that he has left his microscope and other belongings at the Kirsanov place, Maryino, a little trick carefully prepared by Turgenev in order to get Bazarov back to the Kirsanovs so as to complete the Uncle Pavel-Fenichka-Bazarov theme.

There are some splendid little scenes in these Nikolskoe chapters, such as the appearance of Katya, and the greyhound:

"A beautiful greyhound bitch with a blue collar on ran into the drawing room, tapping on the floor with her nails, immediately followed by a girl of eighteen, black-haired and swarthy, with a somewhat round but pleasing face and small dark eyes. She was carrying a basket filled with flowers.

" 'And here's my Katya,' said Anna, indicating her with a motion of her head. Katya made a slight curtsy, settled down beside her sister, and began sorting the flowers. . . .

"When Katya spoke, she had a very endearing smile, timid and candid, and looked up from under her eyebrows with a sort of humorous severity. Every-

With Bazarov and Arkady we now visit Anna's
charming country-seat (chapters Twenty Six to chapters
Twenty Nine) They will spend a fortnight there.
The estate , Nikolino is situated a few
miles from the city, and from there
Bazarov intends to travel on to his father's
bounty place. It will be noted that he has left
his microscope and other belongings at the Kirsanov
place, Marino, a little trick carefully prepared
by Turgenev in order to get Bazarov back to
the Kirsanovs so as to complete the
uncle Paul - Fenichka Bazarov theme.

There some splendid little scenes in the Nikolino
chapters. I recommend to you Katya's apparition
in p. 324 and the greyhound (Read 324)
We now expect from Bazarov and Anna a few
good conversations , and indeed we
get them conversation number one in p 325
of Sixteen ('yes, that seems to suffice - why that kind of love),
conversation number two in the next chapter
and conversation number three in ch. Eighteen

thing about her still had the greenness of youth: her voice and the bloom on her whole face, and her rosy hands with the whitish circles on the palms, and her shoulders just the least bit narrow. She was constantly blushing and breathing rapidly."

We now expect from Bazarov and Anna a few good conversations, and indeed we get them: conversation number one in chapter 16 ("Yes. That seems to surprise you—why?"—that kind of thing), conversation number two in the next chapter, and number three in chapter 18. In conversation number one Bazarov expresses the stock ideas of progressive young men of the time, and Anna is calm and elegant and languid. Notice the charming description of her aunt:

"Princess Kh., a wizened little woman with a pinched-up face that looked like a small clenched fist, and staring malicious eyes under a gray scratch wig, came in, and scarcely bowing to the guests, she sank into a roomy velvet-covered armchair upon which none but she had the right to sit. Katya put a footstool under her feet; the old woman did not thank her, did not even glance at her, her hands merely stirred under the yellow shawl, which practically covered her whole wizened body. The Princess was fond of yellow; her cap, too, had bright yellow ribbons."

We had Schubert played by Arkadi's father. Now Katya plays Mozart's Fantasia in C minor: Turgenev's detailed references to music were one of the things that irritated so dreadfully his enemy Dostoevski. Later they go botanizing and then we pause again for some additional characterization of Anna. That doctor is a strange man, she reflects.

Shortly Bazarov is horribly in love: "His blood was on fire directly if he merely thought of her; he could easily have mastered his blood, but something else had gotten into him, something he had never admitted, at which he had always jeered, at which all his pride revolted. . . . Suddenly he would imagine that those chaste arms would one day twine about his neck, that those proud lips would respond to his kisses, those clever eyes would dwell with tenderness—yes, with tenderness—on his, and his head would start spinning, and for an instant he would forget himself, until indignation flared up in him again. He caught himself in all sorts of 'shameful' thoughts, as though some fiend were mocking him. Sometimes it seemed to him that a change was taking

A page from Nabokov's lecture on *Fathers and Sons* with his map of Bazarov's travels.

place in Anna as well; that a certain something was emerging in the expression of her face; that perhaps—But at that very point he would stamp his foot or gnash his teeth and shake his fist in his own face." (I have never cared much for that gnashing and fist-shaking.) He decides to leave, and "she paled."

A pathetic note is introduced with the appearance of the Bazarovs' old steward whom they have sent to see if Eugene is coming at last. This is the beginning of the Bazarov family theme, which is the most successful one in the whole novel.

We are now ready for conversation number two. The summer night scene is indoors, with a window playing a well-known romanticist role:

" 'Why leave?' asked Anna, dropping her voice.

"He glanced at her. She had thrown back her head on the back of her easy chair, and had crossed her arms, bare to the elbows, on her breast. She seemed paler in the light of the single lamp covered with a perforated paper shade. An ample white gown hid her completely in its soft folds; the tips of her feet, also crossed, were hardly visible.

" 'And why stay?' Bazarov countered.

"Anna turned her head slightly.

" 'You ask why? Haven't you enjoyed yourself here? Or do you think you won't be missed?'

" 'I'm sure of it.'

"Anna was silent a while. 'You're wrong in thinking so. However, I don't believe you. You couldn't have said that seriously.' Bazarov still sat immovable. 'Eugene Vasilyich, why don't you say something?'

" 'Why, what am I to say to you? It isn't worth while missing people, as a general thing—and surely not me.'

. . . " 'Open that window—I feel half stifled somehow.'

"Bazarov got up and gave the window a push. It flew open noisily and suddenly. He had not expected it to open so easily; besides, his hands were shaking. The dark soft night peered into the room with its almost black sky, its faintly rustling leaves, and the fresh fragrance of the pure open air. . . .

" 'We've become such friends—' Bazarov uttered in a stifled voice.

" 'Yes! For I'd forgotten that you wish to leave.'

"Bazarov got up. The lamp burnt dimly in the middle of the dark, fragrant, isolated room; from time to time the blind shook, and the insidious freshness of the night flowed in; one could hear the mysterious whisperings of that night. Anna did not stir a single limb; a secret emotion was overcoming her little by little. It was communicated to Bazarov. He suddenly became aware that he was alone with a young and lovely woman.

" 'Where are you going?' she asked slowly.

"He made no answer and sank into a chair. . . .

" 'Wait a little,' whispered Anna. Her eyes rested on Bazarov; it seemed as though she were examining him intently.

"He strode across the room, then suddenly went up to her, hurriedly said 'Good-by!,' squeezed her hand so that she almost cried out, and left the room. She raised her crushed fingers to her lips, breathed on them, and suddenly, impulsively getting up from her low chair, she went with rapid steps toward the door, as though she wished to bring Bazarov back. . . . Her braid came loose and like a dark snake slithered down on her shoulder. The lamp burned long in Anna's room, and for long did she sit without moving, only running her hands from time to time over her arms, nipped at by the chill of the night.

"Bazarov went back to his bedroom two hours later, his boots wet with dew; he was all muffled up and glum."

In chapter 18 we have the third conversation, with a passionate outburst at the end, and again the window:

"Anna held both her hands out before her, but Bazarov was leaning with his forehead pressed against the window pane. He was gasping; his whole body was visibly trembling. But it was not the tremor of youthful timidity, it was not the delectable dread of a first declaration of love that possessed him; it was passion struggling in him, strong and painful—passion not unlike rancor, and perhaps akin to it. Anna became both afraid of him and sorry for him.

" 'Eugene Vasilyich!' she said, and involuntarily there was the ring of tenderness in her voice.

"He turned quickly, devoured her with his eyes, and snatching both her hands, he drew her suddenly to his breast.

"She did not free herself from his embrace at once, but within an instant she was standing in a distant corner and watching Bazarov from there. He rushed toward her.

" 'You have misunderstood me,' she whispered hurriedly, in alarm. It seemed that were he to make another step she would scream. Bazarov bit his lips and left the room."

In chapter 19 Bazarov and Kirsanov leave Nikolskoe. (The arrival of Sitnikov is for comic relief, and artistically is too pat and not satisfying.) We will spend now three days—three days after three years of separation—with Bazarov's old people:

"Bazarov leaned out of the coach, while Arkadi craned his head over his companion's shoulder and caught sight on the steps of the little manor house of a tall, gaunt man with rumpled hair and a thin aquiline nose; his military coat was unbuttoned. He was standing, his legs wide apart, smoking a long pipe, and his eyes were puckered up from the sun.

"The horses stopped.

" 'So you've favored us at last,' said Bazarov's father, still going on smoking, though his student pipe was fairly dancing up and down in his fingers. 'Come, get out, get out; let me kiss you.'

"He put his arms around his son.

" 'Gene, Gene,' they heard a woman's trembling voice. The door was flung open, and a roly-poly, short little old woman in a white cap and a short striped jacket appeared on the threshold. She 'oh'd,' swayed, and would certainly have fallen if Bazarov had not held her up. Her plump little arms were instantly twined round his neck, her head was pressed to his breast, and there was a complete hush. The only sound to be heard was her broken sobs."

It is a small estate; the Bazarovs have only twenty-two serfs. Old Bazarov, who had served in General Kirsanov's regiment, is an old-fashioned provincial doctor, hopelessly behind the times. In their first conversation he indulges in a pathetic monologue which bores his emancipated, nonchalant son. The mother wonders how long Eugene will stay—after three years. Turgenev closes the chapter with a description of Madame Bazarov's origins and mentality, a device we now know well: the biographical pause.

A second conversation takes place, this time between old Bazarov and Arkadi (Eugene having got up early and gone for a ramble—one wonders if he collected anything). The conversation is permeated on old Bazarov's part by Arkadi's being Eugene's friend and admirer: it is this admiration of his son that the old man touchingly basks in. A third conversation takes place between Eugene and Arkadi in the shade of a haystack, in which we learn a few biographical details concerning Eugene. He had lived there two years on end and from time to time elsewhere; his father being an army doctor, he had led a roving life. The conversation turns philosophical but ends in a slight quarrel.

The real drama begins when Eugene suddenly decides to leave, even though he promises to return in a month's time.

Old Bazarov, "after a few more moments of bravely waving his handkerchief on the steps, sank into a chair and let his head drop on his breast.

" 'He's forsaken us, he's forsaken us!' he babbled. 'He's forsaken us; he became bored here. I'm all alone now, all alone like this!' And each time he said this he thrust out his hand, with the index finger sticking up. Whereupon Arina Vlasievna drew near him and, putting her gray head close to his gray head, said:

" 'There's no help for it Vasya! A son is a slice off the loaf. He's like the falcon—he felt like it, and he winged back to the nest; he felt like it, and he winged away. But you and I are like bumps on a hollow tree, sitting side by side and never budging. Only I shall remain the same to you forever, even as you to me.'

"Vasili Ivanovich took his hands away from his face and embraced his wife, his friend, his mate, harder than he had ever clasped her even in youth: she had consoled him in his grief.''

On Bazarov's whim the two friends make a detour to Nikolskoe where they are not expected. Having spent four unsatisfactory hours there (Katya remaining in her room), they go on to Maryino. Ten days later Arkadi returns to Nikolskoe. The main reason is, Turgenev has to have him out of the way when the expected quarrel between Bazarov and Uncle Pavel takes place. There is no explanation why Bazarov remains: he could have conducted his simple experiments quite as successfully in the home of his parents. The theme of Bazarov and Fenichka now starts, and we have the famous scene in the lilac arbor, complete with the Eavesdropping Device:

" 'I like it when you talk. It's just like a little brook murmuring.' Fenichka turned her head away.

" 'How you talk!' she said, running her fingers over the flowers. 'And why should you listen to me? You've conversed with such clever ladies.'

" 'Ah, Theodosia Nikolaievna! Believe me, all the clever ladies in the world aren't worth the dimple on your little elbow.'

" 'Why, what won't you think of!' murmured Fenichka, and put her hands under her. . . .

" 'Then I'll tell you; I want—one of those roses.'

"Fenichka broke into laughter again and even clapped her hands, so amusing did Bazarov's request seem to her. She laughed, and at the same time felt flattered. Bazarov was looking at her intently.

" 'By all means, by all means,' she said at last and, bending down to the seat, began picking over the roses. 'Which will you have—a red or a white?'

" 'Red—and not too large.' . . .

"Fenichka stretched her little neck forward and put her face close to the flower. The kerchief rolled down from her head on to her shoulders; a soft mass of dark, shining, slightly ruffled hair became visible.

" 'Wait, I want to sniff it with you,' said Bazarov. He bent down and kissed her hard on her parted lips.

"She was startled and thrust him back with both her hands on his breast, but her thrust was weak, and he was able to renew and prolong the kiss.

"There was a dry cough behind the lilac bushes. Fenichka instantaneously moved away to the other end of the seat. Pavel Petrovich appeared, made a slight bow, and having dropped with a sort of malicious despond 'You here?,' he went out of the arbor. . . .

" 'That was wrong of you Eugene Vasilyich,' she whispered as she went. There was a note of unfeigned reproach in her whisper.

"Bazarov remembered another recent scene, and he felt both shame and contemptuous annoyance. But he immediately tossed back his head, ironically congratulated himself 'on his formal induction into the ranks of the Lotharios,' and went on to his own room."

In the duel that follows Uncle Pavel aims directly at Bazarov and fires but misses. Bazarov "took one more step and, without taking aim, pressed the trigger.

"Kirsanov gave a slight start and clutched at his thigh. A thin stream of blood began to trickle down his white trousers.

"Bazarov flung aside his pistol and approached his antagonist. 'Are you wounded?' he asked.

" 'You had the right to call me up to the barrier,' said Pavel Petrovich, 'but this wound is a trifle. According to our agreement, each of us has the right to one more shot.'

" 'Really, you'll excuse me, but that will wait till another time,' answered Bazarov, and he put his arm around Kirsanov, who was beginning to turn pale. 'Now I'm no longer a duelist but a doctor, and I must examine your wound before anything else. . . .

" 'That's all nonsense—I don't need anyone's aid,' Kirsanov declared jerkily, 'and—we must—again—' He tried to pull at his mustache, but his hand failed him, his eyes rolled up, and he lost consciousness. . . . Kirsanov slowly opened his eyes.

". . . 'All I need is something to bind up this scratch and I can reach home on foot, or else you can send a droshky for me. The duel, if you are willing, won't be renewed. You have behaved nobly—today, today, you will note.'

" 'No use raking up the past,' rejoined Bazarov. 'And as for the future, it's not worth racking one's head about that, either, for I intend clearing out without any delay.' " Actually Bazarov would have behaved still more nobly if he had coolly discharged his pistol in the air after enduring Uncle Pavel's fire.

Turgenev now starts his first mopping-up operation when a conversation takes place between Uncle Pavel and Fenichka, and another between Uncle

Pavel and his brother—and Uncle Pavel solemnly asks Nikolay to marry Fenichka. A little moral is stressed, not very artistically. Uncle Pavel decides to go abroad: his soul is dead within him. We shall meet him for a last glimpse in the epilogue, but otherwise Turgenev has done with him.

Now for the mopping-up of the Nikolskoe theme. We move to Nikolskoe where Katya and Arkadi are sitting in the shade of an ash tree. The greyhound Fifi is there, too. The light and shade are beautifully rendered:

"A faint breeze stirring in the leaves of the ash kept pale-gold flecks of light wavering to and fro over the shady path and over Fifi's tawny back; an even shade fell upon Arkadi and Katya, save that now and then a vivid streak would flare up in her hair. Both were silent, but the very way in which they were silent, in which they were sitting together, was expressive of a trustful *rapprochement*; each of them seemed to be not thinking of his companion, yet secretly rejoicing at the other's proximity. Their faces, too, had changed since we saw them last; Arkadi seemed calmer, Katya more animated, more spirited."

Arkadi is getting out and away from Bazarov's influence. The conversation is a functional one—summing up matters, giving results, stating a final situation. It is also an attempt to draw differences between Katya's character and Anna's character. It is all very weak and belated. The moment Arkadi almost proposes marriage but walks away, Anna appears. A page later, Bazarov is announced. What activity!

We are now going to get rid of Anna, Katya, and Arkadi. The final scene is set in the arbor. During another conversation between Arkadi and Katya, the Bazarov-Anna couple is heard discoursing. We have sunk to the level of a comedy of manners. The overhearing device is with us, the pairing device is with us, the summing up device is with us. Arkadi resumes his courtship and is accepted. Anna and Bazarov reach an understanding:

" 'You see,' Anna Sergeievna continued, 'you and I have made a mistake; we're both past our first youth—especially I; we have seen life, we are tired; we're both—why be falsely modest?—clever; at first we aroused each other's interest, our curiosity was stirred, but then—'

" 'But then I became flat,' Bazarov put in.

" 'You know that that was not the cause of our misunderstanding. But be that as it may, we had no need of each other, that's the main thing; there was too much—how should I put it?—similarity in us. We did not realize this immediately. . . . Eugene Vasilyich, we have no power over—' she began; but a gust of wind swooped down, set the leaves rustling, and bore her words away.

" 'Of course, you are free—' Bazarov declared a little later. Nothing more could be distinguished; their steps retreated; everything was stilled."
The next day Bazarov blesses his young friend Arkadi and departs.

———————

We now come to the greatest chapter in our novel, chapter 27, which is the one before the last. Bazarov returns to his family and engages himself to medical activities. Turgenev is preparing his death. Then it comes. Eugene asks his father for some lunar caustic:
" 'Yes, what do you want it for?'
" 'I need it—to cauterize a cut.'
" 'For whom?'
" 'For myself.'
" 'What—yourself? How is that? What sort of a cut? Where is it?'
" 'Right here, on my finger. I went to the village today—you know, where they brought that peasant with typhus from. They were about to perform an autopsy on him for some reason or other, and I've had no practice on that sort of thing for a long while.'
" 'Well?'
" 'Well, so I asked the district doctor to let me do it; and so I cut myself.'
"Vasili Ivanovich suddenly turned all white and, without uttering a word, rushed to his study, from which he returned at once carrying a bit of lunar caustic. Bazarov was about to take it and leave.
" 'For dear God's sake,' said his father, 'let me do this myself.'
Bazarov smiled.
" 'What a devoted practitioner!'
" 'Don't laugh, please. Let me see your finger. The cut isn't so great. Doesn't that hurt?'
" 'Press harder; don't be afraid.'
"Vasili Ivanovich stopped.
" 'What do you think, Eugene—wouldn't it be better to cauterize it with a hot iron?'
" 'That should have been done sooner; but now, if you get down to brass tacks, even the lunar caustic is useless. If I've been infected, it's too late now.'
" 'What—too late—' Vasili Ivanovich could scarcely articulate the words.
" 'Of course! It's more than four hours ago.'
"Vasili Ivanovich cauterized the cut a little more.
" 'Why, didn't the district doctor have any lunar caustic?'
" 'No.'

" 'My God, how is it possible? A doctor—and he hasn't got such an indispensable thing as that!'

" 'You ought to have a look at his lancets,' Bazarov observed, and walked out."

Bazarov has become infected, falls ill, has a partial recovery, and then a relapse that brings him to the crisis of the disease. Anna is sent for, arrives with a German physician, who tells her there is no hope, and she goes to Bazarov's bedside.

" 'Well, thanks,' Bazarov repeated. 'This is a regal action. They say that monarchs visit the dying, too.'

" 'Eugene Vasilyich, I hope—'

" 'Eh, Anna Sergeievna, let's speak the truth. It's all over with me. I'm caught under the wheel. And now it turns out it was useless to think of the future. Death is an old trick, yet it strikes everyone as something new. So far I have no craven fear of it—and later on a coma will come,.and—' he whistled and made a feeble nugatory gesture. 'Well, what am I to say to you? That I loved you? There was no sense in that even before, and less than ever now. Love is a form, and my own form is already decomposing. I'd do better to say how fine you are! Even now you're standing there, so beautiful—'

"Anna gave an involuntary shudder.

" 'Never mind, don't be upset. Sit over there. Don't come close to me— after all, my illness is contagious.'

"Anna swiftly crossed the room and sat down in the armchair near the divan on which Bazarov was lying.

" 'Magnanimous one!' he whispered. 'Oh, how near and how young and fresh and pure . . . in this loathsome room! . . . Well, good-by! Live long, that's the best thing of all, and make the most of it while there is time. Just see, what a hideous spectacle: a worm half crushed, but writhing still. And yet I, too, thought: I'd accomplish so many things, I wouldn't die, not me! If there were any problem—well, I was a giant! And now all the problem the giant has is how to die decently, although that makes no difference to anyone either. Never mind; I'm not going to wag my tail.'. . .

"Bazarov put his hand to his brow.

"Anna bent down to him.

" 'Eugene Vasiliyich, I'm here—'

"He at once took his hand away and raised himself.

" 'Good-by,' he said with sudden force, and his eyes gleamed with a last gleam. 'Good-by. Listen—you know I didn't kiss you that time. Breathe on the dying lamp and let it go out—'

"Anna put her lips to his forehead.

" 'Enough!' he murmured, and dropped back on the pillow. 'Now . . . darkness—'

"Anna went softly out.

" 'Well?' Vasili Ivanovich asked her in a whisper.

" 'He has fallen asleep,' she answered, barely audible.

"Bazarov was not fated to awaken. Toward evening he sank into complete unconsciousness, and the following day he died. . . .

"And when finally he had breathed his last, and a universal lamentation arose throughout the house, Vasili Ivanovich was seized by a sudden frenzy.

" 'I said I would rebel,' he screamed hoarsely, with his face flaming and distorted, shaking his fist in the air, as though threatening someone, 'and I will rebel.'

"But Arina Vlasievna, all in tears, hung upon his neck, and both prostrated themselves together.

" 'Side by side,' Anfisushka related afterward in the servants' quarters, 'they let their poor heads droop, like lambs at noonday—'

"But the sultriness of noonday passes, and evening comes, and night, and then follows the return to the calm refuge, where sleep is sweet for the tortured and the weary."

In the epilogue, chapter 28, everyone is marrying, in the pairing-off device. Notice here the didactic and slightly humorous attitude. Fate takes over but still under Turgenev's direction.

"Anna has recently married, not of love but out of conviction, one of the future leaders of Russia, a very intelligent man, a lawyer, possessed of strong practical sense, firm will, and remarkable eloquence—still young, good-natured, and cold as ice. . . . The Kirsanovs, father and son, live at Maryino; their fortunes are on the mend. Arkadi has become zealous in the management of the estate, and the 'farm' is now yielding a rather good revenue. . . . Katya has a son, little Nikolay, while Mitya runs about ever so lively and talks beautifully. . . . In Dresden, on the Brühl Terrace, between two and four o'clock—the most fashionable time for walking—you may meet a man about fifty, by now altogether gray, and apparently afflicted with gout, but still handsome, exquisitely dressed, and with that special stamp which is gained only by moving a long time in the higher strata of society. That is Pavel Petrovich. From Moscow he had gone abroad for the sake of his health, and has settled down in Dresden, where he associates for the most part with

Englishmen and Russian visitors. . . . Kukshina, too, found herself abroad. . . . With two or three just such young chemists, who don't know oxygen from nitrogen, but are filled with skepticism and self-respect, Sitnikov is knocking about Petersburg, also getting ready to be great, and, according to his own assertions, is carrying on Bazarov's 'work.' . . .

"There is a small village graveyard in one of the remote nooks of Russia. Like almost all our graveyards, it presents a woebegone appearance. . . . But among these graves there is one untouched by man, untrampled by beast; the birds alone perch thereon and sing at dawn. An iron railing runs around it; two young firs are there, one planted at each end.

"Eugene Bazarov is buried in this grave. Often, from the little village not far off, an old couple, decrepit by now, comes to visit it—man and wife. Supporting each other, they move to it with heavy steps; they come close to the railing and get down on their knees. And long and bitterly do they weep, and long and intently do they gaze at the mute stone, under which their son is lying; they exchange some brief phrase, brush the dust from the stone, and set straight a branch on one of the firs, and then pray again, and they cannot forsake this place, where they seem to feel nearer to their son, to their memories of him."

Western reference first next page

We must distinguish between sentimental
and "sensitive". A sentimentalist
may be a perfect brute in his free
time. A sensitive person is never
a cruel person. Sentimental Rousseau
who could weep over a progressive idea,
distributed his many natural
children through various poorhouses and
workhouses and never gave a hoot
for them. So a sentimental old
maid may pamper her parrot and
poison her niece. The sentimental politician
may remember mother's day and
ruthlessly destroy a rival. Stalin
loved babies. Lenin sobbed at
the opera especially at the Traviata. A whole century
of authors praised the simple life of the poor and so on.
Remember now than we speak of
sentimentalist in any writer — Richardson, Rousseau,
Dostoevski — we mean: the non-artistic exaggeration of
familiar emotions meant to provoke automatically
traditional compassion in the reader

FYODOR DOSTOEVSKI (1821-1881)

B elinski from "Letter to Gogol" (1847): ". . . you have not observed that Russia sees its salvation not in mysticism, not in asceticism, not in
pietism, but in the successes of civilization, of enlightenment, of
humanitarianism. It is not preachments that Russia needs (she has heard them),
nor prayers (she has said them over and over), but an awakening among her
common folk of a sense of human dignity, for so many centuries lost amid the
mire and manure, and rights and laws, conforming not with the teachings of
the Church but with common sense and justice, and as strict fulfillment of
them as is possible. But instead of that Russia presents the horrible spectacle of
a land where men traffic in men, not having therefor even that justification
which the American plantation owners craftily avail themselves of, affirming
that the Negro is not a man; the spectacle of a land where people do not call
themselves by names but by ignoble nicknames Jack and Tom (Vankas,
Vaskas, Steshkas, Palashkas); the spectacle of a country, finally, where there
are not only no guarantees whatsoever for one's person, honor, property, but
where there is even no order maintained by the police, instead of which there
are only enormous corporations of various administrative thieves and robbers.
The most pressing contemporary national problems in Russia now are: the
abolition of the right to own serfs, the abrogation of corporal punishment, the
introduction as far as possible of a strict fulfillment of at least those laws which

already exist. This is felt even by the government itself (which is well aware of what the landowners do with their peasants and how many throats of the former are cut every year by the latter), which is proved by its timid and fruitless half-measures for the benefit of our white Negroes. . . ."

My position in regard to Dostoevski is a curious and difficult one. In all my courses I approach literature from the only point of view that literature interests me—namely the point of view of enduring art and individual genius. From this point of view Dostoevski is not a great writer, but a rather mediocre one—with flashes of excellent humor, but, alas, with wastelands of literary platitudes in between. In *Crime and Punishment* Raskolnikov for some reason or other kills an old female pawnbroker and her sister. Justice in the shape of an inexorable police officer closes slowly in on him until in the end he is driven to a public confession, and through the love of a noble prostitute he is brought to a spiritual regeneration that did not seem as incredibly banal in 1866 when the book was written as it does now when noble prostitutes are apt to be received a little cynically by experienced readers. My difficulty, however, is that not all the readers to whom I talk in this or other classes *are* experienced. A good third, I should say, do not know the difference between real literature and pseudo-literature, and to such readers Dostoevski may seem more important and more artistic than such trash as our American historical novels or things called *From Here to Eternity* and such like balderdash.

However, I shall speak at length about a number of really great artists—and it is on this high level that Dostoevski is to be criticized. I am too little of an academic professor to teach subjects that I dislike. I am very eager to debunk Dostoevski. But I realize that readers who have not read much may be puzzled by the set of values implied.

———

Fyodor Mikhailovich Dostoevski was born in 1821 in the family of a rather poor man. His father was a doctor in one of the public hospitals in Moscow, but the position of a doctor of a public hospital in contemporaneous Russia was a modest one and the Dostoevski family lived in cramped quarters and in conditions anything but luxurious.

His father was a petty tyrant who was murdered under obscure circumstances. Freudian-minded explorers of Dostoevski's literary work are inclined to see an autobiographic feature in the attitude of Ivan Karamazov toward the murder of his father: though Ivan was not the actual murderer, yet through his lax attitude, and through his not having prevented a murder he could have prevented, he was in a way guilty of patricide. It seems, according to those critics, that Dostoevski all his life labored under a similar consciousness of indirect guilt after his own father had been assassinated by his coachman. Be it as it may, there is no doubt that Dostoevski was a neurotic, that from his early years he had been subject to that mysterious sickness, the epilepsy. The epileptic fits and his general neurotic condition worsened considerably under the influence of the misfortunes which befell him later.

Dostoevski received his education first at a boarding school in Moscow, then at the Military Engineers' School in Petersburg. He was not particularly interested in military engineering, but his father had desired him to enter that school. Even there he devoted most of his time to the study of literature. After graduation he served at the engineering department just as long as was obligatory in return for the education he had received. In 1844 he resigned his commission and entered upon his literary career. His first book *Poor Folk* (1846) was a hit both with the literary critics and the reading public. There are all sorts of anecdotes concerning its early history. Dostoevski's friend and a writer in his own right, Dmitri Grigorovich, had persuaded Dostoevski to let him show the manuscript to Nikolay Nekrasov, who was at that time publisher of the most influential literary review *Sovremennik (The Contemporary)*. Nekrasov and his lady friend Mrs. Panaiev entertained at the office of the review a literary *salon* which was frequented by all the worthies of contemporaneous Russian literature. Turgenev, and later Tolstoy, were among its constant members. So were the famous left-wing critics Nikolay Chernyshevski and Nikolay Dobrolyubov. Being published in Nekrasov's review was enough to make a man's literary reputation. After leaving his manuscript with Nekrasov, Dostoevski went to bed full of misgivings: "They will poke fun at my *Poor Folk*," he kept telling himself. At four in the morning he was awakened by Nekrasov and Grigorovich, who made an irruption into his apartment and smothered him with smacking Russian kisses: they had begun to read the manuscript in the evening and could not stop until they had read it to the end. Their admiration had been so great that they decided to wake up the author and tell him what they thought of him at once. "What matter that he sleeps: *this* is more important than sleep," they said.

Nekrasov took the manuscript to Belinski and declared that a new Gogol had been born. "Gogols seem to grow like toadstools with you," remarked Belinski dryly. But his admiration after reading *Poor Folk* was unbounded too and he asked immediately to be introduced to the new author and showered upon him enthusiastic praise. Dostoevski was transported with joy; *Poor Folk* was published in Nekrasov's review. Its success was enormous. Unfortunately it did not last. His second novel, or long short story, *The Double* (1846), which is the best thing he ever wrote and certainly far above *Poor Folk*, met with an indifferent reception. In the meantime Dostoevski had developed a tremendous literary vanity, and being very naive, unpolished, and but poorly equipped where manners were concerned, contrived to make a fool of himself in his dealings with his newly acquired friends and admirers and eventually to spoil completely his relations with them. Turgenev dubbed him a new pimple on the nose of Russian literature.

His early inclinations were to the side of the radicals; he leaned more or less toward the Westernizers. He also consorted with a secret society (though apparently did not actually become its member) of young men who had adopted the socialistic theories of Saint-Simon and Fourier. These young men gathered at the house of an official of the State Department, Mikhail Petrashevski, and read aloud and discussed the books of Fourier, talked socialism, and criticized the government. After the upheavals of 1848 in several European countries, there was a wave of reaction in Russia; the government was alarmed and cracked down upon all dissenters. The Petrashevskians were arrested, among them Dostoevski. He was found guilty of "having taken part in criminal plans, having circulated the letter of Belinski [to Gogol] full of insolent expressions against the Orthodox Church and the Supreme Power, and of having attempted, together with others, to circulate anti-Government writings with the aid of a private printing press." He awaited his trial in the Fortress of St. Paul and Peter, of which the commander was a General Nabokov, an ancestor of mine. (The correspondence which passed between this General Nabokov and Tsar Nicholas in regard to their prisoner makes rather amusing reading.) The sentence was severe — eight years of hard labor in Siberia (this was later commuted to four by the Tsar) — but a monstrously cruel procedure was followed before the actual sentence was read to the condemned men: They were told they were to be shot; they were taken to the place assigned for the execution, stripped to their shirts, and the first batch of prisoners were tied to the posts. Only then the actual sentence was read to them. One of the men went mad. A deep scar was left in Dostoevski's soul by the experience of that day. He never quite got over it.

The four years of penal servitude Dostoevski spent in Siberia in the company of murderers and thieves, no segregation having been yet introduced between ordinary and political criminals. He described them in his *Memoirs from the House of Death* (1862). They do not make a pleasant reading. All the humiliations and hardships he endured are described in detail, as also the criminals among whom he lived. Not to go completely mad in those surroundings, Dostoevski had to find some sort of escape. This he found in a neurotic Christianism which he developed during these years. It is only natural that some of the convicts among whom he lived showed, besides dreadful bestiality, an occasional human trait. Dostoevski gathered these manifestations and built upon them a kind of very artificial and completely pathological idealization of the simple Russian folk. This was the initial step on his consecutive spiritual road. In 1854 when Dostoevski finished his term he was made a soldier in a battalion garrisoned in a Siberian town. In 1855 Nicholas I died and his son Alexander became Emperor under the name of Alexander II. He was by far the best of the nineteenth-century Russian rulers. (Ironically he was the one to die at the hands of the revolutionaries, torn literally in two by a bomb thrown at his feet.) The beginning of his reign brought a pardon to many prisoners. Dostoevski was given back his officer's commission. Four years later he was allowed to return to Petersburg.

During the last years of exile, he had resumed literary work with *The Manor of Stepanchikovo* (1859) and the *Memoirs from the House of Death*. After his return to Petersburg, he plunged into literary activity. He began at once publishing, together with his brother Mikhail, a literary magazine *Vremia* (*Time*). His *Memoirs from the House of Death* and yet another work, a novel, *The Humiliated and the Insulted* (1861), appeared in this magazine. His attitude toward the Government had completely changed since the days of his youthful radicalism. "Greek-Catholic Church, absolute monarchy, and the cult of Russian nationalism," these three props on which stood the reactionary political slavophilism were his political faith. The theories of socialism and Western liberalism became for him the embodiments of Western contamination and of satanic sin bent upon the destruction of a Slavic and Greek-Catholic world. It is the same attitude that one sees in Fascism or in Communism — universal salvation.

His emotional life up to that time had been unhappy. In Siberia he had married, but this first marriage proved unsatisfactory. In 1862-1863 he had an affair with a woman writer and in her company visited England, France, and Germany. This woman whom he later characterized as "infernal" seems to have been an evil character. Later she married Rozanov, an extraordinary writer combining moments of exceptional genius with manifestations of astounding naiveté. (I knew Rozanov, but he had married another woman by that time.) This woman seems to have had a rather unfortunate influence on Dostoevski, further upsetting his unstable spirit. It was during this first trip abroad to Germany that the first manifestation of his passion for gambling appeared which during the rest of his life was the plague of his family and an insurmountable obstacle to any kind of material ease or peace to himself.

After his brother's death, the closing of the review which he had been editing left Dostoevski a bankrupt, and burdened by the care of his brother's family, a duty which he immediately and voluntarily assumed. To cope with these overwhelming burdens Dostoevski applied himself feverishly to work. All his most celebrated writings, Crime and Punishment (1866), The Gambler (1867), The Idiot (1868), The Possessed (1872), The Brothers Karamazov (1880), etc., were written under constant stress: he had to work in a hurry, to meet deadlines with hardly any time left to re-read what he had written, or rather what he had dictated to a stenographer he had been obliged to hire. In his stenographer he at last found a woman full of devotion and with such practical sense that by her help he met his deadlines and gradually began to extricate himself from his financial mess. In 1867 he married her. This marriage was on the whole a happy one. For four years, from 1867 to 1871, they had achieved some financial security and were able to return to Russia. From then on to the end of his days Dostoevski enjoyed comparative peace. The Possessed was a great success. Soon after its publication he was offered the editorship of Prince Meshcherski's very reactionary weekly, the Citizen. His last work, The Brothers Karamazov, of which he wrote only the first volume and was working on the second when he died, brought him the greatest fame of all his novels.

But even more publicity fell to the lot of his address at the unveiling of the Pushkin memorial in Moscow in 1880. It was a very great event, the manifestation of the passionate love Russia bore Pushkin. The foremost writers of the time took part in it. But of all the speeches the most popular success fell to Dostoevski. The gist of his speech was Pushkin as the embodiment of the national spirit of Russia, which subtly understands the ideals of other nations but assimilates and digests them in accordance with its own spiritual setup. In this capacity Dostoevski saw the proof of the all-embracing mission of the Russian people, etc. When read, this speech does not explain the great success it enjoyed. But if we consider the fact that it was a time when all Europe was allying itself against Russia's rise in power and influence, we can better understand the enthusiasm Dostoevski's speech provoked in his patriotic listeners.

A year later, in 1881, and but a short time before the assassination of Alexander II, Dostoevski died, enjoying general recognition and esteem.

Through French and Russian translations, Western influence, sentimental and gothic—Samuel Richardson (1689-1761), Ann Radcliffe (1764-1823), Dickens (1812-1870), Rousseau (1712-1778), Eugène Sue (1804-1857)—combines in Dostoevski's works with a religion of compassion merging on melodramatic sentimentality. We must distinguish between "sentimental" and "sensitive." A sentimentalist may be a perfect brute in his free time. A sensitive person is never a cruel person. Sentimental Rousseau, who could weep over a progressive idea, distributed his many natural children through various poorhouses and workhouses and never gave a hoot for them. A sentimental old maid may pamper her parrot and poison her niece. The sentimental politician may remember Mother's Day and ruthlessly destroy a rival. Stalin loved babies. Lenin sobbed at the opera, especially at the *Traviata*. A whole century of authors praised the simple life of the poor, and so on. Remember that when we speak of sentimentalists, among them Richardson, Rousseau, Dostoevski, we mean the nonartistic exaggeration of familiar emotions meant to provoke automatically traditional compassion in the reader.

Dostoevski never really got over the influence which the European mystery novel and the sentimental novel made upon him. The sentimental influence implied that kind of conflict he liked—placing virtuous people in pathetic situations and then extracting from these situations the last ounce of pathos. When after his return from Siberia his essential ideas began to ripen—the idea of salvation to be found through transgression, the ethical supremacy of suffering and submission over struggle and resistance, the defence of free will not as a metaphysical but as a moral proposition, and the ultimate formula of egoism-antichrist Europe on one side and brotherhood-Christ-Russia on the other—when these ideas (which are all thoroughly examined in countless textbooks) suffused his novels, much of the Western influence still remained, and one is tempted to say that in a way Dostoevski, who so hated the West, was the most European of the Russian writers.

Another interesting line of inquiry lies in the examination of his characters in their historical development. Thus the favorite hero of the old Russian folklore, John the Simpleton, who is considered a weak-minded muddler by his brothers but is really as cunning as a skunk and perfectly immoral in his activities, an unpoetical and unpleasant figure, the personification of secret slyness triumphing over the big and the strong, Johnny the Simpleton, that product of a nation which has had more than one nation's share of misery, is a curious prototype of Dostoevski's Prince Myshkin, hero of his novel *The Idiot*, the positively good man, the pure innocent fool, the cream of humility, renunciation, and spiritual peace. And Prince Myshkin, in turn, had for his grandson the character recently created by the contemporary Soviet writer Mikhail Zoshchenko, the type of cheerful imbecile, muddling through a police-state totalitarian world, imbecility being the last refuge in that kind of world.

Dostoevski's lack of taste, his monotonous dealings with persons suffering with pre-Freudian complexes, the way he has of wallowing in the tragic misadventures of human dignity—all this is difficult to admire. I do not like this trick his characters have of "sinning their way to Jesus" or, as a Russian author Ivan Bunin put it more bluntly, "spilling Jesus all over the place." Just as I have no ear for music, I have to my regret no ear for Dostoevski the Prophet. The very best thing he ever wrote seems to me to be *The Double*. It is the story—told very elaborately, in great, almost Joycean detail (as the critic Mirsky notes), and in a style intensely saturated with phonetic and rhythmical expressiveness—of a government clerk who goes mad, obsessed by the idea that a fellow clerk has usurped his identity. It is a perfect work of art, that story, but it hardly exists for the followers of Dostoevski the Prophet, because it was written in the 1840s, long before his so-called great novels; and moreover its imitation of Gogol is so striking as to seem at times almost a parody.

In the light of the historical development of artistic vision, Dostoevski is a very fascinating phenomenon. If you examine closely any of his works, say *The Brothers Karamazov*, you will note that the natural background and all things relevant to the perception of the senses hardly exist. What landscape there is is a landscape of ideas, a moral landscape. The weather does not exist in his world, so it does not much matter how people dress. Dostoevski characterizes his people through situation, through ethical matters, their psychological reactions, their inside ripples. After describing the looks of a character, he uses the old-fashioned device of not referring to his specific physical appearance any more in the scenes with him. This is not the way of an artist, say Tolstoy, who sees his character in his mind all the time and knows exactly the specific gesture he will employ at this or that moment. But there is something more striking still about Dostoevski. He seems to have been chosen by the destiny of Russian letters to become Russia's greatest playwright, but he took the wrong turning and wrote novels. The novel *The Brothers Karamazov* has always seemed to me a straggling play, with just that amount of furniture and other implements needed for the various actors: a round table with the wet, round trace of a glass, a window painted yellow to make it look as if there were sunlight outside, or a shrub hastily brought in and plumped down by a stagehand.

Let me refer to one more method of dealing with literature—and this is the simplest and perhaps most important one. If you hate a book, you still may derive artistic delight from imagining other and better ways of looking at things, or, what is the same, expressing things, than the author you hate does. The mediocre, the false, the poshlust—remember that word*—can at least afford a mischievous but very healthy pleasure, as you stamp and groan through a second-rate book which has been awarded a prize. But the books you like must also be read with shudders and gasps. Let me submit the following practical suggestion. Literature, real literature, must not be gulped down like some potion which may be good for the heart or good for the brain—the brain, that stomach of the soul. Literature must be taken and broken to bits, pulled apart, squashed—then its lovely reek will be smelt in the hollow of the palm, it will be munched and rolled upon the tongue with relish; then, and only then, its rare flavor will be appreciated at its true worth and the broken and crushed parts will again come together in your mind and disclose the beauty of a unity to which you have contributed something of your own blood.

When an artist starts out on a work of art, he has set himself some definite artistic problem that he is out to solve. He selects his characters, his time and his place, and then finds the particular and special circumstances which can allow the developments he desires to occur naturally, developing, so to say, without any violence on the artist's part in order to compel the desired issue, developing logically and naturally from the combination and interaction of the forces the artist has set into play.

The world the artist creates for this purpose may be entirely unreal—as for instance the world of Kafka, or that of Gogol—but there is one absolute demand we are entitled to make: this world in itself and as long as it lasts, must be plausible to the reader or to the spectator. It is quite inessential, for instance, that Shakespeare introduces in *Hamlet* the ghost of Hamlet's father. Whether we agree with those critics who say that Shakespeare's contemporaries believed in the reality of phantoms, and therefore Shakespeare was justified to introduce these phantoms into his plays as realities, or whether we assume that these

---

*"English words expressing several although by no means all aspects of *poshlust* are, for instance: 'cheap, sham, smutty, pink-and-blue, high-falutin', in bad taste.' " See Nabokov's lecture on "Philistines and Philistinism."

ghosts are something in the nature of stage properties, it does not matter: from the moment the murdered king's ghost enters the play, we accept him and do not doubt that Shakespeare was within his right in introducing him into his play. In fact, the true measure of genius is in what measure the world he has created is his own, one that has not been here before him (at least, here, in literature) and, even more important, how plausible he has succeeded in making it. I would like you to consider Dostoevski's world from this point of view.

Secondly, when dealing with a work of art we must always bear in mind that art is a divine game. These two elements—the elements of the divine and that of the game—are equally important. It is divine because this is the element in which man comes nearest to God through becoming a true creator in his own right. And it is a game, because it remains art only as long as we are allowed to remember that, after all, it is all make-believe, that the people on the stage, for instance, are not actually murdered, in other words, only as long as our feelings of horror or of disgust do not obscure our realization that we are, as readers or as spectators, participating in an elaborate and enchanting game: the moment this balance is upset we get, on the stage, ridiculous melodrama, and in a book just a lurid description of, say, a case of murder which should belong in a newspaper instead. And we cease to derive that feeling of pleasure and satisfaction and spiritual vibration, that combined feeling which is our reaction to true art. For example, we are not disgusted or horrified by the bloody ending of the three greatest plays ever written: the hanging of Cordelia, the death of Hamlet, the suicide of Othello give us a shudder, but a shudder with a strong element of delight in it. This delight does not derive from the fact that we are glad to see those people perish, but merely our enjoyment of Shakespeare's overwhelming genius. I would like you further to ponder *Crime and Punishment* and *Memoirs from a Mousehole* also known as the *Notes from Underground* (1864) from this point of view: is the artistic pleasure you derive from accompanying Dostoevski on his excursions into the sick souls of his characters, is it consistently greater than any other emotions, thrills of disgust, morbid interest in a crime thriller? There is even less balance between the esthetic achievement and the element of criminal reportage in Dostoevski's other novels.

Thirdly, when an artist sets out to explore the motions and reactions of a human soul under the unendurable stresses of life, our interest is more readily aroused and we can more readily follow the artist as our guide through the dark corridors of that human soul if that soul's reactions are of a more or less all-human variety. By this I certainly do not wish to say that we are, or should be, interested solely in the spiritual life of the so-called average man. Certainly not. What I wish to convey is that though man and his reactions are infinitely varied, we can hardly accept as human reactions those of a raving lunatic or a character just come out of a madhouse and just about to return there. The reactions of such poor, deformed, warped souls are often no longer human, in the accepted sense of the word, or they are so freakish that the problem the author set himself remains unsolved regardless of how it is supposed to be solved by the reactions of such unusual individuals.

I have consulted doctors' case studies* and here is their list classifying Dostoevski's characters by the categories of mental illnesses by which they are affected:

I. EPILEPSY

The four well-marked cases of epilepsy among Dostoevski's characters are: Prince Myshkin in *The Idiot*; Smerdyakov in *The Brothers Karamazov*; Kirillov in *The Possessed*; and Nellie in *The Humiliated and Insulted*.

1) Myshkin's is the classic case. He has frequent moods of ecstasy . . . a tendency to emotional mysticism, an extraordinary power of empathy which permits him to divine the feelings of others. He shows meticulous attention to detail, particularly in penmanship. In childhood he had had frequent paroxysms, and had been given up by the physicians as a hopeless "idiot". . . .

2) Smerdyakov, the bastard son of old Karamazov by an imbecile woman. As a child Smerdyakov showed great cruelty. He was fond of hanging cats, then burying them with much blasphemous ceremony. As a young man he developed an exaggerated sense of self-esteem, verging at times on megalomania . . . had frequent paroxysms . . . etc.

3) Kirillov, the scapegoat character in *The Possessed*, is an incipient epileptic; though he is noble, gentle, and high-minded, he has a markedly epileptoid personality. He describes clearly the premonitory symptoms which he had often experienced. His case is complicated by suicidal mania.

4) The case of Nellie is unimportant . . . adds nothing of consequence to what the first three cases have revealed of the inward consciousness of the epileptic.

*Nabokov's discussion of the categories of mental illness is interpolated from S. Stephenson Smith and Andrei Isotoff, "The Abnormal From Within: Dostoevsky," *The Psychoanalytic Review*, XXII (October 1939), 361-391.

II. SENILE DEMENTIA

The case of General Ivolgin in *The Idiot* is one of incipient senile dementia, complicated with alcoholism . . . he is irresponsible . . . borrows money on worthless IOUs to procure drinks. When accused of lying, he is nonplussed for a moment, but soon regains his assurance and continues in the same vein. It is the peculiar character of this pathological lying which best reveals the state of mind which goes with this senile decay . . . accelerated by alcoholism.

III. HYSTERIA

1)Liza Khokhlakov in *The Brothers Karamazov*, a girl of fourteen, partially paralyzed, the paralysis presumably hysterical and curable by miracles. . . . She is extremely precocious, impressionable, coquettish, and perverse; is subject to nocturnal fevers—all symptoms in precise accord with classic cases of hysteria. Her dreams are of devils. . . . In her day-dreams she is preoccupied with ideas of evil and destruction. She loves to dwell in her thoughts on the recent patricide with which Dmitri Karamazov is charged; and thinks that everyone "loves him for his having killed his father," etc.

2) Liza Tushin in *The Possessed* is a borderline case of hysteria. She is exceedingly nervous and restless, arrogant, yet capable of unusual efforts to be kind. . . . She is given to fits of hysterical laughter, ending in weeping, and to strange whims, etc.

In addition to these definitely clinical cases of hysteria, Dostoevski's characters include many instances of hysterical tendencies: Nastasya . . . in *The Idiot*, Katerina . . . in *Crime and Punishment*, who is afflicted with "nerves"; most of the women characters, in fact, show more or less marked hysterical tendencies.

IV. PSYCHOPATHS

Among the principal characters in the novels are found many psychopaths: Stavrogin, a case of "moral insanity"; Rogozhin, a victim of erotomania; Raskolnikov, a case . . . of "lucid madness"; Ivan Karamazov, another half lunatic. All these show certain symptoms of dissociation of personality. And there are many other examples, including some characters completely mad.

Incidentally, scientists completely refute the notion advanced by some critics that Dostoevski anticipated Freud and Jung. It can be proved convincingly that Dostoevski used extensively in building his abnormal characters a book by a German, C. G. Carus, *Psyche*, published in 1846. The assumption that Dostoevski anticipated Freud arose from the fact that the terms and hypotheses in Carus' book resemble those of Freud, but actually the parallels between Carus and Freud are not those of central doctrine at all, but merely of linguistic terminology, which in the two authors has a different ideological content.

It is questionable whether one can really discuss the aspects of "realism" or of "human experience" when considering an author whose gallery of characters consists almost exclusively of neurotics and lunatics. Besides all this, Dostoevski's characters have yet another remarkable feature: throughout the book they do not develop as personalities. We get them all complete at the beginning of the tale, and so they remain without any considerable changes although their surroundings may alter and the most extraordinary things may happen to them. In the case of Raskolnikov in *Crime and Punishment*, for instance, we see a man go from premeditated murder to the promise of an achievement of some kind of harmony with the outer world, but all this happens somehow from without: innerly even Raskolnikov does not go through any true development of personality, and the other heroes of Dostoevski do even less so. The only thing that develops, vacillates, takes unexpected sharp turns, deviates completely to include new people and circumstances, is the plot. Let us always remember that basically Dostoevski is a writer of mystery stories where every character, once introduced to us, remains the same to the bitter end, complete with his special features and personal habits, and that they all are treated throughout the book they happen to be in like chessmen in a complicated chess problem. Being an intricate plotter, Dostoevski succeeds in holding the reader's attention; he builds up his climaxes and keeps up his suspenses with consummate mastery. But if you re-read a book of his you have already read once so that you are familiar with the surprises and complications of the plot, you will at once realize that the suspense you experienced during the first reading is simply not there any more.

Crime and Punishment (1866)

Because he can spin a yarn with such suspense, such innuendoes, Dostoevski used to be eagerly read by schoolboys and schoolgirls in Russia, together with Fenimore Cooper, Victor Hugo, Dickens, and Turgenev. I must have been twelve when forty-five years ago I read *Crime and Punishment* for the first time and thought it a wonderfully powerful and exciting book. I read it again at nineteen, during the awful years of civil war in Russia, and thought it long-winded, terribly sentimental, and badly written. I read it at twenty-eight when discussing Dostoevski in one of my own books. I read the thing again when preparing to speak about him in American universities. And only quite recently did I realize what is so wrong about the book.

The flaw, the crack in it, which in my opinion causes the whole edifice to crumble ethically and esthetically may be found in part ten, chapter 4. It is in the beginning of the redemption scene when Raskolnikov, the killer, discovers through the girl Sonya the New Testament. She has been reading to him about Jesus and the raising of Lazarus. So far so good. But then comes this singular sentence that for sheer stupidity has hardly the equal in world-famous literature: "The candle was flickering out, dimly lighting up in the poverty-stricken room the murderer and the harlot who had been reading together the eternal book." "The murderer and the harlot" and "the eternal book"—what a triangle. This is a crucial phrase, of a typical Dostoevskian rhetorical twist. Now what is so dreadfully wrong about it? Why is it so crude and so inartistic?

I suggest that neither a true artist nor a true moralist—neither a good Christian nor a good philosopher—neither a poet nor a sociologist—should have placed side by side, in one breath, in one gust of false eloquence, a killer together with whom?—a poor streetwalker, bending their completely different heads over that holy book. The Christian God, as understood by those who believe in the Christian God, has pardoned the harlot nineteen centuries ago. The killer, on the other hand, must be first of all examined medically. The two are on completely different levels. The inhuman and idiotic crime of Raskolnikov cannot be even remotely compared to the plight of a girl who impairs human dignity by selling her body. The murderer and the harlot reading the eternal book—what nonsense. There is no rhetorical link between a filthy murderer, and this unfortunate girl. There is only the conventional link of the Gothic novel and the sentimental novel. It is a shoddy literary trick, not a masterpiece of pathos and piety. Moreover, look at the absence of artistic balance. We have been shown Raskolnikov's crime in all sordid detail and we

The opening page of Nabokov's lecture on *Crime and Punishment*.

Crime and Punishment

1865-1866

I shall (from today's) say a few words to day about
Crime and Punishment written in the original edition. Crime is obligatory
& Punishment is not — in regard to the final
exams — but the novel is not to long, is
easy to read so that I suppose some of you
will go to the end. Under his pillow lay the
New Testament, the very volume from which Sonia had
read the raising to Lazarus to him — this is, page 341,
in my edition. The scene of Sonia's reading I shall
briefly discuss to day. I believe. After that I
shall plunge into a detailed discussion
of the mousehole Memoirs. [By the way all this is
going to be a monologue from now on, and perhaps lasting on Friday.
You will study Raskolnikov's curious the sunset.
rehearsal of the impending killing,
the seventy hundred and thirty steps from his lodging
house to the house of the old female pawnbroker
the significant coincidence (p. 55) and
the theme of humiliation. Old Marmeladov's
fat red hands with the black fingernails. You will
also notice that Dostoevski use the old fashioned
device of not referring
to his specific physical appearance any more.

Crime and Punishment

There in an [enormous amount] of [illegible]

      Shivering = starting

235 - "For the next few minutes the whole company (R., his friend,
sister, mother) was very cheerful -- its satisfaction was manifested by
in laughter. Dounetchka alone grew pale at intervals and knitted
her brows whilst reflecting on the previous unpleasantness."

    ---

247 - "What are you doing? And to me?" -- stammered Sonia growing
pale with sorrow-smitten heart.

      Upon this he rose. "I did not bow down to you personally,
but to suffering humanity in your person", said he somewhat strangey
going to lean against the window." (cp. original)

    ---

372 - "The dying candle lit up the low-ceilinged room where an
assassin and a harlot had just been reading the Book of Books."

      Analyze the perfectly idiotic scene of the "mad banquet".

    ---

296 - "Amalia (the landlady) ... moved ... in the room, howling
with rage and throwing about her whatever came in her way. Some
of the lodgers commented on the preceding scene, while others
quarrelled; and others, again, struck up refrains" /apparently
ignoring Amalia/.

*at the beginning of Raskolnikov's [redemption] when through Sonia
he discovers the New Testament, there occurs a statement that for sheer
stupidity - moral and artistic stupidity has hardly its equal in
world-famous literature. This is [illegible] To place Raskolnikov's
inhuman crime on the same level as poor Sonia's
degradation is something that neither a moralist nor an artist, in
his right mind, can do. Those who [illegible] Dostoevski [illegible]*

also have been given half a dozen different explanations for his exploit. We have never been shown Sonya in the exercise of her trade. The situation is a glorified cliché. The harlot's sin is taken for granted. Now I submit that the true artist is the person who never takes anything for granted.

Why did Raskolnikov kill? The motivation is extremely muddled. Raskolnikov was, if we believe what Dostoevski rather optimistically wants us to believe, a good young man, loyal to his family, on the one hand, and to high ideals on the other, capable of self-sacrifice, kind, generous, and industrious, though very conceited and proud, even to the point of entirely retiring into his inner life without feeling the need of any human heart-to-heart relations. This very good, generous, and proud young man is dismally poor.

Why did Raskolnikov murder the old money-lending woman and her sister?

Apparently to save his family from misery, to spare his sister, who, in order to help him get through college, was about to marry a rich but brutal man.

But he also committed this murder in order to prove to himself that he was not an ordinary man abiding by the moral laws created by others, but capable of making his own law and of bearing the tremendous spiritual load of responsibility, of living down the pangs of conscience and of using this evil means (murder) toward attaining a good purpose (assistance to his own family, his education which will enable him to become a benefactor of the human kind) without any prejudice to his inner balance and virtuous life.

And he also committed this murder because one of Dostoevski's pet ideas was that the propagation of materialistic ideas is bound to destroy moral standards in the young and is liable to make a murderer even out of a fundamentally good young man who would be easily pushed toward a crime by an unfortunate concurrence of circumstances. Note the curiously fascist ideas developed by Raskolnikov in an "article" he wrote: namely that mankind consists of two parts—the herd and the supermen—and that the majority should be bound by the established moral laws but that the few who are far above the majority ought to be at liberty to make their own law. Thus Raskolnikov first declared that Newton and other great discoverers should not

---

Nabokov's notes on *Crime and Punishment* with his denunciation of the novel's "moral and artistic stupidity. . . ."

---

have hesitated to sacrifice scores or hundreds of individual lives had those lives stood in their way toward giving mankind the benefit of their discoveries. Later he somehow forgets these benefactors of humanity to concentrate on an entirely different ideal. All his ambition suddenly centers in Napoleon in whom he sees characteristically the strong man who rules the masses through his daring to "pick up" power which lies there awaiting the one who "dares." This is a fast transition from an aspiring benefactor of the world toward an aspiring tyrant for the sake of his own power. A transformation which is worth a more detailed psychological analysis than Dostoevski, in his hurry, can afford to make.

The next pet idea of our author happens to be that a crime brings the man who commits it that inner hell which is the inevitable lot of the wicked. This inner solitary suffering, however, for some reason does not lead to redemption. What does bring redemption is actual suffering openly accepted, suffering in public, the deliberate self-abasement and humiliation before his fellow-humans—this can bring the sufferer the absolution of his crime, redemption, new life, and so on. Such actually is to be the road which Raskolnikov will follow, but whether he will kill again is impossible to say. And finally there is the idea of free will, of a crime just for the sake of performing it.

Did Dostoevski succeed in making it all plausible? I doubt it.

Now, in the first place, Raskolnikov is a neurotic, hence the effect that any philosophy can have upon a neurotic does not help to discredit that philosophy. Dostoevski would have better served his purpose if he could have made of Raskolnikov a sturdy, staid, earnest young man genuinely misled and eventually brought to perdition by a too candid acceptance of materialistic ideas. But Dostoevski of course realized too well that this would never work, that even if that sort of a sturdy young man did accept the absurd ideas which turned neurotic Raskolnikov's head, a healthy human nature would inevitably balk before the perpetration of deliberate murder. For it is no accident that all the criminal heroes of Dostoevski (Smerdyakov in *The Brothers Karamazov*, Fedka in *The Possessed*, Rogozhin in *The Idiot*) are not quite sane.*

Feeling the weakness of his position, Dostoevski dragged in every possible human incentive to push his Raskolnikov to the precipice of that temptation to murder which we must presume was opened to him by the German philosophies he had accepted. The dismal poverty, not only his own but that of his dearly beloved mother and sister, the impending self-sacrifice of his sister, the utter moral debasement of the intended victim—this profusion of acciden-

---

*VN deleted the next sentence: "It is further no accident that the rulers of Germany's recently fallen regime based on the theory of Superman and his special rights were, too, either neurotics or ordinary criminals, or both." Ed.

tal causes shows how difficult Dostoevski himself felt it to prove his point. Kropotkin very aptly remarks: "Behind Raskolnikov one feels Dostoevski trying to decide whether he himself, or a man like him, might have been brought to perform personally the act as Raskolnikov did. . . . But writers do *not* murder."

I also entirely subscribe to Kropotkin's statement that ". . . men like the examining magistrate and Svidrigailov, the embodiment of evil, are purely romantic invention." I would go further and add Sonya to the list. Sonya is a good descendant of those romantic heroines who, for no fault of their own, were to live a life outside the bounds established by society and were made by that same society to bear all the burden of shame and suffering attached to such a way of life. These heroines were never extinct in world literature ever since the good Abbé Prévost introduced to his readers the far better written and therefore far more moving *Manon Lescaut* (1731). In Dostoevski the theme of degradation, humiliation, is with us from the start, and in this sense Raskolnikov's sister Dunya and the drunken girl glimpsed on the boulevard, and Sonya the virtuous prostitute, are sisters within the Dostoevskian family of hand-wringing characters.

The passionate attachment of Dostoevski to the idea that physical suffering and humiliation improve the moral man may lie in a personal tragedy: he must have felt that in him the freedom-lover, the rebel, the individualist, had suffered a certain loss, and impairing of spontaneity if nothing else, through his sojourn in his Siberian prison; but he stuck doggedly to the idea that he had returned "a better man."

"Memoirs from a Mousehole" (1864)

The story whose title should be "Memoirs from Under the Floor," or "Memoirs from a Mousehole" bears in translation the stupidly incorrect title of *Notes from the Underground*. The story may be deemed by some a case history, a streak of persecution mania, with variations. My interest in it is limited to a study in style. It is the best picture we have of Dostoevski's themes and formulas and intonations. It is a concentration of Dostoevskiana. Moreover it is very well rendered in English by Guerney.

Its first part consists of eleven small chapters or sections. Its second part, which is twice the length, consists of ten slightly longer chapters containing events and conversations. The first part is a soliloquy but a soliloquy that presupposes the presence of a phantom audience. Throughout this part the mouseman, the narrator, keeps turning to an audience of persons who seem to be amateur philosophers, newspaper readers, and what he calls normal people. These ghostly gentlemen are supposed to be jeering at him, while he is supposed to thwart their mockery and denunciations by the shifts, the doubling back, and various other tricks of his supposedly remarkable intellect. This imaginary audience helps to keep the ball of his hysterical inquiry rolling, an inquiry into the state of his own crumbling soul. It will be noticed that references are made to topical events of the day in the middle of the 1860s. The topicality, however, is vague and has no structural power. Tolstoy uses newspapers too—but he does this with marvelous art when, for example, in the beginning of *Anna Karenin* he not only characterizes Oblonski by the kind of information Oblonski likes to follow in the morning paper but also fixes with delightful historical or pseudo-historical precision a certain point in space and time. In Dostoevski we have generalities substituted for specific traits.

The narrator starts by depicting himself as a rude, waspish man, a spiteful official who snarls at the petitioners who come to the obscure bureau where he works. After making his statemnt, "I am a spiteful official," he retracts it and says that he is not even that: "It was not only that I could not become spiteful; I did not know how to become anything: either spiteful or kind, either a rascal or an honest man, either a hero or an insect." He consoles himself with the thought that an intelligent man does not become anything, and that only rascals and fools become something. He is forty years old, lives in a wretched room, had a very low rank in the civil service, has retired by now after getting a small legacy, and is anxious to talk about himself.

I should warn you at this point that the first part of the story, eleven little chapters, are significant not in what is expressed or related, but in the manner it is expressed and related. The manner reflects the man. This reflection Dostoevski wishes to fix in a cesspool of confessions through the manners and mannerisms of a neurotic, exasperated, frustrated, and horribly unhappy person.

The next theme is human-consciousness (not conscience but consciousness), the awareness of one's emotions. The more aware this mouseman was of goodness, of beauty—of moral beauty—the more he sinned, the deeper he sank in filth. Dostoevski, as so often happens with authors of his type, authors who have a general message to deliver to all men, to all sinners, Dostoevski does not specify the depravity of his hero. We are left guessing. .

After every loathsome act the narrator commits, he says he crawls back into his mousehole and proceeds to enjoy the accursed sweetness of shame, of remorse, the pleasure of his own nastiness, the pleasure of degradation. Delighting in degradation is one of Dostoevski's favorite themes. Here, as elsewhere in his writing, the writer's art lags behind the writer's purpose, since the sin committed is seldom specified, and art is always specific. The act, the sin, is taken for granted. Sin here is a literary convention similar to the devices in the sentimental and Gothic novels Dostoevski had imbibed. In this particular story the very abstractness of the theme, the abstract notion of loathsome action and consequent degradation is presented with a not negligible bizarre force in a manner that reflects the man in the mousehole. (I repeat, it is the manner which counts.) By the end of chapter 2 we know that the mouseman has started writing his memoirs in order to explain the joys of degradation. He is, he says, an acutely conscious mousey man. He is being insulted by a kind of collective normal man—stupid but normal. His audience is mocking him. The gentlemen are jeering. Unsatisfied desires, the burning thirst of parching revenge, hesitations—half-despair, half-faith—all this combines to form a strange morbid bliss for the humiliated subject. Mouseman's rebellion is based not upon a creative impulse but upon his being merely a moral misfit, a moral dwarf, who sees in the laws of nature a stone wall which he cannot break down. But here again we flounder in a generalization, in an allegory, since no specific purpose, no specific stone wall is evoked. Bazarov (*Fathers and Sons*) knew that what a nihilist wishes to break is the old order that among other things sanctioned slavery. The mouse here is merely listing his grudges against a despicable world that he has invented himself, a world of cardboard instead of stone.

Chapter 4 contains a comparison: his pleasure, he says, is the pleasure of a person with a toothache realizing that he is keeping his family awake with his moans—moans that perhaps are those of an imposter. A complicated pleasure. But the point is that the mouseman suggests he is cheating.

So by chapter 5 we have the following situation. The mouseman is filling his life with bogus emotions because he lacks real ones. Moreover, he has no foundation, no starting point from which to proceed to an acceptance of life. He looks for a definition of himself, for a label to stick upon himself, for instance a "lazy-bones," or a "connoisseur of wines," any kind of peg, any kind of nail. But what exactly compels him to look for a label is not divulged by Dostoevski. The man he depicts lives only as a maniac, as a tangle of mannerisms. Dostoevski's mediocre imitators such as Sartre, a French journalist, have continued the trend to-day.

At the beginning of chapter 7 we find a good example of Dostoevski's style, very well rendered by Guerney revising Garnett:

"But these are all golden dreams. Oh, tell me, who was it first announced, who was it first proclaimed, that man only does nasty things because he does not know his own interests; and that if he were enlightened, if his eyes were opened to his real normal interests, man would at once cease to do nasty things, would at once become good and noble because, being enlightened and understanding his real advantage, he would see his own advantage in the good and nothing else, and we all know that not one man can, consciously, act against his own interests, consequently, so to say, through necessity, he would begin doing good? Oh, the babe! Oh, the pure, innocent child! Why, in the first place, when in all these thousands of years has there been a time when man has acted only from his own interest? What is to be done with the millions of facts that bear witness that men, *consciously*, that is, fully understanding their real interests, have left them in the background and have rushed headlong on another path, to meet peril and danger, compelled to this course by nobody and by nothing, but, as it were, simply disliking the beaten track, and have obstinately, willfully, beaten another difficult, absurd path, seeking it almost in the darkness? So, I suppose, this obstinacy and perversity were pleasanter to them than any advantage."

The repetition of words and phrases, the intonation of obsession, the hundred percent banality of every word, the vulgar soapbox eloquence mark these elements of Dostoevski's style.

In this chapter 7 the mouseman, or his creator, hits upon a new series of ideas revolving around the term "advantage." There are, he says, cases when a man's advantage must consist in his desiring certain things that are actually harmful to him. This is all double talk, of course; and just as the enjoyment of degradation and pain have not been easily explained by the mouseman, so the advantage of disadvantage will not be explained by him either. But a set of new mannerisms will be arrayed in the tantalizing approximations that occupy the next pages.

What exactly is this mysterious "advantage"? A journalistic excursion, in Dostoevski's best manner, first takes care of "civilization [which] has made mankind, if not more bloodthirsty, at least more vilely, more loathsomely bloodthirsty." This is an old idea going back to Rousseau. The mouseman evokes a picture of universal prosperity in the future, a palace of crystal for all, and finally there it comes—the mysterious advantage: One's own free unfettered choice, one's own whim no matter how wild. The world has been beautifully rearranged, but here comes a man, a natural man, who says: it is merely my whim to destroy this beautiful world—and he destroys it. In other words, man wants not any rational advantage, but merely the fact of independent choice—no matter what it is—even though breaking the pattern of logic, of statistics, of harmony and order. Philosophically this is all bunkum since harmony, happiness, presupposes and includes also the presence of whim. But the Dostoevskian man may choose something insane or stupid or harmful—destruction and death—because it is at least his own choice. This, incidentally, is one of the reasons for Raskolnikov's killing the old woman in *Crime and Punishment*.

In chapter 9 the mouseman goes on ranting in self-defence. The theme of destruction is taken up again. Perhaps, says he, man prefers destroying to creating. Perhaps it is not the achievement of any goal that attracts him but the process of attaining this goal. Perhaps, says Mouseman, man dreads to succeed. Perhaps he is fond of suffering. Perhaps suffering is the only origin of consciousness. Perhaps man, so to speak, becomes a human being with the first awareness of his awareness of pain.

The palace of crystal as an ideal, as a journalistic symbol of perfect universal life in aftertime, is again projected on the screen and discussed. The narrator has worked himself into a state of utter exasperation, and the audience of mockers, of jeering journalists he confronts, seems to be closing in upon him. We return to one of the points made in the very beginning: it is better to be nothing, it is better to remain in one's mousehole—or rat hole. In the last chapter of part one he sums up the situation by suggesting that the audience he has been evoking, the phantom gentlemen he has been addressing, is an attempt to create readers. And it is to this phantom audience that he will now present a series of disjointed recollections which will, perhaps, illustrate and explain his mentality. Wet snow is falling. Why he sees it as yellow is more emblematic than optical. He means, I suppose, yellow as implying unclean white, "dingy," as he also says. A point to be noticed is that he hopes to obtain relief from writing. This closes the first part, which, I repeat, is important in its manner, not matter.

Why part two is entitled "Concerning Wet Snow" is a question that can be settled only in the light of journalistic innuendoes of the 1860s by writers who liked symbols, allusions to allusions, that kind of thing. The symbol perhaps is of purity becoming damp and dingy. The motto—also a vague gesture—is a lyrical poem by Dostoevski's contemporary Nekrasov.

The events our mouseman is going to describe in the second part go twenty years back to the 1840s. He was as gloomy then as he is now, and hated his fellow men as he does now. He also hated his own self. Experiments in humiliation are mentioned. Whether he hated a fellow or not, he could not look into a person's eyes. He experimented—could he outstare anybody?—and failed. This worried him to distraction. He is a coward, he says, but for some reason or other every decent man of our age, he says, must be a coward. What age? The 1840s or the 1860s? Historically, politically, sociologically, the two eras differed tremendously. In 1844 we are in the age of reaction, of despotism; 1864 when these notes are set down is the age of change, of enlightenment, of great reforms as compared to the forties. But Dostoevski's world despite topical allusions is the gray world of mental illness, where nothing can change except perhaps the cut of a military uniform, an unexpectedly specific detail to meet at one point.

A few pages are devoted to what our mouseman calls "romantics," or more correctly in English "romanticists." The modern reader cannot understand the argument unless he wades through Russian periodicals of the fifties and sixties. Dostoevski and the mouseman really mean "sham idealists," people who can somehow combine what they call the good and the beautiful with material things, such as a bureaucratic career, etc. (Slavophiles attack Westerners for setting up idols rather than Ideals.) All this is very vaguely and tritely expressed by our mouseman, and we need not bother about it. We learn that our mouseman, furtively, in solitude at night, indulged in what he calls filthy vice, and apparently for this purpose he visited various obscure haunts. (We recall St. Preux, the gentleman in Rousseau's *Julie* who also visited a remote room in a house of sin where he kept drinking white wine under the impression it was water, and next thing found himself in the arms of what he calls *une créature*. This is vice as depicted in sentimental novels.)

The "out-staring" theme is then given a new twist: it becomes the out-jostling theme. Our mouseman, apparently a small slender chap, is thrust aside by a passerby, a military man over six feet high. Mouseman keeps meeting him on Nevski Avenue, which is Petersburg's Fifth Avenue, and keeps telling himself that he, mouseman, will not give way; but every time he *would* give way, would step aside, letting the gigantic officer stalk straight past. One day Mouseman dresses up as if for a duel or funeral, and with heart going pit-a-pat tries to assert himself and not step aside. But he is flung aside like an india rubber ball by the military man. He tries again—and manages to retain his balance—they run into each other full tilt, shoulder to shoulder, and pass each other on a perfectly equal footing. Mouseman is delighted. His only triumph in the tale is here.

Chapter 2 starts with an account of his satirical day-dreams and then the story at last is launched. Its prologue has occupied forty pages in Guerney's translation, counting part one. On a certain occasion he visits a certain Simonov, an old schoolfellow. Simonov and two friends are planning a farewell dinner in honor of a fourth schoolfellow Zverkov, who is another military man in the story. (His name is derived from "little beast" *zveryok*.) "This Zverkov, too, had been at school all the time I was there. I had begun to hate him, particularly in the upper grades. In the lower grades he had simply been a pretty, playful boy whom everybody liked. I had hated him, however, even in the lower grades, just because he was a pretty and playful boy. He was always poor at his lessons and got worse and worse as he went on; however, he left with a good certificate, since he had influential people interested in him. During his last year at school he came in for an estate of two hundred serfs, and as almost all of us were poor he took to swaggering among us. He was vulgar in the extreme, but at the same time he was a good-natured fellow, even in his swaggering. In spite of superficial, fantastic and sham notions of honor and dignity, all but very few of us positively groveled before Zverkov, and the more he swaggered the more they groveled. And it was not from any interested motive that they groveled, but simply because he had been favored by the gifts of nature. Moreover, it was, as it were, an accepted idea among us that Zverkov was a specialist in tact and the social graces. This last fact particularly infuriated me. I hated the abrupt self-confident tone of his voice, his admiration of his own witticisms, which were often frightfully stupid, though he was bold in his language; I hated his handsome but stupid face (for which I would, however, have gladly exchanged my intelligent one), and the free-and-easy military manners in fashion in the forties."

The first of the other two schoolfellows is Ferfichkin, a comedy name; he is of German extraction, a vulgar swaggering fellow. (It should be noted that Dostoevski had a kind of pathological hatred of Germans, Poles, and Jews, as depicted in his writings.) The other schoolfellow is yet another army officer, Trudolyubov, whose name means "diligent." Dostoevski here and elsewhere has the eighteenth-century comedy tendency to apply descriptive names to people. Our mouseman, who as we know likes to court insult, invites himself.

" 'It's settled then—the three of us, with Zverkov for the fourth, twenty-one rubles, at the Hôtel de Paris, at five o'clock tomorrow,' Simonov, who had been asked to make the arrangements, concluded finally.

" 'How do you figure twenty-one rubles?' I asked in some agitation, with a show of being offended. 'If you count me it won't be twenty-one but twenty-eight rubles.'

"It seemed to me that to invite myself so suddenly and unexpectedly would be positively graceful, and that they would all be conquered at once and would look upon me with respect.

" 'Do you want to join, too?' Simonov observed, with no appearance of pleasure, seeming to avoid looking at me. He knew me through and through.

"It infuriated me that he knew me so thoroughly.

" 'Why not? I'm an old schoolfellow of his, too, I believe, and I must own I felt hurt at your having left me out,' I said, boiling over again.

" 'And where were we to find you?' Ferfichkin put in rudely.

" 'You never were on good terms with Zverkov,' Trudolyubov added, frowning.

"But I had already grabbed at the idea and would not give it up.

" 'It seems to me that no one has a right to form an opinion upon that,' I retorted in a shaky voice, as though something tremendous had happened. 'Perhaps that is just my reason for wishing it now, that I have not always been on good terms with him.'

" 'Oh, there's no making you out—with all these refinements,' Trudolyubov jeered.

" 'We'll put your name down,' Simonov decided, addressing me. 'Tomorrow at five o'clock at the Hôtel de Paris.' "

That night the mouseman dreams of his school days, a generalized dream that would not do in a modern case-history. Next morning he polished his boots after his servant Apollon had cleaned them once already. Wet snow is symbolically falling in thick flakes. He arrives at the restaurant and learns that they had changed the dinner hour from five to six and nobody had troubled to inform him. Here begins the accumulation of humiliations. Finally the three schoolfellows and Zverkov, the guest, arrive. What follows is one of the best scenes in Dostoevski. He had a wonderful flair for comedy mixed with tragedy; he may be termed a very wonderful humorist, with the humor always on the verge of hysterics and people hurting each other in a wild exchange of insults. A typical Dostoevskian row starts:

" 'Tell me, are you . . . in a government office?' Zverkov went on being attentive to me. Seeing that I was embarrassed, he seriously thought that he ought to be friendly to me, and, so to speak, cheer me up.

" 'Does he want me to throw a bottle at his head?' I thought, in a rage. In my novel surroundings I was unnaturally ready to be irritated.

" 'In the N—— office,' I answered jerkily, with my eyes on my plate.

" 'And ha-ave you a goo-ood berth? I say, what ma-a-de you leave your original job?'

" 'What ma-a-de me was that I wanted to leave my original job,' I drawled more than he, hardly able to control myself. Ferfichkin went off into a guffaw. Simonov looked at me sarcastically. Trudolyubov left off eating and began looking at me with curiosity.

"Zverkov winced, but he tried not to notice anything.

" 'And the remuneration?'

" 'What remuneration?'

" 'I mean your sa-a-lary?'

" 'Why are you cross-examining me?' However, I told him at once what my salary was. I turned horribly red.

" 'It's not very handsome,' Zverkov observed majestically.

" 'Yes, you can't afford to dine at cafes on that,' Ferfichkin added insolently.

" 'To my thinking it's very poor,' Trudolyubov observed gravely.

" 'And how thin you have grown! How you have changed!' added Zverkov, with a shade of venom in his voice, scanning me and my attire with a sort of insolent compassion.

" 'Oh, spare his blushes,' cried Ferfichkin, sniggering.

" 'My dear Sir, allow me to tell you I am not blushing,' I broke out at last: 'Do you hear? I am dining here, at this cafe, at my own expense, not at other people's—note that, Mr. Ferfichkin.'

" 'Wha-at? Isn't everyone here dining at his own expense? You seem to be——' Ferfichkin turned on me, becoming as red as a lobster and looking me in the face with fury.

" 'We won't go into tha-at,' I mimicked in answer, feeling I had gone too far. 'And I imagine it would be better to talk of something more intelligent.'

" 'You intend to show off your intelligence, I suppose?'

" 'Don't upset yourself; that would be quite out of place here.'

" 'Why are you jabbering away like that, my good Sir? eh? Have you gone out of your wits in your office?'

" 'Enough, gentlemen, enough!' Zverkov cried authoritatively.

" 'How stupid all this is!' muttered Simonov.

" 'It really is stupid. We've met here, a party of friends, for a farewell dinner to a comrade, and you carry on a fight,' said Trudolyubov, rudely addressing himself to me alone. 'You invited yourself to join us, so don't disturb the general harmony.'

" . . . No one paid any attention to me, and I sat crushed and humiliated.

" 'Good Heavens, these are not the people for me!' I thought. 'And what a fool I have made of myself before them! . . . But what's the use! I must get up at once, this very minute, take my hat and simply go without a word—with contempt! The scoundrels! As though I cared about the seven rubles. They may think. . . . Damn it! I don't care about the seven rubles. I'll go this minute!'

"Of course I remained. I drank sherry and Lafitte by the glassful in my discomfiture. Being unaccustomed to it, I was quickly affected. My annoyance increased as the wine went to my head. I longed all of a sudden to insult them all in a most flagrant manner and then go away. To seize the moment and show what I could do, so that they would say: 'He's clever, though he's absurd,' and . . . and . . . in fact, damn them all! . . .

" 'Why, aren't you going to drink the toast?' roared Trudolyubov, losing patience and turning menacingly to me. . . .

" 'Lieutenant Zverkov, Sir,' I began, 'let me tell you that I hate phrases, phrasemongers, and men who wear corsets—that's the first point, and there's a second one to follow it.'

"There was a general stir.

" 'The second point is: I hate loose talk and loose talkers. Especially loose talkers! The third point: I love justice, truth, and honesty.' I went on almost mechanically, for I was beginning to shiver with horror myself and had no idea how I had come to be talking like this. 'I love thought, Monsieur Zverkov; I love true comradeship, on an equal footing and not—h'm! I love—but, however, why not? I'll drink your health, too, Monsieur Zverkov. Seduce the Circassian girls, shoot the enemies of the fatherland, and—and here's to your health, Monsieur Zverkov!'

"Zverkov got up from his seat, bowed to me, and said:

" 'I'm very much obliged to you.' He was frightfully offended and had turned pale.

" 'Damn the fellow!' roared Trudolyubov, bringing his fist down on the table.

" 'Well, he ought to get a punch in the nose for that,' squealed Ferfichkin.

" 'We ought to turn him out,' muttered Simonov.

" 'Not a word, gentlemen, not a move!' cried Zverkov gravely, checking the general indignation. 'I thank you all, but I am able to show him myself how much value I attach to his words.'

" 'Mr. Ferfichkin, you will give me satisfaction tomorrow for your words just now!' I said aloud, turning with dignity to Ferfichkin.

" 'A duel, you mean? Certainly,' he answered. But probably I was so ridiculous as I challenged him, and it was so out of keeping with my appearance, that everyone, including Ferfichkin, was prostrate with laughter.

" 'Yes, let him alone, of course! He's quite drunk,' Trudolyubov said with disgust. . . . I was so harassed, so exhausted, that I would have cut my throat to put an end to it. I was in a fever; my hair soaked with perspiration, stuck to my forehead and temples.

" 'Zverkov, I beg your pardon,' I said abruptly and resolutely. 'Ferfichkin, yours, too, and everyone's, everyone's; I have insulted you all!'

" 'Aha! A duel is not in your line, old man,' Ferfichkin got out venomously through clenched teeth.

"It sent a sharp pang to my heart.

" 'No, it's not the duel I'm afraid of, Ferfichkin! I'm ready to fight you tomorrow, after we're reconciled. I insist upon it, in fact, and you cannot refuse. I want to show you that I am not afraid of a duel. You'll fire first and I'll fire into the air.' . . .

"They were all flushed; their eyes were bright; they had been drinking heavily.

" 'I ask for your friendship, Zverkov; I insulted you, but—'

" 'Insulted? *You* insulted *me*? Understand, Sir, that you never, under any circumstances, could possibly insult *me*.'

" 'And that's enough for you. Out of the way!' concluded Trudolyubov. . . .

"I stood there as though they had spat upon me. The party went noisily out of the room. Trudolyubov struck up some stupid song. . . . Disorder, the remains of the dinner, a broken wineglass on the floor, spilt wine, cigarette ends, fumes of drink and delirium in my brain, an agonizing misery in my heart and finally the waiter, who had seen and heard all and was looking inquisitively into my face.

" 'I'm going there!' I cried. 'Either they'll all go down on their knees to beg for my friendship or I'll give Zverkov a slap in the face!' ".

After the great chapter 4 the mouseman's irritation, humiliation, etc., become repetitious, and soon a false note is introduced with the appearance of that favorite figure of sentimental fiction, the noble prostitute, the fallen girl with the lofty heart. Liza, the young lady from Riga, is a literary dummy. Our mouseman, to get some relief, starts the process of hurting and frightening a fellow creature, poor Liza (Sonya's sister). The conversations are very garrulous and very poor, but please go on to the bitter end. Perhaps some of you may like it more than I do. The story ends with our mouseman emitting the idea that humiliation and insult will purify and elevate Liza through hatred, and that perhaps exalted sufferings are better than cheap happiness. That's about all.

———

The Idiot (1868)

In *The Idiot* we have the Dostoevskian positive type. He is Prince Myshkin, endowed with the kindness and the capacity to forgive possessed before him by Christ alone. Myshkin is sensitive to a weird degree: he feels everything that is going on inside other people, even when these people are miles away. Such is his great spiritual wisdom, his sympathy and understanding for the sufferings of others. Prince Myshkin is purity itself, sincerity, frankness; and these qualities inevitably bring him into painful conflicts with our conventional artificial world. He is loved by everyone who knows him; his would-be murderer Rogozhin, who is passionately in love with the heroine Nastasya Filipovna, and is jealous of Myshkin, winds up with admitting Myshkin into the house where he has just murdered Nastasya, and seeks under the protection of Myshkin's spiritual purity to reconcile himself to life and to appease the storm of passions in his own soul.

Yet Myshkin is also a half-imbecile. Since his early childhood he has been a backward child, unable to speak until he was six, a victim of epilepsy, constantly threatened with complete degeneration of the brain unless he leads a quiet relaxed life. (Degeneration of the brain eventually overtakes him in the wake of the events described in the novel.)

Unfit to marry anyway, as the author takes care to make clear, Myshkin is nevertheless torn between two women. One is Aglaia, the innocently pure, beautiful, sincere young girl, unreconciled to the world or rather to her lot as daughter of a wealthy family destined to marry a successful and attractive young man and "live happily ever after." What exactly it is that Aglaia wants, she does not know herself; but she is supposed to be different from her sisters and family, "crazy" in the benevolent Dostoevskian sense of the word (he very much prefers crazy people to the normal ones), in a word a personality with a "quest" of her own, thus with a God's spark in her soul. Myshkin (and to a certain extent Aglaia's mother) are the only people who understand her; while her intuitive and naive mother is only worried by her daughter's unusualness, Myshkin feels with Aglaia the hidden anxiety of her soul. With the obscure urge to save and protect her by blazing for her a spiritual path in life, Myshkin agrees to Aglaia's desire to marry him. But then the complication begins: there is also in the book the demoniac, proud, wretched, betrayed, mysterious, adorable, and, in spite of her degradation, incorruptibly pure Nastasya Filipovna, one of those completely unacceptable, unreal, irritating characters with which Dostoevski's novels teem. This abstract woman indulges in the superlative type of feeling: there are no limits either to her kindliness or to her wickedness. She is the victim of an elderly playboy who, after having made her his mistress and enjoyed her company for several years, has decided to marry a decent woman. He blandly decides to marry Nastasya Filipovna off to his secretary.

All the men around Nastasya know that at bottom she is a decent girl herself; her lover is alone to blame for her irregular position. This does not prevent her fiancé (who is by the way very much in love with her) from despising her as a "fallen" woman and Aglaia's family from being profoundly shocked when they discover that Aglaia has established some clandestine communication with Nastasya. In fact, it does not prevent Nastasya from

126   VLADIMIR NABOKOV

despising herself for her "degradation" and from deciding to take it out on herself by turning into an actual "kept woman." Myshkin alone, like Christ, sees no fault in Nastasya for what is happening to her and redeems her with his profound admiration and respect. (Here again is a hidden paraphrase of the story of Christ and of the fallen woman.) At this point I shall quote a very apt remark by Mirsky about Dostoevski: "His Christianity . . . is of a very doubtful kind. . . . It was a more or less superficial spiritual formation which it is dangerous to identify with real Christianity." If we add to this that he kept throwing his weight about as a true interpreter of Orthodox Christianity, and that for the untying of every psychological or psychopathic knot he inevitably leads us to Christ, or rather to his own interpretation of Christ, and to the holy Orthodox Church, we shall better understand the truly irritating side of Dostoevski as "philosopher."

But to come back to the story. Myshkin at once realizes that of the two women who claim him, Nastasya needs him more, being the more unfortunate. So he quietly leaves Aglaia to save Nastasya. Then Nastasya and he try to outdo each other in generosity, she trying desperately to release him in order that he can be happy with Aglaia, he not releasing her so that she would not "perish" (a favorite word of Dostoevski's). But when Aglaia upsets the apple cart by deliberately insulting Nastasya in her own house (going there on purpose), Nastasya sees no further reason for sacrificing herself for her rival's sake and decides to carry off Myshkin to Moscow. At the last moment the hysterical woman changes her mind again, feeling incapable of allowing him to "perish" through her, and runs away, almost from the very altar, with Rogozhin, a young merchant who squanders upon her the inheritance to which he has just succeeded. Myshkin follows them to Moscow. The next period of their life and doings is cunningly covered with a veil of mystery. Dostoevski never betrays to the reader what exactly happened in Moscow, only keeps dropping here and there significant and mysterious hints. Some great spiritual sufferings are endured by both men because of Nastasya, who is growing more and more insane, and Rogozhin becomes Myshkin's brother in Christ by exchanging crosses with him. We are given to understand that he does this to save himself from the temptation of murdering Myshkin out of jealousy.

Well, eventually Rogozhin, being the most normal of the three, cannot bear it any longer and kills Nastasya. Dostoevski furnishes him with extenuating circumstances: Rogozhin while committing his crime was running a high fever. He spends some time in a hospital and then is sentenced to Siberia, that storeroom for Dostoevski's discarded waxworks. Myshkin, after spending the night in the company of Rogozhin by the side of the murdered Nastasya, suffers a final relapse into insanity and returns to the asylum in Switzerland where he had spent his youth and where he ought to have stayed all along. All this crazy hash is interspersed with dialogues destined to depict the respective points of view of different circles of society upon such questions as capital punishment or the great mission of the Russian nation. The characters never say anything without either paling, or flushing, or staggering on their feet. The religious aspects are nauseating in their tastelessness. The author relies completely on definitions without bothering to support them with proofs: e.g., Nastasya, who is, we are told, a paragon of reserve and distinction and refinement of manner, behaves occasionally like a furious bad-tempered hussy.

But the plot itself is ably developed with many ingenious devices used to prolong the suspense. Some of these devices appear to me, when compared to Tolstoy's methods, like blows of a club instead of the light touch of an artist's fingers, but there are many critics who would not agree with this view.

The Possessed (1872)

The Possessed is the story of Russian terrorists, plotting violence and destruction, and actually murdering one of their own number. It was denounced as a reactionary novel by the radical critics. On the other hand, it has been described as a penetrating study of people who have been sidetracked by their ideas into a bog where they sink. Note the landscapes:

"A mist of fine drizzling rain enveloped the whole country, swallowing up every ray of light, every gleam of color, and transforming everything into one smoky, leaden, indistinguishable mass. It had long been daylight yet it seemed as though it were still night." (The morning after Lebyadkin's murder.)

"It was a very gloomy place at the end of the huge park. . . . How sinister it must have looked on that chill autumn evening! It lay on the edge of an old wood belonging to the Crown. Huge ancient pines stood out as vague sombre blurs in the darkness. It was so dark that they could hardly see each other two paces off. . . .

At some unrecorded date in the past a rather absurd-looking grotto had for some reason been built here of rough unhewn stones. The table and benches in the grotto had long decayed and fallen. Two hundred paces to the right was the bank of the third pond of the park. These three ponds stretched one after another for a mile from the house to the very end of the park." (Before Shatov's murder.)

"The rain of the previous night was over, but it was damp, grey and windy. Low, ragged, dingy clouds moved rapidly across the cold sky. The tree-tops roared with the deep droning sound and creaked on their roots; it was a melancholy day."

I mentioned before Dostoevski's method of dealing with his characters is that of a playwright. When introducing this or that one, he always gives a short description of their appearance, then hardly ever refers to it any more. Thus his dialogues are generally free from any intercalations used by other writers—the mention of a gesture, a look, or any detail referring to the background. One feels that he does not see his characters physically, that they are merely puppets, remarkable, fascinating puppets plunged into the moving stream of the author's ideas.

The misadventures of human dignity which form Dostoevski's favorite theme are as much allied to the farce as to the drama. In indulging this farcical side and being at the same time deprived of any real sense of humor, Dostoevski is sometimes dangerously near to sinking into garrulous and vulgar nonsense. (The relationship between a strong-willed hysterical old woman and a weak hysterical old man, the story of which occupies the first hundred pages of The Possessed, is tedious, being unreal.) The farcical intrigue which is mixed with tragedy is obviously a foreign importation; there is something second-rate French in the structure of his plots. This does not mean, however, that when his characters appear there are not sometimes well written scenes. In The Possessed there is the delightful skit on Turgenev: Karmazinov, the author à la mode, "an old man with a rather red face, thick grey locks of hair clustering under his chimney-pot hat and curling round his clean little pink ears. Tortoise-shell lorgnette, on a narrow black ribbon, studs, buttons, signet ring, all in the best form. A sugary but rather shrill voice. Writes solely in self-display, as for instance in the description of the wreck of some steamer on the English coast. 'Look rather at me, see how I was unable to bear the sight of the dead child in the dead woman's arms etc.' " A very sly dig, for Turgenev has an autobiographical description of a fire on a ship—incidentally associated with a nasty episode in his youth which his enemies delighted in repeating during all his life.

"The next day . . . was a day of surprises, a day that solved past riddles and suggested new ones, a day of startling revelations and still more hopeless perplexity. In the morning . . . I was, by Varvara Petrovna's particular request, to accompany my friend Stepan Trofimovich on his visit to her and at three o'clock in the afternoon I had to be with Lizaveta Nikolavna in order to tell her—I did not know what—and to assist her—I did not know how. And meanwhile it all ended as no one could have expected. In a word, it was a day of wonderful coincidences."

At Varvara Petrovna's the author, with all the gusto of a playwright tackling his climax, crams in, one after the other, all the characters of *The Possessed*, two of them arriving from abroad. It is incredible nonsense, but it is grand booming nonsense with flashes of genius illuminating the whole gloomy and mad farce.

Once collected in one room, these people trample on each other's dignity, have terrific rows (which translators insist on rendering as "scandals," misled by the Gallic root of the Russian "skandal" term) and these rows just fizzle out as the narrative takes a sharp new turn.

It is, as in all Dostoevski's novels, a rush and tumble of words with endless repetitions, mutterings aside, a verbal overflow which shocks the reader after, say, Lermontov's transparent and beautifully poised prose. Dostoevski as we know is a great seeker after truth, a genius of spiritual morbidity, but as we also know he is not a great writer in the sense Tolstoy, Pushkin, and Chekhov are. And, I repeat, not because the world he creates is unreal—all the worlds of writers are unreal—but because it is created too hastily without any sense of that harmony and economy which the most irrational masterpiece is bound to comply with (in order to be a masterpiece). Indeed, in a sense Dostoevski is much too rational in his crude methods, and though his facts are but spiritual facts and his characters mere ideas in the likeness of people, their interplay and development are actuated by the mechanical methods of the earthbound and conventional novels of the late eighteenth and early nineteenth centuries.

I want to stress again the fact that Dostoevski was more of a playwright than a novelist. What his novels represent is a succession of scenes, of dialogues, of scenes where all the people are brought together—and with all the tricks of the theatre, as with the scène à faire, the unexpected visitor, the comedy relief, etc. Considered as novels, his works fall to pieces; considered as plays, they are much too long, diffuse, and badly balanced.

He has little humor in the description of his characters or their relations, or in the situations, but sometimes he displays a kind of caustic humor in certain scenes.

"The Franco-Prussian War," a musical piece composed by Lyamshin, one of the characters in *The Possessed*:

"It began with the menacing strains of the Marseillaise, *Qu'un sang impur abreuve nos sillons*. There is heard the pompous challenge, the intoxication of future victories. But suddenly mingling with the masterly variations of the national hymn, somewhere from some corner quite close, on one side, come the vulgar strains of 'Mein lieber Augustin.' The Marseillaise goes on unconscious of them. It is at the climax of intoxication with its own grandeur; but Augustin gains strength. Augustin grows more and more insolent, and suddenly the melody of Augustin begins to blend with the melody of the Marseillaise. The latter begins, as it were, to get angry; becoming aware of Augustin, at last, it tries to brush him off as a fly. But Mein lieber Augustin holds his ground firmly, he is cheerful and self-confident—and the Marseillaise seems suddenly to become terribly stupid. She can no longer conceal her mortification. It is a wail of indignation, tears and curses, with an appeal to Providence, *pas un pouce de notre terrain, pas une de nos forteresses*.

But she is forced to sing in time with Mein leiber Augustin. Her melody passes foolishly into Augustin. She yields and dies away. And only in snatches it is heard again *qu'un sang impur*. . . . But suddenly it passes over into the vulgar waltz. She submits altogether. It is Jules Favre sobbing on Bismark's bosom and surrendering everything. . . . Here Augustin grows fierce. Hoarse sounds are heard. There is a suggestion of countless gallons of beer, of a frenzy of self-glorification, demand for millions, for fine cigars, champagne and hostages. Augustin becomes a wild yell."

The Brothers Karamazov (1880)

The Brothers Karamazov is the most perfect example of the detective story technique as constantly used by Dostoevski in his other novels. It is a long novel (more than 1,000 pages), and it is a curious novel. The things that are curious about it are numerous; even the chapter headings are curious. It is worth noting that the author not only is well aware of this quaint and weird nature of his book but he even seems to be all the time pointing to it, teasing his reader, using every device to excite the reader's curiosity. Let us look, for instance, at the index of chapters. I have just mentioned how unusual and how puzzling: a man, unfamiliar with the novel, could be easily misled into imagining that the book offered him is not a novel but rather the libretto of some whimsical vaudeville. Chapter 3: "Confession of a Fiery Heart, Expressed in

Verse." Chapter 4: "Confession of a Fiery Heart, Expressed in Anecdotes." Chapter 5: "Confession of a Fiery Heart, 'Upside Down.' " Then in the second volume, Chapter 5: "Nerve Storm in a Drawing Room." Chapter 6: "Nerve Storm in a Peasant Hut." Chapter 7: "And Outofdoors." Some headings surprise us by their odd diminutives: "A Cozy Little Chat Over Brandikins" (*Za kon'yachkom: kon'yak* - brandy; *kon'yachok* - diminutive form), or an elderly lady's aching little foot (*nozhka* - diminutive of *noga*). Most of these titles do not hint even ever so slightly at the contents of the chapter, as "One more reputation destroyed" or "The third and indisputable thing," headings that are meaningless. Finally a number of headings with their flippancy and their bantering choice of words read actually like an index to a collection of humorous stories. Only in part six, in fact, incidentally the weakest part of the book, are the names of chapters in agreement with their content.

In this taunting and teasing way the cunning author quite deliberately entices his reader. However, this is not the only way in which he does it. He is constantly preoccupied with various means for keeping and whetting the reader's attention throughout the book. Take for instance the manner in which he finally discloses the name of the town where the action has been taking place from the very start of the novel. This revelation of the town's name does not occur until close to the end: "Skotoprigonyevsk [place towards which cattle herds are driven, clearing place for cattle, something like oxtown], Skotoprigonyevsk," he says, "such alas is the name of our town, I have been long trying to conceal it." This over-sensitivity, over-concern of the writer in regard to the reader—when the reader is thought of simultaneously as the victim being drawn into a trap by the writer and as a hunter before whose path the writer keeps crossing and recrossing like a fleeing hare—this consciousness of the reader on the part of the writer derives partly from the Russian literary tradition. Pushkin in *Evgeniy Onegin*, Gogol in *Dead Souls*, often apostrophize, address themselves to the reader in a sudden aside, sometimes with an apology, sometimes with a request or with a joke. But it also derives from the tradition of the Western detective story, or rather from its predecessor, the criminal novel. It is in accordance with this latter tradition that Dostoevski uses an amusing device: with deliberate frankness, as if he were putting down before you all his cards, he comes out at the very beginning with the statement that a murder has been committed. "Aleksey Karamazov was the third son of Fyodor Karamazov, a landowner of our county, who became so famous for a time . . . through his tragic and unclarified death." This apparent sincerity on the part of the author is nothing but a stylistic device, the object being to inform the reader from the first of the fact of this "tragic and unclarified death."

The book is a typical detective story, a riotous whodunit—in slow motion. The initial situation is the following. We have the father Karamazov, a lecherous, hideous old man, one of those unlamentable victims neatly prepared for murder by every farsighted writer of detective fiction. And we also have his four sons—three legitimate and one illegitimate—each of whom might be his murderer. The youngest son, the saintly Aleksey (Alyosha) is definitely a positive character, but if for once we accept Dostoevski's world and its rules, we may consider it a possibility that even Alyosha may kill his father, whether for the sake of his brother Dmitri in whose way the old man most deliberately stands, or in a sudden rebellion against the evil which his father represents, or for any other reason. The plot is presented in such a way that for a long time the reader keeps guessing who the murderer is; moreover, when the alleged murderer goes on trial it is the wrong man who is being tried, the eldest son of the murdered man, Dmitri, whereas the actual murderer happens to be the illegitimate son, Smerdyakov.

In accordance with Dostoevski's purpose to entangle the credulous reader in the guesswork that goes with the enjoyment of detective fiction, the author carefully prepares in the reader's mind the necessary portrait of the possible murderer, Dmitri. The pattern of deception begins when Dmitri after feverish and vain attempts to secure the three thousand rubles he desperately needs, seizes on the run a copper pestle seven inches long, shoves it into his pocket, and rushes off. "Oh Lord, he sure wants to murder someone," a woman exclaims.

The girl Dmitri loves, another of those Dostoevskian "infernal" women, Grushenka, has also caught the fancy of the old man, who has promised her money if she pays him a visit, and Dmitri is persuaded that she has accepted the offer. Convinced that Grushenka was with his father, he leaped over the fence into the garden, from where he could see the lighted windows of his father's house; then "he stealthily approached and hid in the shadow, behind a bush. One half of the bush was lit by the lighted window. 'A bush with berries, how red they are,' he whispered, not knowing why." When he went up to the bedroom window, "the whole bedroom of Fyodor Pavlovich, a small chamber, lay before him as if in the palm of his hand." That little room was divided in two by red screens. Fyodor, the father, stood there, beside the window, "in his new striped silk dressing gown belted with a silk cord with tassels. From under the collar of the dressing gown appeared clean smart linen, a shirt of fine Holland cloth with golden studs. . . . "The old man almost climbed out of the window while trying to see the garden door which was further on the right side. . . . Dmitri was looking from the side and stood motionless. The whole detested profile of the old man, with its sagging skin on the Adam's apple, his lips smiling in voluptuous anticipation, all of it was obliquely lit on the left side by the lamp. A terrible boundless fury arose in Dmitri's heart," and losing all self-control, he suddenly snatched the copper pestle he had in his pocket.

Here follows an eloquent line consisting of asterisks, this again in compliance with the technique of entertaining novels built around bloody deeds. Then, as if after catching his breath, the author attacks it again from a different angle. Providence, as Dmitri himself used to say later, "seems to have watched me at the time." This might mean that something stayed his hand at the last moment; but no, immediately after this sentence comes a colon and then a sentence which seems to be there as if to elaborate the previous statement: At that very time Grigori, the old servant, woke up and came out into the garden. So that the sentence about God instead of meaning, as it seemed at first, that some guardian sign stopped him in time on his evil path, may also merely mean that God woke up the old servant to allow him to see and identify the fleeing murderer. And here comes a curious maneuver: from the moment of Dmitri's flight to that when the authorities come to arrest him for murder in the small market town where he is having a drinking bout with Grushenka (and there are seventy-five pages from murder to arrest), the author arranges things in such a way that garrulous Dmitri never once betrays his innocence to the reader. What is more: whenever he remembers Grigori, the servant whom he hit with the pestle and maybe has killed, Dmitri never mentions the man he hit by name but merely describes him as "the old man," so that it actually could have applied to his father. This device may be too crafty; it betrays too much the author's desire to keep Dmitri's speeches confusing enough to deceive the reader into taking him for the murderer of his father.

Later, at the trial, an important angle is whether or not Dmitri is saying the truth when he claims that he had his three thousand rubles with him before he went to the old man's house. Otherwise he may well be suspected of having stolen the three thousand rubles the old man had prepared for the girl, which in turn would serve to prove that he entered the house and committed the murder. And there, at the trial, Alyosha, the younger brother, suddenly remembers that Dmitri when he saw him last—and that was before Dmitri went on his nocturnal expedition to his father's garden—kept slapping himself on the chest and proclaiming that he had right there what was necessary to help him out of his difficult situation. At that time Alyosha had thought that Dmitri meant his heart. But now he suddenly remembered that even then he had observed that the place Dmitri kept slapping was not where the heart would be but much higher. (Dmitri had it in a little bag on a string around his neck.) This observation of Alyosha became the only proof, or rather a hint of proof, that Dmitri actually had obtained the money before and thus had not necessarily murdered his father. Incidentally, Alyosha was wrong: Dmitri meant a charm he had on a chain.

Yet the following circumstance, which would easily have settled the question and saved Dmitri, is completely disregarded by the author. Smerdyakov has confessed to Ivan, another brother, that he was the real murderer, and that in committing his crime he had used a heavy ashtray. Ivan is going all out to save Dmitri; yet this essential circumstance is never mentioned at the trial. Had Ivan told the court about the ashtray, not much skill would have been needed to establish the truth if the ashtray was examined for blood and its shape was compared with the shape of the mortal wound. This is not done, a bad flaw in a mystery novel.

This analysis will suffice to show the characteristic development of the novel's plot where it concerns Dmitri. Ivan, the second brother, who goes away from the town in order to allow the murder to be completed (by Smerdyakov whom he has been actually coaching for murder in a sort of metaphysical way), Ivan who thus becomes so to say an accomplice of Dmitri, Ivan is much more closely integrated in the plot of the book than is the third brother Alyosha. Where Alyosha is concerned, we constantly gain the impression that the author was torn between two independent plots: Dmitri's tragedy on the one side and the story of the almost saintly youth Alyosha. Alyosha is again an exponent (the other was Prince Myshkin) of the author's unfortunate love for the simple-minded hero of Russian folklore. The whole lengthy limp story of the monk Zosima could have been deleted from the novel without impairing it; rather, its deletion would have given the book more unity and a better balanced construction. And again quite independently, sticking quite obviously out of the general scheme of the book, stands the, in itself, very well written story of the schoolboy Ilyusha. But even into that excellent story about the boy Ilyusha, another boy Kolya, the dog Zhuchka, the silver toy cannon, the cold nose of the puppy, the freakish tricks of the hysterical father, even into this story Alyosha introduces an unpleasant unctuous chill.

Generally speaking, whenever the author busies himself with Dmitri his pen acquires exceptional liveliness. Dmitri seems to be constantly illumined by strong lamps, and so do all those who surround him. But the moment we come to Alyosha, we are immersed in a different, entirely lifeless element. Dusky paths lead the reader away into a murky world of cold reasoning abandoned by the spirit of art.

Tolstoy   Lecture One

① 1

Tolstoy is the greatest Russian writer of prose fiction. Leaving aside his precursors Pushkin and Lermontov, we might list the greatest artists in Russian prose thus: first, Tolstoy, second, Gogol, third Chekhov, fourth Turgenev. This is rather like grading students' papers and no doubt ~~~~~~ Dostoevski ~~~~~~ ~~~~~~ ~~~~~~

The ideological poison, the message — to use a term invented by quack reformers — began to affect the Russian novel in the middle of last century, and has killed it by the middle of this one. It would seem at first glance that Tolstoy's fiction is heavily infected with his teachings. Actually, his ideology was so tame and so vague and so far from politics and — on the other hand, his art was so powerful, so tiger-bright, so original and universal that it easily transcends the sermon.

In the long run what interested him as a thinker were Life and Death, and after all no ~~~~~~ artist can avoid treating these themes.

LEO TOLSTOY (1828-1910)

Anna Karenin* (1877)

T olstoy is the greatest Russian writer of prose fiction. Leaving aside his precursors Pushkin and Lermontov, we might list the greatest artists in Russian prose thus: first, Tolstoy; second, Gogol; third, Chekhov; fourth, Turgenev.** This is rather like grading students' papers and no doubt Dostoevski and Saltykov are waiting at the door of my office to discuss their low marks.

The ideological poison, the message—to use a term invented by quack reformers—began to affect the Russian novel in the middle of the last century, and has killed it by the middle of this one. It would seem at first glance that Tolstoy's fiction is heavily infected with his teachings. Actually, his ideology was so tame and so vague and so far from politics, and, on the other hand, his

---

*"Translators have had awful trouble with the heroine's name. In Russian, a surname ending in a consonant acquires a final 'a' (except in the case of such names as cannot be declined) when designating a woman; but only when the reference is to a female stage performer should English feminize a Russian surname (following a French custom: *la Pavlova*, 'the Pavlova'). Ivanov's and Karenin's wives are Mrs. Ivanov and Mrs. Karenin in England and America—not 'Mrs. Ivanova' or 'Mrs. Karenina.' Having decided to write 'Karenina,' translators found themselves forced to call Anna's husband 'Mr. Karenina,' which is about as ridiculous as calling Lady Mary's husband 'Lord Mary.' " Transferred from VN's commentary note. Ed.

**"When you read Turgenev, you know you are reading Turgenev. When you read Tolstoy, you read just because you cannot stop." Bracketed note elsewhere in the section. Ed.

art was so powerful, so tiger bright, so original and universal that it easily transcends the sermon. In the long run what interested him as a thinker were Life and Death, and after all no artist can avoid treating these themes.

———————

Count Leo (in Russian Lev or Lyov) Tolstoy (1828-1910) was a robust man with a restless soul, who all his life was torn between his sensual temperament and his supersensitive conscience. His appetites constantly led him astray from the quiet country road that the ascetic in him craved to follow as passionately as the rake in him craved for the city pleasures of the flesh.

In his youth, the rake had a better chance and took it. Later, after his marriage in 1862, Tolstoy found temporary peace in family life divided between the wise management of his fortune—he had rich lands in the Volga region—and the writing of his best prose. It is then, in the sixties and early seventies, that he produced his immense *War and Peace* (1869) and his immortal *Anna Karenin*. Still later, beginning in the late seventies, when he was over forty, his conscience triumphed: the ethical overcame both the esthetical and the personal and drove him to sacrifice his wife's happiness, his peaceful family life, and his lofty literary career to what he considered a moral necessity: living according to the principles of rational Christian morality—the simple and stern life of generalized humanity, instead of the colorful adventure of individual art. And when in 1910 he realized that by continuing to live on his country estate, in the bosom of his stormy family, he still was betraying his ideal of a simple, saintly existence, he, a man of eighty, left his home and wandered away, heading for a monastery he never reached, and died in the waiting room of a little railway station.

I hate tampering with the precious lives of great writers and I hate Tom-peeping over the fence of those lives—I hate the vulgarity of "human interest," I hate the rustle of skirts and giggles in the corridors of time—and no biographer will ever catch a glimpse of my private life; but this I must say. Dostoevski's gloating pity for people—pity for the humble and the humiliated—this pity was purely emotional and his special lurid brand of the Christian faith by no means prevented him from leading a life extremely removed from his teachings. On the other hand, Leo Tolstoy like his rep-

———————

The beginning of Nabokov's discussion of Tolstoy's life.

———————

2

Count { Leo Lev Lyov } Tolstoy (pronounced Tál-stoy)
a Leon
Elion
Fr Leon
(hardly yet pr Aliosha Levi) Lyóvin in Anna Karenin (misspelt Levin by translator)

— from which he derived the surname of his character Lyóvin in Anna Karenin (misspelt Levin by translator)

which creates some confusion
It has nothing to do with the Jewish name Lévin or Levín

1828 — 1910

[His life was not as adventurous as that of Pushkin or Lermontov.]

He joined the army at twenty three and took part in the fighting at Sebastopol in the crimean war of the mid fifties.

His first admirable piece in which his genius shines with authentic Tolstoyan glamour is "Childhood and Boyhood" — which came out in 1852 and 1854. It is as it were a preview of the Rostov family in War and Peace.

Tolstoy married in 1862 and went to live in his country estate, raising a big family of so called real people and of two immortal characters. In the sixties he wrote War and Peace, not to be confused with the vulgar and ridiculous movie that appeared under that title. In the early seventies — he wrote Anna Karenin.

resentative Lyovin was organically unable to allow his conscience to strike a bargain with his animal nature—and he suffered cruelly whenever this animal nature temporarily triumphed over his better self.

And when he discovered his new religion and in the logical development of this new religion—a neutral blend between a kind of Hindu Nirvana and the New Testament, Jesus minus the Church—he reached the conclusion that art was ungodly because it was founded on imagination, on deceit, on fancy-forgery, he ruthlessly sacrificed the giant of an artist that he was to a rather pedestrian and narrow minded though well-meaning philosopher that he had chosen to become. Thus when he had just reached the uppermost peaks of creative perfection with *Anna Karenin*, he suddenly decided to stop writing altogether, except for essays on ethics. Fortunately he was not always able to maintain in chains that gigantic creative need of his and, succumbing once in a while, added to his output a few exquisite stories untainted by deliberate moralizing among which is that greatest of great short stories, "The Death of Ivan Ilyich."

Many people approach Tolstoy with mixed feelings. They love the artist in him and are intensely bored by the preacher; but at the same time it is rather difficult to separate Tolstoy the preacher from Tolstoy the artist—it is the same deep slow voice, the same robust shoulder pushing up a cloud of visions or a load of ideas. What one would like to do, would be to kick the glorified soapbox from under his sandalled feet and then lock him up in a stone house on a desert island with gallons of ink and reams of paper—far away from the things, ethical and pedagogical, that diverted his attention from observing the way the dark hair curled above Anna's white neck. But the thing cannot be done: Tolstoy is homogeneous, is one, and the struggle which, especially in the later years, went on between the man who gloated over the beauty of black earth, white flesh, blue snow, green fields, purple thunderclouds, and the man who maintained that fiction is sinful and art immoral—this struggle was still confined within the same man. Whether painting or preaching, Tolstoy was striving, in spite of all obstacles, to get at the truth. As the author of *Anna Karenin*, he used one method of discovering truth; in his sermons, he used another; but somehow, no matter how subtle his art was and no matter how dull some of his other attitudes were, truth which he was ponderously groping for or magically finding just around the corner, was always the same truth—this truth was he and this he was an art.

What troubles one, is merely that he did not always recognize his own self when confronted with truth. I like the story of his picking up a book one dreary day in his old age, many years after he had stopped writing novels, and starting to read in the middle, and getting interested and very much pleased, and then looking at the title—and seeing: *Anna Karenin* by Leo Tolstoy. What obsessed Tolstoy, what obscured his genius, what now distresses the good reader, was that, somehow, the process of seeking the Truth seemed more important to him than the easy, vivid, brilliant discovery of the illusion of truth through the medium of his artistic genius. Old Russian Truth was never a comfortable companion; it had a violent temper and a heavy tread. It was not simply truth, not merely everyday *pravda* but immortal *istina*—not truth but the inner light of truth. When Tolstoy did happen to find it in himself, in the splendor of his creative imagination, then, almost unconsciously, he was on the right path. What does his tussle with the ruling Greek-Catholic Church matter, what importance do his ethical opinions have, in the light of this or that imaginative passage in any of his novels?

Essential truth, *istina*, is one of the few words in the Russian language that cannot be rhymed. It has no verbal mate, no verbal associations, it stands alone and aloof, with only a vague suggestion of the root "to stand" in the dark brilliancy of its immemorial rock. Most Russian writers have been tremendously interested in Truth's exact whereabouts and essential properties. To Pushkin it was of marble under a noble sun; Dostoevski, a much inferior artist, saw it as a thing of blood and tears and hysterical and topical politics and sweat; and Chekhov kept a quizzical eye upon it, while seemingly engrossed in the hazy scenery all around. Tolstoy marched straight at it, head bent and fists clenched, and found the place where the cross had once stood, or found—the image of his own self.

One discovery that he made has curiously enough never been noticed by critics. He discovered—and certainly never realized his discovery—he discovered a method of picturing life which most pleasingly and exactly corresponds to our idea of time. He is the only writer I know of whose watch keeps time with the numberless watches of his readers. All the great writers have good eyes, and the "realism," as it is called, of Tolstoy's descriptions, has been deepened by others; and though the average Russian reader will tell you that what seduces him in Tolstoy is the absolute reality of his novels, the sensation of meeting old friends and seeing familiar places, this is neither here nor there. Others were equally good at vivid description. What really seduces the average reader is the gift Tolstoy had of endowing his fiction with such time-values as correspond exactly to our sense of time. It is a mysterious accomplishment which is not so much a laudable feature of genius as something pertaining to the physical nature of that genius. This time balance, absolutely peculiar to

Tolstoy alone, is what gives the gentle reader that sense of average reality which he is apt to ascribe to Tolstoy's keen vision. Tolstoy's prose keeps pace with our pulses, his characters seem to move with the same swing as the people passing under our window while we sit reading his book.

The queer thing about it is that actually Tolstoy was rather careless when dealing with the objective idea of time. In *War and Peace* attentive readers have found children who grow too fast or not fast enough, just as in Gogol's *Dead Souls*, despite Gogol's care in clothing his characters, we find that Chichikov wore a bearskin overcoat in midsummer. In *Anna Karenin*, as we shall see, there are terrific skiddings on the frozen road of time. But such slips on Tolstoy's part have nothing to do with the impression of time he conveys, the idea of time which corresponds so exactly with the reader's sense of time. There are other great writers who were quite consciously fascinated by the idea of time and quite consciously tried to render its movement; this Proust does when his hero in the novel *In Search of Lost Time* arrives at a final party where he sees people he used to know now for some reason wearing gray wigs, and then realizes that the gray wigs are organic gray hairs, that they have grown old while he had been strolling through his memories; or notice how James Joyce regulates the time element in *Ulysses* by the slow gradual passing of a crumpled bit of paper down the river from bridge to bridge down the Liffy to Dublin Bay to the eternal sea. Yet these writers who actually dealt in time values did not do what Tolstoy quite casually, quite unconsciously, does: they move either slower or faster than the reader's grandfather clock; it is the time *by* Proust or the time *by* Joyce, not the common average time, a kind of standard time which Tolstoy somehow manages to convey.

No wonder, then, that elderly Russians at their evening tea talk of Tolstoy's characters as of people who really exist, people to whom their friends may be likened, people they see as distinctly as if they had danced with Kitty and Anna or Natasha at that ball or dined with Oblonski at his favorite restaurant,* as we shall soon be dining with him. Readers call Tolstoy a giant not because other writers are dwarfs but because he remains always of exactly our own stature,** exactly keeping pace with us instead of passing by in the distance, as other authors do.

---

*"Those very particular sensations of reality, of flesh and blood, of characters really living, of living on their own behalf, the main reason for this vividness is due to the fact of Tolstoy's possessing the unique capacity of keeping time with us; so that if we imagine a creature from some other solar system who would be curious about our time conception, the best way to explain matters to him would be to give him to read a novel by Tolstoy—in Russian, or at least in *my* translation with my commentaries." VN deleted passage from the section. Ed.

**"The Russian writer Bunin told me that when he visited Tolstoy for the first time and sat waiting for him, he was almost shocked to see suddenly emerge from a small door a little old man instead of the giant he had involuntarily imagined. And I have also seen myself that little old man. I was a child and I faintly remember my father shaking hands with someone at a street corner, then telling me as we continued our walk, 'That was Tolstoy.' " VN deleted passage from the section. Ed.

And in this connection it is curious to note that although Tolstoy, who was constantly aware of his own personality, constantly intruding upon the lives of his characters, constantly addressing the reader—it is curious to note that nevertheless in those great chapters that are his masterpieces the author is invisible so that he attains that dispassionate ideal of authors which Flaubert so violently demanded of a writer: to be invisible, and to be everywhere as God in His universe is. We have thus the feeling now and then that Tolstoy's novel writes its own self, is produced by its matter, by its subject, not by a definite person moving a pen from left to right, and then coming back and erasing a word, and pondering, and scratching his chin through his beard.*

The intrusion of the teacher into the artist's domain is, as I have remarked already, not always clearly defined in Tolstoy's novels. The rhythm of the sermon is difficult to disentangle from the rhythm of this or that character's personal meditations. But sometimes, rather often in fact, when pages and pages follow which are definitely in the margin of the story, telling us what we ought to think, what *Tolstoy* thinks about war or marriage or agriculture— then the charm is broken and the delightful familiar people who had been sitting all round us, joining in our life, are now shut off from us, the door is locked not to be opened until the solemn author has quite, quite finished that ponderous period in which he explains and reexplains his ideas about marriage, or Napoleon, or farming, or his ethical and religious views.

As an example, the agrarian problems discussed in the book, especially in relation to Lyovin's farming, are extremely tedious to foreign-language readers, and I do not expect you to study the situation with any degree of penetration. Artistically Tolstoy made a mistake in devoting such a number of pages to these matters, especially as they tend to become obsolete and are linked up with a certain historical period and with Tolstoy's own ideas that changed with time. Agriculture in the seventies does not have the eternal thrill of Anna's or Kitty's emotions and motives. Several chapters are devoted to the provincial elections of various administrators. The landowners through an organization called *zemstvo* tried to get into touch with the peasants and to help the peasants (and themselves) by setting up more schools, better hospitals, better machinery, et cetera. There were various participating landowners: conservative, reactionary landowners still looked upon the peasants as slaves—though officially the slaves had been liberated more than ten years before—while liberal, progressive landowners were really eager to improve conditions by having peasants share the landlord's interests and thus helping the peasants become richer, healthier, better educated.

*VN continued, but then deleted, "and then getting cross with his wife Sofia Andrevna for letting a noisy visitor into the neighboring room." Ed.

It is not my custom to speak of plots but in the case of *Anna Karenin* I shall make an exception since the plot of it is essentially a moral plot, a tangle of ethical tentacles, and this we must explore before enjoying the novel on a higher level than plot.

One of the most attractive heroines in international fiction, Anna is a young, handsome, and fundamentally good woman, and a fundamentally doomed woman. Married off as a very young girl by a well-meaning aunt to a promising official with a splendid bureaucratic career, Anna leads a contented life within the most sparkling circle of St. Petersburg society. She adores her little son, respects her husband who is twenty years her senior, and her vivid, optimistic nature enjoys all the superficial pleasures offered her by life.

When she meets Vronski on a trip to Moscow, she falls deeply in love with him. This love transforms everything around her; everything she looks at she sees in a different light. There is that famous scene at the railway station in St. Petersburg when Karenin comes to meet her on her way back from Moscow, and she suddenly notices the size and vexing convexity of his huge homely ears. She had never noticed those ears before because she had never looked at him critically; he had been for her one of the accepted things of life included in her own accepted life. Now everything has changed. Her passion for Vronski is a flood of white light in which her former world looks like a dead landscape on a dead planet.

Anna is not just a woman, not just a splendid specimen of womanhood, she is a woman with a full, compact, important moral nature: everything about her character is significant and striking, and this applied as well to her love. She cannot limit herself as another character in the book, Princess Betsy, does, to an undercover affair. Her truthful and passionate nature makes disguise and secrecy impossible. She is not Emma Bovary, a provincial dreamer, a wistful wench creeping along crumbling walls to the beds of interchangeable paramours. Anna gives Vronski her whole life, consents to a separation from her adored little son—despite the agony it costs her not to see the child—and she goes to live with Vronski first abroad in Italy, and then on his country place in central Russia, though this "open" affair brands her an immoral woman in the eyes of her immoral circle. (In a way she may be said to have put into action Emma's dream of escaping with Rodolphe, but Emma would have experienced no wrench from parting with *her* child, and neither were there any moral complications in *that* little lady's case.) Finally Anna and Vronski return to city life. She scandalizes hypocritical society not so much with her love affair as with her open defiance of society's conventions.

While Anna bears the brunt of society's anger, is snubbed and snobbed, insulted and "cut," Vronski, being a man—a not very deep man, not a gifted man by any means, but a fashionable man, say—Vronski is spared by scandal: he is invited, he goes places, meets his former friends, is introduced to seemingly decent women who would not remain a second in the same room with disgraced Anna. He still loves Anna, but sometimes he is pleased to be back in the world of sport and fashion, and he begins occasionally to avail himself of its favors. Anna misconstrues trivial unloyalties as a drop in the temperature of his love. She feels that her affection alone is no longer enough for him, that she may be losing him.

Vronski, a blunt fellow, with a mediocre mind, gets impatient with her jealousy and thus seems to confirm her suspicions.* Driven to despair by the muddle and mud in which her passion flounders, Anna one Sunday evening in May throws herself under a freight train. Vronski realizes too late what he has lost. Rather conveniently for him and for Tolstoy, war with Turkey is brewing—this is 1876—and he departs for the front with a battalion of volunteers. This is probably the only unfair device in the novel, unfair because too easy, too pat.

A parallel story which develops on seemingly quite independent lines is that of the courtship and marriage of Lyovin and Princess Kitty Shcherbatski. Lyovin, in whom more than in any other of his male characters Tolstoy has portrayed himself, is a man of moral ideals, of Conscience with a capital C. Conscience gives him no respite. Lyovin is very different from Vronski. Vronski lives only to satisfy his impulses. Vronski, before he meets Anna, has lived a conventional life: even in love, Vronski is content to substitute for moral ideals the conventions of his circle. But Lyovin is a man who feels it his duty to understand intelligently the surrounding world and to work out for himself his place within it. Therefore Lyovin's nature moves on in constant evolution, spiritually growing throughout the novel, growing toward those religious ideals which at the time Tolstoy was evolving for himself.

Around these main characters a number of others move. Steve Oblonski, Anna's lighthearted good-for-nothing brother; his wife Dolly, born Shcherbatski, a kindly, serious, long-suffering woman, in a way one of Tolstoy's ideal women, for her life is selflessly devoted to her children and to her shiftless husband; there is the rest of the Shcherbatski family, one of Moscow's old

---

*VN bracketed for reconsideration but did not delete: "Of course he is an incomparably more civilized person than squire Rodolphe, Emma's coarse lover; but still there are moments when, during his mistress' tantrums, he might be ready to say mentally, with Rodolphe's intonation, 'You are losing your time, my good girl.' " Ed.

aristocratic families; Vronski's mother; and a whole gallery of people of St. Petersburg high society. Petersburg society was very different from the Moscow kind, Moscow being the kindly, homey, flaccid, patriarchal old town, and Petersburg the sophisticated, cold, formal, fashionable, and relatively young capital where some thirty years later I was born. Of course there is Karenin himself, Karenin the husband, a dry righteous man, cruel in his theoretical virtue, the ideal civil servant, the philistine bureaucrat who willingly accepts the pseudo-morality of his friends, a hypocrite and a tyrant. In his rare moments he is capable of a good movement, of a kind gesture, but this is too soon forgotten and sacrificed to considerations of his career. At Anna's bedside, when she is very sick after bearing Vronski's child and certain of her impending death (which, however, does not come), Karenin forgives Vronski and takes his hand with a true feeling of Christian humility and generosity. He will change back later to his chilly unpleasant personality, but at the moment the proximity of death illumes the scene and Anna in a subconscious way loves him as much as she loves Vronski: both are called Aleksey, both as loving mates share her in her dream. But this feeling of sincerity and kindliness does not last long, and when Karenin makes an attempt at securing a divorce—a matter of not much consequence to him but which would make all the difference to Anna—and is faced with the necessity of submitting to unpleasant complications in the course of obtaining it, he simply gives up and refuses ever to try again, no matter what this refusal may mean to Anna. Moreover, he manages to find satisfaction in his own righteousness.

Though one of the greatest love stories in world literature, *Anna Karenin* is of course not just a novel of adventure. Being deeply concerned with moral matters, Tolstoy was eternally preoccupied with issues of importance to all mankind at all times. Now, there is a moral issue in *Anna Karenin*, though not the one that a casual reader might read into it. This moral is certainly not that having committed adultery, Anna had to pay for it (which in a certain vague sense can be said to be the moral at the bottom of the barrel in *Madame Bovary*). Certainly not this, and for obvious reasons: had Anna remained with Karenin and skillfully concealed from the world her affair, she would not have paid for it first with her happiness and then with her life. Anna was not punished for her sin (she might have got away with that) nor for violating the conventions of a society, very temporal as all conventions are and having nothing to do with the eternal demands of morality. What was then the moral "message" Tolstoy has conveyed in his novel? We can understand it better if we look at the rest of the book and draw a comparison between the Lyovin-Kitty story and the Vronski-Anna story. Lyovin's marriage is based on a metaphysical, not only physical, concept of love, on willingness for self-sacrifice, on mutual respect. The Anna-Vronski alliance was founded only in carnal love and therein lay its doom.

It might seem, at first blush, that Anna was punished by society for falling in love with a man who was not her husband. Now such a "moral" would be of course completely "immoral," and completely inartistic, incidentally, since other ladies of fashion, in that same society, were having as many love-affairs as they liked but having them in secrecy, under a dark veil. (Remember Emma's blue veil on her ride with Rodolphe and her dark veil in her rendezvous at Rouen with Léon.) But frank unfortunate Anna does not wear this veil of deceit. The decrees of society are temporary ones; what Tolstoy is interested in are the eternal demands of morality. And now comes the real moral point that he makes: Love cannot be exclusively carnal because then it is egotistic, and being egotistic it destroys instead of creating. It is thus sinful. And in order to make his point as artistically clear as possible, Tolstoy in a flow of extraordinary imagery depicts and places side by side, in vivid contrast, two loves: the carnal love of the Vronski-Anna couple (struggling amid their richly sensual but fateful and spiritually sterile emotions) and on the other hand the authentic, Christian love, as Tolstoy termed it, of the Lyovin-Kitty couple with the riches of sensual nature still there but balanced and harmonious in the pure atmosphere of responsibility, tenderness, truth, and family joys.

A biblical epigraph: Vengeance is *mine*; *I* will repay (saith the Lord).

(*Romans* XII, verse 19)

What are the implications? First, Society had no right to judge Anna; second, Anna had no right to punish Vronski by her revengeful suicide.

Joseph Conrad, a British novelist of Polish descent, writing to Edward Garnett, a writer of sorts, in a letter dated the 10th of June, 1902, said: "Remember me affectionately to your wife whose translation of Karenina is splendid. Of the thing itself I think but little, so that her merit shines with the greater lustre." I shall never forgive Conrad this crack. Actually the Garnett translation is very poor.

We may look in vain among the pages of *Anna Karenin* for Flaubert's subtle transitions, within chapters, from one character to another. The structure of *Anna Karenin* is of a more conventional kind, although the book was written twenty years later than Flaubert's *Madame Bovary*. Conversation between characters mentioning other characters, and the maneuvers of intermediate characters who bring about the meetings of main participants—these are the simple and sometimes rather blunt methods used by Tolstoy. Even simpler are his abrupt switches from chapter to chapter in changing his stage sets.

Tolstoy's novel consists of eight parts and each part on the average consists of about thirty short chapters of four pages. He sets himself the task of following two main lines—the Lyovin-Kitty one and the Vronski-Anna one, although there is a third line, subordinate and intermediary, the Oblonski-Dolly one that plays a very special part in the structure of the novel since it is present to link up in various ways the two main lines. Steve Oblonski and Dolly are there to act as go-betweens in the affairs of Lyovin and Kitty and in those of Anna and her husband. Throughout Lyovin's bachelor existence, moreover, a subtle parallel is drawn between Dolly Oblonski and Lyovin's ideal of a mother which he will discover for his own children in Kitty. One should notice, also, that Dolly finds conversation with a peasant woman about children as fascinating as Lyovin finds conversation with male peasants about agriculture.

The action of the book starts in February 1872 and goes on to July 1876: in all, four years and a half. It shifts from Moscow to Petersburg and shuttles among the four country estates (because the country place of the old Countess Vronski near Moscow also plays a part in the book, though we are never taken to it).

The first of the eight parts of the novel has as its main subject the Oblonski family disaster with which the book starts, and as a secondary subject the Kitty-Lyovin-Vronski triangle.

The two subjects, the two expanded themes—Oblonski's adultery and Kitty's heartbreak when her infatuation for Vronski has been ended by Anna*—are introductory notes to the tragic Vronski-Anna theme which will not be so smoothly resolved as are the Oblonski-Dolly troubles or Kitty's bitterness. Dolly soon pardons her wayward husband for the sake of their five children and because she loves him, and because Tolstoy considers that two married people with children are tied together by divine law forever. Two years after her heartbreak over Vronski, Kitty marries Lyovin and begins what

---

*In a sentence that he later deleted VN adds: "It should be noticed that Anna who with wisdom and grace brings on the reconciliation and thus performs a good action, simultaneously performs an evil action by captivating Vronski and breaking up his courtship of Kitty." Ed.

Nabokov's outline of the plot for *Anna Karenin*, part one.

Anna Karenin

Part I

Chapter I	Confusion in Oblonsky household. Steve's dream.	3
Chapter II	Anna to arrive. Matriona's advice.	5
Chapter III	Steve's morning. Children.	9
Chapter IV	Explanation between Steve and Dolly. Unsuccessful.	13
Chapter V	Steve at office. Levin.	18
Chapter VI	About Levin	27
Chapter VII	Levin and Kosnishev	30
Chapter VIII	" "	32
Chapter IX	Skating rink	34
Chapter X	Oblonsky and Levin at the restaurant	41
Chapter XI	" " " "	48
Chapter XII	Kitty. Old Princess Shcherbatsky's thoughts about Kitty and Vronsky	52
Chapter XIII	Levin's proposal.	56
Chapter XIV	At the Shcherbatskis	59
✗ Chapter XV	Scene between Prince and Princess Shcherb. p. 66-67	65
Chapter XVI	Vronsky	68
Chapter XVII	At the station	70
Chapter XVIII	" " " Vronsky meets Anna.	73
Chapter XIX	Dolly and Anna	78
Chapter XX	Anna and Kitty. p. 83-89 ✔	84
✗ Chapter XXI	Oblonskys reconciled. Vronsky calls on Oblonskys	88
✗ Chapter XXII	The Ball p. 93 Anna	90
✗ Chapter XXIII	" " Vronsky and Anna p. 97 Kitty	95
✗ Chapter XXIV	Levin after Kitty's refusal. Levin and his brother N. 99	
Chapter XXV		103
✗ Chapter XXVI	Levin back on his estate p. 111 the calf: cp. Kitty; instinct	109
Chapter XXVII	" "	112
Chapter XXVIII	Anna and Dolly (about Vronsky and the ball). Anna leaves for Petersburg	115
Chapter XXIX	On the train between Moscow and Petersburg	118
Chapter XXX	Seeing Vronsky on train. Reaching Petersburg.	121

January 2-5
1872

Beginning of the dream-death theme (see XXIX)

cont. p. 118 dream-death theme

Tolstoy regards as a perfect marriage. But Anna, who becomes Vronski's mistress after ten months of persuasion, Anna will see the destruction of her family life and will commit suicide four years after the book's start.

"Happy families are all alike; every unhappy family is unhappy in its own way.

"All was confusion in the Oblonski house [in the sense of 'home,' both 'house' and 'home' being *dom* in Russian].* The wife had discovered that the husband had an affair with a French girl, who had been a governess in their house, and she had declared to her husband that she could not go on living in the same house with him. This situation was now in its third day, and not only husband and wife, but all the members of the family and the household, were conscious of it. Every person in the house felt that there was no sense in their living together, and that the stray people brought together by chance in any inn had more in common with one another than they, the members of the family and household of the Oblonskis. The wife did not leave her own rooms, the husband had not been in the house for three days. The children ran wild all over the house; the English governess had quarreled with the housekeeper, and wrote to a friend asking her to find a new place for her; the chef had walked off the day before just at dinner-time; the woman who cooked for the servants and the coachman had given notice.

"Three days after the quarrel, Prince Stepan Arkadyevitch Oblonski—Steve as he was called in the fashionable world—woke up at his usual hour, that is, at eight o'clock in the morning, not in his wife's bedroom, but on the morocco upholstered sofa in his study. He turned over his stout, well-cared-for person on the springy sofa, as though he would sink into a long sleep again; he vigorously embraced the pillow on the other side and pressed his cheek against it; but all at once he gave a start, sat up on the sofa, and opened his eyes.

" 'Yes, yes, how did it go?' he thought, recalling his dream. 'Yes, how did it go? Ah, yes. Alabin was giving a dinner at Darmstadt [in Germany]; no, not Darmstadt, but something American. Yes, but then, Darmstadt was in America. Yes, Alabin was giving a dinner on tables made of glass, and the tables sang, *Il mio tesoro* —not *Il mio tesoro* though, but something better, and there were some sort of little decanters, and these were at the same time women, too.' "**

Steve's dream is the kind of illogical arrangement that is hastily brought

---

*"Dom—Dom—Dom: the tolling bell of the family theme—house, household, home. Tolstoy deliberately gives us on the very first page the key, the clue: the home theme, the family theme." This sentence is drawn from a page of notes for the start of this section. For a more elaborate statement, see VN's Commentary Note Number 2. Ed.

**The passages quoted by VN in these lectures represent his revision of the Garnett translation of the novel, and his occasional abridgements and paraphrases for oral reading. Ed.

about by the dream producer. You must not imagine these tables as merely covered with glass—but made completely of glass. Wine-decanters, of crystal, sing in Italian voices and at the same time these melodious decanters are women—one of those economic combinations that the amateur management of our dreams often employs. It is a pleasant dream, so pleasant in fact, that it is quite out of keeping with reality. He awakes not in the connubial bed but in the exile of his study. This however is not the most interesting point. The interesting point is that Steve's light-hearted, transparent, philandering, epicurean nature is cunningly described by the author through the imagery of a dream. This is the device for introducing Oblonski: a dream introduces him. And another point: this dream with singing little women is going to be very different from the dream about a muttering little man that both Anna and Vronski will see.

We are going to pursue our inquiry as to what impressions went to form a certain dream that both Vronski and Anna had in a later part of the book. The most prominent of these occurs on her arrival in Moscow and her meeting with Vronski.

"Next day at eleven in the morning, Vronski drove to the station to meet his mother who was coming from Petersburg and the first person he came across on the great flight of steps was Steve Oblonski who was expecting his sister by the same train. [She was coming to reconcile Steve and his wife.]

" 'Hallo there,' cried Steve, 'whom are you meeting?'

" 'My mother,' answered Vronski. . . . 'And whom are you meeting?'

" 'A pretty woman,' said Steve.

" 'Oh,' said Vronski.

" 'Shamed be who thinks evil of it,' said Steve. 'It's my sister Anna.'

" 'Ah, that's Karenin's wife,' said Vronski.

" 'Know her?' asked Steve.

" 'I think I do, or perhaps not, I am not sure.' Vronski spoke heedlessly with a vague recollection of something formal and dull evoked by the name Karenin.

" 'But,' Steve went on, 'my celebrated brother-in-law, you surely must know him?' . . .

" 'Well, by reputation, by sight. I know that he is clever, learned, churchy

---

Overleaf, left: The opening pages in Nabokov's teaching copy of *Anna Karenin*.
Right: Nabokov's corrections for the first pages of Garnett's translation of *Anna Karenin*.

---

a complete devastating his translation
which is pretty well and but the trouble of here
but I first distinguished and tried to correct it
from beginning to end, in 3 places here Boris.

Epigraph:

Vengeance is mine; I will repay
(saith the Lord)   "(Romans XII, 19)

1) Stories of Society (to judge Anna
   Anna has no wish to learn
   prince's family by her
   wrongful murder, suicide

2) Red 4th   You may leave out
   373-41 Dr   ch 24 to 32, in part III
   4755-778   ch 26 to 31   in part VI

Joseph Conrad wrote to Edward Garnett
in a letter dated the 10th of June, 1902:
"Remember me affectionately to your wife
whose translation of Karenina is splendid.
Of the thing I have too little, as that has most
shaken with the greatest realm."

I shall never forget the
Conrad your own of one
the translation in a disaster

ANNA KARENINA   begun
March 1873
April 1876

PART I

CHAPTER I

HAPPY families are all alike; every unhappy family is
unhappy in its own way.

Everything was in confusion in the Oblonskys' house.
The wife had discovered that the husband was carrying on
an intrigue with a French girl, who had been a governess in
their family, and she had announced to her husband that she
could not go on living in the same house with him. This
position of affairs had now lasted three days, and not only the
husband and wife themselves, but all the members of their
family and household, were painfully conscious of it. Every
person in the house felt that there was no sense in their living
together, and that the stray people brought together by chance
in any inn had more in common with one another than they,
the members of the family and household of the Oblonskys.
The wife did not leave her own room, the husband had not
been at home for three days. The children ran wild all over
the house; the English governess quarreled with the housekeeper, and wrote to a friend asking her to look out for a new
situation for her; the man-cook had walked off the day before
just at dinner-time; the kitchen-maid, and the coachman had
given warning.

Three days after the quarrel, Prince Stepan Arkadyevitch
Oblonsky—Stiva, as he was called in the fashionable world—
woke up at his usual hour, that is, at eight o'clock in the morning, not in his wife's bedroom, but on the leather-covered sofa
in his study. He turned over his stout, well-cared-for person
on the springy sofa, as though he would sink into a long sleep
again; he vigorously embraced the pillow on the other side and

3

Anna Karenin.   (text corrections)
                        of Garnett version

Part I

Chapter I
p.3,1.3-6 All was confusion in the Oblonskis' house. The wife had discovered
          that the husband had an affair with a French girl who had been a
          governess in their house, and declared to her husband...
                                                                This
          situation had now lasted three days, and not only husband and wife,
          but all the members of the family...
                                                        ...*it*. All
1.10
).11   the members of the family and the household were conscious....
1.13   in any roadside inn...
1.15   ... her own rooms, *the* ...
1.18-19   ... asking her to find her a new place *for*...
1.19   ...; the chef *had*...
1.20-21   ...; the woman who cooked for the servants and the
          coachman had given notice.
1.22   ..., Prince Stepan
).23   Oblonski -- Steve...
1.25   ..., but on the morocco-upholstered sofa...

p.4,1.1   pressed his cheek against it; but all at once he gave a start...
1.3   "Yes, yes, how did it go?" he thought, recalling his dream. "Yes,
7.4   how did it go? Ah, yes! *Alabin*...
1.9   ...decanters,
(.10   and these were at the same time women."
1.11   Steve's eyes......
1.16   cloth blinds, *he* gaily dropped his feet...
1.17-19   ... for his tawny morocco slippers
          embroidered by his wife (a present for his last-year's birthday.)
          And...

or something. But you know that is not in my line,' added Vronski in English. . . .

"Vronski followed the conductor to the car where his mother was, went up the steps and at the entrance of the section he stopped short in the vestibule of the car to make room for a lady who was coming out. With the instinct of a man of the world he at once classified her as belonging to the highest society. He begged her pardon, retreated and was about to proceed on his way when he felt he must glance at her again; not because she was very beautiful, not because of her elegance and subdued grace but because in the expression of her charming face as she passed close by him, there was something peculiarly caressing and soft. As he looked back at her, she too turned her head. Her sparkling eyes that were grey but looked darker because of her thick lashes rested with friendly attention on his face as though she were recognizing him, and then promptly passed away to the passing crowd where she was looking for someone. Vronski had time to notice the suppressed eagerness which played over her face and flitted about her brilliant eyes and the faint smile that curved her red lips. She seemed to be brimming over with something that gleamed against her will in her eyes and her smile. Then deliberately she put out the light in her eyes but it was still there on her lips glimmered against her will in her faintly susceptible smile. . . ."

Vronski's mother who had been traveling with this lady, who is Anna, introduces her son. Oblonski appears. Then, as they are all going out, there is a stir. (Rodolfe saw Emma for the first time over a basin of blood. Vronski and Anna meet also over blood.)

"Several men ran by with frightened faces. The station master too ran by in that cap of his which was of such an unusual color [black and red]. Obviously something unusual had happened." They learned presently that a station guard either drunk or too much muffled up in the bitter frost, had not heard the train as it started to back out of the station and had been crushed. Anna asks if something could be done for his widow—he had a huge family—Vronski immediately glanced at her and said to his mother he would be back in a minute. We find later that he had given two hundred rubles for the man's family. (Mark the muffled-up man being crushed. Mark that his death establishes a kind of connection between Anna and Vronski. We shall need all these ingredients when we discuss the twin dream they have.)

"People coming and going were still talking of what had happened. 'What a horrible death,' said a man who was passing by. 'They say he was cut in two pieces.' 'On the contrary, I think it is the easiest, the quickest,' said another [and Anna marks this]. 'How is it no safety measures are taken?' said a third.

"Anna seated herself in the carriage and Steve saw with surprise that her lips were quivering, and she had difficulty restraining her tears. 'What is it, Anna?' he asked. 'It's an omen of evil.' 'Nonsense,' said Steve." And he goes on to say how glad he is that she has come.

The remaining important formative impressions for the dream come later. Anna has met Vronski again at the ball and danced with him — but that is all for the moment. Now she is on her way back to St. Petersburg, having reconciled Dolly and her brother Steve.

" 'Come, it's all over [her interest in Vronski], and thank God!' was the first thought that came to Anna, when she had said good-bye for the last time to her brother, who had stood blocking up the entrance to the car till the third bell rang. She sat down in her plush seat beside Annushka [her maid], and looked about her in the twilight of the [so-called] sleeping-car. 'Thank God! To-morrow I shall see Sergey and Aleks, and my life will go on in the old way, all nice and as usual.'

"Still in the same anxious frame of mind, as she had been all that day, Anna took pleasure in preparing herself for the journey with great care. With her small deft hands she opened and shut her red handbag, took out a little pillow, laid it on her knees, and carefully wrapping up her legs, made herself comfortable. An invalid lady was already settling down to sleep in her seat. Two other ladies began talking to Anna, and a stout elderly lady who was in the act of wrapping up her legs snugly made observations about the heating of the train [a crucial problem with that stove in the middle and all those icy drafts]. Anna said a few words, but not foreseeing any entertainment from the conversation, she asked Annushka to get out the small traveling lantern, hooked it onto the arm of her fauteuil, and took out from her bag a paper-knife and an English novel [of which the pages were uncut]. At first her reading made no progress. The fuss and bustle were disturbing [people walking down the passage along the doorless sections of that night coach]; then when the train had started, she could not help listening to the sound of the wheels; then her attention was distracted by the snow beating on the left window and sticking to the pane, and the sight of the muffled conductor passing by [an artistic touch this, the blizzard was blowing from the west; but it also goes well with Anna's one-sided mood, a moral loss of balance], and the conversations about the terrific blizzard raging outside. And so it went on and on: the same shaking and knocking, the same snow on the window, the same rapid transitions from steaming heat to cold and back again to heat, the same passing glimpses of the

CHAPTER XXIX

"COME, it's all over, and thank God!" was the first thought that came to Anna when she had said good-bye for the last time to her brother, who had stood blocking up the entrance to the carriage till the third bell rang. She sat down beside Annushka, and looked about her in the twilight of the sleeping-car. "Thank God! to-morrow I shall see Seryozha and Alexey Alexandrovich, and my life will go on in the old way, all nice and as usual."

Still in the same anxious frame of mind as she had been all that day, Anna took pleasure in arranging herself for the journey with great care. With her deft hands she opened and shut her little red bag, took out a ... laid it on her knees, and carefully wrapping up her feet, settled herself comfortably. An invalid lady had already settled down to sleep. Two other ladies began talking to Anna, and a stout elderly lady made observations about the heating of the train. Anna answered a few words, but not foreseeing any ... from the conversation, she asked Annushka to ... the lamp, hooked it onto the arm of her seat, and took from her bag a paper-knife and an English novel. At first her reading made no progress. The fuss and bustle were distracting; then when the train had started, she could not help listening to the ...; then the snow beating on the left window and sticking to the pane, and the sight of the muffled ... passing by, covered with snow on one side, ... distracted her attention. ... continually the same snow on the window, the same rapid ... the same ... heat to cold, and back again to heat, the same passing glimpses of the same figures in the ..., and the same voices, and Anna began to read and to understand what she read. ... was already dozing, the red bag on her lap, clutched by her broad hands, in gloves, of which one was torn ... Anna Arkadyevna read and understood; but

it was distasteful to follow the ... of other people's lives. She had too great a desire to live herself. If she read that the heroine of the novel was nursing a sick man, she longed to move with noiseless steps about the room of a sick man; if she read of a member of Parliament making a speech, she longed to be delivering the speech; if she read of how Lady Mary had ridden after the hounds, and ... her sister-in-law, and had surprised every one by her ... too wished to be doing the same. But there was no chance of doing anything; and ... the paper-knife in her ... hands, she forced herself to read.

The hero of the novel was already reaching his English happiness, a baronetcy and an estate, and Anna was feeling a desire to go with him to the estate, when she suddenly felt that she ought to feel ashamed, and that she was ashamed of the same thing. But what had he to be ashamed of? "What have I to be ashamed of?" she asked herself in injured surprise. She laid down the book and sank against the back of the chair, tightly gripping the paper-knife in both hands. There was nothing. She went over all her Moscow recollections. All were good, pleasant. She remembered the ball, remembered Vronsky and his face of slavish adoration, remembered all her conduct with him: there was nothing shameful. And for all that, at the same point in her memories, the feeling of shame was intensified, as though some inner voice, just at the point when she thought of Vronsky, were saying to her, "Warm, very warm, hot." "Well, what is it?" she said to herself resolutely, shifting her seat in the ... "What does it mean? Am I afraid to look it straight in the face? Why, what is it? Can it be that between me and this officer boy there exist, or can exist, any other relations than such as are common with every acquaintance?" She laughed contemptuously and took up her book again; but now she was definitely unable to follow ... She passed the paper-knife over the window-pane, then laid its smooth, cool surface to her cheek, and almost laughed aloud at the feeling of delight that all at once without cause came over her. She felt as though her nerves were strings being strained tighter same figures [conductors, stove-tenders] in the shifting dusk, and the same voices, and Anna began to read and to understand what she read. Her maid was already dozing, with her mistress's red bag in her lap, clutching it with her broad hands, in woolen gloves, of which one was torn at a finger tip [one of these little flaws that correspond to a flaw in Anna's own mood]. Anna read but she found it distasteful to follow the shadows of other people's lives. She had too great a desire to live herself. If she read that the heroine of the novel was nursing a sick man, she longed to move herself with noiseless steps about the room of a sick man; if she read of a member of Parliament making a speech, she longed to be delivering the speech herself; if she read of how Lady Mary had ridden to the hounds, and had teased her sister-in-law, and had surprised everyone by her pluck, Anna too wished to be doing the same. But there was no chance of doing anything; and she toyed with the smooth ivory knife in her small hands, and forced herself to go on reading. [Was she a good reader from our point of view? Does her emotional participation in the life of the book remind one of another little lady? Of Emma?].

"The hero of the novel was about to reach his English happiness, a baronetcy and an estate, when she suddenly felt that he ought to feel somehow ashamed, and that she was ashamed, too [she identifies the man in the book with Vronski]. But what had he to be ashamed of? 'What have *I* to be ashamed of?' she asked herself in injured surprise. She laid down the book and sank against the back of her fauteuil, tightly gripping the knife in both hands. There was nothing. She went over all her Moscow impressions. All was good, pleasant. She remembered the ball, remembered Vronski's face of slavish adoration, remembered all her conduct with him: there was nothing shameful. And for all that, at this point in her memories, the feeling of shame was intensified, as though some inner voice, just at that point when she thought of Vronski, were saying to her, 'Warm, very warm, hot.' [In a game where you hide an object and hint at the right direction by these thermal exclamations — and mark that the warm and the cold are alternating in the night-coach too.] 'What is it?' she asked herself, shifting her position in the fauteuil. 'What does it mean? Can it be that between me and that officer boy there exist, or can exist, any other relations than those of ordinary acquaintance?' She gave a little snort of contempt and took up her book again; but now she was definitely unable to follow the story. She passed the ivory paper-knife over the window-pane, then

---

Pages from Nabokov's teaching copy of *Anna Karenin*.

---

laid its smooth, cool surface [contrast again of warm and cold] to her cheek, and almost laughed aloud at the feeling of delight that all at once without cause came over her [her sensuous nature takes over]. She felt as though her nerves were violin strings being strained tighter and tighter on their pegs. She felt her eyes opening wider and wider, her fingers and toes twitched, something within her oppressed her, while all shapes and sounds seemed in the uncertain half-light to strike her with unaccustomed vividness. Moments of doubt were continuously coming upon her, when she was uncertain whether the train was going forwards or backwards [compare this to an important metaphor in 'Ivan Ilyich'], or was standing still altogether; whether it was Annushka at her side or a stranger. 'What's that on the arm of the chair, a fur cloak or some big furry beast? And what am I myself? Myself or somebody else?' She was afraid of giving way to this state of oblivion. But something drew her towards it. She sat up to rouse herself, removed her lap robe and took off the cape of her woolen dress. For a moment she regained full consciousness and realized that the working man who had come into the car, wearing a long nankeen coat with one button missing from it [another flaw in the pattern of her mood], was the stove-heater, that he was looking at the thermometer, that it was the wind and snow bursting in after him [telltale flaw] at the door of the car; but then everything was blurred again. That working man seemed to be gnawing at something in the wall, the old lady began stretching her legs the whole length of the section and filling it with a black cloud; then there was a fearful creaking and knocking, as though someone were being torn apart [mark this half-dream]; then there was a blinding dazzle of red fire before her eyes and a wall seemed to rise up and hide everything. Anna felt as though she had fallen through the floor. But it was not terrible, it was delightful. The voice of a man muffled up [note this too] and covered with snow shouted something in her ear. She pulled herself together; she realized that it was a station and that this muffled up man was the conductor. She asked her maid to hand her the cape she had taken off and her warm kerchief, put them on, and moved towards the door.

" 'Do you wish to go out, Ma'am?' asked the maid.

" 'Yes, I want a little air. It's very hot in here.' And she opened the door leading to the open platform of the car. The driving snow and the wind rushed to meet her and struggled with her over the door. But she enjoyed the struggle. [Compare this with the wind struggling with Lyovin at the end of the book.]

"She opened the door and went out. The wind seemed as though lying in wait for her [again the pathetic fallacy about the wind: emotions ascribed to objects by man in distress]; with a gleeful whistle it tried to snatch her up and bear her off, but she clung to the cold iron post at the car's end, and holding her skirt, got down onto the station platform and stood on the lee side of the car. The wind had been powerful on the open end of the car, but on the station platform, sheltered by the cars, there was a lull. . . .

"But then again the raging tempest rushed whistling between the wheels of the cars, and around the corner of the station along its pillars. The cars, pillars, people, everything that was to be seen was covered with snow on one side and was getting more and more thickly covered there. [Now mark the following ingredient of the later dream.] The bent shadow of a man glided by at her feet, and she heard sounds of a hammer upon iron. 'Hand over that telegram!' came an angry voice out of the stormy darkness on the other side. . . . Muffled figures ran by covered with snow. Two gentlemen with lighted cigarettes passed by her. She drew one more deep breath of the fresh air, and had just put her hand out of her muff to take hold of the car platform post and get back into the car, when another man in a military overcoat, quite close beside her, stepped between her and the flickering light of a station lamp. She turned and immediately recognized Vronski. Putting his hand to the peak of his cap, he bowed to her and asked, Was there anything she wanted? Could he be of any service to her? She peered for a few seconds at him without answering, and, in spite of the shadow in which he was standing, she saw, or fancied she saw, the expression of his face and his eyes. It was again that expression of respectful ecstasy which had made such an impression upon her the day before. . . .

" 'I didn't know you were on the train. Why are you here?' she said, letting fall the hand with which she had grasped the iron post. And irrepressible lovely joy lit up her face.

" 'Why am I here?' he said, looking straight into her eyes. 'You know why. I am on this train to be where you are. I can't help it.'

"At that moment the wind, as if surmounting all obstacles, sent the snow flying from the car roofs, and clanked some sheet of iron it had loosened, while the throaty whistle of the engine roared in front, plaintively and gloomily. . . .

"And clutching at the cold post, she clambered up the steps and got rapidly into the hallway of the car. . . .

"At Petersburg, so soon as the train stopped and she got out, the first person that attracted her attention was her husband. 'Oh, mercy! why have his ears become like that?' she thought, looking at his cold and imposing figure, and especially at his ears whose cartilages propped up the brim of his round hat of black felt."

———————

"[Lyovin] walked along the path towards the skating-ground, and kept saying to himself—'You mustn't be excited, you must be calm. What's the matter with you? What do you want? Be quiet, stupid,' he conjured his heart. And the more he tried to compose himself, the more breathless he found himself. An acquaintance met him and called him by his name, but Lyovin did not even recognize him. He went towards the ice-slopes for coasting whence came the clank of the chains of sleighs as they were dragged up, the rumble of the descending sleighs, and the sounds of merry voices. He walked on a few steps, and the skating-ground lay open before his eyes, and at once, amidst all the skaters, he recognized her.

"He knew she was there by the rapture and the terror that seized on his heart. She was standing talking to a lady at the opposite end of the skating-rink. There was nothing striking either in her dress or in her attitude. But for Lyovin she was as easy to find in that crowd, as a wild rose among nettles. . . .

————

"On that day of the week and at that time of day people of one set, all acquainted with one another, used to meet on the ice. There were crack skaters there, showing off their skill, and beginners behind chairs on wooden runners clinging to the backs of these gliding chairs and scuttling along with timid awkward movements; boys, and elderly people skating for their health. They seemed to Lyovin an elect band of blissful beings because they were here, near her. All the skaters, it seemed, with perfect indifference, caught up with her, overtook her, even spoke to her, and, quite apart from her presence, enjoyed the excellent ice and the fine weather.

"Nikolay Shcherbatski, Kitty's cousin, in a short jacket and tight trousers, was sitting on a bench with his skates on. Upon seeing Lyovin, he cried to him:

" 'Ah, the best skater in Russia! Been here long? First-rate ice—put on your skates, old fellow.'

" 'I haven't got my skates with me,' Lyovin answered, marveling at this boldness and ease in her presence, and not for one second losing sight of her, though he did not look at her. He felt that an invisible sun was coming near him. She was at the bend of the rink and, holding together her slender feet in their blunt-toed high skating shoes, with obvious apprehension she glided in his direction. [Ridiculous—Garnett has Kitty turn her toes out.] A young boy in Russian garb, violently swinging his arms and bending low towards the ice, was in the act of overtaking her. She skated uncertainly; taking her hands out of the little muff, that hung on a cord round her neck, she held them ready for emergency, and looking towards Lyovin, whom she had recognized, she smiled at him, and at her own fears. When she had got round the turn, she gave herself a springy push-off with one foot, and skated straight up to her cousin.

Clutching at his arm, she nodded smiling to Lyovin. She was lovelier than he had imagined her. . . . But what always struck him in her as something unlooked for, was the expression of her eyes, mild, calm, and truthful. . . .

" 'Have you been here long?' she said, shaking hands with him. 'Thank you,' she added, as he picked up the handkerchief that had fallen out of her muff. [Tolstoy keeps a keen eye on his characters. He makes them speak and move—but their speech and motion produce their own reaction in the world he has made for them. Is that clear? It is.]

" 'I didn't know you could skate, and skate so well.'

"She looked at him attentively as though wishing to find out the cause of his confusion.

" 'Your praise is worth having,' she said. 'They say you are a crack skater,' and with her little black-gloved hand she brushed off the little spikes of hoar frost which had fallen upon her muff. [Again Tolstoy's cold eye.]

" 'Yes, I used once to skate with passion,' Lyovin answered. 'I wanted to reach perfection.'

" 'You do everything with passion, I think,' she said smiling. 'I should so like to see how you skate. Put on skates, and let us skate together.'

" 'Skate together! Can that be possible?' thought Lyovin, gazing at her.

" 'I'll put them on directly,' he said.

"And he went off to get skates.

" 'It's a long while since we've seen you here, sir,' said the attendant, supporting his foot, and screwing on the skate to the heel. 'There have been no first-rate skaters among the gentlemen since your time. Will that be all right?' said he, tightening the strap."

A little later, "one of the young men, the best of the skaters after Lyovin's time, came out of the coffee-house in his skates, with a cigarette in his mouth. Taking a run, he dashed down the ice crusted steps in his skates, bouncing noisily. He flew down, and without even changing the relaxed position of his arms, skated away over the ice.

" 'Ah, that's a new trick!' said Lyovin, and he promptly ran up to the top to do this new trick.

" 'Don't break your neck! It needs practice!' Kitty's cousin shouted after him.

"Lyovin went on the porch, and running from above to gain impetus, he dashed down, preserving his balance in this unwonted motion with his arms. On the last step he stumbled, but barely touching the ice with his hand, with a violent effort recovered himself, and skated off, laughing."

We are at a dinner party two years after Lyovin had been rejected by Kitty, a dinner party arranged by Oblonski. First let us retranslate the little passage about a slippery mushroom.

" 'You have killed a bear, I've been told!' said Kitty, trying assiduously to spear with her fork a slippery preserved mushroom, every little poke setting the lace quivering over her white arm. [The brilliant eye of the great writer always noting what his puppets are up to after he has given them the power to live.] 'Are there bears on your place?' she added, turning her charming little head to him and smiling."

We come now to the famous chalk scene. After dinner Kitty and Lyovin are for a minute in a separate part of the room.

"Kitty, going up to a card-table, sat down, and, taking up the chalk, began drawing concentric circles upon the immaculate green cloth.

"They began again on the subject that had been started at dinner—the liberty and occupations of women. Lyovin shared Dolly's opinion that a girl who did not marry should find some occupation suitable for a lady, in her own family. . . .

"A silence followed. She was still drawing with the chalk on the table. Her eyes were shining with a soft light. Under the influence of her mood, he was pervaded with an increasing feeling of happiness.

" 'Akh! I have scrawled all over the table!' she said, and laying down the chalk, she made a movement as though to get up.

" 'What! Shall I be left alone—without her?' he thought with horror, and he took the chalk. 'Wait a minute,' he said, 'I've long wanted to ask you one thing.'

"He looked straight into her friendly, though frightened eyes.

" 'Please ask it.'

" 'Here,' he said; and he wrote the initial letters w, y, s, n, d, y, m, n. These letters meant, 'When you said no, did you mean never?' There seemed no likelihood that she could make out this complicated sentence; but he looked at her as though his life depended on her understanding the words. She glanced at him seriously, then puckered her brow and began to read. Once or twice she stole a look at him, as though asking him, 'Is it what I think?'

" 'I understand,' she said, flushing a little.

" 'What is this word?' he said, pointing to the n that stood for *never*.

" 'It means *never*,' she said; 'but that's not true!'

"He quickly rubbed out what he had written, gave her the chalk, and stood up. She wrote, *t*, *i*, *c*, *n*, *a*, *d*. . . . It meant, 'Then I could not answer differently.'

"He glanced at her questioningly, timidly.

" 'Only *then*?'

" 'Yes,' her smile answered.

" 'And now?' he asked.

" 'Well, read this,' she said. She wrote the initial letters *f*, *a*, *f*. This meant, 'Forget and forgive.' "

All this is a little far fetched. Although, no doubt, love may work wonders and bridge the abyss between minds and present cases of tender telepathy— still such detailed thought-reading, even in Russian, is not quite convincing. However, the gestures are charming and the atmosphere of the scene artistically true.

Tolstoy stood for the natural life. Nature, alias God, had decreed that the human female should experience more pain in childbirth than, say, a porcupine or a whale. Therefore Tolstoy was violently opposed to the elimination of this pain.

In *Look* magazine, a poor relation of *Life*, of April 8, 1952, there is a series of photos under the heading, "I Photographed my Baby's Birth." A singularly unattractive baby smirks in a corner of the page. Says the caption: Clicking her own camera as she lies on the delivery table, Mrs. A. H. Heusinkveld, a photography-writer (whatever that is) of Cedar Rapids, Iowa, records (says the caption) these extraordinary views of the birth of her first baby—from the early labor pains to the baby's first cry.

What does she take in the way of pictures? For instance: "Husband [wearing a handpainted philistine tie, with a dejected expression on his simple face] visits wife in the midst of her pains" or "Mrs. Heusinkveld shoots Sister Mary who sprays patient with disinfectants."

Tolstoy would have violently objected to all this.

Except for a little opium, and that did not help much, no anaesthetics were used in those days for relieving the pains of childbirth. The year is 1875, and all over the world women were delivered in the same way as two thousand years ago. Tolstoy's theme here is a double one, first, the beauty of nature's drama; and second, its mystery and terror as perceived by Lyovin. Modern methods of confinement—anaesthetics and hospitalization—would have made this great chapter 15 of part seven impossible, and the dulling of natural pain would have seemed quite wrong to Tolstoy the Christian. Kitty was having her baby at home, of course, Lyovin wanders about the house.

"He did not know whether it was late or early. The candles had all burned out. . . . He sat listening to the doctor's small talk. . . . Suddenly there came an unearthly shriek from Kitty's room. The shriek was so awful that he did not even start but gazed in terrified inquiry at the doctor. The doctor put his head on one side, listened, and smiled approvingly. Everything was so extraordinary that nothing could strike Lyovin as strange. . . . Presently he tiptoed to the bedroom, edged around the midwife [Elizaveta] and Kitty's mother, and stood at Kitty's pillow. The scream had subsided but there was some change now. What it was he did not see and did not understand, and had no wish to see or understand. . . . Kitty's swollen and agonized face, a tress of hair clinging to her moist temple, was turned to him. Her eyes sought his eyes, her lifted hands asked for his hands. Clutching his cold hands in her hot ones, she began squeezing them to her face.

" 'Don't go, don't go! I am not afraid, I am not afraid. Mamma, take off my earrings, they bother me. . . .' [List these earrings with the handkerchief, the frost on the glove, and other little objects that Kitty handles in the course of the novel.] Then suddenly she pushed him away. 'Oh, this is awful, I am dying, go away,' she shrieked. . . .

"Lyovin clutched at his head and ran out of the room.

" 'It's all right, everything is all right,' Dolly called after him. [She had gone through it seven times herself.]

" 'But,' thought Lyovin, 'they might say what they liked.' He knew now that all was over. He stood in the next room, his head leaning against the door-post, and heard someone emitting shrieks, howls, such as he had never heard before and he knew that this howling thing had been Kitty. But now he had long ago ceased to wish for the child, by now he loathed this child. He did not even wish for *her* life now. All he longed for was the end of this awful anguish.

" 'Doctor, what is it, what is it? Good Lord!' he said, snatching at the doctor's arm as the latter came out.

" 'Well,' said the doctor, 'it's the end,' and the doctor's face was so grave as he said it that Lyovin took the end as meaning her death." [Of course, what the doctor meant was: it will be over in a minute now.]

Now comes the part that stresses the beauty of this natural phenomenon. Mark incidentally that the whole history of literary fiction as an evolutionary process may be said to be a gradual probing of deeper and deeper layers of life. It is quite impossible to imagine either Homer in the ninth century B.C. or

Cervantes in the seventeenth century of our era—it is quite impossible to imagine them describing in such wonderful detail childbirth. The question is not whether certain events or emotions are or are not suitable ethically or esthetically. The point I want to make is that the artist, like the scientist, in the process of evolution of art and science, is always casting around, understanding a little more than his predecessor, penetrating further with a keener and more brilliant eye—and this is the artistic result.

"Beside himself he hurried to the bedroom. The first thing he saw was the face of the midwife. It was even more frowning and stern. Kitty's face was not there. In the place where it had been was something that was fearful in its strained distortion and in the sounds that came from it. [Now comes the beauty of the thing.] He fell down with his head on the wooden framework of the bed, feeling that his heart was bursting. The awful scream never paused, it became still more awful, and as though it had reached the utmost limit of terror, suddenly it ceased. Lyovin could not believe his ears, but there could be no doubt; the scream had ceased and he heard a subdued stir and bustle, and hurried breathing, and her voice, gasping, alive, tender, and blissful, uttered softly, 'It's over!'

"He lifted his head. Exhausted, with her hands lying on the quilt, most lovely and serene, she looked at him in silence and tried to smile, and could not.

"And suddenly, from the mysterious and awful far-away world in which he had been living for the last twenty-two hours, Lyovin felt himself all in an instant borne back to the old every-day world, now flooded by such a radiance of happiness that he could not bear it. The strained strings snapped, sobs and tears of joy which he had never foreseen rose up with such violence that his whole body shook. . . . Falling on his knees before the bed, he held his wife's hand before his lips and kissed it, and the hand, with a weak movement of the fingers, responded to his kiss. [The whole chapter is magnificent imagery. What slight figures of speech there are, shade into direct description. But now we are ready for a summation by means of a simile.] And meanwhile, there at the foot of the bed, in the deft hands of the midwife, like a flickering light on the oil of a lamp, there flickered the life of a human being which had never existed before and which would now . . . live and create in its own image."

We shall mark later the image of the light in connection with Anna's death, in the chapter of her suicide. Death is the delivery of the soul. Thus childbirth and soulbirth (death) are expressed in the same terms of mystery, terror, and beauty. Kitty's delivery and Anna's death meet at this point.

The birth of faith in Lyovin, the pangs of faith birth.

"Lyovin with big steps strode along the highroad, absorbed not so much in his tangled thoughts as in his spiritual condition, unlike anything he had experienced before. . . .

[A peasant with whom he had been talking had said of another peasant that he—that other peasant—lived for his belly, and then had said that one must not live for one's belly, but for truth, for God, for one's soul.]

" 'Can I have found a solution for myself, can my sufferings be over?' thought Lyovin striding along the dusty road. . . . He was breathless with emotion. He turned off the road into the forest and sat down on the grass in the shade of an aspen. He took his hat off his hot head and lay propped on his elbow in the lush fluffy woodland grass [which Mrs. Garnett has trampled upon with flat feet: it is not 'feathery grass.']

" 'Yes, I must make it clear to myself,' he thought as he followed the movements of a small green bug creeping up a blade of witch-grass: it was interrupted in its progress by a leaf of gout-wort. 'What have I discovered?' he asked himself [referring to his spiritual condition] and bending aside the leaf out of the beetle's way and turning down another blade of grass to help it cross over onto it. 'What is it makes me glad? What have I discovered?'

" 'I have only found out what I knew all along. I have been set free from falsity, I have found the Master.' "

But what we must mark is not so much the *ideas*. After all we should always bear in mind that literature is not a pattern of *ideas* but a pattern of *images*. Ideas do not matter much in comparison to a book's imagery and magic. What interests us here is not what Lyovin thought, or what Leo thought, but that little bug that expresses so neatly the turn, the switch, the gesture of thought.

We now come to the last chapters of the Lyovin line—to Lyovin's final conversion—but again let us keep an eye on the imagery and leave the ideas to pile up as they please. The word, the expression, the image is the true function of literature. *Not* ideas.

At Lyovin's estate the family and the guests had been on an outing. Then it is time to go back.

"Kitty's father and Sergey, Lyovin's half brother, got into the small cart and

Nabokov's notes on *Anna Karenin*, part eight, chapter 12, with his caution that "literature is *not* a pattern of *ideas* . . ."

drove off; storm clouds were gathering; the rest of the party hastened homeward on foot.

"But the storm-rack, now white, then black, moved upon them so quickly that they had to walk fast to get home before the rain. The foremost clouds, lowering and as black as soot-laden smoke, moved with extraordinary swiftness over the sky. The party was two hundred paces from the house, the wind of the storm was already blowing and now every second the downpour might come.

"The children ran ahead with frightened and gleeful yells. Dolly, struggling as best she could with her skirts that clung round her legs, was more running than walking, her eyes fixed on the children. The men holding onto their hats strode with long steps beside her. They were just at the steps of the porch when a big raindrop fell and splattered on the rim of the iron gutter. The children ran into the shelter of the house talking excitedly.

" 'Is my wife home?' Lyovin asked of the housekeeper who had met them in the hall with kerchiefs and lap-robes that she was about to send to the picnickers.

" 'We thought she was with you,' she said.

" 'And the baby?'

" 'They must be all in the grove, the nurse too.'

"Lyovin snatched up the lap-robes and coats and ran towards the grove.

"In that brief interval of time the thunderhead had engulfed the sun so completely that the day was as dark as during an eclipse. Stubbornly the wind tried to stop him as though insisting on its rights [the pathetic fallacy of the wind, as on Anna's train trip; but direct imagery will now turn into a comparison], and tearing the leaves and flowers off lime-trees, and turning back the foliage of the white birch branches so as to reveal, hideously and strangely, their nakedness, the wind twisted and tossed everything to one side—acacias, flowers, burdocks, long grass, tall tree-tops. The peasant girls working in the garden ran shrieking into the shelter of the servants' quarters. The downpour had already flung its livid veil over all the distant forest and over half the near fields, and was rapidly swooping down upon the grove. The wet of the rain as it spurted up in tiny drops upon touching the ground could be smelled in the air. Bending his head* and struggling with the wind that strove to snatch the wraps he was carrying away from him [pathetic fallacy continued], Lyovin was nearing the grove, and had just caught sight of something white from behind an oak-tree, when there was a sudden flash, the whole earth

---

*The Garnett translation reads: "Holding his head bent down before him," on which VN fastidiously notes, "Mark that Mrs. Garnett has decapitated the man." Ed.

seemed on fire, and the sky seemed to split in two. Opening his blinded eyes, Lyovin gazed through the thick veil of rain and to his horror the first thing he saw was the uncannily changed position of the green crest of the familiar oak-tree in the middle of the grove. [Compare the scene of the race, Vronski feeling "his changed position" when his horse broke its back while jumping an obstacle in the race.]

" 'Can it have been struck?' he hardly had time to think when, moving more and more rapidly, the foliage of the oak vanished behind other trees, and he heard the crash of the great tree falling upon the others.

"The blaze of lightning, the sound of thunder and the sudden chill that ran through him were all merged for him in one pang of terror. 'My God, my God, not on them,' he said.

"And though he thought at once how senseless was his prayer that the falling oak should not have killed them since it had already fallen, he repeated it, knowing that he could do nothing better than utter this senseless prayer. . . .

"They were at the other end of the grove, under an old lime-tree; they were calling him. Two figures in dark dresses (the dresses had been of a light color when they had started out)* stood bending over something. They were Kitty and the nurse. The rain had almost stopped. It was beginning to clear up when he reached them. The nurse's skirt was dry but Kitty was drenched, and her soaked clothes clung to her. Both stood bending in the same position as when the storm broke, over a baby carriage protected by a green umbrella. 'Alive? Safe? Thank God,' he said. His soaked boots slipped and sloshed in the puddles as he ran up to them. . . . [He was angry with his wife.] They gathered up the baby's wet diapers." [Wet from the rain? This is not clear. Note how Jove's shower has been transformed into a beloved babe's wet diaper. The forces of nature have surrendered to the power of family life. The pathetic fallacy has been replaced by the smile of a happy family.]

The Baby's Bath: "With one hand Kitty was supporting the head of the chubby baby: he was floating on his back in the bath and diddling his legs. With her other hand she squeezed the sponge over him, and the muscles of her forearm contracted in measured motion. . . ." (Again mistranslated by Garnett, who leaves out all reference to the muscles.)

The nurse supporting him with one hand under his little belly, lifted him out of the bath, poured a jugful of water over him, he was wrapped in towels, dried and after some piercing screams handed over to his mother.

---

*VN interjects: "The point of this is of course messed up by Garnett," who writes, "they had been light summer dresses when they started out." Ed.

" 'Well, I am glad you are beginning to love him,' said Kitty to her husband, when she had settled comfortably in her usual place, with the baby at her breast. 'You remember you said you had no feeling for him.'

" 'Really? Did I say that? Oh—I only said I was sort of disappointed.'

" 'In him?'

" 'Not in him but well—in my own feeling. I had somehow expected more, some new delightful emotion, a big surprise, and then instead—disgust, pity.'

"She listened attentively looking at him over the baby while she put back on her slender fingers the rings she had taken off while giving the baby his bath. . . . [Tolstoy never misses a gesture.]

"Lyovin on leaving the nursery and finding himself alone,* went back in thought to the blurry something in his mind. Instead of going into the drawing-room where he heard voices, he stopped on the terrace and leaning his elbows on the parapet gazed at the sky. It was quite dark now. The south was free of clouds which had drifted on towards the opposite side. There were flashes of lightning and distant rumbles from that quarter. He listened to the measured drip-drip from the lime-trees in the garden and looked at the triangle of stars he knew so well and the milky way with all its ramifications. [Now comes a delightful comparison to be marked with love and foresight.] At each flash the Milky Way and even the bright stars vanished but as soon as the lightning died away, they reappeared in their places as though a hand had thrown them back with careful aim. [Is this delightful comparison clear?]

" 'Well, what is perplexing me?' Lyovin said to himself. 'I am wondering about the relationship to God of all the different religions of all mankind. But why do I bother? [Why indeed, murmurs the good reader.] To me individually, personally, to my own heart has been revealed a knowledge beyond all doubt, and unattainable by reason, and here am I obstinately trying to use my reason. . . . The question of other creeds and their relations to Divinity I have no right to decide, no possibility of deciding.'

" 'Oh, you have not gone in,' said Kitty's voice all at once as she went by through the terrace on her way to the drawing-room. 'What is the matter?' she said, looking intently at his face in the starlight.

"But she could not have seen his face if a flash of lightning had not hidden the stars and revealed it. In that flash she saw his face clearly and seeing him happy and calm, she smiled at him. [This is the functional after effect of the delightful comparison we have noticed. It helps to clear matters.]

" 'She understands,' he thought. 'Shall I tell her? Yes.' But at that moment

*In a note VN objects to Mrs. Garnett's phrasing of this opening, "Going out of the nursery and being alone again." Ed.

she began speaking. 'Do me a favor,' she said. 'Go into that guest room and see if they have fixed it right for Sergey [his half brother]. I can't very well. See if they have put the new wash-stand there.'

" 'O.K.,' said Lyovin and gave her a kiss.

" 'No, I had better not speak of it,' he thought. 'It is strictly for me alone, vitally for me alone, and not to be put into words.

" 'This new feeling has not changed me, has not made me happy as I had dreamt it would in regard to that feeling for my child. No surprise in this either. But faith or no faith this feeling has come to stay.'

" 'I shall go on, in the same old way, losing my temper with the coachman, falling into angry discussions, being tactless. There will still be the same wall of reticence between my soul and other people, even between me and my wife. I shall still go on blaming her for my own fears and regretting it. I shall still be as unable to understand with my reason why I pray, and I shall still go on praying; but my whole life now, apart from anything that may happen to me, every minute of it is no longer meaningless as it was before. It has acquired now the positive meaning of good which *I* have the power to give it.' "

Thus the book ends, on a mystic note which seems to me rather a part of Tolstoy's own diary than that of the character he created. This is the background of the book, the Milky Way of the book, the Lyovin-Kitty family life line. We shall presently turn to the pattern of iron and blood, to the Vronski-Anna pattern that stands in awful relief against this star-dusted sky.

Although he is mentioned earlier, Vronski makes his first appearance in part one, chapter 14, at the Shcherbatskis. Incidentally, it is here that starts an interesting little line, the line of "spiritualism," table tilting, entranced mediums, and so on, a fashionable pastime in those days. Vronski in a light-hearted mood wishes to try out this fashionable fad; but much later, in chapter 22 of part seven, it is, curiously enough, owing to the mediumistic visions of a French quack who has found patrons among Petersburg society people, it is owing to him that Karenin decides not to give Anna a divorce — and a telegram to that effect during a final period of tragic tension between Anna and Vronski helps to build up the mood that leads to her suicide.

Some time before Vronski met Anna, a young official in her husband's department had confessed his love to her and she had gaily relayed it to her husband; but now, from the very first look exchanged with Vronski at the ball, a fateful mystery enfolds her life. She says nothing to her sister-in-law about Vronski's giving a sum of money for the widow of the killed railway guard, an act which establishes, through death as it were, a kind of secret link between her and her future lover. And further, Vronski has called on the Shcherbatskis my life now, my whole life, apart from anything that can happen to me, every minute of it is no ~~more~~ longer meaningless, as it was before, but it has the positive meaning of goodness, which I have the power to put into it."

Thus the book ends on a mystic note
' which is rather part of Tolstoy own life
than that of a character he ~~had~~ created.

THE END

I Now is this the background of the book,
the milky way of the book — it
might be a good idea to call
the Levin-Kitty line the milky way.

~~the greater goal~~ We shall now see the
~~what~~ pattern of iron and blood
that stands in relief against ~~this~~ this
lucid
starcloth sky.

although
I shall have some more to say about Levin
in connect with agriculture theme in
the book

the evening before the ball at the exact moment when Anna remembers so vividly her child from whom she is separated for the few days she has spent in Moscow smoothing her brother's troubles. It is the fact of her having this beloved child which will later constantly interfere with her passion for Vronski.

The scenes of the horse race in the middle chapters of part two contain all kinds of deliberate symbolic implications. Firstly there is the Karenin slant. In the pavilion at the races a military man, Karenin's social superior, a high-placed general or a member of the royal family, kids Karenin, saying — and you, you're not racing; upon which Karenin replies deferentially and ambiguously, "the race I am running is a harder one," a phrase with a double meaning, since it could simply mean that a statesman's duties are more difficult than competitive sport, but also may hint at Karenin's delicate position as a betrayed husband who must conceal his plight and find a narrow course of action between his marriage and his career. And it is also to be marked that the breaking of the horse's back coincides with Anna's revealing her unfaithfulness to her husband.

A far deeper emblematism is contained in Vronski's actions at that eventful horse race. In breaking Frou-Frou's back and in breaking Anna's life, Vronski is performing analogous acts. You will notice the same "lower jaw trembling" repeated in both scenes: the scene of Anna's metaphysical fall when he is standing over her adulterous body, and the scene of Vronski's physical fall when he is standing over his dying horse. The tone of the whole chapter of the race with the building up of its pathetic climax is echoed in the chapters relating to Anna's suicide. Vronski's explosion of passionate anger — anger with his beautiful, helpless, delicate-necked mare whom he has killed by a false move, by letting himself down in the saddle at the wrong moment of the jump — is especially striking in contrast to the description that Tolstoy gives a few pages earlier, when Vronski is getting ready for the races — "he was always cool and self-controlled" — and then the terrific way he curses at the stricken mare.

"Frou-Frou lay gasping before him, bending her head back and gazing at him with her exquisite eye. Still unable to realize what had happened, Vronski tugged at his mare's reins. Again she struggled like a fish, and making the

---

The final page in Nabokov's teaching copy of *Anna Karenin*, with his concluding comments.

---

saddle flaps creak, she freed her front legs but unable to lift her rump, she quivered all over and again fell on her side. With a face hideous with passion, his lower jaw trembling and his cheeks white, Vronski kicked her with his heel in the stomach and again fell to tugging at the rein. She did not stir, but thrusting her nose into the ground, she simply gazed at her master with her speaking eye.*

" 'A—a—a!' moaned Vronski, clutching at his head. 'Ah! what have I done! The race lost! And my fault! shameful, unpardonable! And this poor, lovely creature killed by me!' "

Anna almost died giving birth to Vronski's child.

I shall not say much about Vronski's attempt to kill himself after the scene with Anna's husband at her bedside. It is not a satisfactory scene. Of course, Vronski's motives in shooting himself may be understood. The chief one was injured pride, since in the moral sense Anna's husband had shown himself, and had seemed to be, the better man. Anna herself had called her husband a saint. Vronski shoots himself much for the same reason as that for which an insulted gentleman of his day would have challenged the insulter to a duel, not to kill his man, but on the contrary to force him to fire at him, the insulted one. Exposing himself to the other man's forced fire would have wiped away the insult. If killed, Vronski would have been revenged by the other's remorse. If still alive, Vronski would have discharged his pistol in the air, sparing the other man's life and thus humiliating him. This is the basic idea of honor behind duels, although of course there have been cases when both men were out to kill each other. Unfortunately, Karenin would not have accepted a duel, and Vronski has to fight his duel with his own self, has to expose himself to his own fire. In other words, Vronski's attempt at suicide is a question of honor, a kind of hara-kiri as understood in Japan. From this general point of view of theoretic morals this chapter is all right.

But it is not all right from the artistic viewpoint, from the point of view of the novel's structure. It is not really a necessary event in the novel; it interferes with the dream-death theme that runs through the book; it interferes technically with the beauty and freshness of Anna's suicide. If I am not mistaken, it seems to me that there is not a single retrospective reference to Vronski's attempted suicide in the chapter dealing with Anna's journey to her death. And this is not natural: Anna ought to have remembered it, somehow, in connec-

---

*Mrs. Garnett translates, "gazed at her master with her speaking eyes," to which VN adds the note in his teaching copy, "A horse can't look at you with both eyes, Mrs. Garnett." Ed.

tion with her own fatal plans. Tolstoy as an artist felt, I am sure, that the Vronski suicide theme had a different tonality, a different tint and tone, was in a different key and style, and could not be linked up artistically with Anna's last thoughts.

The Double Nightmare: A dream, a nightmare, a double nightmare plays an especially important part in the book. I say "*double* nightmare" because both Anna and Vronski see the same dream. (This monogrammatic interconnection of two individual brain-patterns is not unknown in so-called real life.) You will also mark that Anna and Vronski, in that flash of telepathy, undergo technically the same experience as Kitty and Lyovin do when reading each other's thoughts as they chalk initial letters on the green cloth of a card table. But in Kitty-Lyovin's case the brain-bridge is a light and luminous and lovely structure leading towards vistas of tenderness and fond duties and profound bliss. In the Anna and Vronski case, however, the link is an oppressive and hideous nightmare with dreadful prophetic implications.

As some of you may have guessed, I am politely but firmly opposed to the Freudian interpretation of dreams with its stress on symbols which may have some reality in the Viennese doctor's rather drab and pedantic mind but do not necessarily have any in the minds of individuals unconditioned by modern psychoanalytics. Hence I am going to discuss the nightmare theme of our book, in terms of the book, in terms of Tolstoy's literary art. And this is what I plan to do: I shall go with my little lantern through those murky passages of the book where three phases of Anna's and Vronski's nightmare may be traced. First: I shall trace the formation of that nightmare from various parts and ingredients that are found in Anna's and Vronski's conscious life. Second: I shall discuss the dream itself as dreamed both by Anna and Vronski at a critical moment of their intertwined lives — and I shall show that although the ingredients of the twinned dream were not all the same with Anna and with Vronski, the result, the nightmare itself, is the same, although somewhat more vivid and detailed in Anna's case. And third: I shall show the connection between the nightmare and Anna's suicide, when she realizes that what the horrible little man in her dream was doing over the iron is what her sinful life has done to her soul — battering and destroying it — and that from the very beginning the idea of death was present in the background of her passion, in the wings of her love, and that now she will follow the direction of her dream and have a train, a thing of iron, destroy her body.

So let us start by studying the ingredients of the double nightmare, Anna's and Vronski's. What do I mean by the ingredients of a dream? Let me make this quite clear. A dream is a show—a theatrical piece staged within the brain in a subdued light before a somewhat muddleheaded audience. The show is generally a very mediocre one, carelessly performed, with amateur actors and haphazard props and a wobbly backdrop. But what interests us for the moment about our dreams is that the actors and the props and the various parts of the setting are borrowed by the dream producer from our conscious life. A number of recent impressions and a few older ones are more or less carelessly and hastily mixed on the dim stage of our dreams. Now and then the waking mind discovers a pattern of sense in last night's dream; and if this pattern is very striking or somehow coincides with our conscious emotions at their deepest, then the dream may be held together and repeated, the show may run several times as it does in Anna's case.

What are the impressions a dream collects on its stage? They are obviously filched from our waking life, although twisted and combined into new shapes by the experimental producer, who is not necessarily an entertainer from Vienna. In Anna and Vronski's case the nightmare takes the form of a dreadful-looking little man, with a bedraggled beard, bending over a sack, groping in it for something, and talking in French—though he is a Russian proletarian in appearance—about having to beat iron. In order to understand Tolstoy's art in the matter, it is instructive to note the building up of the dream, the accumulation of the odds and ends of which that nightmare is going to consist—this building up starts at their first meeting when the railway worker is crushed to death. I propose to go through the passages where the impressions occur of which this common nightmare will be formed. I call these dream-building impressions the ingredients of the dream.

The recollection of the man killed by the backing train is at the bottom of the nightmare that pursues Anna and that Vronski (although with less detail) also sees. What were the main characteristics of that crushed man? First, he was all muffled up because of the frost and thus did not notice the backward lurch of the train that brought Anna to Vronski. This "muffled up" business is illustrated before the accident actually happens by the following impressions: these are Vronski's impressions at the station as the train bringing Anna is about to come:

Through the frosty haze one could see railway workers in winter jackets and felt boots crossing the rails of the curving lines, and presently as the engine puffs in one could see the engine driver bowing in welcome—all muffled up and gray with frost.

He was a wretched, poor man, that crushed fellow, and he left a destitute family—hence a tattered wretch.

Mark incidentally the following point: this miserable man is the first link between Vronski and Anna, since Anna knows that Vronski gave money for the man's family only to please her—that it was his first present to her—and that as a married woman she should not accept gifts from strange gentlemen.

He was crushed by a great weight of iron.

And here are some preliminary impressions, Vronski's impression as the train draws in: "One could hear the rolling of some great weight." The vibration of the station-platform is vividly described.

Now we shall follow up these images—muffled up, tattered man, battered by iron, through the rest of the book.

The "muffled up" idea is followed up in the curious shifting sensations between sleep and consciousness that Anna experiences on her way back to Petersburg on the night train.

The muffled up conductor covered with snow on one side and the stove-heater whom she sees in her half-dream gnawing the wall with a sound as if something were torn apart, are nothing but the same crushed man in disguise—an emblem of something hidden, shameful, torn, broken, and painful at the bottom of her new-born passion for Vronski. And it is the muffled man who announces the stop at which she sees Vronski. The heavy iron idea is linked up with all this during these same scenes of her homeward journey. At that stop she sees the shadow of a bent man gliding as it were at her feet and testing the iron of the wheels with his hammer, and then she sees Vronski, who has followed her on the same train, standing near her on that station platform, and there is the clanging sound of a loose sheet of iron worried by the blizzard.

The characteristics of the crushed man have by now been amplified and are deeply engraved in her mind. And two new ideas have been added, in keeping with the muffled-up idea, the tattered element and the battered-by-iron element.

The tattered wretch is bending over something.

He is working at the iron wheels.

The Red Bag

Anna's red bag is prepared by Tolstoy in chapter 28 of part one. It is described as "toy-like" or "tiny" but it will grow. When about to leave Dolly's house in Moscow for Petersburg, in a fit of bizarre tearfulness Anna bends her flushed face over the little bag in which she is putting a nightcap and some cambric handkerchiefs. She will open this red bag when she settles down in the railway car to take out a little pillow, an English novel and a paper-knife to cut it, and then the red bag is relinquished into the hands of her maid, who dozes beside her. This bag is the last object she sheds when she gets rid of her life four years and a half later (May 1876) by jumping under a train when this red bag, which she tries to slip off her wrist, delays her for a moment.

We now come to what was technically known as a woman's "fall." From the ethical viewpoint, this scene is far removed from Flaubert, from Emma's euphoria and Rodolphe's cigar in that sunny little pinewood near Yonville. Through this episode runs a sustained ethical comparison of adultery in terms of a brutal murder—Anna's body, in this ethical image, is trampled upon and hacked to pieces by her lover, by her sin. She is the victim of some crushing force.

"That which for Vronski had been almost a whole year the one absorbing desire of his life . . . that which for Anna had been an impossible, awful, and even for that reason most entrancing dream of bliss, that desire had been fulfilled. He stood before her, pale, his lower jaw trembling. . . .

" 'Anna! Anna!' he kept saying in a trembling voice. . . . He felt what a murderer must feel, when he sees the body he has robbed of life. That body, robbed by him of life, was their love, their young love. . . . Shame at their spiritual nakedness crushed her and him. But in spite of all the murderer's horror before the body of his victim, he must hack it to pieces, hide the body, must take advantage of what he has gained by murder.

"With fury, with passion, the murderer falls on the body, and drags it and hacks at it. And thus he covered her face and shoulders with kisses."
This is a further development of the death theme .that started with the muffled-up guard being cut in two by the train that brought Anna to Moscow.

Now we are ready for the two dreams a year later. This is part four, chapter 2.

"When he got home, Vronski found there a note from Anna. She wrote, 'I am ill and unhappy. I cannot come out, but must see you. Come this evening. My husband goes to the Council at seven and will be there till ten.' He was struck by the strangeness of her inviting him despite her husband's insisting on her not receiving him; he decided to go.

"Vronski had that winter got his promotion, was now a colonel, had left the regimental quarters, and was living alone. After having some lunch, he lay down on the sofa, and in five minutes memories of the disgusting scenes he had witnessed during the last few days [he had been attache to a foreign prince visiting Russia, who had been shown all the most lurid sides of gay rich life] got mixed up with the image of Anna and of a peasant [a trapper] who had played an important part in a certain bear-hunt, and Vronski fell asleep. He woke up in the dark [it was evening by now] trembling with horror, and made haste to light a candle. 'What was it? What? What was the dreadful thing I dreamed? Yes, yes; I think a little dirty man resembled that trapper with the disheveled beard, stooping down doing something; and all of a sudden he began saying some strange words in French. 'Yes, there was nothing else in the dream,' he said to himself. 'But why was it so awful?' He vividly recalled the peasant again and those incomprehensible French words the peasant had uttered, and a chill of horror ran down his spine.

"What nonsense!" thought Vronski, and glanced at his watch. [He was late for his visit to Anna. As he entered the house of his mistress he met Karenin coming out.] Vronski bowed, and Karenin, chewing his lips, lifted his hand to his hat and went on. Vronski saw him, without looking round, get into the carriage, the footman handed him the lap-robe and the opera-glass through the window, and the carriage drove off. Vronski went into the hall. His brows were scowling, and his eyes gleamed with a proud and angry light in them. . . .

"He was still in the hall when he caught the sound of her retreating footsteps. He knew she had been expecting him, had listened for him, and was now going back to the drawing-room. [He was late. The dream had delayed him.]

" 'No,' she cried, on seeing him, and at the first sound of her voice the tears came into her eyes. 'No; if things are to go on like this, it will happen much, much sooner.'

" '*What* will happen, my dear?'

" 'What? I've been waiting in agony for an hour, two hours. . . . No, . . . I can't quarrel with you. Of course you couldn't come.' She laid her two hands on his shoulders, and looked a long while at him with a profound, passionate, and at the same time searching look. . . .

[Note that the first thing she says to him is connected vaguely with the idea that she will die.]

" 'A dream?' repeated Vronski, and instantly he recalled the peasant of his dream.

" 'Yes, a dream,' she said. 'It's a long while since I dreamed it. I dreamed that I ran into my bedroom, that I had to get something there, to find out something; you know how it is in dreams,' she said, her eyes wide with horror; 'and in the bedroom, in the corner, stood something.'

" 'Oh, what nonsense! How can you believe . . .'

"But she would not let him interrupt her. What she was saying was too important to her.

" 'And the something turned round, and I saw it was a peasant with a disheveled beard, little, and dreadful-looking. I wanted to run away, but he bent down over a sack, and was fumbling there with his hands . . .' [She uses the same word—disheveled. Vronski in *his* dream had not made out the sack or the words. She had.]

"She showed how he had moved his hands. There was terror in her face. And Vronski, remembering his dream, felt the same terror filling his soul.

" 'He was groping for something in the sack, and kept talking quickly, quickly, in French, you know: *Il faut le battre, le fer, le broyer, le pétrir* [beat it, the iron, crush it into shape]. . . . And in my horror I tried to wake up, and woke up . . . but woke up in the dream. And I began asking myself what it meant. And Korney [a servant] said to me: "In childbirth you'll die, ma'am, you'll die. . . ." And I woke up.' [It is not in childbirth she will die. She will die in soul birth, though, in faith birth.] . . .

"But all at once she stopped. The expression of her face changed instantly. Horror and excitement were suddenly replaced by a look of soft, solemn, blissful attention. He could not understand the meaning of the change. She was listening to the stirring of the new life within her."

[Notice how the idea of death is associated with the idea of childbirth. We should connect it with that of the flickering light symbolizing Kitty's baby and with the light Anna will see just before she dies. Death is soul birth for Tolstoy.]

Now let us compare Anna's dream and Vronski's dream. They are essentially the same of course and both are founded in the long run on those initial railway impressions a year and a half before—on the railway guard crushed by a train. But in Vronski's case the initial tattered wretch is replaced, or let us say acted, by a peasant, a trapper, who had participated in a bear hunt. In Anna's dream there are added impressions from her railway journey to Petersburg— the conductor, the stove-tender. In both dreams the hideous little peasant has a disheveled beard, and a groping, fumbling manner—remnants of the "muffled-up" idea. In both dreams he stoops over something and mutters

---

Nabokov's comparison of Anna's and Vronski's dreams.

Comparison between the two dreams

Now let us compare ~~these~~ Anna's dream and Vronski's
dream. They are essentially the same of course and
both are founded in the long run on those
initial ~~impressions~~ of ~~on the railway guard crushed by a train~~
a year\ before. But
in Vronski's case ~~the~~ the initial "tattered wretch" is ~~acted~~
replaced or ~~let us acted~~.
by a peasant, a trapper, who had ~~played~~
In Anna's dream ~~the tattered prototype~~ is
a ~~actor for~~ participated in a bear hunt.
In Anna's dream there are added ~~impm you use~~ railway sounds. Probably
In both dreams the hideous little peasant ~~of~~
has a disheveled beard, and a groping, fumbly
manner - remnants of the "muffled up" idea
~~both~~ In both dreams he stoops over something
and mutters something in French. ~~And Vronski~~
- the French ~~language~~ patter they both used in
speaking ~~before strangers~~ of everyday things -
in what Tolstoy considered ~~an artificial,~~ asham
~~simple~~ world of sham ~~and size~~; but
Vronski does not catch the sense of those words;
Anna does - and ~~this at~~ the idea
what those French words contain;
of ~~to - t~~ he iron, of something battered and
crushed. - and this something is she.

10.42

something in French—the French patter they both used in speaking of every-day things in what Tolstoy considered a sham world; but Vronski does not catch the sense of those words; Anna does, and what these French words contain is the idea of iron, of something battered and crushed—and this something is she.

Anna's Last Day

The sequence and the events of Anna's last days in the middle of May 1876 in Moscow are quite clear.

Friday she and Vronski quarrelled, then made it up and decided to leave Moscow for Vronski's country estate in Central Russia on Monday or Tuesday, as she desired. Vronski had wished to go later because of some business he had to wind up but had then given in. (He was selling a horse, and also a house belonging to his mother.)

Saturday a telegram comes from Oblonski who is in Petersburg, about 350 miles north of Moscow, telling them that there is very little chance that Karenin will grant Anna a divorce. Anna and Vronski have another quarrel that morning, and Vronski is away all day settling business matters.

On Sunday morning, the last day of her life, she was waked by a horrible nightmare, which had already recurred several times in her dreams, even before she and Vronski had become lovers. A little old man with a rumpled beard was doing something bent down over some iron, muttering meaningless French words, and she, as she always did in this nightmare (it was this that made the horror of it), felt that this peasant was taking no notice of her, but whatever his horrible business with iron, it was something performed over her. After seeing that hideous nightmare for the last time, Anna notices from her window Vronski in a brief pleasant conversation with a certain young lady and her mother whom the old Countess Vronski from her suburban estate had asked to transmit to him some business papers to be signed in connection with the house she is selling. Without any reconciliation with Anna, Vronski leaves. First he drives to the racing stables where he keeps a horse that he is about to sell, then sends the carriage back for Anna's use in the day and proceeds by local train to his mother's estate in the suburbs in order to get her signature in connection with those papers that she has sent him. A first message, urging him not to leave her alone, is sent by Anna with coachman Michael to the stables; but Vronski has already left, the messenger and message come back: Vronski has already gone to the station to take that train to his mother's place a few miles out of town. Anna sends the same Michael with the same note to old Countess Vronski's place and simultaneously sends a telegram to that place, urging him to return at once. The abrupt telegram will come before the pathetic note comes.

In the afternoon around three she goes to Dolly Oblonski in her victoria; driven by coachman Theodore; and we shall analyze in a moment her thoughts on the way. First let us proceed with this scheme. Around six she drives home and finds an answer to her telegram—Vronski wires that he cannot be home before ten in the evening. Anna decides to take a suburban train and get off at the Obiralovka station near his mother's estate; she plans to leave the train there and get in touch with Vronski, and if he does not join her and come back to town with her she plans to travel on, no matter where, and never to see him again. The train leaves Moscow city at eight P.M. and some twenty minutes later she is at Obiralovka, the suburban station. Remember it is a Sunday, and lots of people are around, and the impact of various impressions, festive and coarse, mingles with her dramatic meditations.

At Obiralovka, she is met by Michael, the coachman whom she had sent with the message, and he brings a second answer from Vronski saying again that he cannot return before ten in the evening. Anna also learns from the servant that the young lady, whom the old Countess Vronski wishes her son to marry, is there with Vronski at his mother's place. The situation assumes in her mind the fiery colors of a devilish intrigue against her. It is then that she decides to kill herself; she throws herself under an oncoming freight train, on that sunny Sunday evening in May 1876, forty-five years after Emma Bovary had died.

This is the pattern; now let us go back five hours earlier to the afternoon of that Sunday and to some details of her last day.

The Stream of Consciousness or Interior Monologue is a method of expression which was invented by Tolstoy, a Russian, long before James Joyce, character's mind in its natural flow, now running across personal emotions and recollections and now going underground and now as a concealed spring appearing from underground and reflecting various items of the outer world. It is a kind of record of a character's mind running on and on, switching from one image or idea to another without any comment or explanation on the part of the author. In Tolstoy the device is still in its rudimentary form, with the author giving some assistance to the reader but in James Joyce the thing will be carried to an extreme stage of objective record.

We return to Anna's last afternoon. Sunday in Moscow, May 1876. The weather has just cleared up after a morning drizzle. The iron roofs, the

on, no matter where, but never see him again.
The train leaves, at 8 p.m. and some twenty minutes *moscow city*
later she is at Obiralovka, the suburban station.
Remember it is a ~~just~~ a Sunday, and lots
of people are around, ~~the~~ and the impact
of various impressions, festive and coarse
mingles with her dramatic meditations.

At Obiralovka, she is met by Michael, the
~~coachman~~ *No 1* whom she *had* sent with *the* message ~~simultaneous~~
~~with the telegram~~, but he brings ~~an~~ a
second answer from Vronsky saying *that I again*
that he cannot return before ten. *in the evening* Anna
also learns *from the servant* that the young lady, whom
the old countess *Vronsky* wishes her son to marry
is there with Vronsky at his mother's place ~~estate~~
The situation assumes in her mind the ~~fiery~~ *colors of a devilish wint uguse ageinst her*
place. It is then that she decides
to kill herself, *and* throws herself under
on a railway
a freight train on that sunny Sunday
evening in May 1876, forty five years
after Emma Bovary had died. *no written not all tis towers and so*
go back to the afternoon of that greatly
This is the pattern, now let us look at
some details of her last day. p. 881

sidewalks, the cobble-stones, the wheels, the leather, and the metal plates of carriages—everything glistens brightly in the May sunshine. It is three o'clock on Sunday in Moscow.

As Anna sat in the corner of the comfortable horse-driven carriage, a victoria, she ran over the events of the last days, recalling her quarrels with Vronski. She blamed herself for the humiliation to which she had lowered her soul. Then she fell to reading the signs of the stores. Now comes the device of stream of consciousness: "Office and warehouse. Dentist. Yes, I'll tell Dolly all about it. She does not like Vronski. I shall be ashamed but I'll tell her. She likes me. I'll follow her advice. I won't give in to him. Won't let him teach me. Filipov's bun shop. Somebody said they send their dough to Petersburg. The Moscow water is so good for it. Ah, those cold springs at Mytishchi and those pancakes! . . . Long long ago, I was seventeen, I had gone with my aunt to the monastery there, in a carriage, there was no railway yet there. Was that really me? Those red hands? Everything that seemed to me so wonderful and unattainable is now so worthless, and what I had then is out of my reach forever! Such humiliation. How proud and smug he will be when he gets my note begging him to come. But I'll show him, I'll show him. How awful that paint smells. Why is it they're always painting buildings? Dressmaker. Man bowing. He's Ann Ushka's husband. Our parasites. [Vronski had said that.] Our? Why our? [We have nothing in common now.] What's so awful is that one can't tear up the past. . . . What are those two girls smiling about? Love, most likely. They don't know how dreary it is, how degrading. The boulevard, the children. Three boys running, playing at horses. Seryozha! [her little boy]. And I am losing everything and not getting him back."

After her inconclusive visit to Dolly, where incidentally she sees Kitty, she drives home. On the way home the stream of consciousness resumes its course. Her thoughts shuttle between the incidental (specific) and the dramatic (general). A fat ruddy gentleman takes her for an acquaintance, lifts his glossy top hat above his bald glossy head, then perceives his mistake. "He thought he knew me. Well, he knows me as little as anyone in the world knows me. I don't know my own self. I only know my appetites, as the French say. Those children want that dirty ice cream; this they *do* know. Ice-cream seller, bucket, takes the bucket off his head, wipes the sweat off his face with a towel. Same

---

Nabokov's account of the events preceding Anna's decision to commit suicide.

---

towel. We all want what is sweet: if not expensive candy, then cheap dirty ice-cream in the street, and Kitty's the same: if not Vronski then Lyovin; and we all hate each other, I, Kitty, Kitty me. Yes, that's the truth. [Now she is struck by the grotesque combination of a funny Russian name and the French word for hairdresser. Mark that the little Russian peasant in her nightmare muttered French words.] Tyutkin, coiffeur. *Je me fais coiffer par Tyutkin.* [I go to Tyutkin for my hairdo. She improves upon the impression with this lame little joke.] I'll tell him that when he comes—she smiled. But immediately she remembered that now she had no one to tell anything amusing to." The stream of consciousness flows on. "And there is nothing amusing either. All is hateful. Church bells. How carefully that merchant crosses himself. Slow. Afraid of letting something drop out of his inside pocket. All those churches and ringing, all that humbug. Simply to conceal that we all hate each other like those cab-drivers there who are insulting each other."

With coachman Theodore driving, and footman Peter sitting beside him on the box, she drives to the station to take the train to Obiralovka. The stream of consciousness takes up again on the way to the station. "Yes, what was the last thing I thought of so clearly? Tyutkin hairdresser? No, not that. Yes, hatred, the one thing that holds men together. No use your going [mentally addressing some people in a cab, evidently going on an excursion to the country]. And the dog you are taking with you will be of no help. You can't get away from yourselves. Dead drunk factory worker, lolling head, *he* has found a quicker way. Count Vronski and I did *not* find that intoxication though we expected so much. . . .

"Beggar woman with a baby. She thinks I am sorry for her. Hate, torture. Schoolboys laughing. Seryozha! [Again the lyrical inward cry.] I thought I loved my child, used to be touched by my own tenderness, but I have lived without him, and I gave him up for another love, and did not regret the exchange till that love was satisfied. And with loathing she thought of what she meant by 'that love,' her carnal passion for Vronski.

She arrives at the station, and takes a local train for Obiralovka, the nearest station to Countess Vronski's estate. As she takes a seat in the railway car two things happen simultaneously. She hears some voices talking affected French and at the same moment she sees a hideous little man, with tangled hair and all covered with dirt, stooping toward the wheels of the railway carriage. With an unbearable shock of supernatural recognition she recalls the combination of her old nightmare, the hideous peasant hammering at some iron and muttering French words. The French—symbol of artificial life—and the tattered dwarf—symbol of her sin, filthy and soul-stunting sin—these two images come together in a fateful flash.

You will note that the coaches of this suburban train are of a different type from those of the night express between Moscow and Petersburg. In this suburban train, each carriage is much shorter and consists of five compartments. There is no corridor. Each compartment has a door on either side, so people get in and out, with a great slamming of five doors on each side of the coach. Since there is no corridor, the conductor, when he has to pass while the train is in motion, has to use a footboard on either side of each coach. A suburban train of this kind has a maximum speed of about thirty miles per hour.

She arrives twenty minutes later at Obiralovka and from a message brought by the servant discovers that Vronski is not willing to come at once—as she had pleaded with him to do. She walks along the platform, talking to her own tortured heart.

"Two maid-servants turned their heads, stared, and made some remarks about her dress. 'Real,' they said of the lace she was wearing. . . . A boy selling soft drinks stared at her. She walked further and further along the platform. Some ladies and children who had come to meet a gentleman in spectacles paused in their laughter and chatter and stared at her too. She quickened her pace and walked on to the end of the platform. A freight train was backing in. The platform vibrated. And all at once she thought of the man crushed [the day she had first met Vronski, more than four years ago, as that train of the past came back for her]. And she knew what she had to do. With a swift light motion she went down the steps that led from a water tank to the rails and stopped quite near the train that was lumbering by slowly. [She was now on the level of the tracks.] She looked at the lower part of the cars, at the screws and chains and the tall iron wheels of a car slowly moving by, and her eyes tried to find the middle between the front and back wheels to seize the moment when that middle point would be opposite her [the middle point, the entrance to death, the little archway]. 'Down there,' she said to herself, looking into the shadow of the car, at the coal dust on the sleepers, 'down there, in the very middle, and I will punish him, and escape from everyone and from myself.'

"She meant to fall under the wheels of the first car, as its middle part came level with her, but the little red bag [our old friend] which she tried to slip off her wrist delayed her, and it was too late, the middle entrance had already passed. She waited for the next car. It was like entering the water when bathing in a river, and she crossed herself. This familiar gesture brought back a flood of young memories, and suddenly the fog that had just been covering everything was torn apart, and she glimpsed all the brightness of her past life. But she did not take her eyes from the wheels of the approaching car, and exactly at the moment when the middle point between the wheels came opposite her she flung aside the red bag and, drawing her head in, fell on her hands under the car, and lightly, as though she would rise again at once, dropped to her knees. And at the same instant she was terrified. 'Where am I? What am I doing?' She tried to get up, to turn, but something huge and merciless struck her on the back, and dragged her along. She prayed, feeling it impossible to struggle. [In a last vision] the little peasant muttering to himself was working at his iron, and the candle by which she had read the book of troubles, deceit, grief, and evil, flared up more brightly than ever before, illumed for her all that had been darkness, sputtered, began to dim and went out for ever."

<hr />

CHARACTERIZATION

All was confusion in the Oblonski household, but all is order in Tolstoy's kingdom. A vivid array of people, the main characters of the novel, already start to exist for the reader in part one. Anna's curiously dual nature is already perceptible in the double role she plays at her first appearance when she restores, by means of tender tact and womanly wisdom, harmony in a broken home but simultaneously acts as an evil enchantress by destroying a young girl's romance. With his fond sister's assistance quickly recovering from his despicable plight, the blond-whiskered, moist-eyed bon-vivant Oblonski is already—in his meetings with Lyovin and Vronski—acting the role of master of ceremonies which he will play in the novel. Through a series of deeply poetical images Tolstoy conveys the tenderness and fierceness of Lyovin's love for Kitty, which is at first unrequited, but is to attain later, in the course of the book, what was to Tolstoy the difficult and divine ideal of love, namely marriage and procreation. Lyovin's proposal comes at the wrong time and brings into special relief Kitty's infatuation with Vronski—a kind of sensuous awkwardness which adolescence will live down. Vronski, a strikingly handsome but somewhat stockily built fellow, very intelligent but devoid of talent, socially charming but individually rather mediocre, reveals in his behavior toward Kitty a streak of bland insensitivity which may easily grade into callousness and even brutality later on. And it will be noted by the amused reader that it is not any of the young men of the book, but dignified Karenin of the homely ears, who is the triumphant lover in part one; we approach here the moral of the tale: the Karenin marriage, lacking as it does true affinity between its partners, is as sinful as Anna's love affair is to be.

Here, too, in part one the dawning of Anna's tragic romance is fore-glimpsed; and in thematic introduction and contrast to her case, three different examples of adultery or cohabitation are given by Tolstoy: (1) Dolly, a faded woman of thirty-three with many children, happens to find an amorous billet addressed by her husband, Steve Oblonski, to a young French woman who some time ago had been the governess of their children; (2) Lyovin's brother Nikolay, a pitiful figure, lives with a kind-hearted albeit uncultured woman whom, in an ecstasy of social reform common to his time, he took from a low-class brothel of which she had been a passive inmate; (3) in the last chapter of part one Tolstoy clinches it with the Petritski-Baroness Shilton case of cheerful adultery in which no deceit and no family ties are involved.

These three illustrations of irregular amours, Oblonski's, Nikolay Lyovin's, and Petritski's, are traced in the margin of Anna's own ethical and emotional troubles. It will be marked that Anna's troubles start the minute she meets Vronski. Indeed, Tolstoy arranges matters in such a manner that the events in part one (which occur about a year before Anna actually becomes Vronski's mistress) foreshadow Anna's tragic destiny. With an artistic force and subtlety unknown to Russian letters before his day, Tolstoy introduces the theme of violent death simultaneously with that of violent passion in Vronski's and Anna's life: the fatal accident to a railway employee, coincident with their first meeting, becomes a grim and mysterious link between them through Vronski's quietly helping the dead man's family merely because Anna happens to think of it. Married ladies of fashion should not accept presents from strange gentlemen, but here is Vronski making Anna the gift, as it were, of that railway guard's death. And it will also be marked that this act of gallantry, this flash of connivance (with a chance death for chance subject), is something that Anna regards as shameful in retrospection, as if it were a first stage in her unfaithful-ness to her husband, an event not to be mentioned either to Karenin or to the young girl Kitty who is in love with Vronski. And more tragically still, Anna feels all at once, as she and her brother are leaving the station, that the accident (coincident with her meeting Vronski and her coming to arrange the affairs of her adulterous brother) is an omen of evil. She is strangely upset. One passerby says to another that such an instantaneous death is also the easiest one: this Anna happens to overhear; this sinks into her mind; this impression will breed.

Not only is unfaithful Oblonski's state of mind in the beginning of the book a grotesque parody of his sister's destiny, but another striking theme is foreglimpsed in the events of his morning—the theme of significant visions in sleep. In regard to Steve's fickle and carefree mind the dream he dreams has exactly the same value of characterization as has, in regard to Anna's deep and rich and tragic personality, a certain fateful nightmare she will be made to see later.

TOLSTOY'S TIMING

The chronology of *Anna Karenin* is based on a sense of artistic timing unique in the annals of literature. Upon perusing part one of the book (thirty-four small chapters making in all 135 pages), the reader is left with the impression that a number of mornings, afternoons, and evenings, at least a week in the lives of several people, have been described in vigorous detail. We shall presently look at the actual time data, but before discussing them, it may be advisable to get the question of meals out of the way.

This, then, was their sequence in the course of a well-to-do Moscovite's or Petersburgian's day in the seventies of the last century. Breakfast, around 9 A.M., consisted of tea or coffee, with bread and butter: the former might be—as it was at Oblonski's table—some kind of fancy roll (e.g., *kalach*, a flour-powdered, crusty outside and soft inside, glorified doughnut, served hot in a napkin). A light lunch between 2 and 3 P.M. would be followed by a large dinner around 5:30 P.M. with Russian liquor and French wines. Evening tea with cakes, jams, and various tasty Russian tidbits would be served between 9 and 10 P.M., after which the family would retire; but its more frivolous members might crown the day with supper in town at 11 P.M. or later.

The action of the novel starts at 8 A.M., Friday, February the 11th (old calendar), 1872. This date is not mentioned anywhere in the text but it is easily arrived at by the following computation:

1. The political events on the eve of the Turkish War, as alluded to in the last part of the novel, set its end at July 1876. Vronski becomes Anna's lover in December 1872. The steeplechase episode occurs in August 1873. Vronski and Anna spend the summer and winter of 1874 in Italy, and the summer of 1875 on Vronski's estate; then, in November, they go to Moscow, where Anna commits suicide on a Sunday evening in May 1876.

2. We are told in chapter 6 of part one that Lyovin had spent the two first months of the winter (i.e., from mid-October to the second week of December 1871) in Moscow, then had retired to his country estate for two months, and now, i.e., in February, is back in Moscow. About three months later, a late spring is mentioned as breaking into exuberant life (chapter 12, part two).

The cover of Nabokov's folder of notes for his projected textbook edition of *Anna Karenin*.

65 pages

Two copies of this stuff · 5 v.p.

June 1975

Anna Karenin

(and most)

1. Its timing
2. Names
3. Notes (mostly referring to Part One)

(Before using this material I must
find a modern English translation of
the novel and carefully check
inaccuracies and bloomers. In 1940-50
I used the dreadful Garnett version with
my unpublished corrections)

BIELLA

3. Oblonski reads in his morning paper about Count Beust, Austrian Ambassador to London, traveling through Wiesbaden on his way back to England. (See note 18 below.) This would be just before the thanksgiving service for the recovery of the Prince of Wales, which took place Tuesday, February 15/27, 1872; and the only possible Friday is Friday 11/23 of February, 1872.

Of the thirty-four small chapters, of which part one consists, the first five are devoted to an unbroken account of Oblonski's doings. He awakes at 8 A.M., breakfasts between 9 and 9:30, and around 11 A.M. arrives at his office. Shortly before 2 P.M. Lyovin unexpectedly turns up there. Beginning with chapter 6 and to the end of chapter 9, Oblonski is set aside and Lyovin is taken up. Tolstoy's device of going back chronologically to handle the Lyovin theme here comes into play for the first time in the book. We go back four months in a brief recapitulation, and then (chapters 7-9) follow Lyovin from the moment of his arrival in Moscow Friday morning through his talk with his half-brother at whose house he is staying, to his (recapitulated) visit to Oblonski's office, and thence to the skating rink, at 4 P.M., where he skates with Kitty. Oblonski reappears at the end of chapter 9: he comes around 5 to fetch Lyovin for dinner; their meal at the Hotel d'Angleterre occupies chapters 10 and 11. Then Oblonski is dismissed again. We know Lyovin has gone to change into evening clothes and is heading for the soirée at the Shcherbatskis, and there we go to wait for him (chapter 12). He appears there (chapter 13), at 7:30 P.M., and in the next chapter Lyovin's meeting with Vronski is described. We have now been with Lyovin and Kitty for a dozen pages (chapters 12-14); Lyovin leaves around 9 P.M. Vronski stays on for another hour or so. The Shcherbatskis before retiring discuss the situation (chapter 15), and the rest of Vronski's evening, till, say, midnight, is described in chapter 16. The reader will note at this point that Lyovin's evening, after he leaves the Shcherbatskis, is to be described later. In the meantime this first day of the novel, Friday, February 11, after a series of sixteen chapters, has been brought to a close for Vronski, who is sound asleep after supper in his hotel room, and for Oblonski, who is winding up his dramatic and cheerful day at a night restaurant.

The next day, Saturday, February 12, starts at 11 A.M. with Vronski and Oblonski arriving separately at the railway station to meet the Petersburg express bringing Vronski's mother and Oblonski's sister (chapters 17-18). After dropping Anna at his house, Oblonski goes to his office around noon, and we follow Anna through her first day in Moscow, till 9:30 P.M. These chapters (17-18), dealing with Saturday events, occupy a score of pages.

Chapters 22-23 (about ten pages) are devoted to the ball which takes place three or four days later, say, Wednesday, February 16, 1872.

In the next chapter (24) Tolstoy uses a device which was adumbrated in chapters 6-8 and which will figure prominently throughout the book, namely that of going back in time where Lyovin's doings are concerned. We go back to Friday night, February 11, to follow Lyovin from the Shcherbatskis to his brother's where he arrives at 9:30 and stays for supper with him (chapters 24-25). Next morning, from another station (the Nizhegorodski) than the one (Peterburgski) at which that same Saturday Anna arrives, Lyovin travels back to his estate in Central Russia, presumably near Tula, some three hundred miles south of Moscow, and his evening there is depicted in chapters 26-27.

Then we leap forward to Thursday, February 17, 1872, in order to follow Anna, who on the next day after the ball leaves for Petersburg where she arrives after a night journey (chapters 29-31), around 11 A.M., Friday, the 18th of February. (This Friday is fully described in chapters 31-33), and here precise timing is deliberately used by Tolstoy to characterize, with ironic overtones, Karenin's scrupulously ordered existence that will be shattered before long. Immediately after meeting Anna at the station, he drives away to preside at a Committee, comes home at 4 P.M., they have guests to dinner at 5, he drives off around 7 P.M. to attend a Cabinet meeting, returns at 9:30 P.M., has evening tea with his wife, then retires to his study, and punctually at midnight proceeds to the conjugal bedroom. The last chapter (34) takes care of Vronski's homecoming that same Friday.

It will be seen from this brief account of the time pattern in part one that Tolstoy uses time as an artist's tool in various ways and for different purposes. The regular course of Oblonski's time through the first five chapters is instrumental in stressing the easy-going routine of his week day, from eight in the morning to dinner time around half-past five in the evening, a flowing course of animal existence which his wife's misfortune cannot mar. With this routine part one begins and is symmetrically closed by the more stately and rigid order of another day, the day of Karenin, Oblonski's brother-in-law. No apprehension of Anna's complete inner change affects the timetable of her husband as through a series of committee meetings and other administrative chores he quietly and steadily makes his way toward bedtime and its lawful joys. Lyovin's "time" erratically interrupts the smooth history of Oblonski's day, and the quality of Lyovin's highstrung and moody nature is reflected in the curious jerks given here to the threads of the chronological web Tolstoy is weaving. Finally we note the striking harmony in which two special scenes in part one fall: the night of the ball with Kitty's dreamlike, exaggerated awareness of Anna's enchantments; and the night of the train journey to Petersburg with its strange fancies passing through the chiarascuro of Anna's mind. These two scenes form as it were the two inner pillars of the edifice of which Oblonski's "time" and Karenin's "time" are the wings.

––––––––––

STRUCTURE

What is the key to an intelligent appreciation of the structure of Tolstoy's huge *Anna Karenin*? The key to its structure is consideration in terms of time. Tolstoy's purpose, and Tolstoy's achievement, is the synchronization of seven major lives, and it is this synchronization that we have to follow in order to rationalize the delight that his magic produces in us.

The first twenty-one chapters have for their main subject the Oblonski disaster. It helps to introduce two budding subjects: (1) the Kitty-Lyovin-Vronski triangle, and (2) the beginning of the Vronski-Anna theme. Mark that Anna, who (with the grace and wisdom of a bright-eyed goddess Athena) brings on the reconciliation between her brother and his wife, simultaneously and demoniacally breaks up the Kitty-Vronski combination by captivating Vronski. The Oblonski adultery and the Shcherbatskis' heartbreak prepare the Vronski-Anna theme which will not be so naturally resolved as are the Oblonski-Dolly trouble and Kitty's bitterness. Dolly pardons her husband for the sake of their children and because she loves him; Kitty two years later marries Lyovin, and it proves to be a perfect match, a marriage after Tolstoy's heart; but Anna, the dark beauty of the book, will see the destruction of her family life, and shall die.

Throughout the first part of the book (thirty-four chapters), seven lives are abreast in time: Oblonski, Dolly, Kitty, Lyovin, Vronski, Anna, and Karenin. In the case of two pairs (the Oblonskis and the Karenins) the pairing has been impaired at the start: it is then patched up in the Oblonski pair, but it is just beginning to break up in the Karenin pair. A complete break-up has taken place in the two possible pairs, in the vestigial Vronski-Kitty pair and in the likewise vestigial Lyovin-Kitty pair. In consequence, Kitty is mateless, Lyovin is mateless, and Vronski (tentatively paired off with Anna) threatens to break up the Karenin pair. So let us mark the following important points in this first part: there is a reshuffling of seven relationships; there are seven lives to take care of (between them the little chapters shuttle); and these seven lives are abreast in time, the time being the beginning of February 1872.

Part two, which consists of thirty-five chapters, starts for everybody in mid-March of the same year, 1872; but then we witness a curious phenomenon: the Vronski-Karenin-Anna triangle lives faster than the still mateless Lyovin, or the still mateless Kitty. This is a very fascinating point in the structure of the novel—the mated existing faster than the mateless. If we follow first the Kitty line we find that mateless Kitty, who is wilting away in Moscow, is examined by a famous doctor around March 15; despite her own woes she helps to nurse back to health Dolly's six children (the baby is two months old) who are down with scarlet fever; and then Kitty will be taken by her parents to Soden, a German resort, in the first week of April 1872. These matters are taken care of in the first three chapters of this part two. Only in chapter 30 do we actually follow the Shcherbatskis to Soden, where time and Tolstoy completely cure Kitty. Five chapters are devoted to this cure and then Kitty returns to Russia, to the Oblonski-Shcherbatski country place a few miles from Lyovin's place, by the end of June 1872, and this is the end of part two as far as Kitty is concerned.

In this same part two Lyovin's life in the Russian countryside is correctly synchronized with Kitty's existence in Germany. We read of his activities on his country estate in a set of six chapters, 12 to 17. He is sandwiched between two sets of chapters dealing with the lives of Vronski and the Karenins in St. Petersburg; and the very important point to be marked is that the Vronski-Karenin team lives faster than Kitty or Lyovin by more than a year. In the first set of chapters of this part two, from chapters 5 to 11, the husband broods and Vronski perseveres, and by chapter 11, after almost a year of pursuit, Vronski becomes technically Anna's lover. This is October 1872. But in Lyovin's life and in Kitty's life, the time is only spring 1872. They lag behind by several months. Another leap forward is taken by the Vronski-Karenin time-team (a good Nabokovian term—time-team; use it with acknowledgments) in a set of twelve chapters, 18 to 29, in which the famous episode of the steeplechase, followed by Anna's confession to her husband, takes place in August 1873 (with three years to go to the end of the whole novel). Then again the shuttle: we go back to the spring of 1872, to Kitty in Germany. So that at the end of part two we have a curious situation: Kitty's life, and Lyovin's life, are about fourteen or fifteen months behind that of the Vronski-Karenins. To repeat, the mated move faster than the mateless.

In part three, which consists of thirty-two chapters, we stay for a little while with Lyovin, then we visit Dolly with him on the Oblonski estate just before Kitty arrives, and finally in chapter 12, summer 1872, Lyovin has a charming glimpse of Kitty arriving in a coach from the railway station, back from Germany. The next set of chapters takes us to Petersburg to Vronski and to the

Karenins just after the races (this is the summer 1873), and then we move back in time to September 1872, to Lyovin's estate, which he leaves in October 1872 for a somewhat vague journey in Germany, France, and England.

I wish now to stress the following point. Tolstoy is in difficulties. His lovers and betrayed husband live fast—they have left single Kitty and single Lyovin far behind in time: it is mid-winter 1873 in Petersburg during the first sixteen chapters of part four. But nowhere does Tolstoy give us the exact length of Lyovin's stay abroad, and the difference of more than a year between the Lyovin-Kitty time and the Vronski-Anna time hangs only upon one chronological remark in chapter 11, part two, concerning Anna's becoming Vronski's mistress: for about a year Vronski had been courting her before she fell—and this is the gap of time by which Lyovin-Kitty lag. But the reader does not keep a keen eye on the timetable, even good readers seldom do so and so we are misled into thinking and feeling that the Vrsonski-Anna episodes are perfectly synchronized with the Lyovin and Kitty episodes and that the various events in the two sets of lives happen at more or less the same time. The reader is aware, of course, that we shuttle in space, from Germany to Central Russia, and from the countryside to Petersburg or Moscow and back again; but he is not necessarily aware that we also shuttle in time—forward for Vronski-Anna, backward for Lyovin-Kitty.

In the first five chapters of part four we attend the developments of the Vronski-Karenin theme in St. Petersburg. It is now mid-winter 1873, and Anna is going to have a baby, Vronski's child. In chapter 6 Karenin visits Moscow on political business, and at the same time Lyovin comes to Moscow too, after his visit abroad. Oblonski in chapters 9 to 13 arranges a dinner at his house, first week of January 1874, where Lyovin and Kitty meet each other again. The chalk writing scene occurs, as this time-keeper will tell you, exactly two years after the beginning of the novel; but somehow for the reader, and for Kitty (see various references in her conversation with Lyovin at the card table while they fiddle with the chalk) only a year has passed. We are thus confronted by the following marvelous fact: there exists a tell-tale difference between the Anna physical time on one side and the Lyovin spiritual time on the other.

By part four, exactly in mid-book, all the seven lives are abreast again as they were in the beginning, February 1872. It is now January 1874 by Anna's and my calendar but 1873 by the reader's and Kitty's calendar. The second half of part four (chapters 17 to 23) shows us Anna in Petersburg almost dying in childbed, and then Karenin's temporary reconciliation with Vronski and Vronski's attempt to commit suicide. Part four ends in March 1874: Anna breaks with her husband; she and her lover go to Italy.

Part five consists of thirty-three chapters. Not for long have the seven lives been abreast. Vronski and Anna in Italy again take the lead. This is quite a race. Lyovin's marriage in the first six chapters takes place in early spring 1874; and when we see the Lyovins again, in the country and then at Lyovin's brother's deathbed (chapters 14-20), it is the beginning of May 1874. But Vronski and Anna (sandwiched in between these two sets of chapters) are two months ahead and somewhat insecurely enjoying a southern July in Rome.

The synchronizing link between the two time-teams is now the mateless Karenin. Since there are seven major people involved and since the action of the novel depends upon pairing them, and since seven is an odd number, one person will obviously be out and bound to be without a mate. In the beginning Lyovin was the outcast, the superfluous one; now it is Karenin. We go back to the Lyovins in the spring of 1874 and then we attend to Karenin's various activities, and this brings us gradually to as late as March 1875. By now Vronski and Anna have returned to Petersburg after a year in Italy. She visits her little son on his tenth birthday, say, March 1, a pathetic scene. Soon after, she and Vronski go to live on Vronski's country estate which very conveniently is in the same district as the Oblonski and Lyovin country places.

Lo and behold, our seven lives are abreast again in part six, which consists of thirty-three chapters, from June to November 1875. We spend the first half of the summer of 1875 with the Lyovins and their relatives; then in July Dolly Oblonski gives us a lift in her carriage to Vronski's estate for some tennis. Oblonski, Vronski, and Lyovin are brought together in the rest of the chapters at some country elections on the second of October 1875, and a month later Vronski and Anna go to Moscow.

Part seven consists of thirty-one chapters. It is the most important one in the book, the book's tragic climax. We are now all abreast in Moscow, end of November 1875: six of us are in Moscow, three pairs, the insecure, already embittered Vronski-Anna, the breeding Lyovins, and the Oblonskis. Kitty's baby is born, and in the beginning of May 1876 we visit, with Oblonski, Karenin in St. Petersburg. Then back again to Moscow. Now begins a series of chapters, from 23 to the end of part seven, devoted to Anna's last days. Her death, by suicide, is in mid-May 1876. I have already given my account of those immortal pages.

Part eight, the last one, is a rather cumbersome machine, consisting of nineteen chapters. Tolstoy uses a device that he has used several times in the course of the novel, the device of having a character move from one place to another place and thus transfer the action from one set of people to another.* Trains and coaches play a significant part in the novel: we have Anna's two train journeys in the first part, from Petersburg to Moscow and back to Petersburg. Oblonski and Dolly are at various points the traveling agents of the story, taking the reader with them wherever Tolstoy wants the reader to be. In fact, Oblonski is finally given a soft job with a big salary for services rendered to the author. Now in the first five chapters of the last, eighth, part, we have Lyovin's half-brother Sergey travel on the same train with Vronski. The date is easy to establish because of the various allusions to war news. The Slavs of Eastern Europe, the Serbians and Bulgarians, were fighting the Turks. This is August 1876; a year later Russia will actually proclaim war with Turkey. Vronski is seen at the head of a detachment of volunteers leaving for the front. Sergey, on the same train, is on his way to visit the Lyovins, and this takes care not only of Vronski but also of Lyovin. The last chapters are devoted to Lyovin's family life in the country and to his conversion when he gropes for God with Tolstoy giving directions.

From this account of the structure of Tolstoy's novel it will be seen that the transitions are far less supple, far less elaborate, than the transitions from group to group in *Madame Bovary* within chapters. The brief abrupt chapter in Tolstoy replaces the flowing paragraph in Flaubert. But it will be also noted that Tolstoy has more lives on his hands than had Flaubert. With Flaubert a ride on horseback, a walk, a dance, a coach drive between village and town, and innumerable little actions, little movements, make those transitions from scene to scene within the chapters. In Tolstoy's novel great, clanging, and steaming trains are used to transport and kill the characters—and any old kind of transition is used from chapter to chapter, for instance beginning the next part or next chapter with the simple statement that so much time has passed and now this or that set of people are doing this or that in this or that place. There is more melody in Flaubert's poem, one of the most poetical novels ever composed; there is more might in Tolstoy's great book.

This is the moving skeleton of the book, which I have given in terms of a race, with the seven lives at first abreast, then Vronski and Anna pressing forwards, leaving Lyovin and Kitty behind, then again all seven are abreast, and again with the funny jerking movement of a brilliant toy Vronski and Anna take the lead, but not for long. Anna does not finish the race. Of the six others, only Kitty and Lyovin retain the interest of the author.

*VN interlines but deletes a remark to the class, "You remember what we called the 'sifting agent.' " The reference is to his Dickens lecture the preceding semester where he analyzed the structural function of characters whom he called "perries," used chiefly to bring characters together or to provide information by conversing with them. See the first volume, *Lectures on Literature*, p. 98. Elsewhere he calls Oblonski a kind of "perry."—Ed.

IMAGERY

Imagery may be defined as the evocation, by means of words, of something that is meant to appeal to the reader's sense of color, or sense of outline, or sense of sound, or sense of movement, or any other sense of perception, in such a way as to impress upon his mind a picture of fictitious life that becomes to him as living as any personal recollection. For producing these vivid images the writer has a wide range of devices from the brief expressive epithet to elaborate word pictures and complex metaphors.

1) *Epithets*. Among these to be noted and admired are the "limply plopping" and "scabrous" as applied so magnificently to the slippery insides and rough outsides of the choice oysters Oblonski enjoys during his restaurant meal with Lyovin. Mrs. Garnett omitted to translate these beautiful *shlyupayushchie* and *shershavye*; we must restore them. Adjectives used in the scene of the ball to express Kitty's adolescent loveliness and Anna's dangerous charm should also be collected by the reader. Of special interest is the fantastic compound adjective, literally meaning "gauzily-ribbonly-lacily-iridescent" (*tyulevo-lento-kruzhevno-tsvetnoy*), used to describe the feminine throng at the ball. The old Prince Shcherbatski calls a flabby type of elderly clubman, shlyupik, pulpy thing, a child's word for a hardboiled egg that has become quite pulpy and spongy from too much rolling in a Russian Easter game where eggs are rolled and knocked at each other.

2) *Gestures*. Oblonski, while his upper lip is being shaved, answering his valet's question (Is Anna coming with her husband or alone) by lifting one finger; or Anna, in her talk with Dolly, illustrating Steve's spells of moral oblivion by making a charming blurred gesture of obliteration before her brow.

3) *Details Of Irrational Perception*. Many examples in the account of Anna's half dream on the train.

4) *Colorful Comedy Traits*. As when the old Prince *thinks* he is mimicking his wife as he grotesquely simpers and curtseys when speaking of matchmaking.

5) *Word Pictures*. These are innumerable: Dolly miserably sitting at her dressing table and the rapid deep-chested voice in which, disguising her distress, she asks her husband what he wants; Grinevich's convexedly-tipped fingernails; the old sleepy blissful hound's sticky lips—are all delightful and unforgettable images.

6) *Poetical Comparisons*. Seldom used by Tolstoy, appealing to the senses, such as the charming allusions to diffuse sunlight and a butterfly, when Kitty is described on the skating rink and at the ball.

7) *Utilitarian Comparisons*. Appealing to the mind rather than to the eye, to the ethical sense rather than to the esthetical one. When Kitty's feelings before the ball are compared to those of a young man before a battle, it would be ridiculous to visualize Kitty in a lieutenant's uniform; but as a rational black-and-white verbal scheme the comparison works nicely and has the parable note that Tolstoy cultivates so assiduously in certain later chapters.

Not all is direct imagery in Tolstoy's text. The parable comparison grades insensibly into the didactic intonations with their meaningful repetitions that characterize Tolstoy's accounts of situations and states of mind. In this respect, the direct statements of chapter openings should be especially marked: "Oblonski had learned easily at school" or "Vronski had never had any real home life."

8) *Similes And Metaphors*. The old curly birches of the gardens, with all their branches weighed down by snow, seemed decked in new festive vestments (Part one, chapter 9).

But for Lyovin she was as easy to find in that crowd as a wild rose among nettles. Everything was made bright by her. She was the smile that shed light on all around her. The place where she stood seemed to him a holy shrine. . . . He walked down, for a long while avoiding looking at her as at the sun, but seeing her, as one does the sun, without looking (Chapter 9).

He felt as though the sun were coming near him (Chapter 9).

like the sun going behind a cloud, her face lost all its friendliness (Chapter 9).

The Tatar . . . instantly, as though worked by springs, laying down one bound bill of fare, he took up another, the list of wines (Chapter 10).

she was unable to believe it, just as she would have been unable to believe that, at any time whatever, the most suitable playthings for children five years old ought to be loaded pistols (Chapter 12).

Kitty experienced a sensation akin to the sensation of a young man before battle (Chapter 13).

Anna speaking: "I know that blue haze like the mist on the mountains in Switzerland. That mist which covers everything in that blissful time when childhood is just ending, and out of that vast circle, happy and gay [there is a path growing narrower and narrower]" (Chapter 20).

the rustle of movement like an even humming stir as from a hive (Chapter 22).

this air she had of a butterfly clinging to a grass blade, and just about to flutter up again with iridescent wings spread (Chapter 23).

And on Vronski's face . . . she [Kitty] saw that look that had struck her . . . like the expression of an intelligent dog when it has done wrong (Chapter 23).

But immediately as though slipping his feet into old slippers, he [Vronski] dropped back into the light-hearted, pleasant world he had always lived in (Chapter 24).

Comparisons may be similes or metaphors, or a mixture of both. Here are some models of comparison:

The *simile* model:

Between land and sea the mist was like a veil

This is a simile. Such links as "like" or "as" are typical of the simile: one object is like another object.

If you go on to say the mist was like the veil of a bride, this is a *sustained* simile with elements of mild poetry; but if you say, the mist was like the veil of a fat bride whose father was even fatter and wore a wig, this is a *rambling* simile, marred by an illogical continuation, of the kind Homer used for purposes of epic narration and Gogol used for grotesque dream-effects.

Now the *metaphor* model:

The veil of the mist between land and sea.

The link "like" has gone; the comparison is integrated. A *sustained* metaphor would be:

The veil of the mist was torn in several places

since the end of the phrase is a logical continuation. In a rambling metaphor there would be an illogical continuation.

————

The Functional Ethical Comparison.

A peculiar feature of Tolstoy's style is that whatever comparisons, whatever similes, or metaphors, he uses, most of them are used not for an esthetical purpose but for an ethical one. In other words his comparisons are utilitarian, are functional. They are employed not to enhance the imagery, to give a new slant to our artistic perception of this or that scene; they are employed to bring out a moral point. I call them, therefore, Tolstoy's moral metaphors or similes—ethical ideas expressed by means of comparisons. These similes and metaphors are, I repeat, strictly functional, and thus rather stark, and constructed according to a recurrent pattern. The dummy, the formula, is: "He felt like a person who. . . ." A state of emotion—this is the first part of the formula—and then a comparison follows: "a person who . . ." etc. I shall give some examples.

(Lyovin thinking of married life.) At every step he experienced what a man would experience who, after admiring the smooth, happy course of a little boat on a lake, should enter that little boat himself. He discovered that it was not enough to sit still, keeping balance; that one had also to maintain, without a moment's inattention, the right direction, that there was water underneath and one had to row, that one's unaccustomed hands hurt; and that only looking at it had been easy; but that doing all this, though very delightful, was very difficult (Part five, chapter 14).

(During a tiff with his wife.) He was offended for the first instant, but the very same second he felt that he could not be offended by her, that she was himself. During that first instant he felt as a man feels when, having suddenly received a violent blow from behind, he turns round, angry and eager to avenge himself, to look for his antagonist, and finds that he has merely struck himself accidentally, and there is no one to be angry with, and he must endure and soothe the pain (*ibid.*).

To remain under such undeserved reproach was a wretched situation, but to make her suffer by justifying himself was worse still. Like a man half-awake in an agony of pain, he craved to tear out and fling away the aching part, and upon awaking, felt that the aching part was himself. (*ibid.*).

. . . the saintly image of Madame Stahl which she [Kitty] had carried for a whole month in her heart, vanished, never to return, just as a human figure seen in some clothing carelessly thrown on a chair vanishes the moment one's eye unravels the pattern of its folds (Part two, chapter 34).

He [Karenin] experienced a feeling like a man who, after calmly crossing a precipice by a bridge, should suddenly discover that the bridge was dismantled, and that there was an abyss below (Part two, chapter 8).

He experienced a feeling such as a man might have, returning home and finding his own house locked up (Part two, chapter 9).

Like an ox with head bent, submissively he awaited the blow [of the *obukh*] which he felt was lifted over him (Part two, chapter 10).

He [Vronski] very quickly perceived that though society was open to him personally, it was closed to Anna. Just as in the parlor game of cat and mouse [with one person in a circle of players and the other outside], the linked hands raised for him were lowered to bar the way for her (Part five, chapter 28).

He could not go anywhere without running into Anna's husband. So at least it seemed to Vronski, just as it seems to a man with a sore finger continually, as though on purpose, grazing his sore finger on everything (*ibid.*).

NAMES

In speaking to a person, the most ordinary and neutral form of address among cultured Russians is not the surname but the first name and patronymic, Ivan Ivanovich (meaning "Ivan, son of Ivan") or Nina Ivanovna (meaning "Nina, daughter of Ivan"). The peasant may hail another as "Ivan" or "Vanka," but otherwise only kinsmen or childhood friends, or people who in their youth served in the same regiment, etc., use first names in addressing each other. I have known a number of Russians with whom I have been on friendly terms for two or three decades but whom I would not dream of addressing otherwise than Ivan Ivanovich or Boris Petrovich as the case may be; and this is why the ease with which elderly Americans become Harrys and Bills to each other after a couple of highballs strikes formal Ivan Ivanovich as impossibly absurd.

A man of parts whose full name is, say, Ivan Ivanovich Ivanov (meaning "Ivan, son of Ivan, surnamed Ivanov"; or in American parlance, "Mr. Ivan Ivanov, Jr.") will be Ivan Ivanovich (often contracted to "Ivan Ivanych": "y" pronounced as "u" in "nudge") to his acquaintances and to his own servants; *barin* (master) or "Your Excellency" to servants in general; "Your Excellency" also to an inferior in office if he happens to occupy a high bureaucratic position; *Gospodin* (Mr.) Ivanov to a wrathful superior—or to somebody who in desperation has to address him but does not know his first name and patronymic; Ivanov to his teachers at high school; Vanya to his relatives and close childhood friends; Jean to a simpering female cousin; Vanyusha or Vanyushenka to his fond mother or wife; Vanechka Ivanov, or even Johnny Ivanov, to the beau monde if he is a sportsman or a rake, or merely a good-natured, elegant nonentity. This Ivanov may belong to a noble but not very old family since surnames derived from first names imply comparatively short genealogical trees. On the other hand, if this Ivan Ivanovich Ivanov belongs to the lower classes—is a servant, a peasant, or a young merchant—he may be called Ivan by his superiors, Vanka by his comrades, and Ivan Ivanych ("Mr. Johnson") by his meek kerchiefed wife; and if he is an old retainer, he may be addressed as Ivan Ivanych in sign of deference by the family he has served for half a century; and a respectable old peasant or artisan may be addressed by the weighty "Ivanych."

In the matter of titles, Prince Oblonski or Count Vronski or Baron Shílton meant in old Russia exactly what a prince, a count, or a baron would mean in continental Europe, prince corresponding roughly to an English duke, count to earl, baron to baronet. It should be noted, however, that titles did not imply any kinship to the Tsar's family, the Romanovs (the Tsar's immediate relatives were called Grand Dukes) and that many families of the oldest nobility never had a title. Lyovin's nobility was older than Vronski's. A man of comparatively unglamorous origin but a favorite of the Court might receive the title of Count from the Tsar and it seems likely that Vronski's father had been ennobled that way.

To force upon a foreign reader the use of a dozen names, mostly unpronounceable to him, for the designation of one person is both unfair and unnecessary. In the appended list I have given full names and titles as employed by Tolstoy in the Russian text; but in my revised translation* I have ruthlessly simplified addresses and allowed a patronymic to appear only when the context absolutely demanded it. (See also Notes 6, 21, 30, 68, 73, 79, 89.)

A complete list of characters that appear, or are mentioned, in part one of *Anna Karenin* (note stress accents and the revised spelling of names):

The Oblónski-Shcherbátski Group

Oblónski, Prince Stepán Arkádievich ("son of Arkádi"); anglicized diminutive of first name: Steve; aged 34; of ancient nobility; formerly (till 1869) served in Tver, his home town, a city north of Moscow; is now (1872) head of one of the several government bureaus in Moscow; office hours: from around 11 A.M. to 2 P.M. and from 3 P.M. to around 5 P.M.; may also be seen on official business at his residence; has a house in Moscow and a country estate (his wife's dowry), Ergushóvo, twenty miles from Lyovin's estate Pokróvskoe (presumably in the Province of Túla, south of Moscow, Central Russia).

His wife, Dolly (anglicized diminutive of Dária; the Russian diminutive is Dásha or Dáshenka); full name: Princess Dária Aleksandrovna ("daughter of Aleksandr") (wife of) Oblónski, born Princess Shcherbátski; aged 33; has been married nine years in part one.

Their five children (in February 1872), three girls and two boys: the eldest (aged eight) Tánya (diminutive of Tatiána); Grísha (diminutive of Grigóri); Másha (María); Lili (Elizaveta); and baby Vásya (Vasilí). A sixth child is to be born in March, and two children have died, making eight in all. In part three when they go to their country place Ergushóvo in late June 1872, the baby is three months old.

Dolly's brother, unnamed, drowned around 1860 in the Baltic; and two sisters: Natália (French form: Nathalie), married to Arséni Lvov, a diplomat and later an official at the Palace Offices (they have two boys, one

*Along with the other sections of what is called the Commentary in this volume, Nabokov intended the account of names to be part of the prefatory matter to a textbook edition of *Anna Karenin* that would have contained a new translation. It is particularly unfortunate that this project was never completed. Ed.

called Mísha, diminutive of Mihaíl); and Kitty (anglicized diminutive of Ekaterína; Russian diminutive: Katya, Kátenka), aged 18.

Prince Nikoláy Shcherbátski, a cousin.

Countess María Nórdston, a young married woman, Kitty's friend.

Prince Aleksándr Shcherbátski, a Moscow nobleman, and his wife ("the old Princess") are the parents of Dolly, Nathalie, and Kitty.

Filip Ivanych Nikítin and Mihaíl Stanislavich Grinévich, officials of Oblónski's bureau.

Zahar Nikítich (first name and patronymic), Oblónski's secretary.

Fomín, a shady character in a case under discussion at Oblónski's office.

Alábin, a society friend of Oblónski.

Prince Golitsyn, a gentleman dining with a lady at the Hotel d'Angleterre.

A Mr. Brénteln who married a Princess Shahovskóy.

Countess Bánin, a lady at whose house Oblónski attends a rehearsal of some private theatricals.

Mrs. Kalínin, a staff captain's widow, with a petition.

Mlle. Roland, formerly the French governess of Oblónski's children, now his mistress. She will be replaced in part four, chapter 7, about two years later (winter 1873-1874) by a young ballerina Masha Chibisova.

Miss Hull, their English governess.

Mlle. Linon, the old French governess of Dolly, Nathalie, and Kitty.

Matryóna Filimónovna ("daughter of Filimón"), no surname; diminutive: Matryósha; the old nurse of the Shcherbatski girls, now nursing the Oblónski children. Her brother, a cook.

Matvey(the English would be Matthew), Oblónski's old valet and butler.

Other servants of the Oblónski household: Már'ya, a housekeeper of sorts; a chef; an assistant (female) cook, who prepares the servants' meals; several anonymous maids; a footman; a coachman; a daily barber, and a weekly clockwinder.

The Bóbrishchevs, the Nikítins, the Mezhkóvs, Moscow families mentioned by Kitty in connection with gay and dull balls. Kórsunski, Egórushka (diminutive of Geórgi), an amateur conductor of dances at the balls given by his friends.

His wife, Lydíe (Lídia).

Miss Elétski, Mr. Krivin, and other guests at the ball.

———

The Karénin Group

Karénin (rhymes with "rainin' "), Alekséy Aleksándrovich ("son of Aleksandr"), Russian nobility of unspecified ancientry, formerly (around 1863) Governor of Tver; now a statesman occupying a high rank in one of the Ministries, apparently Interior or Imperial Estates; has a house in Petersburg.

His wife, Ánna Arkádievna ("daughter of Arkádi") Karénin, born Princess Oblónski, Steve's sister. Married eight years.

Seryózha (diminutive of Sergéy), their son, in his eighth year in 1872.

Countess Lídia Ivánovna ("daughter of Iván"), no surname mentioned, a friend of the Karenins, fashionably interested in the union of Catholic religions (Greek and Roman) and of the Slav nations.

Právdin, a vaguely Masonic correspondent of hers.

Princess Elizavéta Fyódorovna Tverskóy; anglicized diminutive: Betsy; Vronski's first cousin, married to Anna's first cousin.

Iván Petróvich (first name and patronymic), no surname given, a gentleman from Moscow, Anna's acquaintance, who happens to travel on the same train with her.

An anonymous railway guard, crushed by a backing train; leaves a widow and a large family.

A number of people, passengers and officials, on trains and railway stations.

Ánnushka (lowly diminutive of Ánna), Ánna Karénin's maid.

Mariette, Seryózha's French governess, surname not given; at end of part four is replaced by Miss Edwards.

Kondráti (first name), one of the Karénins' coachmen.

The Vrónski Group

Vrónski, Count Alekséy Kirílych, son of Count Kiríl Ivánovich Vrónski; diminutive Alyósha; a Cavalry Captain (*rotmistr*) of the Guards and aide-de-camp at the Court; stationed in Petersburg; in Moscow on leave of absence; has an apartment in St. Petersburg in the Morskáya Street (a fashionable quarter) and a country estate Vozdvízhenskoe, some fifty miles from Lyovin's estate, presumably in the Province of Túla, Central Russia.

His elder brother, Aleksándr (French: Alexandre), living in St. Petersburg, Commander of a Regiment of the Guards, father of at least two daughters (the elder is called Marie) and of a newborn boy; his wife's name is Várya (diminutive of Varvára), née Princess Chirkóv, daughter of a Decembrist. Keeps a dancing-girl.

Countess Vrónski, mother of Aleksándr and Alekséy, has an apartment or house in Moscow and a country estate nearby, reached from a station (Obirálovka), a few minutes from Moscow on the Nizhegorodski line.

Alekséy Vrónski's servants: a German valet and an orderly; old Countess Vrónski's maid and her butler Lavrénti, both traveling with her back to

Moscow from Petersburg; and an old footman of the Countess who comes to meet her at the Moscow station.

Ignátov, a Moscow pal of Vrónski.

Lieutenant "Pierre" Petrítski, one of Vrónski's best friends, staying in Vrónski's Petersburg flat.

Baroness Shílton, a married lady, Pierre's mistress.

Captain Kameróvski, a comrade of Petrítski's.

Various acquaintances mentioned by Petrítski: fellow officers Berkóshev and Buzulúkov; a woman, Lóra; Fertingóf and Miléev, her lovers; and a Grand Duchess. (Grand Dukes and Grand Duchesses were Románovs, i.e., relatives of the Tsar.)

The Lyóvin Group

Lyóvin, Konstantín Dmítrich ("son of Dmítri"), scion of a noble Moscow family older than the Count Vronski's; Tolstoy's representative in the world of the book; aged 32; has an estate, Pokróvskoe, in the "Karázinski" District and another in the Seleznyovski District, both in Central Russia. ("Province of Káshin"—presumably the Province of Túla.)

Nikoláy, his elder brother, a consumptive crank.

María Nikoláevna, first name and patronymic, no surname given; diminutive: Másha; she is Nikoláy's mistress, a reformed prostitute.

Nikoláy's and Konstantín's sister, unnamed; living abroad.

Their elder half brother, Sergéy Ivanóvich Kóznyshev, a writer on philosophic and social questions; has a house in Moscow and an estate in the Province of Káshin.

A professor from the University of Kharkov, South Russia.

Trúbin, a cardsharp.

Krítski, an acquaintance of Nikoláy Lyóvin, embittered and leftist.

Vanyúshka, a boy, adopted at one time by Nikoláy Lyóvin, now a clerk in the office of Pokróvskoe, the Lyóvins' estate.

Prokófi, Kóznyshev's man servant.

Menials on Konstantín Lyóvin's estate: Vasíli Fyódorovich (first name and patronymic), the steward; Agáfia Miháylovna (first name and patronymic), formerly nurse of Lyóvin's sister, now his housekeeper; Filíp, a gardener; Kuzmá, a house servant; Ignát, a coachman; Semyón, a contractor; Próhor, a peasant.

––––––––

Commentary Notes (part one)*

No. 1 *All was confusion in the Oblonski's house*
In the Russian text, the word *dom* (house, household, home) is repeated eight times in the course of six sentences. This ponderous and solemn repetition, *dom*, *dom*, *dom*, tolling as it does for doomed family life (one of the main themes of the book), is a deliberate device on Tolstoy's part (p.3).

No. 2 *Alabin, Darmstadt, America*
Oblonski with several of his friends, such as Vronski and presumably Alabin, is considering arranging a restaurant supper in honor of a famous songstress (see note 75); these pleasant plans permeate his dream and mingle with recollections of recent news in the papers: he is a great reader of political hodge-podge. I find that about this time (February 1872) the Cologne *Gazette* at Darmstadt (capital of the Grand Duchy of Hesse, part of the new German Empire in 1866) was devoting much discussion to the so-called Alabama claims (generic name applied to claims for indemnity made by the U. S. upon Great Britain because of the damage done to American shipping during the Civil War). In result Darmstadt, Alabin, and America get mixed up in Oblonski's dream (p.4).

No. 3 *Il mio tesoro*
"My Treasure." From Mozart's *Don Giovanni* (1787), it is sung by Don

---

*Page references are to the 1935 Modern Library Edition; but the key phrases sometimes represent Nabokov's retranslations.

Ottavio, whose attitude toward women is considerably more moral than Oblonski's (p.4).

No. 4 *But while she was in the house I never took any liberties. And the worst of the matter is that she is already* . . .
The first "she" refers to Mlle. Roland, the second to Oblonski's wife Dolly, who is already eight months pregnant (Dolly is to be delivered of a girl at the end of the winter, that is in March) (p.6).

No. 5 *Livery stable*
Where the Oblonskis rented a carriage and a pair. Now the rent is due (p.7).

No. 6 *Anna Arkadievna, Daria Aleksandrovna*
In speaking to a servant, Oblonski refers to his sister and wife by their first names and patronymics. In the reference to Dolly, there would not have been much difference had he said *knyaginya* (the Princess) or *barynya* (the Mistress) instead of "Daria Aleksandrovna" (p.7).

No. 7 *Side whiskers*
Fashionable in the seventies throughout Europe and America (p.7).

No. 8 *You want to try*
Matvey reflects that his master wishes to see if his wife will react to the news in the same way as she would have before their estrangement (p.8).

No. 9 *Things will arrange themselves*
The old servant uses a comfortably fatalistic folksy term: *obrazuetsya*, things will take care of themselves, it will be all right in the long run, this too will pass (p.8).

No.10 *He who likes coasting* . . .
The nurse quotes the first part of a common Russian proverb: "He who likes coasting should like dragging his little sleigh" (p.8).

No. 11 *Flushing suddenly*
Cases of flushing, blushing, reddening, crimsoning, coloring, etc. (and the opposite action of growing pale), are prodigiously frequent throughout this novel and, generally, in the literature of the time. It might be speciously argued that in the nineteenth century people blushed and blanched more readily and

more noticeably than today, mankind then being as it were younger; actually, Tolstoy is only following an old literary tradition of using the act of flushing, etc., as a kind of code or banner that informs or reminds the reader of this or that character's feelings (p.9). Even so the device is a little overdone and clashes with such passages in the book where, as in Anna's case, "blushing" has the reality and value of an individual trait.

This may be compared to another formula Tolstoy makes much use of: the "slight smile," which conveys a number of shades of feeling—amused condescension, polite sympathy, sly friendliness, and so on.

No. 12 *A merchant*
The name of this merchant (p.9), who eventually does acquire that forest at Ergushovo (the Oblonski's estate), is Ryabinin: he is to appear in part two, chapter 16.

No. 13 *Still damp*
In the old system of making-ready, as employed in Russia and elsewhere by printers of newspapers, it was necessary to dampen paper before it could be satisfactorily printed. Hence a newspaper copy fresh from the press would be dampish to the touch (p.9).

No. 14 *Oblonski's newspaper*
The mildly liberal newspaper Oblonski read was no doubt the *Russian Gazette* (*Russkie Vedomosti*), a Moscow daily (since 1868) (p.9).

No. 15 *Ryurik*
In the year A.D. 862, Ryurik, a Northman, the chief of a Varangian (Scandinavian) tribe, crossed the Baltic from Sweden and founded the first dynasty in Russia (862-1598). This was followed, after a period of political confusion, by the reign of the Romanovs (1613-1917), a much less ancient family than the descendants of Ryurik. In Dolgorukov's work on Russian genealogy, only sixty families descending from Ryurik are listed as existing in 1855. Among these are the Obolenskis of which name "Oblonski" is an obvious and somewhat slatternly imitation. (p.10).

No. 16 *Bentham and Mill*
Jeremy Bentham (1740-1832), English jurist, and James Mill (1773-1836), Scotch economist; their humane ideals appealed to Russian public opinion (p.11).

No. 17 *Beust rumored to have traveled to Wiesbaden*
Count Friedrich Ferdinand von Beust (1809-1886), Austrian statesman. Austria was at the time a regular wasp's nest of political intrigue, and much speculation was aroused in the Russian press when on November 10 new style, 1871, Beust was suddenly relieved of his function as Imperial Chancellor and appointed Ambassador to the Court of St. James. Just before Christmas, 1871, immediately after presenting his credentials, he left England to spend two months with his family in North Italy. According to the gazettes of the day and to his own memoirs (London, 1887), his return to London via Wiesbaden coincided with preparations for the thanksgiving service to be held in St. Paul's Tuesday, February 17/15, 1872, for the recovery (from typhoid fever) of the Prince of Wales. Of Beust's passage through Wiesbaden on his way back to England Oblonski read on a Friday; and the only Friday available is obviously February 23/11, 1872—which fixes nicely the opening day of the novel (p. 11).

Some of you may still wonder why I and Tolstoy mention such trifles. To make his magic, fiction, look *real* the artist sometimes places it, as Tolstoy does, within a definite, specific historical frame, citing fact that can be checked in a library—that citadel of illusion. The case of Count Beust is an excellent example to bring into any discussion about so-called real life and so-called fiction. There on the one hand is a historical fact, a certain Beust, a statesman, a diplomat, who not only has existed but has left a book of memoirs in two volumes, wherein he carefully recalls all the witty repartees, and political puns, which he had made in the course of his long political career on this or that occasion. And here, on the other hand, is Steve Oblonski whom Tolstoy created from top to toe, and the question is which of the two, the "real-life" Count Beust, or the "fictitious" Prince Oblonski is more alive, is more real, is more believable. Despite his memoirs—long-winded memoirs full of dead clichés—the good Beust remains a vague and conventional figure, whereas Oblonski, who never existed, is immortally vivid. And furthermore, Beust himself acquires a little sparkle by his participating in a Tolstoyan paragraph, in a fictitious world.

No. 18 *They (Grisha and Tanya) were in the act of propelling something, and then something fell. . . . All is confusion, thought Oblonski.*
This little accident to a simulated train against a background of confusion in the adulterer's home will be marked by the good reader as a subtle premonition, devised by Tolstoy's farsighted art, of a considerably more tragic catastrophe in part seven of the book. And what is especially curious is that Anna's little boy Seryozha, later in the book, plays at school at an invented game

where the boys represent a moving train; and when his house-tutor finds him despondent, the despondency is due not to his having hurt himself in that game but to his resenting the family situation (p.11).

No. 19 *She is up . . . that means she's not slept again all night.*
Dolly usually rose later and would never have been up as early as that (it is now around 9:30 A.M.) had she slept normally through the night (p.12).

No. 20 *Tanchúrochka*
A further diminution fanciful and endearing, of the common diminutive "Tanya" or "Tanechka." Oblonski crosses it with one of the *dochúrochka*, tender diminutives of *dochka*, the Russian word for "daughter" (p.12).

No. 21 *Petitioner*
Oblonski, as any high official, was in a position to hasten the proceedings of a case or to cut through the red tape, or sometimes even to influence a dubious issue. The petitioner's visit may be compared to seeing one's Congressman in quest of a special favor. Naturally, there were more plain people among petitioners than high-born and influential ones, since Oblonski's personal friend or social equal could ask him for a favor at a dinner or through a common friend (p.12).

No. 22 *The clockman*
There was, in the homes of Russian gentlemen, a custom of having a clockmaker (who happens to be a German here) come once a week, generally on Fridays, to check and wind the desk clocks, wall clocks, and grandfather clocks in the house. This paragraph defines the day of the week on which the story begins. For a novel in which time plays such an important part, a clockman is just the right person to start it on its way (p.17).

No. 23 *Ten rubles*
In the early seventies of the last century, one ruble was about three-quarters of a dollar, but the purchasing power of a dollar (one ruble thirty) was in some respects considerably higher than today. Roughly speaking, the government salary of six thousand per year that Oblonski was paid in 1872 would correspond to four thousand five hundred dollars of 1872 (at least fifteen thousand dollars of today, untaxed).*

*Perhaps more than $60,000 as of 1980. Ed.

No. 24 *And the worst of the matter* . . .

The worst of the matter, Dolly reflects, is that in a month or so she is going to have a child (p.18). This is on Tolstoy's part a nicely devised echo of Oblonski's thoughts on the same subject (p.6).

No. 25 *Complete liberalism*

Tolstoy's own notion of "liberalism" did not coincide with Western democratic ideals and with true liberalism as understood by progressive groups in old Russia. Oblonski's "liberalism" is definitely on the patriarchal side and we shall also note that Oblonski is not immune to conventional racial prejudice (p.20).

No. 26 *Uniform*

Oblonski changed from a lounge coat he wore into a government official's uniform (e.g., a green frock coat) (p.20).

No. 27 *The Penza Provincial Office*

Penza, main city in the Province of Penza, east central Russia (p.20).

No. 28 *Kamer-yunker*

German *Kammerjunker*, English (approximately) gentleman of the King's bedchamber. One of the several Russian court ranks, of an honorary nature, with such tame privileges as, for instance, the right to attend court balls. The mention of this title in connection with Grinevich merely implies that he belonged, and prided himself in belonging, to a socially more prominent set than his colleague, the plodding old bureaucrat Nikitin (p.21). The latter is not necessarily related to the Nikitins mentioned by Kitty on p. 86.

No. 29 *Kitty's education*

Though high schools for women began to come into existence as early as 1859, a noble family of the Shcherbatski type would either send their daughters to one of the "Institutes for Young Noblewomen," that dated back to the eighteenth century, or have them educated at home by governesses and visiting teachers. The programme would consist of a thorough study of French (language and literature), dancing, music, drawing. In many families, especially in St. Petersburg and Moscow, English would run a close second to French.

A young woman of Kitty's set would never go out-of-doors unattended either by a governess or by her mother or by both. She would be seen walking only at a certain fashionable hour on a certain fashionable boulevard, and on these occasions a footman would be following a few steps behind—both for protection and prestige.

No. 30 *Lyovin*

Tolstoy wrote "Levin," deriving the surname of this character (a Russian nobleman and the representative of a young Tolstoy in the imaginary world of the novel) from his own first name "Lev" (Russian for "Leo"). Alphabetically the Russian "e" is pronounced "ye" (as in "yes"), but in a number of instances it may have the sound of "yo" (as in "yonder"). Tolstoy pronounced his first name (spelled "Lev" in Russian) as "Lyov" instead of the usual "Lyev." I write "Lyovin" instead of "Levin," not so much to avoid any confusion (the possibility of which Tolstoy apparently did not realize) with a widespread Jewish surname of a different derivation, as to stress the emotional and personal quality of Tolstoy's choice (p.21).

Lvov

In giving to Nathalie Shcherbatski's husband, a diplomat with extremely sophisticated manners, the surname Lvov, Tolstoy used a common derivative from "Lev" as if to point out another side of his, Tolstoy's, personality in his youth, namely the desire to be absolutely *comme il faut*.

No. 31 *Oblonski was on familiar terms*

Russians (as well as the French and the Gemans) when addressing intimates use the singular "thou" (French *tu*, German *du*) instead of "you." This is *ty* in Russian, the "y" being pronounced somewhat as "u" in "tug." Although generally speaking the *ty* would go with the use of the interlocutor's first name, a combination of *ty* with the surname, or even with first name and patronymic, occurs not infrequently (p.22).

No. 32 *An active member of the zemstvo, a new type of man in this respect*

The *zemstvos* (created by a government act of January 1, 1864) were district and provincial assemblies with councils elected by three groups: landowners, peasants, and townspeople. Lyovin had been at first an eager supporter of these administrative boards but now objected to them on the grounds that landowner members were steering their needier friends into various lucrative positions (p.23).

No. 33 *New suit*

According to fashion plates of the time, Lyovin probably wore a well-cut short coat ("sack coat") with a braid edge, and then changed into a frock coat for his evening visit to the Shcherbatskis (p.24).

No. 34 *Gurin*
A merchant name implying a good but not smart restaurant, adequate for a friendly lunch around the corner (p.24).

No. 35 *Eight thousand acres in the Karazinski district*
The allusion is clearly to a district in the Province of Tula (further disguised as "Kashin"), Central Russia, south of Moscow, where Tolstoy possessed a considerable amount of land himself. A "province" (or "government," *guberniya*) consisted of districts (*uezdy*), and this one consisted of twelve such districts. Tolstoy invented "Karazinski," fancifully deriving it from Karazin (the name of a famous social reformer, 1773-1842), and combining Krapivenski District, where his own estate, *Yasnaya Polyana*, was situated (about eight miles from Tula on the Moscow-Kursk line), with the name of a neighboring village (Karamyshevo) (p.26). Lyovin had also land in the "Seleznyovski" district of the same ("Kashin") province.

No. 36 *Zoological Garden*
Tolstoy has in view a skating rink on the Presnenski Pond or some part of it, just south of the Zoo, in the north-west corner of Moscow (p.26).

No. 37 *Red stockings*
According to my source (*Mode in Costume*, by R. Turner Wilcox, New York, 1948, p. 308) purple and red in petticoats and stockings were great favorites with Parisian young ladies around 1870—and fashionable Moscow, of course, followed Paris. The shoe in Kitty's case would probably be a buttoned bottine of fabric or leather (p.28).

No. 38 *A very important philosophical question*
Tolstoy did not bother to go very far for a suitable subject. Problems of mind versus matter are still discussed all over the world; but the actual question as defined by Tolstoy was by 1870 such an old and obvious one, and is stated here in such general terms, that it hardly seems likely a professor of philosophy would travel all the way (over 300 miles) from Kharkov to Moscow to thrash it out with another scholar (p.30).

No. 39 *Keiss, Wurst, Knaust, Pripasov*

Although according to the *Allgemeine Deutsche Biographie* (Leipzig, 1882), there was a German educator Raimond Jacob Wurst (1800-1845) and a sixteenth-century song-maker Heinrich Knaust (or Knaustinus), I can find no Keiss, let alone Pripasov, and prefer to think that Tolstoy wittily invented wholesale that string of materialistic philosophers with—in plausible percentage—one Russian name in the wake of three German ones (p.31).

No. 40 *The skating ground*

Ever since the beginning of history, when the first skates were fashioned from the cannon bone of a horse, boys and young men used to play on the ice of frozen rivers and fens. The sport was extremely popular in old Russia, and by 1870 had become fashionable for both sexes. Club-skates of steel, round-toed or pointed, were strapped to the shoe and kept firm by clamps, spikes, or screws that entered the sole. This was before the time that special skating-boots, with skates permanently fixed to them, were used by good skaters (p.34).

No. 41 *The old curly birches of the garden, with all their branches weighed down by snow, seemed decked in new festive vestments*

As previously noted, Tolstoy's style, while freely allowing the utilitarian ("parabolic") comparison, is singularly devoid of poetical similes or metaphors intended to appeal primarily to the artistic sense of the reader. These birch-trees (with the "sun" and "wild rose" comparisons further) are an exception. They will presently cast a few spicules of their festive frost onto the fur of Kitty's muff (p.35).

It is curious to compare Lyovin's awareness of these emblematic trees here, at the commencement of his courtship, with certain other old birches (to be first mentioned by his brother Nikolay), that are worried by a crucial summer storm in the last part of the book.

No. 42 *Behind chairs*

A beginner might toddle along in his awkward skates clinging to the back of a chair painted green, on wooden runners, and in these same chairs ladies might be driven around by a friend or paid attendant (p.35).

Nabokov's drawing of a costume such as Kitty wore when she skated with Lyovin.

---

skating costume. Polonaise[(1)] and skirt of[(2)]
waterproof tweed, with military trimming[(3)]
and muff [(4)]   1872

Copied from C. W. Cunnington's "English women's clothing in
the nineteenth century", London, 1937, p. 266

No. 43 *Russian garb*

This lad, a gentleman's son, wears for skating the winter attire of the lower classes, or a stylized version of it—high boots, short belted coat, sheepskin cap (p.36).

No. 44 *We are at home on Thursdays. . . . "Which means to-day?" said Lyovin*

This is a slip on Tolstoy's part; but then, as previously mentioned, Lyovin's time throughout the book is prone to lag behind the time of the other characters. The Oblonskis, and we, know it is Friday (chapter 4), and later references to Sunday confirm this (p.40).

No. 45 *The Hotel d'Angleterre or the Ermitage*

The *Ermitage* is mentioned but not chosen, since it would have been hardly seemly for a novelist to advertise one of the best Moscow restaurants (where, according to Karl Baedeker, writing in the nineties, i.e., twenty years later, a good dinner minus wine cost two rubles twenty-five, or a couple of old-time dollars). Tolstoy mentions it, along with his invented Angleterre, merely to point out the latter's gastronomic rank. It will be noted that dinner is at the old-fashioned time between five and six (p.40).

No. 46 *Sleigh*

Cabs for hire as well as private vehicles other than the *kareta* (a closed carriage on wheels, such as Oblonski used) were more or less snug sleighs for two people. Snow permitting the use of sleighs covered the streets of Moscow and Petersburg approximately from November to April (p.40).

No. 47 *Tatars*

Or, less, correctly, Tartars—a name given to nearly three million inhabitants of the former Russian Empire, chiefly Moslems and mostly of Turkic origin, remnants of the Mongol (Tatar) invasions of the thirteenth century. From the Province of Kazan, East Russia, a few thousand migrated in the nineteenth century to Petersburg and Moscow where some of them pursued the calling of waiters (p.41).

No. 48 *The French girl at the buffet board*

Her job would be to supervise the buffet, and sell flowers (p.41).

No. 49 *Prince Golitsyn*

A generalized gentleman here. The moralist in Tolstoy had such a distaste for "inventing" (although actually the artist in him invented a greater number of plausible people than any man before him except Shakespeare) that often in his drafts we find him using "real names" instead of the slightly camouflaged ones he superimposed later. Golitsyn is a well-known name, and in this case Tolstoy apparently did not bother to twist it into Goltsov or Litsyn in his final text (p.42).

No. 50 *Oysters*

Flensburg oysters: these came from German beds (on the North Sea coast of Schleswig Holstein, just south of Denmark), which from 1859 to 1879 were rented to a company in Flensburg on the Denmark border.

Ostend oysters: ever since 1765 seed oysters had been brought from England to Ostend in Belgium.

Both "Flensburg" and "Ostend" were small products in the seventies, and these imported oysters were highly esteemed by Russian epicures (p.42).

No. 51 *Cabbage soup and groats*

Shchi—a soup consisting mainly of boiled cabbage—and *grechnevaya kasha*—boiled buckwheat meal—were, and presumably still are, the staple food of Russian peasants, whose rustic fare Lyovin would partake of in his capacity of gentleman farmer, man of the soil, and advocate of his simple life. In my time, forty years later, to slurp *shchi* was as chic as to toy with any French fare (p.42).

No. 52 *Chablis, Nuits*

Burgundy wines, white and red respectively. The white wines known to us as Chablis are made in the Department of Yonne (eastern France) situated in the oldest viticultural district of Europe, namely the ancient province of Burgundy. Nuits (place name) St. Georges, which presumably was the waiter's suggestion, comes from vineyards north of Beaune, in the center of the Burgundy district (p.43).

No. 53 *Parmesan*

Cheese was eaten with bread as an hors-d'oeuvre and in between courses (p.43).

No. 54 *Gallant steeds*

Russia's greatest poet Aleksandr Pushkin (1799-1837) translated into Russian (from a French version) Ode LIII of the so-called *Anacreontea*, a collection of poems attributed to Anacreon (born in the sixth century B.C. in Asia Minor, died at the age of 85), but lacking the peculiar forms of Ionic Greek in which he wrote according to authentic fragments quoted by ancient writers. Oblonski misquotes Pushkin horribly. Pushkin's version reads:

Gallant steeds one recognizes
By the markings branded on them;
Uppish Parthians one can tell
By their elevated mitres;
As to me I recognize
Happy lovers by their eyes . . . (p.45).

No. 55 *And with disgust the scroll of my past life*
I read, and shudder, and denounce it
And bitterly complain. . . .

Lyovin quotes a passage from Pushkin's poignant "Recollection" (1828) (p.48).

No. 56 *Recruits*

In the summary of the week's news of the *Pall Mall Budget* for December 29, 1871, I find the following: "An Imperial decree has been issued at St. Petersburg fixing the levy of recruits of the year 1872 at the rate of six per 1000 for the whole empire including the Kingdom of Poland. This is the usual levy in order to raise the army and navy to their proper standard" etc.

This note has little direct bearing on our text but is of some interest in itself (p.48).

No. 57 *Himmlisch ist's* . . .

"To conquer my earthly lust would have been divine but if I have not succeeded, I experience all the same lots of pleasure."

According to a brief note in Maude's translation of the novel (1937), Oblonski quotes these lines from the libretto of the *Fledermaus* which, however, was first produced two years after that dinner.

The exact reference would be: *Die Fledermaus, komische Operette in drei Akten nach Meilhac und Halevy* (authors of *Le Réveillon*, a French vaudeville, which itself was taken from a German comedy *Das Gefängnis* by Benedix), *bearbeitet von Haffner und Genée, Musik von Johann Strauss*. First produced in Vienna on April 5, 1874 (according to Loewenberg's *Annals of Opera*,

1943). I have not discovered this anachronistic quotation in the score but it may be in the complete book (p.50).

No. 58 *That gentleman in Dickens . . .*

The reference is to the pompous and smug Mr. John Podsnap in Dickens' *Our Mutual Friend*, which had first appeared in London in twenty monthly parts from May 1864 to November 1865. Podsnap, who was "happily acquainted with his own merit and importance, [had] settled that whatever he put behind him he put out of existence. . . . [He] had even acquired a peculiar flourish of the right arm in often clearing the world of its most difficult problems by sweeping them behind him . . ." (p.50).

No. 59 *Plato's "Symposium"*

In this dialogue Plato, a notorious Athenian philosopher (died in 347 B.C. at the age of eighty), has several banqueters discuss love. One of them rhetorically distinguishes earthly from heavenly love; another sings of Love and Love's works; a third, Socrates, speaks of two kinds of love, one ("being in love") which desires beauty for a peculiar end, and the other enjoyed by creative souls that bring into being not children of their body but good deeds (culled from an old edition of the *Encyclopaedia Britannica*) (p.51).

No. 60 *The dinner bill*

This literary dinner had cost twenty-six rubles including the tip, so Lyovin's share was thirteen rubles (about ten dollars of the time). The two men had two bottles of champagne, a little vodka, and at least one bottle of white wine (p.52).

No. 61 *Princess Shcherbatski had been married thirty years ago*

A slip on Tolstoy's part. Judging by Dolly's age, it should be at least thirty-four (p.53).

No. 62 *Changes in the manner of society*

In 1870, the first institution of higher learning for women (the Lubianski Courses: *Lubyanskie Kursy*) was inaugurated in Moscow. In general it was a time of emancipation for Russian women. Young women were claiming a freedom they did not have until then—among other things the freedom to choose their own husbands instead of having their parents arrange the match (p.54).

No. 63 *Mazurka*

One of the dances at balls of the time ("Gentlemen commencing with left foot, ladies with right, slide, slide, slide, slide, bring feet together, leap-turn" etc.). Tolstoy's son Sergey, in a series of notes on *Anna Karenin* (*Literaturnoe nasledstvo*, vols. 37-38, pp. 567-590, Moscow, 1939), says: "The mazurka was a favorite with ladies: to it the gentlemen invited those ladies to whom they were particularly attracted"(p.55).

No. 64 *Kaluga*

A town south of Moscow in the Tula direction (Central Russia) (p.60).

No. 65 *Classic, modern*

"Classic" (*klassicheskoe*) education in reference to Russian schools meant the study of Latin and Greek, whereas "Modern" (*realnoe*) implied their replacement by living languages, with the stress laid on the "scientific" and practical in other subjects (p.62).

No. 66 *Spiritualism*

The talk (at the Shcherbatskis) about table turning in part one, chapter 14, with Lyovin criticizing "spiritualism" and Vronski suggesting they all try, and Kitty looking for some small table to use—all this has a strange sequel in part four, chapter 13, when Lyovin and Kitty use a card table to write in chalk and communicate in fond cipher. This was a fashionable fad of the day—ghost rapping, table tilting, musical instruments performing short flights across the room, and other curious aberrations of matter and minds, with well-paid mediums making pronouncements and impersonating the dead in simulated sleep (p.62). Although dancing furniture and apparitions are as old as the world, their modern expression stems from the hamlet Hydesville near Rochester, New York State, where in 1848 raps had been recorded, produced by the ankle bones or other anatomical castanets of the Fox sisters. Despite all denouncements and exposures, "spiritualism" as it unfortunately became known fascinated the world and by 1870 all Europe was tilting tables. A committee appointed by the Dialectical Society of London to investigate "phenomena alleged to be spiritual manifestations" had recently reported thereon—and at one seance the medium Mr. Home had been "elevated eleven inches." In a later part of the book we shall meet this Mr. Home under a transparent disguise, and see how strangely and tragically spiritualism, a mere game suggested by Vronski in part one, will affect Karenin's intentions and his wife's destiny.

No. 67 *Ring game*
A parlor game played by young people in Russia and presumably elsewhere: the players form a circle all holding the same string, along which a ring is passed from hand to hand while a player in the middle of the circle tries to guess whose hands conceal the ring (p.65).

No. 68 *Prince*
Princess Shcherbatski's way of addressing her husband as *knyaz* (Prince) is an old-fashioned Moscovism. Note also that the Prince calls his daughters "Katenka" and "Dashenka" in the good Russian manner, i.e., having no use, as it were, for new-fangled English diminutives ("Kitty" and "Dolly") (p.66).

No. 69 *Tyutki*
A plural noun applied by the gruff Prince to the young scatterbrains, with connotations of fatuousness and foppery. It does not really suit Vronski whom Kitty's father seems to have in mind here; Vronski may be vain and frivolous but he is also ambitious, intelligent, and persevering. Readers will note the curious echo of this fancy word in the name of the hairdresser ("Tyutkin coiffeur") whose sign Anna reads with a roaming eye on the day of her death while driving through the streets of Moscow (p. 885); she is struck by the absurd contrast of "Tyutkin," a Russian comedy name, with the stiff French epithet "coiffeur," and for a second reflects she might amuse Vronski by making a joke of this (p.66).

No. 70 *Corps of pages*
Pazheski ego imperatorskogo velichestva korpus (His Imperial Majesty's Corps of Pages), a military school for the sons of noblemen in old Russia, founded 1802, reformed 1865 (p.68).

No. 71 *Chateau des Fleurs, can-can*
Allusion to a night restaurant with vaudeville performances on a stage. "The notorious can-can . . . is only a quadrille danced by gross people" (Allen Dodworth in *Dancing and its Relations to Education and Social Life*, London, 1885) (p.69).

No. 72 *The station*
The Nikolaevski or Peterburgski railway station in the north-central part of Moscow. The line was built by the government in 1843-1851. A fast train

covered the distance between Petersburg and Moscow (about 400 miles) in twenty hours in 1862 and in thirteen hours in 1892. Leaving Petersburg around 8 P.M., Anna arrived in Moscow a little after 11 A.M. the following day (p.70).

No. 73 *Ah, your Serenity*
An inferior—servant, clerk, or tradesman—would address a titled person (prince or count) as "your Serenity," *vashe siyatel'stvo* (German "Durchlaucht"). The use which Prince Oblonski (who is a *siyatel'stvo* in his own right, of course) makes of the term in greeting Count Vronski is playfully patronizing: he mimics an elderly attendant stopping a young scapegrace in his tracks, or—as more precisely, perhaps—acts the staid family man speaking to a flighty bachelor (p.70).

No. 74 *Honi soit qui mal y pense*
The motto of the Order of the Garter, "Shame to him who thinks evil of it," as pronounced by Edward the Third in 1348 when rebuking the mirth of some noblemen over a lady's fallen garter (p.70).

No. 75 *Diva*
This Italian word ("the divine one") was applied to celebrated singers (e.g., *la diva* Patti); by 1870, in France and elsewhere, the term was often used in reference to flashy ladies of the variety stage; but here I think a respectable singer or actress is implied. This diva, reflected and multiplied, takes part in Oblonski's dream—the dream from which he awakes Friday at 8 A.M., February 11 (p. 4). Here, on page 71 Oblonski and Vronski talk of the supper to be given in her honor next day, Sunday, February 13. On page 77 Oblonski talks about her ("the new singer") with Countess Vronski at the station, that same Saturday morning, February 12. Finally, on page 90, he tells his family, at 9:30 P.M. the same Saturday, that Vronski has just called to inquire about the dinner they are to give next day to a celebrity from abroad. It seems that Tolstoy could not quite make up his mind whether the occasion was to be formal or frivolous (p.71).

It should be noted that at the end of part five, the appearance of a famous singer (the *diva* Patti, this time she is named) occurs in a critical passage of Anna's romance with Vronski.

No. 76 *Through the frosty haze one could distinguish a number of railway workers, wearing short sheepskin coats and felt snowboots, in the act of stepping across the rails of the curving tracks*

Here commences a sequence of subtle moves on Tolstoy's part aiming at bringing about a gruesome accident and, simultaneously, adducing the impressions from which later a crucial nightmare seen both by Anna and Vronski will be formed. The poor visibility among the frosty vapors is connected with various muffled-up figures such as these railway workers and, a little further, the muffled-up, frost-covered engine driver. The death of the railway guard which Tolstoy is preparing occurs on page 77: "a guard . . . too much muffled up against the severe frost had not heard a train backing [the optical haze becomes an auditory one] and had been crushed." Vronski views the mangled body (p.77) and he (and possibly Anna) has also noticed a peasant with a bag over his shoulder emerge from the train (p.72)—a visual impression that will breed. The theme of "iron" (which is beaten and crushed in the subsequent nightmare) is also introduced here in terms of a station platform vibrating under a great weight (p.71).

No. 77 *The locomotive came rolling by*

In the famous photograph (1869) of the first two transcontinental trains meeting at Promontory Summit, Utah, the engine of the Central Pacific (building from San Francisco eastward) is seen to have a great flaring funnel stack, while the engine of the Union Pacific (building from Omaha westward) sports but a straight slender stack topped by a spark-arrester. Both types of chimneys were used on Russian locomotives. According to Collignon's *Chemins de Fer Russes* (Paris, 1868), the seven and a half meters long locomotive, with wheels oOOo, of the fast train connecting Petersburg and Moscow had a straight funnel two and a third meters high, i.e., exceeding by thirty centimeters the diameter of its driving wheels whose action is so vigorously described by Tolstoy (p.72).

No. 78 *This lady's appearance . . .*

It is not necessary for the reader to look at Anna with Vronski's eyes, but for those who are anxious to appreciate all the details of Tolstoy's art, it is necessary to realize clearly what he meant his heroine to look like. Anna was rather stout but her carriage was wonderfully graceful, her step singularly light. Her face was beautiful, fresh, and full of animation. She had curly black hair that was apt to come awry, and gray eyes glistening darkly in the shadow of thick lashes. Her glance could light up with an enchanting glow or assume a serious and woeful expression. Her unpainted lips were a vivid red. She had plump arms, slender wrists and tiny hands. Her handshake was vigorous, her motions rapid. Everything about her was elegant, charming and real (p.73).

No. 79 *Oblonski! Here!*

Two men of fashion, close friends or messmates, might call each other by their surnames, or even by their titles—count, prince, baron—reserving first names or nicknames for special occasions. When Vronski calls to Steve "Oblonski!" he is using an incomparably more intimate form of address than if he had shouted out Stepan Arkadyevich's name and patronymic (p.74).

No. 80 *Vous filez le parfait amour. Tant mieux, mon cher*

You are engrossed in perfect love-making. So much the better, my dear (p.75).

No. 81 *Unusual color, unusual event*

There is of course no actual connection between the two, but the repetition is characteristic of Tolstoy's style with its rejection of false elegancies and its readiness to admit any robust awkwardness if that is the shortest way to sense. Cp. the somewhat similar clash of "unhasting" and "hastily" some fifty pages further on. The station master's cap was of a bright red color (p.76).

No. 82 *Bobrishchevs*

We may infer that *they* were giving this particular ball (p.86).

No. 83 *Anna's dress*

Perusal of an article on "Paris fashions for February" in the *London Illustrated News*, 1872, reveals that whereas *toilettes de promenade* just touched the ground, an evening dress had a long square-cut train. Velvet was most fashionable, and for a ball a lady would wear a *robe princesse* of black velvet over a skirt of faille, edged with chantilly lace, and a tuft of flowers in the hair (p.93).

No. 84 *Waltz*

Sergey Tolstoy, in the series of notes already mentioned (see note 63), describes the order of dances at a ball of the type described here: "The ball would start with a light waltz, then there would come four quadrilles, then a mazurka with various figures. . . . The final dance would be a cotillion . . . with such figures as grand-rond, chaine, etc., and with interpolated dances—waltz, galop, mazurka."

Dodworth in his book (*Dancing*, 1885) lists as many as two hundred and fifty figures in the "Cotillion or German." The grand-rond is described under Nr. 63 as: "Gentlemen select gentlemen; ladies select ladies; a grand round is formed, the gentlemen joining hands on one side of the circle, the ladies on the other; the figure is begun by turning to the left; then the conductor who holds his lady by the right hand, advances, leaving the other [dancers] and cuts through the middle of the round . . . [then] he turns to the left with all the gentlemen while his partner turns to the right with all the ladies, continuing down the side of the room, thus forming two lines facing. When the last two have passed out [!] the two lines advance, each gentleman dancing with opposite lady." Various "chains" —double, uninterrupted, etc. —can be left to the reader's imagination (p.95).

No. 85 *People's theatre*
According to a note in Maude's translation, a people's theatre (or more exactly a privately financed theatre—Moscow having only State theatres at that time) was initiated "at the Moscow Exhibition of 1872" (p.95).

No. 86 *She had refused five partners*
She had also refused Lyovin a few days before. The whole ball (with its wonderful break [p.95] "the music stopped") is subtly emblematic of Kitty's mood and situation (p.97).

No. 87 . . . *Enchanting [was] the firm-fleshed neck with its row of pearls [zhemchug] . . . enchanting [her] animation [ozhivlenie] but there was something terrifying [uzhasnoe] and cruel [zhestokoe] about her charm*
This "zh" repetition (phonetically coinciding with "s" in "pleasure"—the buzzing ominous quality of her beauty—is artistically followed up in the penultimate paragraph of the chapter: ". . . the uncontrollable [neuderzhimy], quivering [drozhashchi] glow of her eyes and smile burned [obzhog] him. . . ." (pp.98-99).

No. 88 *Dance leader*
"The conductor [or "leader"] should exercise constant watchfulness and be ever on the alert to urge the tardy, prompt the slow, awake the inattentive, signal those occupying the floor too long, superintend the preparatory formation of the figure, see that each dancer is on the proper side of his partner, and, if simultaneous movement is required, give the signal for that movement to commence etc. He is thus compelled to fulfill the duties of a 'whipper-in,' as well as those of conductor, instructor, and superintendent." Toned down by the social position and expert dancing of the people involved in the present ball, this was more or less Korsunski's function (p.99).

No. 89 *There is some gentleman, Nikolay Dmitrich*
Nikolay's lowly mistress uses the first name and abridged patronymic as a respectful wife would in a petty bourgeois household (p.101).

When Dolly, in speaking of her husband calls him by his first name and patronymic, she is doing something else: she chooses the most formal and neutral manner of reference to him to stress the estrangement.

No. 90 *And the birches, and our schoolroom*
With keen nostalgic tenderness recalling the rooms in the ancestral manor, where as boys he and his brother used to have lessons with a tutor or a governess (p.107).

No. 91 *Gypsies*
Night restaurants had Gypsy (*Tzygan*) entertainers who sang and danced. Good-looking female Gypsy performers were extremely popular with Russian rakes (p.108).

No. 92 *His low-slung carpet sleigh*
A type of rustic comfortable sleigh which looked as if it consisted of a rug on runners (p.109).

No. 93 *Heated*
Lyovin's manor house was heated by means of wood-burning Dutch stoves, a stove per room, and there were double windows with wads of cotton wool between the panes (p.112).

No. 94 *Tyndall*
John Tyndall (1820-1893), author of *Heat as a Mode of Motion* (1863 and later editions). This was the first popular exposition of the mechanical theory of heat which in the early sixties had not reached the text books (p.113).

No. 95 *Third bell*
The three Russian station bells had already become in the seventies a national institution. The first bell, a quarter of an hour before departure, introduced the idea of a journey to the would-be passenger's mind; the second, ten minutes later, suggested the project might be realized; immediately after the third, the train whistled and glided away (p.118).

No. 96 *Car*

Roughly speaking, two notions of night-traveling comfort were dividing the world in the last third of the century: the Pullman system in America, which favored curtained sections and which rushed sleeping passengers feet foremost to their destination; and the Mann system in Europe, which had them speed sidewise in compartments; but in 1872, a first-class car (euphemistically called sleeping-car by Tolstoy) of the night express between Moscow and Petersburg was a very primitive affair still wavering between a vague Pullman tendency and Colonel Mann's "boudoir" scheme. It had a lateral corridor, it had water closets, it had stoves burning wood; but it also had open-end platforms which Tolstoy calls "porches" (*krylechki*), the vestibule housing not having yet been invented. Hence the snow driving in through the end doors when conductors and stove-tenders passed from car to car. Night accommodations were draughty sections, semi-partitioned off from the passage, and it is evident from Tolstoy's description that six passengers shared one section (instead of the four in sleeping compartments of a later day). The six ladies in the "sleeping" section reclined in fauteuils, three facing three, with just enough space between opposite fauteuils to permit the extension of footrests. As late as 1892, Karl Baedeker speaks of first-class cars on that particular line as having fauteuils which can be transformed into beds at night but he gives no details of the metamorphosis, and anyway, in 1872, the simulacrum of full-length repose did not include any bedding. To comprehend certain important aspects of Anna's night journey, the reader should clearly visualize the following arrangement: Tolstoy indiscriminately calls the plush seats in the section either "little divans" or "fauteuils"; and both terms are right since, on each side of the section, the divan was divided into three armchairs. Anna sits facing north, in the right-hand (south-east) window corner, and she can see the left-hand windows, across the passage. On her left she has her maid Annushka (who this time travels with her in the same section, and not second-class, as she had on her journey to Moscow) and on the other side, further west, there is a stout lady, who being closest to the passage on the left-hand side of the section, experiences the greatest discomfort from heat and cold. Directly opposite Anna, an old invalid lady is making the best she can of the sleeping arrangements; there are two other ladies in the seats opposite to Anna, and with these she exchanges a few words (p.118).

No. 97 *Small traveling lantern*

This was, in 1872, a very primitive gadget, with a candle inside, a reflector, and a metallic handle that could be fixed to the arm of a railway fauteuil at the reader's elbow (p.118).

LEO TOLSTOY   231

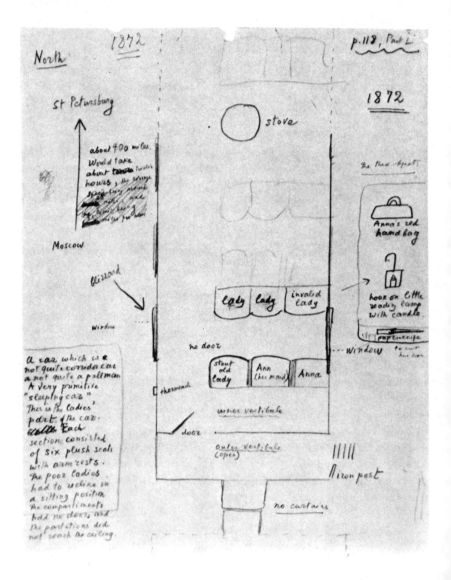

No. 98 *The stove-heater*
Here is a further set of impressions going back to the muffled-up guard who got crushed ("someone being torn part") and going forward to Anna's suicide (the blinding wall, the "sinking"). The wretched stove-heater seems to somnolent Anna to be gnawing at something in the wall, and this will be twisted into the groping and crushing motion of the disgusting dwarf in her later nightmare (p.118).

No. 99 *A stop*
The station is Bologoe, midway between Moscow and St. Petersburg. In the 1870s this was a twenty-minute stop in the small hours for some bleak refreshments (see also note 72) (p.120).

No. 100 *Round hat*
In 1850, there appeared a hard hat with a low crown designed by William Bowler, an English hatter, and this was the original model of the bowler, or derby—its American name stemming from the fact that the Earl of Derby wore a gray bowler with a black band to the English races. It was generally adopted in the seventies.
Karenin's ears should be noted as the third item in the series of the "wrong things" which underscore Anna's mood (p.123).

No. 101 *Panslavist*
Promoter of a spiritual and political union of all Slavs (Serbs, Bulgarians, etc.), with Russia at its head (p.128).

No. 102 *Put [Seryozha] to bed*
The time is around 9 p.m. (see end of paragraph). For some reason Seryozha has been put to bed earlier than usual (see above where "around ten" is mentioned as his bedtime—a singularly late one for a child of eight) (p.131).

No. 103 *Duc de Lille's* Poesie des Enfers
Possibly a disguised allusion on Tolstoy's part to the French writer Count Mathias Philippe Auguste Villiers de L'Isle Adam (1840-1889). Tolstoy invented the title, "The Poesie of Hades," (p.132).

Nabokov's sketch of the sleeping car in which Anna rode from Moscow to St. Petersburg.

No. 104 *Vronski's teeth*

In the course of the novel, Tolstoy refers several times to Vronski's splendid regular teeth, *sploshnye zuby*, which make a smooth solid ivory front when he smiles; but before he disappears from the pages of the novel in part eight, his creator, punishing Vronski in his brilliant physique, inflicts upon him a marvelously described toothache (p.137).

No. 105 *A special note on the game of tennis*

At the end of chapter 22 of part six, Dolly Oblonski watches Vronski, Anna, and two male guests play tennis. This is July 1875 and the tennis they are playing on the Vronski country estate is the modern game, which a Major Wingfield introduced in England in 1873. It was an immediate success and was played in Russia and in this country as early as 1875. In England, tennis is often called lawn tennis because at first it was played on croquet lawns, hard or turfy, and also in order to distinguish it from the ancient game of tennis, played in special tennis halls and called sometimes court-tennis. Court-tennis is mentioned both by Shakespeare and Cervantes. Ancient kings played it, stamping and panting in resounding halls. But this (lawn tennis), I repeat, is our modern game. You will notice Tolstoy's neat description: the players divided into two teams of two stood on opposite sides of a tightly drawn net with gilt poles (I like the gilt—an echo of the game's royal origin and genteel resurrection) on the nicely rolled croquet-ground. The various personal tricks of playing are described. Vronski and his partner Sviazhski played a good game and played it very earnestly: keeping a sharp eye on the ball as it came their way and without haste or delay they ran nimbly up to it, waited for the rebound, and neatly hit it back—most of the shots were more or less lobs I'm afraid. Anna's partner, a young man called Veslovski, whom Lyovin had thrown out of his house a couple of weeks before, played worse than the others. Now comes a nice detail: the men with the ladies' permission took their coats off and played in their shirt sleeves. Dolly found the whole performance unnatural—grown-up people running after a ball like children. Vronski is a great admirer of English ways and fads, and the tennis illustrates this. Incidentally, the game was much tamer in the seventies than it is today. A man's service was a stiff pat, with the

knitted jersey

tennis costume
c. 1875

C. Willett Cunnington
English Women's clothing
in the nineteenth century
London 1937
p. 293

racquet held vertically at eye level; a lady's sevice was a feeble underhand stroke.

No. 106 *A special note on the question of religion*

The people in the book belong to the Russian church, the so-called Greek Orthodox—or more correctly Greek Catholic—Church, which separated from the Roman communion a thousand years ago. When we first meet one of the minor characters in the book, Countess Lidia, she is interested in the union of the two churches and so is the pietist lady Madame Stahl affecting Christian devotion, whose influence Kitty soon gets rid of at Soden. But as I say, the main faith in the book is the Greek Catholic creed. The Shcherbatskis, Dolly, Kitty, their parents, are shown combining the traditional ritual with a kind of natural, old-fashioned, easy-going faith which Tolstoy approved of, for in the seventies when Tolstoy was writing this novel he had not evolved yet his fierce contempt for church ritual. The marriage ceremony for Kitty and Lyovin, and the priests, are described sympathetically. It is at his marriage that Lyovin, who had not gone to church for years and had considered himself an atheist, feels the first pangs of faith birth, then doubt again—but at the end of the book we leave him in a state of bewildered grace, with Tolstoy gently pushing him into the Tolstoyan sect.

———

The Death of Ivan Ilyich (1884-1886)

To a greater or lesser extent there goes on in every person a struggle between two forces: the longing for privacy and the urge to go places: introversion, that is, interest directed within oneself toward one's own inner life of vigorous thought and fancy; and extroversion, interest directed outward, toward the external world of people and tangible values. To take a simple example: the university scholar—and by scholar I mean professors and students alike—the university scholar may present sometimes both sides. He may be a bookworm and he may be what is called a joiner—and the bookworm and the joiner may fight within one man. A student who gets or wishes to get prizes for acquired knowledge may also desire, or be expected to desire, prizes for what is called leadership. Different temperaments make different decisions, of course, and there are minds in which the inner world persistently triumphs over the outer one, and vice versa. But we must take into account the very fact of a struggle going on or liable to go on between the two versions of man in one man— introversion and extroversion. I have known students who in the pursuit of the inner life, in the ardent pursuit of knowledge, of a favorite subject had to clap their hands to their ears in order to shut out the booming surf of dormitory life; but at the same time they would be full of a gregarious desire to join in the fun, to go to the party or to the meeting, to give up the book for the band.

From this state of affairs there is really not a very far cry to the problems of writers like Tolstoy in whom the artist struggled with the preacher; the great introvert with the robust extrovert. Tolstoy surely realized that in him as in many writers there did go on the personal struggle between creative solitude and the urge to associate with all mankind—the battle between the book and band. In Tolstoyan terms, in the symbols of Tolstoyan later philosopy after he finished *Anna Karenin*, creative solitude became synonymous with sin: it was egoism, it was the pampering of one's self and therefore a sin. Conversely, the idea of *all mankind* was in Tolstoyan terms the idea of God: God is in men and God is universal love. And Tolstoy advocated the loss of one's personality in this universal God-Love. He suggested, in other words, that in the personal struggle between the godless artist and the godly man the latter should better win if the synthetic man wishes to be happy.

We must retain a lucid vision of these spiritual facts in order to appreciate the philosophy of the story "The Death of Ivan Ilyich." Ivan is of course the Russian for John, and John in Hebrew means God is Good, God is Gracious. I know it's not easy for non-Russian-speaking people to pronounce the patronymic Ilych, which of course means the son of Ilya, the Russian version of the name Elias or Elijah, which incidentally means in Hebrew, Jehovah is God. Ilya is a very common Russian name, pronounced very much like the French *il y a*; and Ilyich is pronounced Ill-Itch—the ills and itches of mortal life.

Now comes my first point: this is really the story not of Ivan's Death but the story of Ivan's Life. The physical death described in the story is part of mortal Life, it is merely the last phase of mortality. According to Tolstoy, mortal man, personal man, individual man, *physical* man, goes his physical way to nature's garbage can; according to Tolstoy, *spiritual* man returns to the cloudless region of universal God-Love, an abode of neutral bliss so dear to Oriental mystics. The Tolstoyan formula is: Ivan lived a bad life and since a bad life is nothing but the death of the soul, then Ivan lived a living death; and since beyond death is God's living light, then Ivan died into new Life—Life with a capital L.

My second point is that this story was written in March 1886, at a time when Tolstoy was nearly sixty and had firmly established the Tolstoyan fact that writing masterpieces of fiction was a sin. He had firmly made up his mind that if he would write anything, after the great sins of his middle years, *War and Peace* and *Anna Karenin*, it would be only in the way of simple tales for the people, for peasants, for school children, pious educational fables, moralistic fairy tales, that kind of thing. Here and there in "The Death of Ivan Ilyich" there is a half-hearted attempt to proceed with this trend, and we shall find samples of a pseudo-fable style here and there in the story. But on the whole it is the artist who takes over. This story is Tolstoy's most artistic, most perfect, and most sophisticated achievement.

Thanks to the fact that Guerney has so admirably translated the thing I shall have the opportunity at last to discuss Tolstoy's style. Tolstoy's style is a marvelously complicated, ponderous instrument.

You may have seen, you must have seen, some of those awful text books written not by educators but by educationalists—by people who talk about books instead of talking within books. You may have been told by them that the chief aim of a great writer, and indeed the main clue to his greatness, is "simplicity." Traitors, not teachers. In reading exam papers written by misled students, of both sexes, about this or that author, I have often come across such phrases—probably recollections from more tender years of schooling—as "his style is simple" or "his style is clear and simple" or "his style is beautiful and simple" or "his style is quite beautiful and simple." But remember that "simplicity" is buncombe. No major writer is simple. The *Saturday Evening Post* is simple. Journalese is simple. Upton Lewis is simple. Mom is simple. Digests are simple. Damnation is simple. But Tolstoys and Melvilles are not simple.

One peculiar feature of Tolstoy's style is what I shall term the "groping purist." In describing a meditation, emotion, or tangible object, Tolstoy follows the contours of the thought, the emotion, or the object until he is perfectly satisfied with his re-creation, his rendering. This involves what we might call creative repetitions, a compact series of repetitive statements, coming one immediately after the other, each more expressive, each closer to Tolstoy's meaning. He gropes, he unwraps the verbal parcel for its inner sense, he peels the apple of the phrase, he tries to say it one way, then a better way, he gropes, he stalls, he toys, he Tolstoys with words.

Another feature of his style is his manner of weaving striking details into the story, the freshness of the descriptions of physical states. Nobody in the eighties in Russia wrote like that. The story was a forerunner of Russian modernism just before the dull and conventional Soviet era. If there is the fable noted, there is too a tender, poetical intonation here and there, and there is the tense mental monologue, the stream of consciousness technique that he had already invented for the description of Anna's last journey.

A conspicuous feature of the structure is that Ivan is dead when the story starts. However, there is little contrast between the dead body and the existence of the people who discuss his death and view his body, since from Tolstoy's point of view their existence is not life but a living death. We discover at the very beginning one of the many thematic lines of the story, the pattern of trivialities, the automatic mechanism, the unfeeling vulgarity of the bureaucratic middle-class city life in which so recently Ivan himself had participated. Ivan's civil service colleagues think of how his death will affect their careers: "So on receiving the news of Ivan Ilyich's death the first thought of each of the gentlemen in those chambers was of the changes and promotions it might occasion among themselves or their acquaintances.

" 'I'll be sure to get Shtabel's place or Vinnikov's,' thought Fyodor Vasilievich. 'I was promised that long ago, and the promotion means an extra eight hundred rubles a year for me besides the allowance.'

" 'Now I must apply for my brother-in-law's transfer from Kaluga,' thought Peter Ivanovich. 'My wife will be very glad, and then she won't be able to say that I never do anything for her relatives.' "

Note the way the first conversation has gone but this selfishness after all is a very normal and humble human trait because Tolstoy is an artist, above castigation of morals—note, I say, the way the conversation about Ivan's death then slips into a piece of innocent kidding when the self-seeking thoughts have ended. After the seven introductory pages of chapter 1, Ivan Ilyich, as it were, is revived, is made to live his whole life again, in thought, and then he is made to revert, physically, to the state depicted in the first chapter (for death and bad life are synonymous) and spiritually to pass into the state so beautifully adumbrated in the last chapter (for there is no death once this business of physical existence is over).

Egotism, falsity, hypocrisy, and above all automatism are the most important moments of life. This automatism puts people on the level of inanimate objects—and this is why inanimate objects also go into action and become characters in the story. Not symbols of this or that character, not attributes as in Gogol's work, but acting agents on a par with the human characters.

Let us take the scene between Ivan's widow Praskovya and Ivan's best friend Peter. "Peter Ivanovich sighed still more deeply and despondently, and Praskovya Fyodorovna pressed his arm gratefully. When they reached the drawing room, upholstered in pink cretonne and lighted by a dim lamp, they sat down at the table—she on a sofa and Peter Ivanovich on a low, soft ottoman, the springs of which yielded spasmodically under his weight. Praskovya Fyodorovna had been on the point of warning him to take another seat, but felt that such a warning was out of keeping with her present condition and so changed her mind. As he sat down on the ottoman Peter Ivanovich recalled how Ivan Ilyich had arranged this room and had consulted him regarding this pink cretonne with green leaves. The whole room was full of furniture and knickknacks, and on her way to the sofa the lace of the widow's black shawl caught on the carved edge of the table. Peter Ivanovich rose to detach it, and the springs of the ottoman, relieved of his weight, rose also and gave him a bounce. The widow began detaching her shawl herself, and Peter Ivanovich again sat down, suppressing the rebellious springs of the ottoman under him. But the widow had not quite freed herself, and Peter Ivanovich got up again, and again the ottoman rebelled and even creaked. When this was all over she took out a clean cambric handkerchief and began to weep. . . . 'You may smoke,' she said in a magnanimous yet crushed voice, and turned to discuss with Sokolov the price of the plot for the grave. . . .

" 'I look after everything myself,' she told Peter Ivanovich, shifting the albums that lay on the table; and noticing that the table was endangered by his cigarette ash, she immediately passed him an ash tray. . . ."

As Ivan, with Tolstoy's assistance, revises his life, he sees that the culmination of his happiness in that Life (before he fell ill, never to recover) was when he got a nice fat official position and rented an expensive bourgeois apartment for himself and his family. I use the word bourgeois in the philistine sense, not in a class sense. I mean the kind of apartment that would strike the conventional mind in the eighties as moderately luxurious, with all kinds of knickknacks and ornaments. Today, of course, a philistine might dream of glass and steel, videos or radios disguised as book shelves and dumb pieces of furniture.

I said that this was the peak of Ivan's philistine happiness, but it was upon this peak that death pounced upon him. In falling from a stepladder when he was hanging a curtain, he had fatally injured his left kidney (this is my diagnosis—the result was probably cancer of the kidney); but Tolstoy, who disliked doctors and medicine in general, deliberately confuses matters by alluding to various other possibilities—floating kidney, some stomach ailment, even appendicitis, which could hardly have been in the left side as mentioned several times. Ivan makes later a wry joke that he was mortally wounded when storming the curtain, as if it were a fortress.

From now on nature, in the disguise of physical disintegration, enters the picture and destroys the automatism of conventional life. Chapter 2 had begun with the phrase, "Ivan's life had been most simple and most ordinary—and therefore most terrible." It was terrible because it had been automatic, trite, hypocritical—animal survival and childish contentment. Nature now introduces an extraordinary change. Nature to Ivan is uncomfortable, filthy, indecent. One of the props of Ivan's conventional life was propriety, superficial decency, elegant and neat surfaces of life, decorum. These are gone now. But nature comes in not only as the villain of the piece: it also has its good. Very good and sweet side. This leads us to the next theme, of Gerasim.

Tolstoy, as the consistent dualist he was, draws a contrast between the conventional, artificial, false, intrinsically vulgar, superficially elegant city life and the life of nature personified here by Gerasim, a clean, calm, blue-eyed young peasant, one of the lowly servants in the house, doing the most repellant jobs—but performing them with angelic indifference. He personifies the natural goodness in Tolstoy's scheme of things and he is thus closer to God. He appears here first as the embodiment of swift, soft-walking but vigorous nature. Gerasim understands and pities the dying Ivan but he pities him lucidly and dispassionately.

"Gerasim did it all easily, willingly, simply, and with a good nature that touched Ivan Ilyich. Health, strength, and vitality in other people were offensive to him, but Gerasim's strength and vitality did not mortify but soothed him.

"What tormented Ivan Ilyich most was the deception, the lie, which for some reason they all accepted, that he was not dying but was simply ill, and that he only need keep quiet and undergo treatment and then the results would be very good. . . . He saw that no one felt for him, because no one even wished to grasp his position. Only Gerasim recognized and pitied him, and so Ivan Ilyich felt at ease only with him. . . . Gerasim alone did not lie; everything showed that he alone understood the facts of the case and did not consider it necessary to disguise them, but simply felt sorry for his emaciated and enfeebled master. Once when Ivan Ilyich was sending him away he even said straight out: 'We shall all of us die, so why should I grudge a little trouble?'—expressing the fact that he did not think his work burdensome, because he was doing it for a dying man and hoped someone would do the same for him when his time came."

The final theme may be summed up in Ivan Ilyich's question: What if my whole life has been wrong? For the first time in his life he feels pity for others. Then comes the resemblance to the fairy tale pathos of the Beast and Beauty ending, to the magic of metamorphosis, the magic of return tickets to princedoms and faith as rewards for spiritual reform.

"Suddenly some force struck him in the chest and side, making it still harder to breathe, and he fell through the hole, and there at the bottom was a light. . . .

" 'Yes, it was all not the right thing,' he said to himself, 'but that doesn't matter. It can be so. But what *is* the right thing?' he asked himself, and suddenly grew quiet.

"This occurred at the end of the third day, two hours before his death. Just then his schoolboy son had crept softly in and gone up to the bedside. . . .

"At that very moment Ivan Ilyich fell through and caught sight of the light, and it was revealed to him that though his life had not been what it should have been, this could still be rectified. He asked himself: 'What *is* the right thing?' and grew still, listening. Then he felt that someone was kissing his hand. He opened his eyes, looked at his son, and felt sorry for him. His wife came up to him, and he glanced at her. She was gazing at him open-mouthed, with undried tears on her nose and cheeks and a despairing look on her face. He felt sorry for her, too.

" 'Yes, I'm making them wretched,' he thought. 'They're sorry, but it will be better for them when I die.' He wished to say this but had not the strength to utter it. 'Besides, why speak? I must act,' he thought. With a look at his wife, he indicated his son and said: 'Take him away—sorry for him—sorry for you, too—' He tried to add: 'Forgive me,' but said 'Forego—' and waved his hand, knowing that He whose understanding mattered would understand.

"And suddenly it grew clear to him that what had been oppressing him and would not leave him was all dropping away at once from two sides, from ten sides, and from all sides. He was sorry for them, he must act so as not to hurt them: release them and free himself from these sufferings. 'How good and how simple!' he thought. . . .

"He sought his former accustomed fear of death and did not find it. 'Where is it? What death?' There was no fear because he could not find death.

"In place of death there was light.

" 'So that's what it is!' he suddenly exclaimed aloud. 'What joy!'

To him all this happened in a single instant, and the meaning of that instant did not change. For those present his agony continued for another two hours. Something rattled in his throat, his emaciated body twitched, then the gasping and rattle became less and less frequent.

242   VLADIMIR NABOKOV

" 'It's all over!' said someone near him.

"He heard these words and repeated them in his soul.

" 'Death is all over,' he said to himself. 'It's no more.'

"He drew in a breath, stopped in the midst of a sigh, stretched out, and died."

Chehov

study
closely { The Lady with the Dog

In the Ravine } Viking Pun

read
(passages
discussed
in class) The House with the Mezzanīnē

The Three Sisters

vs Guerney (a pachinal story
between flux and
cutty of a man's story;
estranny only over one
part of a man's flus)

Reading Period

Discussed
in class. The Sea Gull (outright choice:
Dostoevsey Double
and Tolstoy's Kage m wrad)

or what edition?

Chapter 3 to end of the Merry book with the
editors post script.

ANTON CHEKHOV (1860-1904)

Anton Pavlovich Chekhov's grandfather had been a serf but for 3,500 rubles had bought his own and his family's freedom. His father was a petty merchant who lost his money in the 1870s, whereupon the whole family went to live in Moscow while Anton Pavlovich remained behind in Taganrog (Southeast Russia) to finish high-school. He supported himself by his own work. After finishing school, in the autumn of 1879 he too went to Moscow and entered the university.

Chekhov's first stories were written in order to ease the poverty endured by his family.

He studied medicine and after graduating from the Moscow university became an assistant of the district doctor in a small provincial town. It was there that he began to accumulate his wealth of subtle observations of the peasants who came to his hospital in search of medical assistance, of the army officers (for a battery was stationed in the little town—you will find some of these army men in *The Three Sisters*), and of those innumerable characters typical of provincial Russia of his time whom he recreated later in his short stories. But at this period he wrote mostly humoristic little bits which he signed with different pen-names, reserving his true signature for medical articles. The little humoristic bits of writing were published in various dailies, often belonging to violently antagonistic political groups.

Chekhov himself never took part in political movements, not because he was indifferent to the plight of the simple people under the old regime, but because he did not feel political activity to be his predestined path: he too was serving his people, but in a different way. He believed that the first thing needed was justice, and all his life he raised his voice against every kind of injustice; but he did it as a writer. Chekhov was in the first place an individualist and an artist. He was therefore no easy "joiner" of parties: his protest against existing injustice and brutality came in his individual way. Usually critics who write about Chekhov repeat that they are quite unable to understand what induced him, in 1890, to undertake a dangerous and fatiguing trip to Sakhalin Island to study the life of those sentenced to terms of penal servitude there.*

His first two collections of short stories—*Speckled Stories* and *In the Twilight*—appeared in 1886 and 1887 and were immediately acclaimed by the reading public. From that time on he belonged among the leading writers, could publish his stories in the best periodicals, and was able to abandon his medical career and give all his time to literature. He soon bought a small estate near Moscow where all his family could live. The years spent there belong among the happiest. He thoroughly enjoyed his own independence, the comforts he was able to provide for his aging parents, fresh air, work in his own garden, visits from numerous friends. The Chekhov family seems to have been full of fun, full of jokes: fun and laughter were the main feature of their life.

"Not only was Chekhov eager to turn everything green, to plant trees and flowers, to make the soil fruitful, he was always eager to create something new in life. With all his life-confirming, dynamic, inexhaustibly active nature, he gave himself up not merely to describing life but to transforming it, to building it up. He would bustle about the building of Moscow's first People's Home, with a library, reading room, auditorium, and theatre; he would see about getting Moscow a clinic for skin diseases; with the help of the painter Ilya Repin he would organize a Museum of Painting and Fine Arts in Taganrog; he would initiate the building of Crimea's first biological station; he would collect books for the schools on the Pacific island of Sakhalin and ship them there in large consignments; he would build three schools for peasant children, not far from Moscow, one after the other, and at the same time a belfry and a fire department for the peasants. Later, when he moved to the Crimea, he built a fourth school there. And, generally, any construction work fascinated him,

*At the beginning of this lecture, VN interpolated passages from Kornei Chukovski's "Friend Chekhov," *Atlantic Monthly*, 140 (September 1947), 84-90. Ed.

for in his opinion such activity always increased the sum total of man's happiness. He wrote to Gorki: 'If every man did what he could on his little bit of soil, how marvelous our world would be!'

"In his notebook he made this entry: 'The Turk digs a well for the salvation of his soul. It would be good if each of us left after him a school, a well, or something of the kind so that our life would not pass into eternity without leaving any trace behind.' This activity often demanded much hard labor of him. When, for instance, he was building the schools, he himself had all the fuss and bother of dealing with the laborers, bricklayers, stove-installers, and carpenters; he bought all the building material himself down to the tiles and doors for the stoves, and he personally supervised the construction work.

"Or take his work as a doctor. During the cholera epidemic he worked all alone as a district doctor; without any assistant he took care of twenty-five villages. And take the help he gave to the starving during the years when the harvest failed. He had many years of practice as a doctor, chiefly among the peasants of the Moscow suburbs. According to his sister, Maria Pavlovna, who helped him as a trained nurse, he 'treated more than a thousand sick peasants a year at his home, gratis, and he supplied them all with medicines.' " A whole book could be written about his work in Yalta as a member of the Board of Guardians for the Visiting Sick. "He burdened himself to such an extent that he was practically the entire institution in himself. Many tubercular people came to Yalta at that time, without a copper in their pockets, and they came all the way from Odessa, Kishinev, and Kharkov just because they had heard that Chekhov was living in Yalta. 'Chekhov will fix us up. Chekhov will arrange lodging for us, and a dining room, and treatment' (Chukovski)."

This great kindness pervades Chekhov's literary work, but it is not a matter of program, or of literary message with him, but simply the natural coloration of his talent. And he was adored by all his readers, which practically means by all Russia, for in the late years of his life his fame was very great indeed. "Without this phenomenal sociability of his, without his constant readiness to hobnob with anyone at all, to sing with singers and to get drunk with drunkards; without that burning interest in the lives, habits, conversations, and occupations of hundreds and thousands of people, he would hardly have been able to create that colossal, encyclopedically detailed Russian world of the 1880s and 1890s which goes by the name of Chekhov's *Short Stories*."

" 'Do you know how I write my short stories?' he said to Korolenko, the radical journalist and short-story writer, when the latter had just made his acquaintance. 'Here's how!'

" 'He glanced at his table,' Korolenko tells us, 'took up the first object that met his eye—it happened to be an ash tray—placed it before me and said: 'If you want it, you'll have a story to-morrow. It will be called "The Ash Tray." ' "

And it seemed to Korolenko right then and there that a magical transformation of that ash tray was taking place: "Certain indefinite situations, adventures which had not yet found concrete form, were already beginning to crystallize about the ash tray."

Chekhov's health which had never been strong (and which had suffered in consequence of the hardships of his trip to Sakhalin) soon made it imperative for him to seek a milder climate than that of the Moscow region. He had tuberculosis. He went away, first to France, but then settled down in Yalta, in the Crimea, where he bought a country-house with an orchard. The Crimea in general, and Yalta in particular, are very beautiful places, with a comparatively mild climate. There Chekhov lived from the late eighties to almost the very end, leaving Yalta but rarely to visit Moscow.

The famous Moscow Art Theatre, founded in the nineties by two amateurs—one an amateur performer Stanislavski, the other a man of letters Nemirovich-Danchenko—who both were endowed with an extraordinary talent for stage-management, was famous before it began the production of Chekhov's plays, but it is nevertheless true that this theatre truly "found itself" and reached a new height of artistic perfection through Chekhov's plays which it made famous. "Chaika," the Seagull, became a symbol of the theatre: a stylized reproduction of a seagull came to stay on the theatre's curtain and programs. *The Cherry Orchard*, *Uncle Vanya*, *The Three Sisters* all became triumphs for the theatre as well as for the author. Mortally sick with consumption, Chekhov would appear for the first performance, listen to the passionate acclaim of the audience, enjoy the success of his play, and then, sicker than ever, return to his Yalta retirement. His wife, Miss Knipper, one of the leading, I can even say *the* leading actress of the theatre, came sometimes to him in the Crimea on short visits. It was not a happy marriage.

In 1904 a very sick man, he thus put in an appearance at the first performance of *The Cherry Orchard*. He had not been expected by the public and his appearance provoked thunderous applause. Then he was fêted by the elite of Moscow's intelligentsia. There were endless speeches. He was so weak from sickness and it was so perceptible that cries arose in the audience, "Sit down, sit down. . . . Let Anton Pavlovich be seated."

Soon after he made his last trip in search of cure, this time to Badenweiler in the German Black Forest. When he got there he had exactly three more weeks to live. On the 2nd of July, 1904, he died far from his family and friends, amidst strangers, in a strange town.

A difference exists between a real artist like Chekhov and a didactic one like Gorki, one of those naive and nervous Russian intellectuals who thought that a little patience and kindness with the miserable, half savage, unfathomable Russian peasant would do the trick. One may compare Chekhov's story "The New Villa."

A rich engineer has built a house for himself and his wife; there is a garden, a fountain, a glass ball, but no arable land—the purpose is fresh air and relaxation. A couple of his horses, splendid, sleek, healthy, snow-white beasts, fascinatingly alike, are led by the coachman to the blacksmith.

"Swans, real swans," says the latter, contemplating them with sacred awe.

An old peasant comes up. "Well," he says with a cunning and ironic smile, "white they are, but what of it? If my two horses were stuffed with oats, they would be quite as sleek. I'd like to see those two put to plow and whipped up."

Now, in a didactic story, especially in one with good ideas and purposes, this sentence would be the voice of wisdom, and the old peasant who so simply and deeply expresses the idea of a modus of life regulating existence would be shown further on as a good fine old man, the symbol of the peasant class consciousness as a rising class, etc. What does Chekhov do? Very probably he did not notice himself that he had put into the old peasant's mind a truth sacred to the radicals of his day. What interested him was that it was true to life, true to the character of the man as a character and not as a symbol—a man who spoke so not because he was wise but because he was always trying to be unpleasant, to spoil other people's pleasures: he hated the white horses, the fat handsome coachman; he was himself a lonely man, a widower, his life was dull (he could not work because of an illness that he called either "gryz'" (hernia) or "glisty" (worms). He got his money from his son who worked in a candy-shop in a big town, and all day long he wandered about idly and if he met a peasant bringing home a log or fishing, he would say, "That log is rotten" or "In this weather fish don't bite."

In other words, instead of making a character the medium of a lesson and instead of following up what would seem to Gorki, or to any Soviet author, a socialistic truth by making the rest of the man beautifully good (just as in an ordinary bourgeois story if you love your mother or your dog you cannot be a bad man), instead of this, Chekhov gives us a living human being without bothering about political messages or traditions of writing.* Incidentally, we might note that his wise men are usually bores, just as Polonius is.

The fundamental idea of Chekhov's best and worst characters seems to have been that until real moral and spiritual culture, physical fitness and wealth, come to the Russian masses, the efforts of the noblest and best-meaning intellectuals who build bridges and schools while the vodka pub is still there, will come to naught. His conclusion was that pure art, pure science, pure learning, being in no direct contact with the masses, will, in the long run, attain more than the clumsy and muddled attempts of benefactors. It is to be noted that Chekhov himself was a Russian intellectual of the Chekhovian type.

———————

No author has created with less emphasis such pathetic characters as Chekhov has, characters who can often be summed up by the quotation from his story "In the Cart": "How strange, she reflected, why does God give sweetness of nature, sad, nice, kind eyes, to weak, unhappy useless people — and why are they so attractive?" There is the old village messenger in the story "On Official Business" who tramps through the snow miles and miles on trifling and useless errands which he neither understands nor questions. There is that young man in "My Life" who left his comfortable home and became a miserable house-painter because he could not endure any longer the nauseating and cruel smugness of small-town life, symbolized for him by the dreadful straggling houses that his father the architect builds for the town. What author would have withstood the temptation of drawing the tragic parallel: father builds houses, son is doomed to paint them? But Chekhov does not so much as allude to this point, which if stressed would have put a pin through the story. There is in the story "The House with the Mezzanine" the frail young girl with a name unpronounceable in English, frail Misyus, shivering in her muslin frock in the autumn night and the "I" of the story putting his coat on her thin shoulders — and then her lighted window and then romance somehow fizzling out. There is the old peasant in "The New Villa" who misunderstands in the most atrocious way the futile and lukewarm kindness of an eccentric squire, but at the same time blesses him from all his heart; and when the master's doll-like pampered little girl bursts into tears as she feels the hostile attitude of

———————

*VN closes this section with a deleted paragraph: "To conclude: Chekhov together with Pushkin are the purest writers that Russia has produced in the sense of the complete harmony that their writings convey. I feel it was rather hard upon Gorki to have spoken of him in the same lecture, but the contrast between the two is extremely instructive. In the twenty-first century, when I hope Russia will be a sweeter country than it is just now, Gorki will be but a name in a textbook, but Chekhov will live as long as there are birchwoods and sunsets and the urge to write." Ed.

the other villagers, he produces from his pocket a cucumber with crumbs sticking to it and thrusts it into her hand, saying to that pampered bourgeois child, "Now don't cry, lassy, or else Mummy will tell Daddy, and Daddy will give you a thrashing"—which suggests the exact habits of his own life without having them stressed or explained. There is in the story "In the Cart" that village school mistress whose pathetic day-dreaming is broken by the accidents of a rough road and the vulgar though good-natured nickname by which the driver addresses her. And in his most astounding story "In the Ravine" there is the tender and simple young peasant mother Lipa whose naked red baby is murdered with one splash of boiling water by another woman. And how wonderful the preceding scene when the baby was still healthy and gay and the young mother played with it—would go to the door, return, respectfully bow to the child from afar, saying good-morning Mister Nikifor, and then would rush to it and hug it with a scream of love. And in the same wonderful tale there is the wretched peasant bum telling the girl of his wanderings over Russia. One day a gentleman, probably exiled from Moscow for his political views, meeting him somewhere on the Volga, and casting a glance at his rags and face, burst into tears and said aloud, so the peasant relates, "Alas," said the gentleman to me, "black is your bread, black is your life."

Chekhov was the first among writers to rely so much upon the undercurrents of suggestion to convey a definite meaning. In the same story of Lipa and the child there is her husband, a certain swindler, who is condemned to hard labor. Before that, in the days when he was still successfully engaged in his shady business, he used to write letters home in a beautiful hand, not his own. He casually remarks one day that it is his good friend Samorodov who pens those letters for him. We never meet that friend of his; but when the husband is condemned to hard labor, his letters come from Siberia in the same beautiful hand. That is all, but it is perfectly clear that the good Samorodov, whoever he was, had been his partner in crime and is now undergoing the same punishment.

———

A publisher once remarked to me that every writer had somewhere in him a certain numeral engraved, the exact number of pages which is the limit of any one book he would ever write. My number, I remember, was 385. Chekhov could never write a good long novel—he was a sprinter, not a stayer. He could not, it seems, hold long enough in focus the pattern of life that his genius perceived here and there: he could retain it in its patchy vividness just long enough to make a short story out of it, but it refused to keep bright and detailed as it should keep if it had to be turned into a long and sustained novel. His qualities as a playwright are merely his qualities as a writer of long short stories: the defects of his plays are the same that would have been obvious had he attempted to write full-bodied novels. Chekhov has been compared to the second-rate French writer Maupassant (called for some reason de Maupassant); and though this comparison is detrimental to Chekhov in the artistic sense, there is one feature common to both writers: they could not afford to be long-winded. When Maupassant forced his pen to run a distance that far outreached his natural inclination and wrote such novels as *Bel Ami* (*Sweet Friend*) or *Une Vie* (*A Woman's Life*), they proved to be at the best a series of rudimental short stories more or less artificially blended, producing a kind of uneven impression with none of that inner current driving the theme along that is so natural to the style of such born novelists as Flaubert or Tolstoy. Except for one faux-pas in his youth, Chekhov never attempted to write a fat book. His longest pieces, such as "The Duel" or "Three Years," are still short stories.

Chekhov's books are sad books for humorous people; that is, only a reader with a sense of humor can really appreciate their sadness. There exist writers that sound like something between a titter and a yawn—many of these are professional humorists, for instance. There are others that are something between a chuckle and a sob—Dickens was one of these. There is also that dreadful kind of humor that is consciously introduced by an author in order to give a purely technical relief after a good tragic scene—but this is a trick remote from true literature. Chekhov's humor belonged to none of these types; it was purely Chekhovian. Things for him were funny and sad at the same time, but you would not see their sadness if you did not see their fun, because both were linked up.

Russian critics have noted that Chekhov's style, his choice of words and so on, did not reveal any of those special artistic preoccupations that obsessed, for instance, Gogol or Flaubert or Henry James. His dictionary is poor, his combination of words almost trivial—the purple patch, the juicy verb, the hothouse adjective, the crême-de-menthe epithet, brought in on a silver tray, these were foreign to him. He was not a verbal inventor in the sense that Gogol was; his literary style goes to parties clad in its everyday suit. Thus Chekhov is a good example to give when one tries to explain that a writer may be a perfect artist without being exceptionally vivid in his verbal technique or exceptionally preoccupied with the way his sentences curve. When Turgenev sits down to discuss a landscape, you notice that he is concerned with the trouser-crease of his phrase; he crosses his legs with an eye upon the color of his socks. Chekhov does not mind, not because these matters are not important—for some writers they are naturally and very beautifully important when the right temperament is there—but Chekhov does not mind because his temperament is quite foreign to verbal inventiveness. Even a bit of bad grammar or a slack newspaperish sentence left him unconcerned.* The magical part of it is that in spite of his tolerating flaws which a bright beginner would have avoided, in spite of his being quite satisfied with the man-in-the-street among words, the word-in-the-street, so to say, Chekhov managed to convey an impression of artistic beauty far surpassing that of many writers who thought they knew what rich beautiful prose was. He did it by keeping all his words in the same dim light and of the same exact tint of gray, a tint between the color of an old fence and that of a low cloud. The variety of his moods, the flicker of his charming wit, the deeply artistic economy of characterization, the vivid detail, and the fade-out of human life—all the peculiar Chekhovian features—are enhanced by being suffused and surrounded by a faintly iridescent verbal haziness.

His quiet and subtle humor pervades the grayness of the lives he creates. For the Russian philosophical or social-minded critic he was the unique exponent of a unique Russian type of character. It is rather difficult for me to explain what that type was or is, because it is all so linked up with the general psychological and social history of the Russian nineteenth century. It is not quite exact to say that Chekhov dealt in charming and ineffectual people. It is a little more true to say that his men and women are charming because they are ineffectual. But what really attracted the Russian reader was that in Chekhov's heroes he recognized the type of the Russian intellectual, the Russian idealist, a queer and pathetic creature that is little known abroad and cannot exist in the Russia of the Soviets. Chekhov's intellectual was a man who combined the deepest human decency of which man is capable with an almost ridiculous inability to put his ideals and principles into action; a man devoted to moral beauty, the welfare of his people, the welfare of the universe, but unable in his private life to do anything useful; frittering away his provincial existence in a haze of utopian dreams; knowing exactly what is good, what is worth while living for, but at the same time sinking lower and lower in the mud of a humdrum existence, unhappy in love, hopelessly inefficient in everything—a good man who cannot make good. This is the character that passes—in the

*VN first wrote "less concerned" and then continued with a passage worth preserving for its interest, though he deleted it: "less concerned than for instance Conrad was when (according to Ford Madox Ford) he tried to find a word of two syllables and a half—not merely two and not merely three, but exactly two and a half—which he felt was absolutely necessary to end a certain description. And being Conrad he was perfectly right, for that was the nature of his talent. Chekhov would have ended that sentence with an "out" or an "in" and never have noticed his ending—and Chekhov was a much greater writer than good old Conrad." Ed.

guise of a doctor, a student, a village teacher, many other professional people—all through Chekhov's stories.

What rather irritated his politically minded critics was that nowhere does the author assign this type to any definite political party or give him any definite political program. But that is the whole point. Chekhov's inefficient idealists were neither terrorists, nor Social Democrats, nor budding Bolsheviks, nor any of the numberless members of numberless revolutionary parties in Russia. What mattered was that this typical Chekhovian hero was the unfortunate bearer of a vague but beautiful human truth, a burden which he could neither get rid of nor carry. What we see is a continuous stumble through all Chekhov's stories, but it is the stumble of a man who stumbles because he is staring at the stars. He is unhappy, that man, and he makes others unhappy; he loves not his brethren, not those nearest to him, but the remotest. The plight of a negro in a distant land, of a Chinese coolie, of a workman in the remote Urals, affects him with a keener pang of moral pain than the misfortunes of his neighbor or the troubles of his wife. Chekhov took a special artistic pleasure in fixing all the delicate varieties of that pre-war, pre-revolution type of Russian intellectual. Those men could dream; they could not rule. They broke their own lives and the lives of others, they were silly, weak, futile, hysterical; but Chekhov suggests, blessed be the country that could produce that particular type of man. They missed opportunities, they shunned action, they spent sleepless nights in planning worlds they could not build; but the mere fact of such men, full of such fervor, fire of abnegation, pureness of spirit, moral elevation, this mere fact of such men having lived and probably still living somewhere somehow in the ruthless and sordid Russia of to-day is a promise of better things to come for the world at large—for perhaps the most admirable among the admirable laws of Nature is the survival of the weakest.

It is from this point of view that those who were equally interested in the misery of the Russian people and in the glory of Russian literature, it is from this point of view that they appreciated Chekhov. Though never concerned with providing a social or ethical message, Chekhov's genius almost involuntarily disclosed more of the blackest realities of hungry, puzzled, servile, angry peasant Russia than a multitude of other writers, such as Gorki for instance, who flaunted their social ideas in a procession of painted dummies. I shall go further and say that the person who prefers Dostoevski or Gorki to Chekhov will never be able to grasp the essentials of Russian literature and Russian life, and, which is far more important, the essentials of universal literary art. It was quite a game among Russians to divide their acquaintances into those who liked Chekhov and those who did not. Those who did not were not the right sort.

I heartily recommend taking as often as possible Chekhov's books (even in the translations they have suffered) and dreaming through them as they are intended to be dreamed through. In an age of ruddy Goliaths it is very useful to read about delicate Davids. Those bleak landscapes, the withered sallows along dismally muddy roads, the gray crows flapping across gray skies, the sudden whiff of some amazing recollection at a most ordinary corner—all this pathetic dimness, all this lovely weakness, all this Chekhovian dove-gray world is worth treasuring in the glare of those strong, self-sufficient worlds that are promised us by the worshippers of totalitarian states.

"The Lady with the Little Dog" (1899)

Chekhov comes into the story "The Lady with the Little Dog" without knocking. There is no dilly-dallying. The very first paragraph reveals the main character, the young fair-haired lady followed by her white Spitz dog on the waterfront of a Crimean resort, Yalta, on the Black Sea. And immediately after, the male character Gurov appears. His wife, whom he has left with the children in Moscow, is vividly depicted: her solid frame, her thick black eyebrows, and the way she had of calling herself "a woman who thinks." One notes the magic of the trifles the author collects—the wife's manner of dropping a certain mute letter in spelling and her calling her husband by the longest and fullest form of his name, both traits in combination with the impressive dignity of her beetle-browed face and rigid poise forming exactly the necessary impression. A hard woman with the strong feminist and social ideas of her time, but one whom her husband finds in his heart of hearts to be narrow, dull-minded, and devoid of grace. The natural transition is to Gurov's constant unfaithfulness to her, to his general attitude toward women—"that inferior race" is what he calls them, but without that inferior race he could not exist. It is hinted that these Russian romances were not altogether as light-winged as in the Paris of Maupassant. Complications and problems are unavoidable with those decent hesitating people of Moscow who are slow heavy starters but plunge into tedious difficulties when once they start going.

Then with the same neat and direct method of attack, with the bridging formula "and so . . .",* we slide back to the lady with the dog. Everything about her, even the way her hair was done, told him that she was bored. The spirit of adventure—though he realized perfectly well that his attitude toward a

---

*VN follows with the deleted "or perhaps still better rendered in English by that 'Now' which begins a new paragraph in straightforward fairy tales." Ed.

1

Chekhov. The lady with the little dog. (1899).

Chekhov comes, into his story, so to speak, without knocking.
There is no dilly-dallying. The very first paragraph reveals the
main character, the young fairhaired lady followed by her white
Pomeranian on the seafront of a Crimean resort, Yalta, with the
prompt simplicity of a door thrown open. And immediately after
this the male character, is shown. His wife, whom he has left
with the children in Moscow, is vividly depicted: her solid frame,
her thick black eyebrows and the way she had of calling herself:
a woman who thinks. Note the magic of the trifles the author
collects -- her manner of dropping a certain mute letter in spelling and her calling her husband by the longest and fullest form
of his name, both traits in combination with the impressive dignity
of her beetle-browed face and rigid poise forming exactly the
necessary impression a hard woman with the strong feminist and
social ideas of her time, but whom her husband finds in his
heart of hearts, flat, narrow, dull-minded and devoid of grace.
Then the natural transition is to Gurov's constant unfaithfulness
to her, his general attitude towards women -- "that inferior race"
is what he calls them, but without that inferior race he could not
exist. The surroundings, the color and a hint that these romances
were not altogether as lightwinged as in the Paris of Maupassant,
are beautifully rendered in the allusion that complications and
problems are unavoidable for those decent hesitating people of
Moscow who are slow heavy starters but plunge into tedious difficulties when once they start going.

Then, with the same neat and direct method of attack, with
the transitional words "and so..." or perhaps still better rendered
by the "now..." which begins a new paragraph in straightforward

lone woman in a fashionable sea town was based on vulgar stories, generally false—this spirit of adventure prompts him to call the little dog, which thus becomes a link between her and him. They are both in a public restaurant.

"He beckoned invitingly to the Spitz, and when the dog approached him, shook his finger at it. The Spitz growled; Gurov threatened it again.

"The lady glanced at him and at once dropped her eyes.

" 'He doesn't bite,' she said and blushed.

" 'May I give him a bone?' he asked; and when she nodded he inquired affably, 'Have you been in Yalta long?'

" 'About five days.' "

They talk. The author has hinted already that Gurov was witty in the company of women; and instead of having the reader take it for granted (you know the old method of describing the talk as "brilliant" but giving no samples of the conversation), Chekhov makes him joke in a really attractive, winning way. "Bored, are you? An average citizen lives in . . . (here Chekhov lists the names of beautifully chosen, super-provincial towns) and is not bored, but when he arrives here on his vacation it is all boredom and dust. One could think he came from Grenada" (a name particularly appealing to the Russian imagination). The rest of their talk, for which this sidelight is richly sufficient, is conveyed indirectly. Now comes a first glimpse of Chekhov's own system of suggesting atmosphere by the most concise details of nature, "the sea was of a warm lilac hue with a golden path for the moon"; whoever has lived in Yalta knows how exactly this conveys the impression of a summer evening there. This first movement of the story ends with Gurov alone in his hotel room thinking of her as he goes to sleep and imagining her delicate weak-looking neck and her pretty gray eyes. It is to be noted that only now, through the medium of the hero's imagination, does Chekhov give a visible and definite form to the lady, features that fit in perfectly with her listless manner and expression of boredom already known to us.

"Getting into bed he recalled that she had been a schoolgirl only recently, doing lessons like his own daughter; he thought how much timidity and angularity there was still in her laugh and her manner of talking with a stranger. It must have been the first time in her life that she was alone in a setting in which she was followed, looked at, and spoken to for one secret purpose alone, which

---

The opening page of Nabokov's lecture on "The Lady with the Little Dog."

---

she could hardly fail to guess. He thought of her slim, delicate throat, her lovely gray eyes.

" 'There's something pathetic about her, though,' he thought, and dropped off."

The next movement (each of the four diminutive chapters or movements of which the story is composed is not more than four or five pages long), the next movement starts a week later with Gurov going to the pavilion and bringing the lady iced lemonade on a hot windy day, with the dust flying; and then in the evening when the sirocco subsides, they go on the pier to watch the incoming steamer. "The lady lost her lorgnette in the crowd," Chekhov notes shortly, and this being so casually worded, without any direct influence on the story—just a passing statement—somehow fits in with that helpless pathos already alluded to.

Then in her hotel room her awkwardness and tender angularity are delicately conveyed. They have become lovers. She was now sitting with her long hair hanging down on both sides of her face in the dejected pose of a sinner in some old picture. There was a watermelon on the table. Gurov cut himself a piece and began to eat unhurriedly. This realistic touch is again a typical Chekhov device.

She tells him about her existence in the remote town she comes from and Gurov is slightly bored by her naiveté, confusion, and tears. It is only now that we learn her husband's name: von Dideritz—probably of German descent.

They roam about Yalta in the early morning mist. "At Oreanda they sat on a bench not far from the church, looked down at the sea, and were silent. Yalta was barely visible through the morning mist; white clouds rested motionlessly on the mountaintops. The leaves did not stir on the trees, the crickets chirped, and the monotonous muffled sound of the sea that rose from below spoke of the peace, the eternal sleep awaiting us. So it rumbled below when there was no Yalta, no Oreanda here; so it rumbles now, and it will rumble as indifferently and hollowly when we are no more. . . . Sitting beside a young woman who in the dawn seemed so lovely, Gurov, soothed and spellbound by these magical surroundings—the sea, the mountains, the clouds, the wide sky—thought how everything is really beautiful in this world when one reflects: everything except what we think or do ourselves when we forget the higher aims of life and our own human dignity.

"A man strolled up to them—probably a watchman—looked at them and walked away. And this detail, too, seemed so mysterious and beautiful. They saw a steamer arrive from Feodosia, its lights extinguished in the glow of dawn.

" 'There is dew on the grass,' said Anna Sergeievna, after a silence.

" 'Yes, it's time to go home.' "

Then several days pass and then she has to go back to her home town. " 'Time for me, too, to go North,' thought Gurov as he returned after seeing her off." *And there the chapter ends.

The third movement plunges us straight into Gurov's life in Moscow. The richness of a gay Russian winter, his family affairs, the dinners at clubs and restaurants, all this is swiftly and vividly suggested. Then a page is devoted to a queer thing that has happened to him: he cannot forget the lady with the little dog. He has many friends, but the curious longing he has for talking about his adventure finds no outlet. When he happens to speak in a very general way of love and women, nobody guesses what he means, and only his wife moves her dark eyebrows and says: "Stop that fatuous posing; it does not suit you."

And now comes what in Chekhov's quiet stories may be called the climax. There is something that your average citizen calls romance and something he calls prose—though both are the meat of poetry for the artist. Such a contrast has already been hinted at by the slice of watermelon which Gurov crunched in a Yalta hotel room at a most romantic moment, sitting heavily and munching away. This contrast is beautifully followed up when at last Gurov blurts out to a friend late at night as they come out of the club: If you knew what a delightful woman I met in Yalta! His friend, a bureaucratic civil servant, got into his sleigh, the horses moved, but suddenly he turned and called back to Gurov. Yes? asked Gurov, evidently expecting some reaction to what he had just mentioned. By the way, said the man, you were quite right. That fish at the club was decidedly smelly.

This is a natural transition to the description of Gurov's new mood, his feeling that he lives among savages where cards and food are life. His family, his bank, the whole trend of his existence, everything seems futile, dull, and senseless. About Christmas he tells his wife he is going on a business trip to St. Petersburg, instead of which he travels to the remote Volga town where the lady lives.

Critics of Chekhov in the good old days when the mania for the civic problem flourished in Russia were incensed with his way of describing what they considered to be trivial unnecessary matters instead of thoroughly examining and solving the problems of bourgeois marriage. For as soon as Gurov arrives in the early hours to that town and takes the best room at the local hotel, Chekhov, instead of describing his mood or intensifying his difficult moral position, gives what is artistic in the highest sense of the word: he notes the gray carpet, made of military cloth, and the inkstand, also gray with dust, with

---

*In the margin VN adds for the benefit of his Cornell class, "From Florida back to Ithaca." Ed.

a horseman whose hand waves a hat and whose head is gone. That is all: it is nothing but it is everything in authentic literature. A feature in the same line is the phonetic transformation which the hotel porter imposes on the German name von Dideritz. Having learned the address Gurov goes there and looks at the house. Opposite was a long gray fence with nails sticking out. An unescapable fence, Gurov says to himself, and here we get the concluding note in the rhythm of drabness and grayness already suggested by the carpet, the inkstand, the illiterate accent of the porter. The unexpected little turns and the lightness of the touches are what places Chekhov, above all Russian writers of fiction, on the level of Gogol and Tolstoy.

Presently he saw an old servant coming out with the familiar little white dog. He wanted to call it (by a kind of conditional reflex), but suddenly his heart began beating fast and in his excitement he could not remember the dog's name—another delightful touch. Later on he decides to go to the local theatre, where for the first time the operetta *The Geisha* is being given. In sixty words Chekhov paints a complete picture of a provincial theatre, not forgetting the town-governor who modestly hid in his box behind a plush curtain so that only his hands were visible. Then the lady appeared. And he realized quite clearly that now in the whole world there was none nearer and dearer and more important to him than this slight woman, lost in a small-town crowd, a woman perfectly unremarkable, with a vulgar lorgnette in her hand. He saw her husband and remembered her qualifying him as a flunkey—he distinctly resembled one.

A remarkably fine scene follows when Gurov manages to talk to her, and then their mad swift walk up all kinds of staircases and corridors, and down again, and up again, amid people in the various uniforms of provincial officials. Neither does Chekhov forget "two schoolboys who smoked on the stairs and looked down at him and her."

" 'You must leave,' Anna Sergeievna went on in a whisper. 'Do you hear, Dmitri Dmitrich? I will come and see you in Moscow. I have never been happy; I am unhappy now, and I never, never shall be happy, never! So don't make me suffer still more! I swear I'll come to Moscow. But now let us part. My dear, good, precious one, let us part!'

"She pressed his hand and walked rapidly downstairs, turning to look round at him, and from her eyes he could see that she really was unhappy. Gurov stood for a while, listening, then when all grew quiet, he found his coat and left the theatre."

The fourth and last little chapter gives the atmosphere of their secret meetings in Moscow. As soon as she would arrive she used to send a red-capped messenger to Gurov. One day he was on his way to her and his daughter was with him. She was going to school, in the same direction as he. Big damp snowflakes were slowly coming down.

The thermometer, Gurov was saying to his daughter, shows a few degrees above freezing point (actually 37° above, fahrenheit), but nevertheless snow is falling. The explanation is that this warmth applies only to the surface of the earth, while in the higher layers of the atmosphere the temperature is quite different.

And as he spoke and walked, he kept thinking that not a soul knew or would ever know about these secret meetings.

What puzzled him was that all the false part of his life, his bank, his club, his conversations, his social obligations—all this happened openly, while the real and interesting part was hidden.

"He had two lives: an open one, seen and known by all who needed to know it, full of conventional truth and conventional falsehood, exactly like the lives of his friends and acquaintances; and another life that went on in secret. And through some strange, perhaps accidental, combination of circumstances, everything that was of interest and importance to him, everything that was essential to him, everything about which he felt sincerely and did not deceive himself, everything that constituted the core of his life, was going on concealed from others; while all that was false, the shell in which he hid to cover the truth—his work at the bank for instance, his discussions at the club, his references to the 'inferior race,' his appearances at anniversary celebrations with his wife—all that went on in the open. Judging others by himself, he did not believe what he saw, and always fancied that every man led his real, most interesting life under cover of secrecy as under cover of night. The personal life of every individual is based on secrecy, and perhaps it is partly for that reason that civilized man is so nervously anxious that personal privacy should be respected."

The final scene is full of that pathos which has been suggested in the very beginning. They meet, she sobs, they feel that they are the closest of couples, the tenderest of friends, and he sees that his hair is getting a little gray and knows that only death will end their love.

"The shoulders on which his hands rested were warm and quivering. He felt compassion for this life, still so warm and lovely, but probably already about to begin to fade and wither like his own. Why did she love him so much? He always seemed to women different from what he was, and they loved in him not himself, but the man whom their imagination had created and whom they had been eagerly seeking all their lives; and afterwards, when they saw their mistake, they loved him nevertheless. And not one of them had been happy with him. In the past he had met women, come together with them, parted from them, but he had never once loved; it was anything you please, but not love. And only now when his head was gray he had fallen in love, really, truly—for the first time in his life."

They talk, they discuss their position, how to get rid of the necessity of this sordid secrecy, how to be together always. They find no solution and in the typical Chekhov way the tale fades out with no definite full-stop but with the natural motion of life.

"And it seemed as though in a little while the solution would be found, and then a new and glorious life would begin; and it was clear to both of them that the end was still far off, and that what was to be most complicated and difficult for them was only just beginning."

All the traditional rules of story telling have been broken in this wonderful short story of twenty pages or so. There is no problem, no regular climax, no point at the end. And it is one of the greatest stories ever written.

We will now repeat the different features that are typical for this and other Chekhov tales.

First: The story is told in the most natural way possible, not beside the after-dinner fireplace as with Turgenev or Maupassant but in the way one person relates to another the most important things in his life, slowly and yet without a break, in a slightly subdued voice.

Second: Exact and rich characterization is attained by a careful selection and careful distribution of minute but striking features, with perfect contempt for the sustained description, repetition, and strong emphasis of ordinary authors. In this or that description one detail is chosen to illume the whole setting.

Third: There is no special moral to be drawn and no special message to be received. Compare this to the special delivery stories of Gorki or Thomas Mann.

Fourth: The story is based on a system of waves, on the shades of this or that mood. If in Gorki's world the molecules forming it are matter, here, in Chekhov, we get a world of waves instead of particles of matter, which, incidentally, is a nearer approach to the modern scientific understanding of the universe.

Fifth: The contrast of poetry and prose stressed here and there with such insight and humor is, in the long run, a contrast only for the heroes; in reality we feel, and this is again typical of authentic genius, that for Chekhov the lofty and the base are *not* different, that the slice of watermelon and the violet sea, and the hands of the town-governor, are essential points of the "beauty plus pity" of the world.

Sixth: The story does not really end, for as long as people are alive, there is no possible and definite conclusion to their troubles or hopes or dreams.

Seventh: The storyteller seems to keep going out of his way to allude to trifles, every one of which in another type of story would mean a signpost denoting a turn in the action—for instance, the two boys at the theatre would be eavesdroppers, and rumors would spread, or the inkstand would mean a letter changing the course of the story; but just because these trifles are meaningless, they are all-important in giving the real atmosphere of this particular story.

"In the Gully" (1900)

The action of "In the Gully" (usually translated as "In the Ravine") takes place half-a-century ago—the story was written in 1900. The place, some-where in Russia, is a village called Ukléyevo: *kley* sounds like *clay* and means "glue." The only thing to tell about the village was that one day at a wake "the old sexton saw among the side dishes some large-grained caviar and began eating it greedily; people nudged him, tugged at his sleeve, but he seemed petrified with enjoyment: felt nothing, and only went on eating. He ate up all the caviar, and there were some four pounds in the jar. And years had passed since then, the sexton had long since been dead, but the caviar was still remembered. Whether life was so poor here or people had not been clever enough to notice anything but that unimportant incident that had occurred ten years before, anyway the people had nothing else to tell about the village of Ukléyevo." Or, rather, there was nothing good to tell except this. Here at least was a beam of fun, a smile, something human. All the rest was not only drab, it was also evil—a gray wasp nest of deception and injustice. "There were only two decent houses built of brick with iron roofs; one of them was occupied by the rural administration; in the other, a two-storied house just opposite the church, lived Grigori Petrovich Tsybukin, a merchant who hailed from Yepi-fan." Both of these houses were abodes of evil. Everything in the story, except the children and the child-wife Lipa, is going to be a succession of deceptions, a succession of masks.

Mask One: "Grigori kept a grocery, but that was only for the sake of appearances: in reality he dealt in vodka, cattle, hides, grain, and pigs; he traded in anything that came to hand, and when, for instance, magpies were wanted abroad for ladies' hats, he made thirty kopeks on every brace of birds; he bought timber for felling, lent money at interest, and altogether was a resourceful old man." This Grigori will also undergo a very interesting metamorphosis in the course of the story.

Old Grigori has two sons, a deaf one around the house, married to what seems a pleasant, cheerful young woman but in reality a malicious devil of a woman; the other son is a detective in town, a bachelor as yet. You will notice that Grigori is immensely appreciative of his daughter-in-law Aksinia: we shall see why in a minute. Old Grigori, a widower, has married again, a new wife named Varvara (Barbara): "No sooner had she moved into a little room in the upper story than everything in the house seemed to brighten up as though new glass had been put into all the windows. The oil lamps burned brightly before the sacred pictures, the tables were covered with snow-white cloths, flowers flecked with red made their appearance in the windows and in the front garden, and at dinner, instead of eating from a single bowl, each person had a separate plate set for him." She also seems, at first, a good woman, a delightful woman, and, anyway, she has a kinder heart than the old man. "When on the eve of a fast or during the local church festival, which lasted three days, Grigori's store palmed off on the peasants tainted salt meat, smelling so strong it was hard to stand near the tub of it, and took scythes, caps, and their wives' kerchiefs in pledge from the drunken men; when the factory hands, stupefied with bad vodka, lay in the mud, and degradation seemed to hover thick like a fog in the air, then it was a kind of relief to think that up there in the house there was a quiet, neatly dressed woman who had nothing to do with salt meat or vodka."

Grigori is a hard man, and though now in the lower middle class is of direct peasant descent—his father was probably a well-to-do peasant—and naturally he hates peasants. Now comes:

Mask Two: Under her gay appearance Aksinia is also hard and that is why old Grigori admires her so much. This pretty woman is a swindler: "Aksinia attended to the shop, and from the yard could be heard the clink of bottles and of money, her laughter and loud talk, and the angry voices of customers whom she had cheated, and at the same time it could be seen that the illicit sale of vodka was already going on in the shop. The deaf man sat in the shop, too, or walked about the street bareheaded, with his hands in his pockets looking

---

The opening page of Nabokov's lecture on "In the Gully."

Known? In the Ravine (Gully, Gulch)
Chapter 1. (consists of nine small chapters, about fifty pages each)

The action takes place half a century ago — the story was written
in 1900 — (somewhere in Russia), is a village called Ukleyevo
The place;
(некваш на Доне) Kley sounds like Clay and meaning Glue
[p. 461 [You will please change, in l. 10, "savories" to "sidedishes".]

The only thing to tell about the village was that once day at a
wake (remnant) ... "the old sexton .... nothing else to tell about
that village." Or rather: there was nothing good to tell except
this. Here at least was a beam of fun, a smile, something
human. All the rest was not only dead, it was also evil
grey deception
a wavy net of deceit and injustice.

p. 462, l. 9, change "the district government office to "rural administration".]
Herborí

There were only two decent homes and both of them
were abodes of evil. Everything in the story, except the children
and the child-wife Lipa, is going to be a succession of deceptions
a succession of
masks.

Mask One — middle paragraph p. 462 Gregor
The store 70
Gregor
kept a grocery ...§ of This Gregor will also undergo a
Try interesting metamorphosis in the course of the
story. I keep was [baffled by my own ability
at discovery intentioned, intentioned themes on the
stories I choose for you] return: Gregor kept a grocery ....
man.

Clefts
p. 463, abacus, one of the first words in the dictionary; an
instrument for calculating by sliding counters of bone or wood along
rods of metal in a wooden frame.

absent-mindedly now at the log cabins, now at the sky overhead. Six times a day they had tea; four times a day they sat down to meals. And in the evening they counted their takings, wrote them down, went to bed, and slept soundly."

Now comes a transition to the calico-printing mills of the place and to their owners. Let us call them collectively the Khrymin family.

Mask Three (adultery): Aksinia not only deceives customers in the store, she also deceives her husband with one of those mill owners.

Mask Four: This is just a little mask, a kind of self-deception. "A telephone was installed in the rural administration, too, but it soon went out of order when it started to harbor bedbugs and cockroaches. The district elder was semiliterate and wrote every word in the official documents with a capital. But when the telephone went out of order he said: 'Yes, now we shall find it hard to be without a telephone.' "

Mask Five: This refers to Grigori's elder son, the detective Anísim. We are now deep in the deception theme of the story. But Chekhov keeps back some important information about Anísim: "The elder son, Anísim, came home very rarely, only on great holidays, but he often sent by a returning villager presents and letters written by someone else in a very beautiful hand, always on a sheet of foolscap that looked like a formal petition. The letters were full of expressions that Anísim never made use of in conversation: 'Dear papa and mamma, I send you a pound of orange pekoe tea for the satisfaction of your physical needs.' " There is a little mystery here that will be gradually cleared up, as in the "someone else in a very beautiful hand."

It is curious that when he arrives home one day and there is something about him suggesting that he has been dismissed from the police force, nobody bothers about it. On the contrary, the occasion seems festive, encouraging ideas of marriage. Says Varvara, Grigori's wife and Anísim's stepmother: " 'How is this, my goodness!' she said. 'The lad's in his twenty-eighth year, and he is still strolling about a bachelor. . . .' From the adjacent room her soft, even speech continued to sound like a series of sighs. She began whispering with her husband and Aksinia, and their faces, too, assumed a sly and mysterious expression as though they are conspirators. It was decided to marry Anísim."

Child Theme: This is the transition to the main character of the story, the girl Lipa (pronounced Leepa). She was the daughter of a working widow, charwoman, and helped her mother in her various chores. "She was pale, thin, and frail, with soft, delicate features, tanned from working in the open air; a shy, melancholy smile always hovered about her face, and there was a childlike look in her eyes, trustful and curious. She was young, still a child, her bosom still scarcely perceptible, but she could be married because she had reached the legal age [eighteen]. She really was beautiful, and the only thing that might be thought unattractive was her big masculine hands which hung idle now like two big claws."

Mask Six: This refers to Varvara, who though pleasant enough, is but a hollow shell of superficial kindness beneath which there is nothing.

Thus Grigori's whole family is a masquerade of deceit.

Now comes Lipa, and with Lipa a new theme starts—the theme of trust, childish trust.

The second chapter ends with another glimpse of Anísim. Everything about him is false: there is something very wrong, and he conceals it not too well. "After the visit of inspection the wedding day was fixed. Anísim kept walking about the rooms at home whistling, or suddenly remembering something, would fall to brooding and would look at the floor fixedly, silently, as though he would probe to the depths of the earth. He expressed neither pleasure that he was to be married, married so soon, the week of St. Thomas [after Easter], nor a desire to see his bride, but simply went on whistling through his teeth. And it was evident that he was only getting married because his father and stepmother wished him to, and because it was a country custom to marry off the son in order to have a woman to help in the house. When he went away he seemed in no haste, and behaved altogether not as he had done on previous visits; he was unusually jaunty and said the wrong things."

In the third chapter observe Aksinia's green and yellow print dress for the wedding of Anísim and Lipa. Chekhov is going to describe her consistently in the terms of a reptile. (A kind of rattlesnake is found in eastern Russia called the yellow belly.) "The dressmakers were making for Varvara a brown dress with black lace and glass beads on it, and for Aksinia a light green dress with a yellow front, and a train." Although these dressmakers are described as belonging to the Flagellant Sect, this did not mean much by 1900—it did not mean that the members actually whipped themselves—it was just one of the numerous sects in Russia, as there are numerous sects in this country. Grigori even practices a deception on the two poor girls: "When the dressmakers had finished their work Grigori paid them not in money but in goods from the shop, and they went away depressed, carrying parcels of tallow candles and tins of sardines which they did not in the least need, and when they got out of the village into the open country they sat down on a hillock and cried."

"Anísim arrived three days before the wedding, rigged out in new togs from top to toe. He wore glistening rubbers, and instead of a tie a red metal cord with little balls hanging on it, and on his shoulders, loosely, its sleeves empty, hung a short overcoat, also new. After crossing himself sedately before the icon, he greeted his father and gave him ten silver rubles and ten half-rubles; to Varvara he gave as much, and to Aksinia twenty quarter-rubles. The chief charm of the present lay in the fact that all the coins, as though carefully matched, were new and glittered in the sun." These were counterfeit coins. An allusion is made to Samorodov, Anísim's friend and co-faker, a dark little man with the beautiful handwriting in which Anísim's letters home were written. It becomes gradually clear that Samorodov is the mastermind in this counter-feiting business, but Anísim tries hard to puff himself up, boasting of his wonderful powers of observation and of his talents as a detective. As a detective, and a mystic, he knows, however, that "anybody can steal but there is no place to hide stolen goods." A streak of curious mysticism runs through this strange character.

You will enjoy the delightful description of the wedding preparations and then of Anísim's mood in church during the wedding is worth noting. "Here he was being married, he had to take a wife for the sake of doing the proper thing, but he was not thinking of that now, he had somehow forgotten his wedding completely. Tears dimmed his eyes so that he could not see the icons, he felt heavy at heart; he prayed and besought God that the misfortunes that threatened him, that were ready to burst upon him tomorrow, if not today, might somehow pass him by as storm-clouds in time of drought bypass a village without yielding one drop of rain. [He knew how good detectives were, being one himself.] And so many sins were heaped up in the past, so many sins, and getting out of it all was so beyond hope that it seemed incongruous even to ask forgiveness. But he did ask forgiveness, and even gave a loud sob, but no one took any notice of that, since they supposed he had had a drop too much."

For a moment the child theme appears: "There was the sound of a fretful childish wail. 'Take me away from here, mamma darling!' 'Quiet there!' cried the priest."

Then a new character is introduced; Yelizarov (nicknamed Crutch), a carpenter and contractor. He is a childish person, very gentle and naive, and a little cracked. He and Lipa are both on the same level of meekness, simplicity, and trust—and he and she are real human beings despite their not having the cunning of the evil characters in the tale. Crutch, who seems vaguely to be endowed with second sight, might be trying intuitively to avert the disaster which the wedding itself will result in: " 'Anísim and you, my child, love one another, lead a godly life, little children, and the Heavenly Mother will not abandon you. . . . Children, children, children,' he muttered rapidly. 'Aksinia my dear, Varvara darling, let's all live in peace and harmony, my dear little hatchets. . . .' " He calls people by the pet names of his pet tools.

Mask Eight: Yet another mask, another deception, relates to the elder of the rural district and his clerk, "who had served together for fourteen years, and who had during all that time never signed a single document for anybody or let a single person out of the office without deceiving him or doing him harm. [They] were sitting now side by side, both fat and replete, and it seemed as though they were so steeped in injustice and falsehood that even the skin of their faces was of a peculiar, thievish kind." "Steeped in falsehood"—this is one of the two main notes of the whole story.

You will notice the various details of the wedding: poor Anísim brooding over his predicament, over the doom that is closing upon him; the peasant woman who shouts outside "You've sucked the blood out of us, you monsters; a plague on you!"; and the wonderful description of Aksinia: "Aksinia had naive gray eyes which rarely blinked, and a naive smile played continually on her face. And in those unblinking eyes, and in that little head on the long neck, and in her slenderness there was something snakelike; all in green, with the yellow front of her bodice and the smile on her lips, she looked like a viper that peers out of the young rye in the spring at the passers-by, stretching itself and lifting its head. The Khrymins were free in their behavior to her, and it was very noticeable that she had long been on intimate terms with the eldest of them. But her deaf husband saw nothing, he did not look at her; he sat with his legs crossed and ate nuts, cracking them with his teeth so loudly that it seemed he was shooting a pistol.

"But, behold, old Grigori himself walked into the middle of the room and waved his handkerchief as a sign that he, too, wanted to dance the Russian dance, and all over the house and from the crowd in the yard rose a hum of approbation:

" 'It's *himself* has stepped out! *Himself!*'. . .

"It was kept up till late, till two o'clock in the morning. Anísim, staggering, went to take leave of the singers and musicians, and gave each of them a new half-ruble. His father, who was not staggering, but treading more heavily on one leg, saw his guests off, and said to each of them, 'The wedding has cost two thousand.'

"As the party was breaking up, someone took the Shikalova innkeeper's good overcoat instead of his own old one, and Anísim suddenly flew into a rage and began shouting: 'Stop, I'll find it at once; I know who stole it! Stop!'

He ran out into the street in pursuit of someone, but he was caught, brought back home, shoved, drunken, red with anger and drenched with sweat, into the room where the aunt was undressing Lipa, and there he and she were locked in."

After five days Anísim, who respects Varvara for being a decent woman, confesses to her that he may be arrested at any moment. When he leaves for town, we have the following beautiful description:

"When they drove up out of the gully Anísim kept looking back toward the village. It was a warm, bright day. The cattle were being driven out for the first time, and the peasant girls and women were walking by the herd in their holiday dresses. The brown bull bellowed, glad to be free, and pawed the ground with his forefeet. On all sides, above and below, the larks were singing. Anísim looked back at the graceful little white church—it had only lately been whitewashed—and he thought how he had been praying in it five days before; he looked back at the school with its green roof, at the little river in which he used to bathe and catch fish, and there was a stir of joy in his heart, and he wished that a wall might rise up from the ground and prevent him from going farther, and that he might be left with nothing but the past."

It is his last glimpse.

And now the delightful transformation that comes over Lipa. Anísim's conscience had not only weighed upon him but had been impersonated in him and had been a dreadful weight on Lipa although she knew nothing of his complicated life. Now he and his burden are removed and she is free.

"Wearing an old skirt, her feet bare and her sleeves tucked up to her shoulders, she was scrubbing the stairs in the entry and singing in a silvery little voice, and when she brought out a big tub of slops and looked up at the sun with her childlike smile it seemed as though she, too, were a lark."

Now Chekhov is going to do something quite difficult from the author's point of view. He is going to take advantage of Lipa's silence being broken in order to have her, the silent one, the wordless one, now find words and bring out the facts that will lead to the disaster. She and Crutch are coming back from a long excursion on foot to a remote church, her mother is lagging behind, and Lipa says: "And now I am afraid of Aksinia. It's not that she does anything, she is always smiling, but sometimes she glances at the window, and her eyes are so angry and there is a greenish gleam in them—like the eyes of the sheep in the dark pen. The Juniors are leading her astray: 'Your old man,' they tell her, 'has a bit of land at Butyokino, a hundred acres,' they say, 'and there is sand and water there, so you, Aksinia,' they say, 'build a brickyard there and we will go shares in it.' Bricks now are twenty rubles the thousand, it's a profitable business. Yesterday at dinner Aksinia said to the old man: 'I want to build a brickyard at Butyokino; I'm going into the business on my own account.' She laughed as she said it. And Grigori Petrovich's face darkened, one could see he did not like it. 'As long as I live,' he said, 'the family must not break up, we must keep together.' She gave him a look and gritted her teeth. . . . Fritters were served, she would not eat them."

When they come to a boundary post, Crutch touches it to see that it is firm, an act in keeping with his character. At this point he, Lipa, and some girls who are collecting toadstools are representative of Chekhov's happy people, naive gentle people against a background of unhappiness and injustice. They meet people coming from the fair: "A cart would drive by stirring up the dust and behind it would run an unsold horse, and it seemed glad it had not been sold." There is a subtle emblematic connection here between Lipa and the happy "unsold" horse. Lipa's owner has disappeared. And another point, reflecting the child theme: "An old woman led a little boy in a big cap and big boots; the boy was tired out with the heat and the heavy boots which prevented him from bending his legs at the knees, but yet he blew a tin trumpet unceasingly with all his might. They had gone down the slope and turned into the street, but the trumpet could still be heard." Lipa sees and hears that little boy because she herself is going to have a baby. In the passage "Lipa and her mother who were born to poverty and prepared to live so till the end, giving up to others everything except their frightened, gentle souls, may perhaps have fancied for a minute that in this vast, mysterious world, among the endless series of lives, they too counted for something," I recommend to your attention the words "their frightened, gentle souls." And notice too the beautiful little picture of the summer evening:

"At last they reached home. The mowers were sitting on the ground at the gates near the shop. As a rule the Ukleyevo peasants refused to work for Grigori, and he had to hire strangers, and now in the darkness it seemed as though there were men with long black beards sitting there. The shop was open, and through the doorway they could see the deaf man playing checkers with a boy. The mowers were singing softly, almost inaudibly, or were loudly demanding their wages for the previous day, but they were not paid for fear they should go away before tomorrow. Old Grigori, with his coat off, was sitting in his waistcoat with Aksinia under the birch-tree, drinking tea; a lighted lamp was on the table.

" 'I say, grandfather,' a mower called from outside the gates, as though teasing him, 'pay us half anyway! Hey, grandfather.' "

On the next page Grigori realizes the silver rubles are false and gives them to Aksinia to throw away, but she uses them to pay the mowers. "You mischievous woman," cries Grigori, dumbfounded and alarmed. "Why did you marry me into this family?" Lipa asks her mother. There is a certain gap in time after chapter 5.

One of the most striking passages in the story occurs in chapter 6, when absolutely and divinely indifferent to what is happening around her (the deserved fate of her idiotic husband and the terrible snake-evil coming from Aksinia), absolutely and divinely indifferent to all this evil, Lipa is engrossed in her child and proceeds to promise her little pinched baby her own most vivid vision, her only knowledge of life. She tosses him up and down and in rhythm with the tossing says in singsong tones: "You will grow ever so big, ever so big. You will be a man, we shall work together! We shall wash floors together!" Just as her own most vivid childhood memories are linked up with washing floors. " 'Why do I love him so much, Mamen'ka? Why do I feel so sorry for him!' she went on in a quivering voice, and her eyes glistened with tears. 'Who is he? What is he like? As light as a little feather, as a little crumb, but I love him, I love him as if he were a real person. Here he can do nothing, he can't talk, and yet I always know what his darling eyes tell me he wants.' "

This chapter ends with the news that Anísim is to get six years of hard labor in Siberia. Then a nice touch is added; says old Grigori:

" 'I am worried about the money. Do you remember before his wedding Anísim's bringing me some new rubles and half-rubles? One parcel I put away at the time, but the others I mixed with my own money. When my uncle Dmitri Filatych—the kingdom of Heaven be his—was alive, he used to go to Moscow and to the Crimea to buy goods. He had a wife, and this same wife, when he was away buying goods, used to take up with other men. They had half a dozen children. And when uncle was in his cups he would laugh and say, "I never can make out," he used to say, "which are my children and which are other people's." An easy-going disposition, to be sure; and now I can't tell which are genuine rubles and which are false ones. And they all seem false to me. . . . I buy a ticket at the station, I give the man three rubles, and I keep fancying they are counterfeit. And I am frightened. I must be ill.' "

From that moment he is mentally deranged and is redeemed, in a sense.

"He opened the door and crooking his finger, beckoned to Lipa. She went up to him with the baby in her arms.

" 'If there is anything you want, Lipynka, you ask for it,' he said. 'And eat anything you like, we don't grudge it, so long as it does you good. . . .' He made the sign of the cross over the baby. 'And take care of my grandchild. My son is gone, but my grandson is left.'

"Tears rolled down his cheeks; he gave a sob and went away. Soon afterwards he went to bed and slept soundly after seven sleepless nights."

This was poor Lipa's happiest night—before the awful events that were to follow.

Grigori makes arrangements to give the land at Butyokino, which Aksinia wants for a brickyard, to his grandson. Aksinia is in a fury.

" 'Hey! Stepan,' she called to the deaf man, 'let us go home this minute! Let us go to my father and mother; I don't want to live with convicts. Get ready!'

"Clothes were hanging on lines stretched across the yard; she snatched off her petticoats and blouses still wet and flung them across the deaf man's stretched arms. Then in her fury she dashed about the yard where the linen hung, tore down all of it, and what was not hers she threw on the ground and trampled upon.

" 'Holy Saints, stop her,' moaned Varvara. 'What a woman! Give her Butyokino! Give it to her, for Christ's sake.' "

We come now to the climax.

"Aksinia ran into the kitchen where laundering was being done. Lipa was washing alone, the cook had gone to the river to rinse the clothes. Steam was rising from the trough and from the caldron near the stove, and the air in the kitchen was close and thick with vapor. On the floor was a heap of unwashed clothes, and Nikifor, kicking up his little red legs, lay on a bench near them, so that if he fell he should not hurt himself. Just as Aksinia went in Lipa took the former's shirt out of the heap and put it into the trough, and was just stretching out her hand to a big panlike dipper full of boiling water which was standing on the table.

" 'Give it here,' said Aksinia, looking at her with hatred, and snatching the shirt out of the trough; 'it is not your business to touch my linen! You are a convict's wife, and ought to know your place and who you are!'

"Lipa gazed at her in utter bewilderment; she did not understand, but suddenly she caught the look Aksinia turned upon the child, and at once she understood and went numb all over.

" 'You've taken my land, so here you are!' Saying this Aksinia snatched up the dipper with the boiling water and splashed it over Nikifor.

"There followed a scream such as had never been heard before in Ukleyevo,

---

Overleaf: Pages from Nabokov's teaching copy of "In the Gully."

---

stand, but suddenly she caught the look Aksinya turned
upon the child, and at once she understood and went
numb all over.

"You've taken my land, so here you are!" Saying this
Aksinya snatched up the pitcher with the boiling water
and flung it over Nikifor. There followed

After this there was heard a scream such as had never
been heard before in Ukleyevo, and no one would have
believed that a little weak creature like Lipa could
scream like that. And it was suddenly quiet in the yard.
Askinya walked into the house in silence with the old
naive smile on her lips. . . . The deaf man kept moving about the yard with his arms full of linen, then he
began hanging it up again, silently, without haste. And
until the cook came back from the river no one ventured
to go into the kitchen to see what had happened there.

VIII

Nikifor was taken to the district hospital, and toward
evening he died there. Lipa did not wait to be fetched
but wrapped the dead baby in its little quilt and carried
it home.

The hospital, a new one recently built, with big windows, stood high up on a hill; it was glittering in the
setting sun and looked as though it were on fire
inside. There was a little village below. Lipa went down
the road, and before reaching the village sat down by a
pond. A woman brought a horse to water but the horse
would not drink.

"What more do you want?" the woman said to
softly, in perplexity. "What more do you want?"

A boy in a red shirt, sitting at the water's edge, was
washing his father's boots. And not another soul was in
sight either in the village or on the hill.

[...]'s not drinking," said Lipa, looking at the horse.

[...]en the woman with the horse and the boy with the [...]s walked away, and there was no one left at all. The [...] went to sleep, covering itself with cloth of gold and [...]le, and long clouds, red and lilac, stretched across [...]ky, guarded its rest. Somewhere far away a bittern [...], a hollow, melancholy sound as of a cow shut up in [...]rn. The cry of that mysterious bird was heard every [...]ng, but no one knew what it was like or where it [...]d. At the top of the hill by the hospital, in the bushes [...] to the pond, and in the fields, the nightingales [...] trilling. The cuckoo kept reckoning someone's [...]s and losing count and beginning again. In the pond [...] frogs called angrily to one another, straining them-[...]es to bursting, and one could even make out the [...]ds: "That's what you are! That's what you are!" [...]at a noise there was! It seemed as though all these [...]tures were singing and shouting so that no one [...]ht sleep on that spring night, so that all, even the [...]ry frogs, might appreciate and enjoy every minute: [...] is given only once.

[...] silver half-moon was shining in the sky; there were [...]y stars. Lipa had no idea how long she sat by the [...]d, but when she got up and walked on everybody [...] asleep in the little village, and there was not a single [...]t. It was probably about eight miles' walk home, but [...] her body nor mind seemed equal to it. The moon [...]med now in front, now on the right, and the same [...]koo kept calling in a voice grown husky, with a [...]ckle as though gibing at her: "Hey, look out, you'll [...] your way!" Lipa walked rapidly; she lost her ker-[...]f . . . she looked at the sky and wondered where [...] baby's soul was now: was it following her, or float-[...] aloft yonder among the stars and not thinking of [...], the mother, any more? Oh, how lonely it is in the and no one would have believed that a little weak creature like Lipa could scream like that. And it was suddenly quiet in the yard. Aksinia walked into the house in silence with the old naive smile on her lips. . . . The deaf man kept moving about the yard with his arms full of linen, then be began hanging it up again, silently, without haste. And until the cook came back from the river no one ventured into the kitchen to see what had happened there."

The enemy is destroyed, Aksinia smiles once more; automatically the land is hers now. The deaf man hanging up the linen again is a stroke of genius on Chekhov's part.

The child theme is continued when Lipa comes on foot the long long way back from the hospital. Her baby has died; she carries his little body wrapped in a blanket.

"Lipa went down the road, and before reaching the hamlet sat down by a small pond. A woman brought a horse to water but the horse would not drink.

" 'What more do you want?' the woman said to it softly, in perplexity. 'What more do you want?'

"A boy in a red shirt, sitting at the water's edge, was washing his father's jack boots. And not another soul was in sight, either in the village or on the hill.

" 'Doesn't drink,' said Lipa, looking at the horse."

This little group should be noted. The boy, not her boy. All of it is emblematic of the simple family happiness that might have been hers. Notice the unobtrusive symbolism of Chekhov.

"Then the woman with the horse and the boy with the boots walked away, and there was no one left at all. The sun went to sleep, covering itself with a skeined cloth of gold, and long clouds, red and lilac, stretched across the sky, guarded its rest. Somewhere far away a bittern boomed, a hollow, melancholy sound as that made by a cow shut up in a barn. The cry of that mysterious bird was heard every spring, but no one knew what it was like or where it lived. At the top of the hill by the hospital, in the bushes close to the pond, and in the fields, the nightingales were singing their heads off. The cuckoo kept reckoning someone's years and losing count and beginning again. In the pond the frogs called angrily to one another, straining themselves to bursting and one could even make out the words: 'That's what you are! That's what you are!' What a noise there was! It seemed as though all these creatures were singing and shouting so that no one might sleep on that spring night, so that all, even the angry frogs, might appreciate and enjoy every minute: life is given only once." Among European writers you may distinguish the bad one from the good one by the simple fact that the bad one has generally one nightingale at a time, as happens in conventional poetry, while the good one has several of them sing together, as they really do in nature.

The men Lipa meets on the road are probably bootleggers but Lipa sees them otherwise in the moonlight.

" 'Are you holy men?' Lipa asked the old man.

" 'No. We are from Firsanovo.'

" 'You looked at me just now and my heart was softened. [An almost Biblical intonation in the Russian text.] And the lad is so gentle. I thought you must be holy men.'

" 'Have you far to go?'

" 'To Ukleyevo.'

" 'Get in, we will give you a lift as far as Kuzmenki, then you go straight on and we turn off to the left.'

"Vavila [the young man] got into the cart with the barrel and the old man and Lipa got into the other. They moved at a walking pace, Vavila in front.

" 'My baby was in torment all day,' said Lipa. 'He looked at me with his little eyes and said nothing; he wanted to speak and could not. Lord God! Queen of Heaven! In my grief I kept falling down on the floor; I would be standing there and then I would fall down by the bedside. And tell me, grandfather, why should a little one be tormented before his death? When a grown-up person, a man or woman, is in torment, his sins are forgiven, but why a little one, when he has no sins? Why?'

" 'Who can tell?' answered the old man.

"They drove on for half an hour in silence.

" 'We can't know everything, how and why,' said the old man. 'A bird is given not four wings but two because it is able to fly with two; and so man is not permitted to know everything but only a half or a quarter. As much as he needs to know in order to live, so much he knows.' . . .

" 'Never mind,' he repeated. 'Yours is not the worst of sorrows. Life is long, there is good and bad yet to come, there is everything to come. Great is mother Russia,' he said, and looked round on either side of him. 'I have been all over Russia, and I have seen everything in her, and you may believe my words, my dear. There will be good and there will be bad. I went as a messenger from my village to Siberia, and I have been to the Amur River and the Altay Mountains and I emigrated to Siberia; I worked the land there, then I got homesick for mother Russia and I came back to my native village. . . . And when I got home, as the saying is, there was neither stick nor stone; I had a wife, but I left her behind in Siberia, she was buried there. So I am a hired man now. And I tell you: since then I have had it good as well as bad. I do not want to die, my dear, I would be glad to live another twenty years; so there has been more of the good. And great is our mother Russia!' and again he gazed on either side and looked back. . . .

"When Lipa reached home the cattle had not yet been driven out; everyone was asleep. She sat down on the steps and waited. The old man was the first to come out; he understood what had happened from the first glance at her, and for a long time he could not utter a word, but only smacked his lips.

" 'Oh Lipa,' he said, 'you did not take care of my grandchild. . . .'

Varvara was awakened. She struck her hands together and broke into sobs, and immediately began laying out the baby.

" 'And he was such a pretty child . . .' she said. 'Oh dear, dear. . . . You had the one child, and you did not take enough care of him, you silly thing.' "

In her innocence Lipa never thought of telling people it was Aksinia who had killed her baby. Apparently the family believed that Lipa had just been careless and had accidentally scalded the child by overturning a pot of hot water.

After the requiem service "Lipa waited at table, and the priest, lifting his fork on which there was a salted mushroom, said to her: 'Don't grieve for the babe. For such is the kingdom of Heaven.'

"And only when they had all left Lipa realized fully that there was no Nikifor and never would be, she realized it and broke into sobs. And she did not know what room to go into to sob, for she felt that now her child was dead there was no place for her in the house, that she had no reason to be there, that she was in the way; and the others felt it, too.

" 'Now what are you bellowing for?' Aksinia shouted, suddenly appearing in the doorway; because of the funeral she was dressed up in new clothes and had powdered her face. 'Shut up!'

"Lipa tried to stop but could not, and sobbed louder than ever.

" 'Do you hear?' shouted Aksinia, and stamped her foot in violent anger. 'Who is it I am speaking to? Get out of the house and don't set foot here again, you convict. Get out.'

" 'There, there, there,' the old man put in fussily. 'Aksinia, don't make such an outcry, my dear. . . . She is crying, it is only natural . . . her child is dead. . . .'

" 'It's only natural,' Aksinia mimicked him. 'Let her stay the night here, and don't let me see a trace of her tomorrow! "It's only natural" . . .' she mimicked him again, and, laughing, went into the shop."

Lipa has lost the frail link that connected her to the household and leaves the house for ever.

In all cases, except Aksinia's, the truth gradually comes out.*

The mechanical quality of Varvara's virtues is nicely exemplified by the jams she keeps making; there is too much of it, it goes sugary and uneatable. We recall that poor Lipa had been so fond of it. The jam turned against Varvara.

The letters from Anísim still come in that beautiful hand—evidently his friend Samorodov is doing time with him in the mines of Siberia, so that here too the truth comes out. "I am ill here all the time; I am wretched, for Christ's sake help me!"

Old Grigori, half-crazy, wretched, unloved, is the most vivid representative here of truth coming into its own.

"One fine autumn day toward evening old Grigori was sitting near the church gates, with the collar of his fur coat turned up and nothing of him could be seen but his nose and the peak of his cap. At the other end of the long bench sat Yelizarov the contractor, and beside him Yakov the school watchman, a toothless old man of seventy. Crutch and the watchman were talking.

" 'Children ought to give food and drink to the old. . . . Honor thy father and mother . . .' Yakov was saying with irritation, 'while she, this woman [Aksinia] has turned her father-in-law out of his own house; the old man has neither food nor drink, where is he to go? He has not had a morsel these three days.'

" 'Three days!' said Crutch, amazed.

" 'Here he sits and does not say a word. He has grown feeble. And why be silent? He ought to prosecute her, they wouldn't praise her in court.'

" 'Who praised whom in court?' asked Crutch, who was hard of hearing.

" 'What?' from the watchman.

" 'The woman's all right,' said Crutch, 'she does her best. In their line of business they can't get on without that . . . without cheating, I mean. . . .'

" 'Kicked out of his own house!' Yakov went on with irritation. 'Save up and buy your own house, then turn people out of it! She is a nice one, to be sure! A pla-ague!'

"Grigori listened and did not stir. . . .

" 'Whether it is your own house or others' it makes no difference so long as it is warm and the women don't scold . . .' said Crutch, and he laughed. 'When I was young I was very fond of my Nastasya. She was a quiet woman. And she used to be always at it: "Buy a house, Makarych! Buy a house,

*VN prefaces this section by the following remark to his class: "There is again a time gap between chapters 8 and 9. You will observe the delightful Chekhovian detail when the Khrymins, one of whom, if not all, is or are on intimate terms with his wife have 'presented the deaf man with a gold watch, and he is constantly taking it out and putting it to his ear.' " Ed.

Makarych! Buy a horse, Makarych!" She was dying and yet she kept on saying, "Buy yourself a racing droshky, Makarych, so that you don't have to walk." And all I did was to buy her gingerbread.'

" 'Her husband's deaf and stupid,' Yakov went on, not listening to Crutch; 'a regular fool, just like a goose. He can't understand anything. Hit a goose on the head with a stick and even then it does not understand.'

"Crutch got up to go home. Yakov also got up, and both of them went off together, still talking. When they had gone fifty paces old Grigori got up, too, and walked after them, stepping uncertainly as though on slippery ice."

In this last chapter the introduction of a new character in the toothless old watchman is another stroke of genius on the part of Chekhov, suggesting the continuity of existence, even though this is the conclusion of the story—but the story will go on with old and new characters, it will flow on as life flows on.

Note the synthesis at the end of this tale: "The village was already sinking in the dusk of evening and the sun only gleamed on the upper part of the road which ran wriggling like a snake up the slope." The brilliant, snakelike trail, an emblem of Aksinia, fades and vanishes in the serene bliss of the night. "Old women were coming back from the woods and children with them; they were bringing baskets of mushrooms. Peasant women and girls came in a crowd from the station where they had been loading the cars with bricks, whose red dust had settled upon their skin under their eyes. They were singing. Ahead of them was Lipa, with her eyes turned toward the sky, she was singing in a high voice, carolling away as though exulting in the fact that at last the day was over and one might rest. Among the crowd, holding by the knot something tied up in a kerchief, breathless as usual, walked Praskovya, her mother, who still went out to work by the day.

" 'Good evening, Makarych!' cried Lipa, seeing Crutch. 'Good evening, dear!'

" 'Good evening, Lipynka,' cried Crutch delighted. 'Girls, women, love the rich carpenter! Ho-ho! My little children, my little children. (Crutch gave a sob.) My dear little hatchets!' " Crutch is the not very efficient but on the whole good spirit of the tale—in the dazed state he usually lives in, he had spoken words of peace at the marriage, as if trying, in vain, to avert the disaster.

Old Grigori dissolves in tears—a weak and silent King Lear.

The final page of "In the Gully" in Nabokov's teaching copy.

---

kovya had dropped a little behind, and when the old man was abreast of them Lipa bowed down low and said:

"Good evening, Grigory Petrovich."

Her mother, too, bowed. The old man stopped and, saying nothing, looked at the two; his lips were quivering and his eyes full of tears. Lipa took out of her mother's bundle a piece of pie stuffed with buckwheat and gave it to him. He took it and began eating.

The sun had set by now: its glow died away on the upper part of the road too. It was getting dark and cool. Lipa and Praskovya walked on and for some time kept crossing themselves.

1900

Note the synthesis at the end of the story. The brilliant trail, snake-like, a symbol of Aksinia, fades and vanishes in the serene bliss of the night. Crutch is the not very efficient but good genius good spirit who earlier had, in the dazed state he usually lives, spoken words of peace at the marriage :476 as if trying to avert the coming disaster. Tsibukin dissolves in tears — a weak and silent King Lear (Lear was strong in a way and a poet). Lipa is her old self dissolving in song, happy in the tiny enclosure of her world, sensitive to her dead baby in the coolness of nightfall — and innocently, unwittingly, carries to God the pink dust of the bricks that are making the fortune of the evil Aksinia.

"Crutch and Yakov passed and could still be heard talking as they receded. Then old Grigori passed in their wake and there was a sudden hush in the crowd. Lipa and Praskovya dropped a little behind, and when the old man was abreast of them Lipa bowed down low and said: 'Good evening, Grigori Petrovich.' Her mother, too, bowed. The old man stopped and, saying nothing, looked at the two; his lips were quivering and his eyes full of tears. Lipa took out of her mother's knotted bundle a piece of pie stuffed with buckwheat and gave it to him. He took it and began eating.

"The sun had set by now: its glow died away on the upper part of the road too. It was getting dark and cool. Lipa and Praskovya walked on and for some time kept crossing themselves."

Lipa is her old self, she dissolves in song, happy in the tiny enclosure of her limited world, united with her dead baby in the coolness of nightfall—and innocently, unconsciously, carrying to her God the pink dust of the bricks that are making the fortune of Aksinia.

Notes on *The Seagull* (1896)

In 1896 *The Seagull* (Chaika) was a complete failure at the Alexandrine Theatre in St. Petersburg, but at the Moscow Art Theatre in 1898 it was a tremendous success.

The first exposition—talk between two minor characters, the girl Masha and the village teacher Medvedenko—is thoroughly permeated by the manner and mood of the two. We learn about them and about the two major characters, the budding actress Nina Zarechny and the poet Treplev, who are arranging some amateur theatricals in the alley of the park: "They are in love with each other and to-night their souls will unite in an effort to express one and the same artistic vision," says the teacher in the ornate style so typical of a Russian semi-intellectual. He has his reasons to allude to this, being in love too. Nevertheless, we must admit that this introduction is decidedly blunt. Chekhov, like Ibsen, was always eager to get done with the business of explaining as quickly as possible. Sorin, the flabby and good-natured landowner, drops by with Treplev, his nephew, who is nervous about the play he is staging. The workmen who have built the platform come and say, we are going for a dip. And meanwhile old Sorin has asked Masha to tell her father (who is his own employee on the estate) to have the dog kept quiet at night. Tell him yourself, she says, rebuffing him. The perfectly natural swing in the play, the association of odd little details which at the same time are perfectly true to life—this is where Chekhov's genius is disclosed.

In the second exposition Treplev talks to his uncle about his mother, the professional actress, who is jealous of the young lady who is going to act in his play. Nor can one even mention Duse in her presence. My goodness, just try, exclaims Treplev.

With another author the complete picture of the woman in this expository dialogue would be a dreadful piece of traditional technique, especially seeing that it is to her own brother that the young man is speaking; but by sheer force of talent Chekhov manages to pull it through. The details are all so amusing: she has seventy thousand in the bank, but if you ask her for a loan she starts crying. . . . Then he speaks of the routine theatre, of its smug household morals and of the new thing he wants to create; and he talks about himself, about his sense of inferiority because his mother is always surrounded by famous artists and writers. It is quite a long monologue. By a judiciously placed question he is further made to speak of Trigorin, his mother's friend, the author. Charm, talent, but—but somehow after Tolstoy and Zola one does not want to read Trigorin. Note the placing of Tolstoy and Zola on one level—typical for a young author like Treplev in those days, the late nineties.

Nina appears. She was afraid her father, a neighboring squire, would not let her come. Sorin goes to call the household, for the moon is rising and it is time to start Treplev's play. Note two typical Chekhov moves: first, Sorin sings a few bars of a Schubert song, then checks himself and tells with a laugh the nasty thing somebody once said about his singing voice; second, then when Nina and Treplev are left alone they kiss and immediately after she asks, "What's that tree there?" The answer, an elm. "Why is the tree so dark?" she goes on. These trifles disclose better than anything invented before Chekhov the wistful helplessness of human beings—the old man who made a mess of his life, the delicate girl who will never be happy.

The workmen come back. It is time to begin. Nina refers to her stage-fright emotion—she will have to be acting in front of Trigorin, the author of those wonderful short stories. "Dunno, haven't read them," Treplev says curtly. It has been pointed out by critics, who like noting such things, that while the elderly actress Arkadina is jealous of the amateur Nina who as yet is only dreaming of a stage career, her son, the unsuccessful and not very gifted young writer, is jealous of a really fine writer, Trigorin (incidentally, a kind of double of Chekhov the professional himself). The audience arrives. First Dorn, the old doctor, and the wife of Shamraev, the manager of Sorin's estate, who is an old flame of Dorn. Then Arkadina, Sorin, Trigorin, Masha, and Medvedenko flock in. Shamraev asks Arkadina about an old comic he used to applaud. "You keep asking me about antediluvian nobodies," she replies, rather testily.

Presently the curtain rises. There is a real moon and a view of the lake instead of a backdrop. Nina sitting on a stone makes a lyrical speech in a Maeterlinck style, mystically commonplace, obscurely trite. ("It is something in the decadent manner," whispers Arkadina. "Mother!" says her son in pleading tones.) Nina goes on. The idea is that she is a spirit talking after all life has ceased on earth. The red eyes of the devil appear. Arkadina makes fun of it and Treplev loses his temper, shouts for the curtain, and goes away. The others rebuke her for having hurt her son. But she feels insulted herself—that bad-tempered, vain boy . . . wants to teach me what the theatre ought to be. . . . The subtle point is that though Treplev has a real desire to destroy the old forms of art, he has not the talent to invent new ones to take their place. Note what Chekhov does here. What other author would have dared to make his main character—a positive character, as they say, that is, one which is expected to win the audience's sympathy—who else would have dared to make him a minor poet, at the same time giving real talent to the least pleasant persons of the play, to the nasty self-sufficient actress and the egotistical, supercritical, emphatically professional writer?

Some singing is heard on the lake. Arkadina recalls the days when youth and gaiety filled the place. She regrets having hurt her son. Nina appears and Arkadina introduces her to Trigorin. "Oh, I always read you." Now comes a delightful little parody of Chekhov's own method of contrast between poetry and prose. "Yes, the setting was beautiful," says Trigorin, and adds after a pause, "That lake must be full of fish." And Nina is puzzled to learn that a man who, as she says, has experienced the delights of creative work, can be amused by angling.

Without any special connection (again a typical device with Chekhov and beautifully true to life), but evidently continuing the line of thought of his previous conversation, Shamraev recalls a certain funny incident in a theatre years ago. There is a pause after this when the joke falls flat and nobody laughs. Presently they disperse, with Sorin complaining without effect to Shamraev about the dog barking at night, Shamraev repeating an earlier anecdote about a church singer, and Medvedenko, the socialist-minded, needy village teacher, inquiring how much such a singer earns. The fact that the question is unanswered shocked many critics who required facts and figures from plays. I remember reading somewhere the solemn statement that a playwright must tell his audience quite clearly the income of his respective characters, for otherwise their moods and action cannot be understood in full. But Chekhov, the genius of the casual, attains in the harmonious interplay of these trivial remarks much greater heights than the ordinary slaves of cause and effect.

Dorn tells Treplev, who now appears again, that he liked his play—or what he heard of the play. He goes on expounding his own views about life, ideas, and art. Treplev, who was at first touched by his praise, now interrupts him twice. Where is Nina? He rushes away almost in tears. "Oh, youth, youth!" sighs the doctor. Masha retorts, "When people can't find anything else to say, they say, Oh youth, youth." She takes a pinch of snuff to the vast disgust of Dorn. Then she becomes suddenly hysterical and tells him she is desperately and hopelessly in love with Treplev. "Everybody is so nervous," the doctor repeats. "So very nervous. And everybody is in love. . . . This magic lake. But how can I help you, my poor child, how?"

So ends the first act, and we may well understand that the average audience in Chekhov's time, as well as the critics—those priests of the average—were left rather irritated and puzzled. There has been no definite line of conflict. Or rather there have been several vague lines and a futility of conflict, for one cannot expect any special conflict from a quarrel between a quick-tempered but soft son and a quick-tempered but equally soft mother, each always regretting his or her hasty words. Nothing special further is suggested by Nina meeting Trigorin, and the romances of the other characters are blind alleys. Finishing the act with an obvious dead end seemed an insult to people eager for a good tussle. But notwithstanding the fact that Chekhov was still tied up by the very traditions he was flaunting (the rather flat expositions, for instance), what seemed nonsense and faults to the average critic are really the grain from which some day a really great drama will grow, for with all my fondness for Chekhov I cannot hide the fact that in spite of his authentic genius he did not create the perfect masterpiece. His achievement was that he showed the right way to escape the dungeon of deterministic causation, of cause and effect, and burst the bars holding the art of drama captive. What I hope of future playwrights is not that they will merely repeat the actual methods of Chekhov, for these belong to him, to his type of genius, and cannot be imitated, but that other methods tending with even more power to the same freedom of drama will be found and applied. This said, let us turn to the next act and see what surprises it reserved for an irritated and puzzled audience.

Act II. A croquet lawn and part of the house and lake. Arkadina is giving Masha a few hints as to how a woman keeps fit. From a chance remark we learn that she has been Trigorin's mistress for quite a while. Sorin comes, together with Nina who has the opportunity of being here because her father and stepmother have gone away for three days. A rambling conversation is set rolling about Treplev's low spirits, about Sorin's poor health.

MASHA. When he reads something aloud, his eyes burn and his face becomes pale. He has a beautiful sad voice and his manners are those of a poet.

(SORIN *reclining in a garden chair is heard snoring.*) [*The contrast!*]

DR. DORN. Good night, baby.

ARKADINA. Hello Peter!

SORIN. Eh? What's that? (*Sits up.*)

ARKADINA. You are sleeping?

SORIN. Not at all.

(*A pause.*) [*Great master of pauses, Chekhov.*]

ARKADINA. You do nothing for your health—that's bad, brother.

SORIN. But I'd like to—only the doctor here is not interested.

DR. DORN. What's the use of seeing a doctor at sixty.

SORIN. A man of sixty wants to live, too.

DR. DORN (*testily*). Oh, all right. Try something for the nerves.

ARKADINA. I keep thinking that he ought to go to some German watering place.

DR. DORN. Well. . . . Well, yes, he might go. And then he might not.

ARKADINA. Do you see what he means? I don't.

SORIN. There is nothing to see. It is all perfectly clear.

That's the way it goes. The wrong audience may get the impression that the author is frittering away his precious twenty minutes, his second act, while conflict and climax are fretting in the wings. But it is quite all right. The author knows his business.

MASHA (*gets up*). Time for lunch, I think. (*Moves indolently.*) My foot is asleep. (*Exit.*)

Presently Shamraev turns up and is annoyed that his wife and Arkadina want to go to town when the horses are needed for the harvest. They quarrel; Shamraev loses his temper and refuses to manage the estate any longer. Can this be called a conflict? Well, there has been something leading up to it—that little thing about refusing to stop the dog barking at night—but really, really, says the smug critic, what parody is this?*

Here quite simply and with great aplomb Chekhov, the novator, reverts to the old old trick of having Nina, the heroine (who now remains alone on the stage) speaking her thoughts aloud. Well, she is a budding actress—but not even that can be an excuse. It is rather a flat little speech. She is puzzling over the fact that a famous actress weeps because she cannot have her own way and a famous writer spends the whole day fishing. Treplev comes back from hunting

---

*Not even could a moralist note here the paradox, typical, one might say, of a decaying class: the employee bullying his master—for this was *not* typical of Russian country life: it is a mere incident based on such and such characters, who may crop up and who may not. (VN deleted marginal note. Ed.)

and throws a dead sea gull at Nina's feet. "I was a cad to kill this bird." Then he adds, "Soon I shall kill myself in the same way." Nina is cross with him: "These last few days you talk in symbols. This bird is apparently a symbol, too. (*She removes it onto a bench.*) But excuse me, I am too simple; I don't understand symbols." (Note that this line of thought will have a very neat ending—Nina herself will turn out to be the live subject of this symbol, which she does not see and which Treplev applies wrongly.) Treplev raves at her for becoming cold and indifferent to him after the flop of his play. He refers to his own oafishness. There is a faint hint at a Hamlet complex, which Chekhov suddenly turns inside out by Treplev applying another Hamlet motive to the figure of Trigorin, who stalks in with a book in his hands. "Words, words, words," Treplev shouts and exits.

Trigorin jots down in his book an observation about Masha: "Takes snuff, drinks strong liquors. . . . Always in black. The schoolteacher is in love with her." Chekhov himself kept such a notebook for jotting down characters that might come in handy. Trigorin tells Nina that he and Arkadina are, apparently, leaving (because of the quarrel with Shamraev). In reply to Nina, who thinks "it must be so wonderful to be a writer," Trigorin delivers a delightful speech, almost three pages long. It is so good and so typical for an author who finds a chance to talk about himself that the general aversion to long monologues in the modern theatre is forgotten. All the details of his profession are remarkably well brought out: ". . . . Here I am, talking to you and I am moved, but at the same time I keep remembering that an unfinished long short story awaits me on my desk. I see, for instance, a cloud; I see it looks like a piano, and immediately I tell myself, I must use that in a story. A passing cloud that had the form of a piano. Or, say, the garden smells of heliotrope. Straightway I collect it: a sickly sweet smell, widow blossom, must mention it when describing summer dusk. . . ." Or this bit: "When in the beginning of my career I used to have a new play staged, it always seemed to me that the dark spectators were opposed to me and that the blond spectators were coldly indifferent. . . ." Or this: "Oh, yes, it is pleasant to write, while you write . . . but afterwards. . . . The public reads and says: Yes, charming, talented. . . . Nice—but so inferior to Tosltoy; . . . yes, a beautiful story— but Turgenev is better." (This was Chekhov's own experience.)

Nina keeps telling him that she could readily undergo all such troubles and disappointments if she could have fame. Trigorin glancing at the lake and taking in the air and the landscape, remarks that it is such a pity he must leave. She points out to him the house on the opposite bank where her mother had lived.

NINA. I was born there. I spent all my life near that lake and know every little island on it.

TRIGORIN. Yes, it's beautiful here. (*Noticing the sea gull on the bench.*) And what's that?

NINA. A sea gull. Treplev killed it.

TRIGORIN. A fine bird. Really, I don't want one bit to go. Look here, try and persuade Madame Arkadin to stay. (*He proceeds to note something down in his book.*)

NINA. What are you writing?

TRIGORIN. Oh, nothing. . . . Just an idea. (*He puts the book into his pocket.*) An idea for a short story: lake, house, girl loves lake, happy and free like a sea gull. Man happens to pass, a glance, a whim, and the sea gull perishes. (*Pause*)

ARKADINA (*from window*). Hullo, where are you?

TRIGORIN. Coming!

ARKADINA. We remain.

(*He goes into the house*)

(*NINA is left alone and broods awhile on the stage-front.*)

NINA. A dream. . . .

Curtain.

Now three things must be said about the ending of this second act. First of all, we have already noticed Chekhov's weak point: the featuring of young poetical women. Nina is slightly false. That last sigh over the footlights dates, and it dates just because it is not on the same level of perfect simplicity and natural reality as the rest of the things in the play. We are aware, certainly, that she is actressy and all that, but still it does not quite click. Trigorin says to Nina, among other things, that he rarely happens to meet young girls and that he is too far gone in life to imagine clearly the feelings of sweet eighteen, so that in his stories, he says, his young girls are generally not true to life. (We may add, something wrong about the mouth, as Sargent the painter used to say the family of his sitters invariably observed.) What Trigorin says may be curiously enough applied to Chekhov, the playwright; for in his short stories, as for instance "The House with the Mezzanine," or "The Lady with the Little Dog," the young women are wonderfully alive. But that's because he does not make them talk much. Here they talk, and the weak spot is felt: Chekhov was not a talkative writer. That's one thing.

Another thing to be remarked is this. To all appearances, and judging by his own subtle approach to the writer's trade, his power of observation, and so on, Trigorin is really a good writer. But somehow the notes he takes about the bird and the lake and the girl do not impress one as the making of a good story. At the same time, we already guess that the plot of the play will be exactly that story and no other. The technical interest is now centered on the point: will Chekhov manage to make a good story out of material which in Trigorin's notebook sounds a little trite. If he succeeds, then we were right in assuming that Trigorin is a fine writer who will succeed in making of a banal theme a fine story. And finally a third remark. Just as Nina herself did not realize the real import of the symbol when Treplev brought the dead bird, so Trigorin does not realize that by remaining in the house near the lake he will become the hunter who kills the bird.

In other words, the end of the act is again obscure to the average audience because nothing can be expected yet. All that has really happened is that there has been a quarrel, a departure settled, a departure put off. The real interest lies in the very vagueness of the lines, and in artistic half-promises.

Act III, a week later. A dining room in Sorin's country house. Trigorin is breakfasting and Masha is telling him about herself so that "you, a writer, can make use of my life." From her very first words it transpires that Treplev has attempted to commit suicide but his wound is not serious.*

Apparently Masha's love for Treplev goes, for now she decides to marry the school teacher in order to forget Treplev. We learn further that Trigorin and Arkadina are about to leave for good now. A scene between Nina and Trigorin follows. She makes him a present, a medallion with, engraved, the title of one of his books and the number of a page and line. As Arkadina and Sorin come in, Nina hurriedly leaves, asking Trigorin to grant her a few minutes before he goes. But note, not a word of love has been spoken, and Trigorin is a little obtuse. As the play proceeds, Trigorin keeps muttering under his breath, trying to remember what was that line on that page. Are there any books of mine in this house? There are, in Sorin's study. He wanders off to find the required volume, which is the perfect way of getting him off the stage.

Sorin and Arkadina discuss the reasons for Treplev's attempted suicide: jealousy, idleness, pride. . . . When he suggests she give him some money she starts crying, as her son has predicted she does in such cases. Sorin gets excited and has a fit of dizziness.

After Sorin is led away, Treplev and Arkadina talk. This is a slightly hysterical and not very convincing scene. First move: he suggests to his mother that she lend some money to Sorin and she retorts that she is an actress and not a banker. A pause. Second move: he asks her to change the bandage on his head

*Note that according to the rules, which I dislike so intensely, you cannot make a man kill himself between the acts, but you can make him make the attempt if he does not die; and vice-versa, you cannot have a man bungle his shot in the last act when he retires behind the scenes to make an end of it. (VN in a deleted passage. Ed.)

and as she does so very tenderly he reminds her of an act of great kindness which she once performed, but she does not remember. He tells how much he loves her but—and now the third move: why is she under the influence of that man? This makes her cross. He says that Trigorin's literature makes him sick; she retorts, you are an envious nonentity; they quarrel fiercely; Treplev starts crying; they make up again (forgive your sinful mother); he confesses he loves Nina but she does not love him; he cannot write any more, all hope is lost. The undulation of moods here is a little too obvious—it is rather a demonstration—the author putting the characters through their tricks. And there is a bad blunder directly afterwards. Trigorin comes in, turning the pages of the book, looking for the line, and then he reads, for the benefit of the audience: "Here it is: ' . . . if any time you need my life, just come and take it.' "

Now it is quite clear that what really would have happened is that Trigorin, hunting for the book in Sorin's study on the lower shelf and finding it, would, normally, crouch and there and then read the lines. As often happens, one mistake leads to another. The next sentence is very weak again. Trigorin thinking aloud: "Why do I seem to hear such sadness in the call of this pure young soul? why does my own heart sink so painfully?" This is definitely poor stuff, and a good writer like Trigorin would hardly indulge in such pathos. Chekhov was faced with the difficult task of making his author suddenly human, and he bungled it completely by making him climb up on stilts so that the spectators might see him better.

Trigorin tells his mistress very bluntly that he wants to remain and have a go at Nina. Arkadina falls on her knees and in a very well imagined speech pleads with him: My king, my beautiful god. . . . You are the last page of my life, etc. You are the best contemporary writer, you are Russia's only hope, etc. Trigorin explains to the audience that he has no will-power—weak, slack, always obedient. Then she notices him writing something in his notebook. He says: "This morning I happened to hear a good expression—the pine grove of maidens. It may come in useful. . . . (*He stretches himself.*) Again railway carriages, stations, station-meals, cutlets, conversations. . . ."*

Shamraev who comes in to say that the carriage is ready speaks of an old actor he used to know. This is his being true to type, as in the first act, but a curious thing seems to have happened here. We have noted that Chekhov found a new device for making his characters live by giving them some silly joke or foolish observation or casual recollection instead of making the miser

---

*Note again, that just as in the demonstration of changing moods in the scene between mother and son, we get here the demonstration of the man reverting to the professional author—a little too obvious. There follows another demonstration: Shamraev . . . (VN in a deleted passage. Ed.)

always talk of his gold and the doctors of their pills. But what happens now is that the thwarted goddess of determinism takes her revenge, and what seemed to be a delightful casual remark indirectly disclosing the nature of the speaker now becomes as unescapable and all-powerful a feature as the miser's stinginess. Trigorin's notebook, Arkadina's tears when money questions are raised, Shamraev's theatrical recollections—these become fixed labels as unpleasant as the recurring oddities in traditional plays—you know what I mean—some special gag which a character repeats throughout the play at the most unexpected or rather expected moments. This goes to show that Chekhov, though he almost managed to create a new and better kind of drama, was cunningly caught in his own snares. I have the definite impression that he would not have been caught by these conventions—by the very conventions he thought he had broken—if he had known a little more of the numerous forms they take. I have the impression that he had not studied the art of drama completely enough, had not studied a sufficient number of plays, was not critical enough about certain technical aspects of his medium.

During the bustle of departure (with Arkadina giving a ruble, then worth about fifty cents, for the three servants, and repeating that they should share it) Trigorin manages to have a few words with Nina. We find him very eloquent about her meekness, her angel like purity, etc. She tells him she has decided to become an actress and to go to Moscow. They fix a date there and embrace. Curtain. There can be no question that though this act has a few good things in it, mainly in the wording, it is far below the two first ones.*

Act IV. Two years pass. Chekhov quietly sacrifices the ancient law of unity of time to secure unity of place, for in this last respect there is something quite natural in going over to next summer when Trigorin and Arkadina are expected to come again to stay with her brother in his country house.

A drawing room converted by Treplev into his den—lots of books. Masha and Medvedenko enter. They are married and have a child. Masha is concerned about Sorin, who is afraid to be alone. They refer to the skeleton of the theatre standing in the dark garden. Mrs. Shamraev, Masha's mother, suggests to Treplev that he be nicer to her daughter. Masha still loves him but now hopes that when her husband gets transferred to another place she will forget.

*Note very carefully, please, the queer revenge which I have just described [of the goddess of determinism]. There is always such a devil awaiting the unwary author just as he thinks he has succeeded. And most important, it is just now when from the point of tradition the author has come back to the fold and when something like a climax looms and the audience expects if not *the* obligatory scene (which would be too much to ask of Chekhov), at least *some* obligatory scene, (which queerly enough is much the same thing—what I mean is, such a scene that, though not consciously defined in the expectancy, is felt to be satisfying the "just what we wanted" when it comes—we may call it the satisfying scene), it is just at this moment that Chekhov is at his worst. (VN deleted passage. Ed.)

Incidentally we learn that Treplev writes for magazines. Old Sorin has his bed made here in Treplev's room. This is a very natural thing for a man suffering from asthma to want, a craving for some change—it must not be confused with the "keeping on the stage" device. A delightful conversation ensues between the doctor, Sorin, and Medvedenko. (Arkadina has gone to the station to meet Trigorin.) For instance, the doctor alludes to his having spent some time and a lot of money in foreign countries. Then they speak of other things. There is a pause. Then Medvedenko speaks.

MEDVEDENKO. May I inquire, Doctor, what foreign town did you like best?
DORN. Genoa.
TREPLEV. Why Genoa—of all towns?

The doctor explains: just an impression, lives there seemed to meander and fuse—rather in the ways, he adds, as the world-soul in your play—by the way where is she now, that young actress? (A very natural transition.) Treplev tells Dorn about Nina. She had a love affair with Trigorin, had a baby, the baby died; she is not a good actress though quite a professional one by now, plays big parts but acts them coarsely, no taste, gasps, gesticulates. There are moments when one feels talent in some outcry of hers, as in the way she dies, but these are but moments.

Dorn inquires whether she has talent and Treplev answers that it is difficult to say. (Note that Nina is much in the same position as Treplev in their artistic achievements.) He goes on to tell that he has followed her from town to town wherever she played, but she never let him come near. Sometimes she writes. After Trigorin left her she has seemed a little wrong in the head. She signs her letters sea gull. (Note that Treplev has forgotten the connection.) He adds that she is here now, roams about, does not dare come, nor does she want anyone to speak to her.

SORIN. She was a charming girl.
DORN. What's that?
SORIN. I said she was a charming girl.

Then Arkadina comes back from the station with Trigorin. (Intertwined with these scenes we are shown the pitiful plight of Medvedenko whom his father-in-law bullies.) Trigorin and Treplev manage to shake hands. Trigorin has brought a copy of a monthly review from Moscow with a story by Treplev, and with the flippant geniality of a famous writer to a lesser star tells him that people are interested, find him mysterious.

Presently all of them but Treplev sit down to play a game of lotto as they always do on rainy evenings. Treplev to himself, looking through the monthly: "Trigorin has read his own stuff but has not even cut the pages of my story." We follow the lotto game, and this is a very typical and beautiful Chekhov scene. It seems that in order to attain the heights of his genius he must put his people at ease, make them feel at home, make them comfortable, though this does not preclude slight boredom, gloomy little thoughts, stirring recollections, etc. And though here again the characters are shown in their oddities or habits—Sorin again dozes, Trigorin talks of angling, Arkadina recalls her stage successes—this is much more naturally done than in the false dramatic background of the preceding act, because it is quite natural that in the same place, with the same people collected, two years later, the old tricks would be gently and rather pathetically repeated. It is hinted that critics have handled Treplev, the young author, very roughly. The numbers of the lotto are called out. Arkadina has never read a line of her son's stuff. Then they interrupt the game to go and have supper, all except Treplev, who remains brooding over his manuscripts. A monologue—it is so good that we do not mind the convention: "I have talked so much about new forms—and now I feel that little by little I myself slip into routine." (This may be applied—like most of the professional observations in the play—to Chekhov himself, in a way certainly, but only when he has lapses as in the previous act.) Treplev reads: " 'Her pale face framed by her dark hair.' That's rotten, that 'framed,' " he exclaims and strikes it out. "I shall begin with the hero being awakened by the sound of rain—and to hell with the rest. The description of the moonshine is much too long and elaborate. Trigorin has created his own tricks; for him it is easy. He will show the neck of a broken bottle glistening on a river-dam and the black shadow under the mill-wheel—that's all and the moonlight is ready, but with me it is all the 'tremulous light' and 'softly twinkling stars' and the distant sounds of a piano, which 'dissolved in the soft intoxicating night air.' It is horrible, awful. . . ." (Here we get, incidentally, a beautifully defined difference between Chekhov's art and that of his contemporaries.)

Next follows the meeting with Nina, which from the point of view of the traditional stage may be considered the main and what I called satisfying scene of the play. Actually it is very fine. Her way of talking is much more in Chekhov's line here, when he is no more concerned with depicting pure, eager, romantic maidens. She is tired, upset, unhappy, a jumble of recollections and details. She loves Trigorin still and ignores the tremendous emotion of Treplev, who tries for the last time to make her consent to stay with him. "I am a sea gull," she says without any special connection. "Now I'm mixing things up. You remember you once shot a sea gull? A man happened to pass, saw the bird, and killed it. Idea for a short story. No . . . I'm getting mixed up again." "Stay a bit, I shall give you something to eat," says Treplev, clinging at a last straw. It is all very finely done. She refuses, speaks again of her love for Trigorin who has so grossly dropped her, then switches to the monologue of Treplev's play, in the beginning of the first act, and hurriedly departs.

The end of the act is magnificent.

TREPLEV (*after a pause*). Pity if somebody meets her in the garden and then tells mamma. It may distress mamma. [Note these are his last words, because now after coolly destroying his writings he opens the door on the right and goes out into an inner room, where presently he will shoot himself.]

DORN (*struggling to push open the door on the left [against which a few moments ago* TREPLEV *had moved an armchair so as not to be disturbed while talking to* NINA]). Queer. . . . The door seems locked. (*At last he comes in and pushes away the armchair.*) Hm. . . . Kind of a steeplechase.

[The others too come back from supper] (ARKADINA, *the* SHAMRAEVS, MASHA, TRIGORIN, *the servant with the wine and beer.*)

ARKADINA. Place it here. The beer is for Trigorin. We shall drink and go on with the game. Let us sit down.

[*Candles are lighted.*] (SHAMRAEV *leads* TRIGORIN *toward a chest of drawers.*)

SHAMRAEV. Look, here's the bird you asked me to stuff last summer.

TRIGORIN. What bird? I don't remember. (*Thinks it over.*) No, really, I don't remember.

(*A shot is heard on the right. They all start.*)

ARKADINA (*frightened*). What was that?

DORN. I know. Something has probably exploded in that medicine chest of mine. Don't worry. (*He goes out and half a minute later [while the rest are settling down to their game] comes back.*) Yes, I was right. A bottle of ether has burst. (*He hums*) "Oh, maiden, again I am bound by your charms. . . ."

ARKADINA (*as she sits down at the table*). Ugh, it gave me a fright. It reminded me of that time when. . . . (*She covers her face with her hands.*) It has made me quite faint.

DORN (*perusing the review, to* TRIGORIN). A month or two ago there was an article here . . . a letter from America . . . and I wanted to ask you . . . (*He leads* TRIGORIN [gently] toward the front of the stage.) . . . because, you see, I am very much interested in the question. (*In a slightly lower voice*)—Will you, please, take Mrs. Arkadin to some other room? The fact is that her son had shot himself.

Curtain.

This is, I repeat, a remarkable ending. Note that the tradition of the backstage suicide is broken by the chief character concerned not realizing what has happened but imitating, as it were, the real reaction by recalling a former occasion. Note, too, that it is the doctor speaking, and so there is no need to call one in order to have the audience quite satisfied. Note, finally, that whereas before his unsuccessful suicide Treplev spoke of doing it, there has not been a single hint in the scene—and still it is perfectly and completely motivated.*

*This final paragraph was deleted by VN. Ed.

if you look up the word "lucid" you will find the
following example: Gorky's "luridly cheap style," and
if you look up the word "cheap" you will find
"Gorky's cheaply lucid style. That was Courtenay's little
way of cornering the writer he disliked just as in
the explanation of political terms he very cleverly made fun of the Tsar's government.

Let us select and examine a typical Gorky
short story for instance the one called "On the
raft: Consider the author's method
of exposition. A certain Mitia and a certain Sergei
are steering the raft across the wide and misty Volga.
The owner of the raft who is somewhere on the forward
part, is heard yelling angrily, and the man Sergei
mutters for the reader to hear: Shout away! Here's
your miserable devil of a son (the other chap,
Mitia) who could not break a straw across his knee
and you put him to steer a raft; and then
you yell so that all the river (and the reader)
hears you. You were mean enough (Sergei goes on
to explain in monologue) not to take a second steersman
(but have your son instead) so now you may
shout as much as you like." These last words — the
author notes and how many authors have used this
particular turn — these last words were growled out
loud enough to be heard forward as if Sergei (the
author adds) wished them to be heard (heard by the →)

MAXIM GORKI (1868-1936)

I n *My Childhood* Gorki has left an account of his life in the house of his maternal grandfather, Vasili Kashirin. It is a dismal story. The grandfather was a tyrannical brute; his two sons—Gorki's uncles—though terrified of their father, in turn terrorized and maltreated their wives and children. The atmosphere was that of never-ending abuse, senseless reproaches, brutal floggings, money-grabbing, and dreary supplications to God.

"Between the barracks and the gaol," says Gorki's biographer, Alexander Roskin, "amidst a sea of mud, stood rows of houses—dun-colored, green, white. And in every one of them, just as in the Kashirin household, people fought and squabbled because the pudding was burnt or the milk had curdled, in every one of them the same petty interests prevailed—about pots and pans and samovars and pancakes—and in every one of them people just as religiously celebrated birthdays and commemorations days, guzzling until they were ready to burst and swilling like hogs."*

This was in Nizhni-Novgorod, and in the social milieu of the worst description—that of the *meshchane*, in status just above the peasants and on the lowest step of the middle class—a social milieu which had already lost the wholesome relation to the soil but had acquired nothing to fill the vacuum thus

---

From the Banks of the Volga, trans. D. L. Fromberg (New York: Philosophical Library, 1946), p. 11.

created, and therefore one that became a prey to the worst vices of the middle classes without their redeeming qualities.

Gorki's father had also had a dismal childhood but afterwards had grown into a fine kind man. He died when Gorki was four, and this was why his widowed mother had gone back to live with her dreadful family. The only happy memory of those days for Gorki was that of his grandmother, who in spite of her terrible surroundings carried in her a kind of happy optimism and a great kindness; only owing to her did the boy ever come to know that there could be happiness, indeed that life was happiness in spite of anything.

At the age of ten Gorki started working for a living. He was in turn an errand-boy in a shoe-store, a dishwasher on a steamboat, an apprentice draftsman, an icon-painter's apprentice, a rag-and-bone man, and a bird-catcher. Then he discovered books and began to read everything he could get hold of. At first he read indiscriminately, but very early he developed fine and sensitive feeling for real literature. He felt a passionate desire to study, but soon realized that he had no chance to be admitted to the university, for which he had gone to Kazan. In his complete destitution he was thrown upon the company of the *bosyaki* —Russian for bums—and made there invaluable observations which he later exploded like a bomb-shell in the face of the dumbfounded reading public of the capitals.

He had eventually to go to work again and served as assistant baker in a basement bakery, where the working day lasted fourteen hours. Soon he became associated with the revolutionary underground where he met more congenial people than the bakery workers. And he continued to read all he could—literature and science and books on social and medical subjects, anything he could get.

At the age of nineteen he attempted to kill himself. The wound was dangerous, but he recovered. The note found in his pocket began thus: "I lay the blame of my death on the German poet Heine, who invented toothache of the heart. . . ."

He tramped on foot all over Russia, to Moscow, and once there made straight for Tolstoy's house. Tolstoy was not at home, but the Countess invited him into the kitchen and treated him to coffee and rolls. She observed that a great number of bums kept coming to see her husband, to which Gorki politely agreed. Back in Nizhni he roomed with a couple of revolutionaries who had been exiled from Kazan because they had participated in student rioting. When the police received an order to arrest one of these and found that he had given them the slip, they arrested Gorki for questioning.

"What odd kind of a revolutionary are you?" said the Gendarme-general during the interrogation. "You write poems and the like. . . . When I let you out, you had better show that stuff of yours to Korolenko." After a month in prison, Gorki was released and, taking the policeman's advice, went to see Vladimir Korolenko. Korolenko was a very popular but quite second-rate writer, loved by the intelligentsia, suspected of revolutionary sympathies by the police—and a very kind man. His criticism, however, was so severe that it frightened Gorki, who gave up writing for a long time and went to Rostov where he worked for a while as a longshoreman. And it was not Korolenko, but a revolutionary named Alexander Kaluzhny, a chance acquaintance in Tiflis in the Caucasus, who helped Gorki to find his way in literature. Charmed by Gorki's vivid narrations of all he had witnessed on his endless tramps, Kaluzhny insisted that Gorki write it down in simple words, the same in which he used to tell it. And when a tale was written, the same man took it to the local newspaper and had it printed. They year was 1892, and Gorki was twenty-four.

Later, however, Korolenko proved a great help—not only with valuable advice, but also by finding Gorki a job at the office of a newspaper with which Korolenko was connected. During this year of journalism in Samara, Gorki devoted himself to work. He studied, he tried to perfect his style, poor man, and he regularly wrote stories which appeared in the paper. By the end of this year he became a well-known writer and received many offers from Volga region newspapers. He accepted an offer from Nizhni and returned to his native town. In his writings he stressed savagely the bitter truth of contemporary Russian life. And yet every line he wrote was permeated with his unconquerable faith in man. Strange though it sounds, this painter of the darkest sides of life, of the cruelest brutalities, was also the greatest optimist Russian literature produced.

His revolutionary bias was quite clear. It added to his popularity among the radical intelligentsia but it also made the police redouble their vigilance in respect to a person who had already for a long time figured on the lists of the suspect. He was soon arrested because a photograph of his with a line of dedication had been found in the lodgings of another man arrested for revolutionary activity, however he was shortly released in the absence of incriminating evidence. He returned to Nizhni again. The police kept an eye on him. Strange individuals were always hovering around the two-storied wooden house in which he lived. One of them would be sitting on a bench, making believe that he was idly surveying the sky. Another would be leaning against a lamp post, ostensibly engrossed in the contents of a newspaper. The coachman of the cab drawn up near the front door also behaved strangely; he would readily agree to take Gorki, or any of his visitors, wherever they pleased, free of charge if need be. But he would never take another fare. All these men were merely police observers.

Gorki became engaged in philanthropic work. He organized a Christmas party for hundreds of the poorest children; opened a comfortable daytime shelter for the unemployed and homeless, with library and piano; started a movement for sending scrapbooks with pictures cut out of magazines to the village children. And also he began to take an active part in revolutionary work. Thus he smuggled a mimeograph for a secret press from St. Petersburg to the Nizhni-Novgorod revolutionary group. This was a serious offence. He was arrested and put in jail. He was a very sick man at the time.

Public opinion, which was a force not to be easily discarded in pre-revolutionary Russia, came out for Gorki in full strength. Tolstoy came out to his defence, and a wave of protest swept through Russia. The Government was forced to yield to public opinion: Gorki was released from prison and confined in his own home instead. "Policemen were posted in his hall and in the kitchen. One of them would constantly intrude into his study," gushes the biographer. Yet a little further we find out that Gorki "settled down to his work, often writing until late at night" and also that he "happened to meet" a friend in the street and, undisturbed, to hold with him a talk about the imminence of revolution. Not such a terrible treatment, I would say. "The police and secret police were powerless to restrain him." (The Soviet police would have restrained him in a twinkle.) Alarmed, the Government ordered him to go and live at Arzamas, a sleepy little town in Southern Russia. "The reprisals against Gorki evoked a wrathful protest from Lenin," Mr. Roskin goes on. " 'One of Europe's foremost writers,' wrote Lenin, 'whose only weapon is freedom of speech, is being banished by the autocratic government without trial.' "

His sickness—consumption, as in Chekhov's case—had become worse during his imprisonment, and his friends, Tolstoy included, brought pressure to bear on the authorities. Gorki was allowed to go to the Crimea.

Earlier back in Arzamas, Gorki, under the very noses of the secret police, had participated actively in revolutionary activities. He also wrote a play, *The Philistines*, which pictures the drab and stuffy milieu in which his own childhood had passed. It never became as famous as his next play, *The Lower Depths*. "While still in the Crimea, sitting one evening on the porch in the gathering dusk, Gorki had mused aloud about his new play: the hero is a former butler to a wealthy family whom the vicissitudes of life have brought to the poorhouse, from which he has never been able to extricate himself. The man's most treasured possession is the collar of a dress shirt—the one object that links him with his former life. The poorhouse is crowded, everybody there hates everyone else. But in the last act spring comes, the stage is flooded with sunlight and the inmates of the poorhouse leave their squalid dwelling and forget the hatred they bear for each other. . ." (Roskin, *From the Banks of the Volga*).

When *The Lower Depths* was finished, it amounted to more than this sketch suggests. Every character depicted is alive and offers an advantageous part to a good actor. It was the Moscow Art Theatre that gave it theatrical realization and, scoring with it a tremendous success, made the play familiar to everybody.

Perhaps it is appropriate at this juncture to say a few words about this amazing Theatre. Before it came into existence, the best theatrical food the Russian theatre-goer could obtain was largely confined to the Imperial companies of Petersburg and Moscow. These had at their disposal considerable means, sufficient to engage the best available talent, but the administration of these theatres was very conservative, which, in art, may often mean very stuffy, and the productions, at best, were on extremely conventional lines. For a really talented actor, however, there was no higher achievement than to "make" the Imperial scene, for the private theatres were very poor and could not compete in any way with the Imperial ones.

When Stanislavski and Nemirovich-Danchenko founded their little Moscow Theatre, everything soon began to change. From the rather hackneyed affair that the theatre had become, it began to pick its way again to what it should be: a temple of careful and genuine art. The Moscow Theatre was backed only by the private fortune of its founders and of a few of their friends, but it did not need elaborate funds. The basic idea that it embodied was to serve the Art, not for the purpose of gain or fame, but for the high purpose of artistic achievement. No part was considered more important than another, every detail was considered to be as worthy of attention as the very choice of the play. The best actors never declined the smallest parts which happened to be allotted them because their talents were best suited to make the greatest success of these parts. No play was performed until the stage-manager was sure that the very best results obtainable had been obtained in regard to artistic realization and perfection of every detail of the production—no matter how many rehearsals had taken place. Time was no object. The enthusiastic spirit of this high service animated every single member of the troupe; and if any other consideration became to him or her of greater importance than the search for artistic perfection, then he or she had no place in this theatrical community. Carried away by the profound artistic enthusiasm of its founders, living like one big family, the actors worked away at every one of the productions as if this were to be the one and only production in their lives. There was religious awe in their approach; there was moving self-sacrifice. And there also was amazing teamwork. For no actor was supposed to care more for his personal performance or success than for the general performance of the troupe, for the general success of the performance. No one was allowed to enter after the curtain went up. No applause was tolerated between acts.

So much for the spirit of the Theatre. As for the basic ideas which revolutionized the Russian theatre and transformed it from a mildly imitative sort of institution always ready to adopt foreign methods *after* they had been soundly established in foreign theatres, into a great artistic institution which soon became a pattern and an inspiration to foreign stage-managers, the main idea was this: the actor should dread above all the rigid techniques, the accepted methods, and should instead give all his attention and effort to an attempt at penetrating the soul of the theatrical type he was going to represent. In this attempt to give a convincing picture of dramatic type, the actor entrusted with the part would try for the period of training to live an imagined life which would be likely to suit the character in question; he would develop in real life mannerisms and intonations suitable for the occasion, so that when he was called upon to speak the words on the stage, these words would come to him as naturally as if he were the man himself and was speaking for himself by an entirely natural impulse.

Whatever may be said for or against the method, one thing is essential: whenever talented people approach art with the sole idea of serving it sincerely to the utmost measure of their ability, the result is always gratifying. Such was the case of the Moscow Theatre. Its success was tremendous. Lines formed days in advance to secure admission to the little hall; the most talented young people began to seek a chance to join the "Moscovites" in preference to the Imperial dramatic troupes. The Theatre soon developed several branches: the first, second, and third "workshops," which remained tightly associated with the parent institution, although each pushed out its artistic investigations in different directions. It also developed a special workshop in Hebrew, the Habima, in which the best producer as well as several actors were non-Jews and which achieved some amazing artistic results of its own.

One of the best actors of the Moscow Theatre was incidentally its founder and stage-director, and, I would almost add, its dictatorial head, Stanislavski, while Nemirovich remained a co-dictator and alternating stage-director.

The Theatre's outstanding successes were Chekhov's plays, Gorki's *Lower Depths*, and of course many other plays. But Chekhov's plays and Gorki's *Lower Depths* have never been removed from the lists and probably will forever be mainly connected with the name of the Theatre.

In the beginning of 1905—the year of the so-called First Revolution—the Government ordered soldiers to shoot at a large gathering of workmen who were marching with the peaceful object of presenting a petition to the Tsar. Later, it became known that the procession had in the first place been organized by a double agent, an *agent provocateur*, of the Government. There were a great number of people, including many children, deliberately killed in the shooting. Gorki wrote a vigorous appeal "To All Russian Citizens and to the Public Opinion of the Countries of Europe" denouncing the "deliberate murders" and implicating the Tsar. Naturally—he was arrested.

This time protests against his arrest poured from all over Europe, from famous scientists, politicians, artists, and again the Government yielded and released him (imagine the Soviet government yielding to-day), after which he went to Moscow and openly helped prepare the Revolution, collecting funds for the purchase of arms and turning his apartment into an arsenal. Revolutionary students set up a rifle range in his lodgings and actively practised shooting.

When the Revolution failed, Gorki quietly slipped over the frontier and went to Germany, then to France, and then America. In the United States he addressed meetings and continued to denounce the Russian government. He also wrote here his long novel, *The Mother*, a very second-rate production. From that time on, Gorki lived abroad, chiefly on Capri in Italy. He remained closely connected with the Russian revolutionary movement, attended revolutionary congresses abroad, and became a close friend of Lenin. In 1913 the Government proclaimed an amnesty and Gorki not only returned to Russia but published there, during the war, a big periodical of his own, *Letopis' (The Chronicle)*.

After the Bolshevik Revolution in the fall of 1917, Gorki enjoyed considerable esteem with Lenin and the other Bolshevik leaders. He also became the chief authority in literary matters. He used this authority with modesty and moderation, realizing that in many literary matters his scanty education did not allow him to impose good judgment. He also used his connections repeatedly to intercede for people who were persecuted by the new government. From 1921 to 1928 he lived again abroad, chiefly in Sorrento—partly on account of his failing health, partly because of political differences with the

Soviets. In 1928 he was more or less ordered back. From 1928 to his death in 1936 he lived in Russia, edited several magazines, wrote several plays and stories, and continued to drink heavily as he had done most of his life. In June 1936 he became very ill and died in the comfortable dacha put to his use by the Soviet government. A good deal of evidence points to the fact that he died of poison administered to him by the Cheka, the Soviet secret police.

As a creative artist, Gorki is of little importance. But as a colorful phenomenon in the social structure of Russia he is not devoid of interest.

"On the Rafts" (1895)

Let us select and examine a typical Gorki short story, for instance the one called "On the Rafts."* Consider the author's method of exposition. A certain Mitya and a certain Sergey are steering the raft across the wide and misty Volga. The owner of the raft, who is somewhere on the forward part, is heard yelling angrily, and the man Sergey mutters for the reader to hear: "Shout away! Here's your miserable devil of a son Mitya who could not break a straw across his knee and you put him to steer a raft; and then you yell so that all the river [and the reader] hears you. You were mean enough [Sergey goes on to explain in monologue] not to take a second steersman [but make your son help me instead], so now you may shout as much as you like." These last words the author notes—and God knows how many authors have used this particular turn—these last words were growled out loud enough to be heard forward as if Sergey (the author adds) wished them to be heard (heard by the audience, we add, for this kind of exposition looks uncommonly like the opening scene of some old faded play with the valet and the maid dusting the furniture and talking about their masters).

Presently we learn from Sergey's sustained monologue that the father had first found a pretty wife for his son Mitya and then had made his daughter-in-law his mistress. Sergey, your healthy cynic, mocks poor moping Mitya and both talk at length in the rhetorical and false style which Gorki reserved for such occasions. Mitya explains that he is going to join a certain religious sect, and the depths of the good old Russian soul are forcibly conveyed to the reader. The scene shifts to the other end of the raft, and now the father is shown with his sweetheart Maria, his son's wife. He is the vigorous and colorful old

---

*This sentence begins handwritten text on page 5 of a manuscript, beneath a deleted incomplete passage remarking Courtenay's description of Gorki's "lurid cheap style." The preceding pages are not preserved. Ed.

man, a well-known figure in fiction. She, the alluring female, twists her body with the movement of that much quoted animal, the cat (lynx is a later variation), and leans toward her lover who proceeds to deliver a speech. We not only hear again the author's high-faluting tones, but almost see him stalking this way and that between his characters and giving them the cue. "I am a sinner, I know," the old father says. "Mitya my son is suffering I know, but is my own position a pleasant one?"—and so on. In both dialogues, the one between Mitya and Sergey, and the one between the father and Maria, the author is trying to make it all less improbable, is careful to make his characters say, as an old playwright would, "we have talked about it more than once already," for otherwise the author might expect the reader to wonder why on earth it was necessary to place two couples on a raft in the middle of the Volga to make them talk of their conflicts. On the other hand, if the constant repetition of such conversation is accepted, one cannot help wondering whether the raft ever got anywhere. People do not talk very much when they steer in a fog across a wide and powerful river—but this, I suppose, is what is called stark realism.

Dawn breaks, and here is what Gorki manages to do in the way of nature description: "The emerald green fields along the Volga glittered with dew diamonds" (quite a jeweller's display). Meanwhile, on the raft the father suggests killing Mitya and "a mysterious charming smile plays on the woman's lips." Curtain.

We must note here that Gorki's schematic characters and the mechanical structure of the story are lined up with such dead forms as the fabliau or the moralité of medieval times. We must also note the low level of culture—what we call in Russia "semi-intelligentsia"—which is disastrous in a writer whose essential nature is *not* vision and imagination (which can work wonders even if an author is not educated). But logical demonstration and a passion for reasoning require, to be successful, an intellectual scope which Gorki completely lacked. Feeling that he had to find some compensation for the poverty of his art and the chaos of his ideas, he always went after the striking subject, the contrast, the conflict, the violent and the harsh—and because what reviewers call "a powerful story" distracts the gentle reader from any true appreciation, Gorki made a strong exotic impression on his readers in Russia and then on his readers abroad. I have heard intelligent people maintain that the utterly false and sentimental story "Twenty-Six Men and a Girl" is a masterpiece. These twenty-six miserable outcasts are working in an underground bakery, rough, coarse, foul-mouthed men surrounding with an almost religious adoration a young girl who comes every day for her bread—then fiercely insulting her when she is seduced by a soldier. This *seemed* something new, but a closer examination reveals that the story is as traditional and flat as the worst examples of the old school of sentimental and melodramatic writing. There is not a single live word in it, not a single sentence that is not ready-made; it is all pink candy with just that amount of soot clinging to it to make it attractive.

From here on there is but one step to so-called Soviet literature.

The conclusion of Nabokov's lecture on Gorki.

We must note here that Gorki's ~~schematic~~ and mechanical structure of the story (characters ~~are~~ the ~~revelations~~ are given with such dead form as the babbian or the monastic, of mediaeval times prototypes of ~~the heroes of modern Soviet fiction~~.) We must also note the low level of culture — what we call in Russia "semi-intelligentsia" — which is disastrous in a writer whose ~~main feature~~ essential nature is not vision and imagination, (which can work wonders even if an author ~~has never is not~~ is not educated). But logical demonstration and a passion for reasoning ~~which~~ require, to be successful, an intellectual scope which Gorky completely lacked. Feeling that he had to find some compensation for the poverty of his art and the chaos of his ideas, he always went after the ~~too~~ striking subject, the contrast, the conflict, the violent and the harsh, — and because what reviewers call "a powerful story" distracts the gentle reader from any true appreciation, Gorky made a strong exotic impression on his readers in Russia and then on his readers abroad. I have heard intelligent people maintain that the utterly false and sentimental story "Twenty six men and a girl" is a masterpiece. ~~The~~ These Twenty six miserable outcasts ~~are~~ ~~who are working in an underground bakery~~ ~~making breads on a damp cellar~~, rough, coarse, foul-mouthed men surround with an almost religious ~~devotedly pour~~ adoration a young girl who comes every day for her ~~bread~~ — then fiercely insult her when she is seduced by a soldier. This seemed something new to the reader ~~who~~ hath forgotten ~~Beauty and the Beast~~). A close examination reveals that the story is as traditional and flat as the worst examples of the old ~~trash~~ school of sentimental and melodramatic writing. There is not a single live word in it, not a single sentence that is not ready made, ~~and~~ it is all pink candy with just that amount of soot clinging to it to make it attractive..

Philistines and Philistinism

Here is the briefest definition of a philistine (pronounced also
"philisteen" and even "philistine"):

A philistine is a full-grown person
whose interests are of a material and commonplace
nature, and whose mentality is formed of
the stock ideas and conventional ideals of his or her group and time.
I have said "full-grown person" because the child
or the adolescent who may look like a small philistine
is only a small parrot mimicking the ways
of confirmed vulgarians. "Vulgarian" is more
or less synonymous with "philistine": the stress
in vulgarian is not so much on the conventionalism of
a philistine as on the vulgarity of some of
his conventional notions. I may also use
the terms genteel and bourgeois. Genteel
implies the lace-curtain, the refined vulgarity
which is worse than simple coarseness. To
burp in company may be rude but to say "excuse me"
after a burp is genteel, and thus worse than
vulgar. The term "bourgeois" I use following
Flaubert, not Marx. Bourgeois in Flaubert's
sense is a state of mind, not a state of
pocket. A bourgeois is a smug philistine,
a dignified vulgarian.

Philistines
and Philistinism

A philistine is a full-grown person whose interests are of a material and commonplace nature, and whose mentality is formed of the stock ideas and conventional ideals of his or her group and time. I have said "full-grown person" because the child or the adolescent who may look like a small philistine is only a small parrot mimicking the ways of confirmed vulgarians, and it is easier to be a parrot than to be a white heron. "Vulgarian" is more or less synonymous with "philistine": the stress in a vulgarian is not so much on the conventionalism of a philistine as on the vulgarity of some of his conventional notions. I may also use the terms *genteel* and *bourgeois*. *Genteel* implies the lace-curtain refined vulgarity which is worse than simple coarseness. To burp in company may be rude, but to say "excuse me" after a burp is genteel and thus worse than vulgar. The term *bourgeois* I use following Flaubert, not Marx. *Bourgeois* in Flaubert's sense is a state of mind, not a state of pocket. A bourgeois is a smug philistine, a dignified vulgarian.

A philistine is not likely to exist in a very primitive society although no doubt rudiments of philistinism may be found even there. We may imagine, for instance, a cannibal who would prefer the human head he eats to be artistically colored, just as the American philistine prefers his oranges to be painted orange, his salmon pink, and his whisky yellow. But generally speaking philistinism presupposes a certain advanced state of civilization where throughout the ages certain traditions have accumulated in a heap and have started to stink.

Philistinism is international. It is found in all nations and in all classes. An English duke can be as much of a philistine as an American Shriner or a French bureaucrat or a Soviet citizen. The mentality of a Lenin or a Stalin or a Hitler in regard to the arts and the sciences was utterly bourgeois. A laborer or a coal miner can be just as bourgeois as a banker or a housewife or a Hollywood star.

Philistinism implies not only a collection of stock ideas but also the use of set phrases, clichés, banalities expressed in faded words. A true philistine has nothing but these trivial ideas of which he entirely consists. But it should be admitted that all of us have our cliché side; all of us in everyday life often use words not as words but as signs, as coins, as formulas. This does not mean that we are all philistines, but it does mean that we should be careful not to indulge too much in the automatic process of exchanging platitudes. On a hot day every other person will ask you, "Is it warm enough for you?" but that does not necessarily mean that the speaker is a philistine. He may be merely a parrot or a bright foreigner. When a person asks you "Hullo, how *are* you?" it is perhaps a sorry cliché to reply, "Fine"; but if you made to him a detailed report of your condition you might pass for a pedant and a bore. It also happens that platitudes are used by people as a kind of disguise or as the shortest cut for avoiding conversation with fools. I have known great scholars and poets and scientists who in the cafeteria sank to the level of the most commonplace give and take.

The character I have in view when I say "smug vulgarian" is, thus, not the part-time philistine, but the total type, the genteel bourgeois, the complete universal product of triteness and mediocrity. He is the conformist, the man who conforms to his group, and he also is typified by something else: he is a pseudo-idealist, he is pseudo-compassionate, he is pseudo-wise. The fraud is the closest ally of the true philistine. All such great words as "Beauty," "Love," "Nature," "Truth," and so on become masks and dupes when the smug vulgarian employs them. In *Dead Souls* you have heard Chichikov. In *Bleak House* you have heard Skimpole. You have heard Homais in *Madame Bovary*. The philistine likes to impress and he likes to be impressed, in consequence of which a world of deception, of mutual cheating, is formed by him and around him.

The philistine in his passionate urge to conform, to belong, to join, is torn between two longings: to act as everybody does, to admire, to use this or that thing because millions of people do; or else he craves to belong to an exclusive set, to an organization, to a club, to a hotel patronage or an ocean liner community (with the captain in white and wonderful food), and to delight in the knowledge that there is the head of a corporation or a European count sitting next to him. The philistine is often a snob. He is thrilled by riches and rank—"Darling, I've actually talked to a duchess!"

A philistine neither knows nor cares anything about art, including literature—his essential nature is anti-artistic—but he wants information and he is trained to read magazines. He is a faithful reader of the *Saturday Evening Post*, and when he reads he identifies himself with the characters. If he is a male philistine he will identify himself with the fascinating executive or any other big shot—aloof, single, but a boy and a golfer at heart; or if the reader is a female philistine—a philistinette—she will identify herself with the fascinating strawberry-blonde secretary, a slip of a girl but a mother at heart, who eventually marries the boyish boss. The philistine does not distinguish one writer from another; indeed, he reads little and only what may be useful to him, but he may belong to a book club and choose beautiful, *beautiful* books, a jumble of Simone de Beauvoir, Dostoevski, Marquand, Somerset Maugham, *Dr. Zhivago*, and Masters of the Renaissance. He does not much care for pictures, but for the sake of prestige he may hang in his parlor reproductions of Van Gogh's or Whistler's respective mothers, although secretly preferring Norman Rockwell.

In his love for the useful, for the material goods of life, he becomes an easy victim of the advertisement business. Ads may be very good ads—some of them are very artistic—that is not the point. The point is that they tend to appeal to the philistine's pride in possessing things whether silverware or underwear. I mean the following kind of ad: just come to the family is a radio set or a television set (or a car, or a refrigerator, or table silver—anything will do). It has just come to the family: mother clasps her hands in dazed delight, the children crowd around all agog: junior and the dog strain up to the edge of the table where the Idol is enthroned; even Grandma of the beaming wrinkles peeps out somewhere in the background; and somewhat apart, his thumbs gleefully inserted in the armpits of his waistcoat, stands triumphant Dad or Pop, the Proud Donor. Small boys and girls in ads are invariably freckled, and the smaller fry have front teeth missing. I have nothing against freckles (in fact I find them very becoming in live creatures) and quite possibly a special survey might reveal that the majority of small American-born Americans *are* freckled, or else perhaps another survey might reveal that all successful executives and handsome housewives had been freckled in their childhood. I repeat, I have really nothing against freckles as such. But I do think there is considerable philistinism involved in the use made of them by advertisers and other agen-

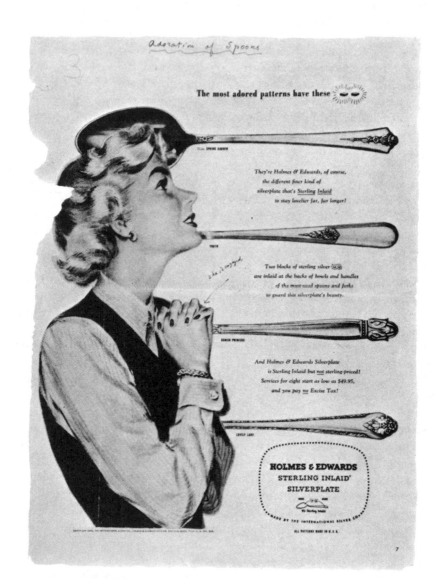

Adoration of Spoons

The most adored patterns have these

They're Holmes & Edwards, of course,
the different finer kind of
silverplate that's Sterling Inlaid
to stay lovelier far, far longer!

Two blocks of sterling silver
are inlaid at the backs of bowls and handles
of the most-used spoons and forks
to guard this silverplate's beauty.

And Holmes & Edwards Silverplate
is Sterling Inlaid but not sterling-priced!
Services for eight start as low as $49.95,
and you pay no Excise Tax!

HOLMES & EDWARDS
STERLING INLAID*
SILVERPLATE

MADE BY THE INTERNATIONAL SILVER CO.

ALL PATTERNS MADE IN U.S.A.

7

cies. I am told that when an unfreckled, or only slightly freckled, little boy actor has to appear on the screen in television, an artificial set of freckles is applied to the middle of his face. Twenty-two freckles is the minimum: eight over each cheekbone and six on the saddle of the pert nose. In the comics, freckles look like a case of bad rash. In one series of comics they appear as tiny circles. But although the good cute little boys of the ads are blond or redhaired, with freckles, the handsome young men of the ads are generally dark haired and always have thick dark eyebrows. The evolution is from Scotch to Celtic.

The rich philistinism emanating from advertisements is due not to their exaggerating (or inventing) the glory of this or that serviceable article but to suggesting that the acme of human happiness is purchasable and that its purchase somehow ennobles the purchaser. Of course, the world they create is pretty harmless in itself because everybody knows that it is made up by the seller with the understanding that the buyer will join in the make-believe. The amusing part is not that it is a world where nothing spiritual remains except the ecstatic smiles of people serving or eating celestial cereals, or a world where the game of the senses is played according to bourgeois rules, but that it is a kind of satellite shadow world in the actual existence of which neither sellers nor buyers really believe in their heart of hearts—especially in this wise quiet country.

Russians have, or had, a special name for smug philistinism—*poshlust*. *Poshlism* is not only the obviously trashy but mainly the falsely important, the falsely beautiful, the falsely clever, the falsely attractive. To apply the deadly label of *poshlism* to something is not only an esthetic judgment but also a moral indictment. The genuine, the guileless, the good is never *poshlust*. It is possible to maintain that a simple, uncivilized man is seldom if ever a *poshlust* since *poshlism* presupposes the veneer of civilization. A peasant has to become a townsman in order to become vulgar. A painted necktie has to hide the honest Adam's apple in order to produce *poshlism*.

It is possible that the term itself has been so nicely devised by Russians because of the cult of simplicity and good taste in old Russia. The Russia of today, a country of moral imbeciles, of smiling slaves and poker-faced bullies, has stopped noticing *poshlism* because Soviet Russia is so full of its special brand, a blend of despotism and pseudo-culture; but in the old days a Gogol, a

---

A 1950 ad selected by Nabokov to illustrate philistinism.

Tolstoy, a Chekhov in quest of the simplicity of truth easily distinguished the vulgar side of things as well as the trashy systems of pseudo-thought. But *poshlists* are found everywhere, in every country, in this country as well as in Europe—in fact *poshlism* is more common in Europe than here, despite our American ads.

The Art
Of Translation

Three grades of evil can be discerned in the queer world of verbal transmigration. The first, and lesser one, comprises obvious errors due to ignorance or misguided knowledge. This is mere human frailty and thus excusable. The next step to Hell is taken by the translator who intentionally skips words or passages that he does not bother to understand or that might seem obscure or obscene to vaguely imagined readers; he accepts the blank look that his dictionary gives him without any qualms; or subjects scholarship to primness: he is as ready to know less than the author as he is to think he knows better. The third, and worst, degree of turpitude is reached when a masterpiece is planished and patted into such a shape, vilely beautified in such a fashion as to conform to the notions and prejudices of a given public. This is a crime, to be punished by the stocks as plagiarists were in the shoebuckle days.

The howlers included in the first category may be in their turn divided into two classes. Insufficient acquaintance with the foreign language involved may transform a commonplace expression into some remarkable statement that the real author never intended to make. "*Bien être general*" becomes the manly assertion that "it is good to be a general"; to which gallant general a French translator of "Hamlet" has been known to pass the caviar. Likewise, in a German edition of Chekhov, a certain teacher, as soon as he enters the classroom, is made to become engrossed in "his newspaper," which prompted a pompous reviewer to comment on the sad condition of public instruction in pre-Soviet Russia. But the real Chekhov was simply referring to the classroom "journal" which a teacher would open to check lessons, marks and absentees. And inversely, innocent words in an English novel such as "first night" and "public house" have become in a Russian translation "nuptial night" and "a brothel." These simple examples suffice. They are ridiculous and jarring, but they contain no pernicious purpose; and more often than not the garbled sentence still makes some sense in the original context.

The other class of blunders in the first category includes a more sophisticated kind of mistake, one which is caused by an attack of linguistic Daltonism suddenly blinding the translator. Whether attracted by the far-fetched when the obvious was at hand (What does an Eskimo prefer to eat—ice cream or tallow? Ice cream), or whether unconsciously basing his rendering on some false meaning which repeated readings have imprinted on his mind, he manages to distort in an unexpected and sometimes quite brilliant way the most honest word or the tamest metaphor. I knew a very conscientious poet who in wrestling with the translation of a much tortured text rendered "is sicklied o'er with the pale cast of thought" in such a manner as to convey an impression of pale moonlight. He did this by taking for granted that "sickle" referred to the form of the new moon. And a national sense of humor, set into motion by the likeness between the Russian words meaning "arc" and "onion," led a German professor to translate "a bend of the shore" (in a Pushkin fairy tale) by "the Onion Sea."

The second, and much more serious, sin of leaving out tricky passages is still excusable when the translator is baffled by them himself; but how contemptible is the smug person who, although quite understanding the sense, fears it might stump a dunce or debauch a dauphin! Instead of blissfully nestling in the arms of the great writer, he keeps worrying about the little reader playing in a corner with something dangerous or unclean. Perhaps the most charming example of Victorian modesty that has ever come my way was in an early English translation of *Anna Karenin*. Vronsky had asked Anna what was the matter with her. "I am *beremenna*" (the translator's italics), replied Anna, making the foreign reader wonder what strange and awful Oriental disease that was; all because the translator thought that "I am pregnant" might shock some pure soul, and that a good idea would be to leave the Russian just as it stood.

But masking and toning down seem petty sins in comparison with those of the third category; for here he comes strutting and shooting out his bejeweled cuffs, the slick translator who arranges Scheherazade's boudoir according to his own taste and with professional elegance tries to improve the looks of his victims. Thus it was the rule with Russian versions of Shakespeare to give Ophelia richer flowers than the poor weeds she found. The Russian rendering of

> *There with fantastic garlands did she come*
> *Of crowflowers, nettles, daisies and long purples*

if translated back into English would run like this:

> *There with most lovely garlands did she come*
> *Of violets, carnations, roses, lilies.*

The splendor of this floral display speaks for itself; incidentally it bowdlerized the Queen's digressions, granting her the gentility she so sadly lacked and dismissing the liberal shepherds; how anyone could make such a botanical collection beside the Helje or the Avon is another question.

But no such questions were asked by the solemn Russian reader, first, because he did not know the original text, second, because he did not care a fig for botany, and third, because the only thing that interested him in Shakespeare was what German commentators and native radicals had discovered in the way of "eternal problems." So nobody minded what happened to Goneril's lapdogs when the line

> *Tray, Blanche and Sweetheart, see, they bark at me*

was grimly metamorphosed into

> *A pack of hounds is barking at my heels.*

All local color, all tangible and irreplaceable details were swallowed by those hounds.

But, revenge is sweet—even unconscious revenge. The greatest Russian short story ever written is Gogol's "Overcoat" (or "Mantle," or "Cloak," or "She-nel"). Its essential feature, that irrational part which forms the tragic undercurrent of an otherwise meaningless anecdote, is organically connected with the special style in which this story is written: there are weird repetitions of the same absurd adverb, and these repetitions become a kind of uncanny incantation; there are descriptions which look innocent enough until you discover that chaos lies right round the corner, and that Gogol has inserted into this or that harmless sentence a word or a simile that makes a passage burst into a wild display of nightmare fireworks. There is also that groping clumsiness which, on the author's part, is a conscious rendering of the uncouth gestures of our dreams. Nothing of these remains in the prim, and perky, and very matter-of-fact English version (see—and never see again—"The Mantle," translated by Claude Field). The following example leaves me with the impression that I am witnessing a murder and can do nothing to prevent it:

Gogol: . . . his [a petty official's] third or fourth-story flat . . . displaying a few fashionable trifles, *such as a lamp for instance* —trifles purchased by many sacrifices. . . .

Field: . . . fitted with some pretentious articles of furniture purchased, etc. . . .

Tampering with foreign major or minor masterpieces may involve an innocent third party in the farce. Quite recently a famous Russian composer asked me to translate into English a Russian poem which forty years ago he had set to music. The English translation, he pointed out, had to follow closely the very sounds of the text—which text was unfortunately K. Balmont's version of Edgar Allan Poe's "Bells." What Balmont's numerous translations look like may be readily understood when I say that his own work invariably disclosed an almost pathological inability to write one single melodious line. Having at his disposal a sufficient number of hackneyed rhymes and taking up as he rode any hitch-hiking metaphor that he happened to meet, he turned something that Poe had taken considerable pains to compose into something that any Russian rhymester could dash off at a moment's notice. In reversing it into English I was solely concerned with finding English words that would sound like the Russian ones. Now, if somebody one day comes across my English version of that Russian version, he may foolishly retranslate it into Russian so that the Poe-less poem will go on being balmontized until, perhaps, the "Bells" become "Silence." Something still more grotesque happened to Baudelaire's exquisitely dreamy "Invitation au Voyage" ("*Mon enfant, ma soeur, Songe à la douceur. . . .*") The Russian version was due to the pen of Merezhkovski, who had even less poetical talent than Balmont. It began like this:

My sweet little bride,
Let's go for a ride ;

Promptly it begot a rollicking tune and was adopted by all the organ-grinders of Russia. I like to imagine a future French translator of Russian folksongs re-Frenchifying it into:

Viens, mon p'tit,
A Nijni

and so on, *ad malinfinitum*.

Barring downright deceivers, mild imbeciles and impotent poets, there exist, roughly speaking, three types of translators—and this has nothing to do with my three categories of evil; or, rather, any of the three types may err in a similar way. These three are: the scholar who is eager to make the world appreciate the works of an obscure genius as much as he does himself; the well meaning hack; and the professional writer relaxing in the company of a foreign confrere. The scholar will be, I hope, exact and pedantic: footnotes—on the *same* page as the text and not tucked away at the end of the volume—can never be too copious and detailed. The laborious lady translating at the eleventh hour the eleventh volume of somebody's collected works will be, I am afraid, less exact and less pedantic; but the point is not that the scholar commits fewer blunders than a drudge; the point is that as a rule both he and she are hopelessly devoid of any semblance of creative genius. Neither learning nor diligence can replace imagination and style.

Now comes the authentic poet who has the two last assets and who finds relaxation in translating a bit of Lermontov or Verlaine between writing poems of his own. Either he does not know the original language and calmly relies upon the so-called "literal" translation made for him by a far less brilliant but a little more learned person, or else, knowing the language, he lacks the scholar's precision and the professional translator's experience. The main drawback, however, in this case is the fact that the greater his individual talent, the more apt he will be to drown the foreign masterpiece under the sparkling ripples of his own personal style. Instead of dressing up like the real author, he dresses up the author as himself.

We can deduce now the requirements that a translator must possess in order to be able to give an ideal version of a foreign masterpiece. First of all he must have as much talent, or at least the same kind of talent, as the author he chooses. In this, though only in this, respect Baudelaire and Poe or Jhukovski and Schiller made ideal playmates. Second, he must know thoroughly the two nations and the two languages involved and be perfectly acquainted with all details relating to his author's manner and methods; also, with the social background of words, their fashions, history and period associations. This leads to the third point: while having genius and knowledge he must possess the gift of mimicry and be able to act, as it were, the real author's part by impersonating his tricks of demeanor and speech, his ways and his mind, with the utmost degree of verisimilitude.

I have lately tried to translate several Russian poets who had either been badly disfigured by former attempts or who had never been translated at all.

The English at my disposal is certainly thinner than my Russian; the difference being, in fact, that which exists between a semi-detached villa and a hereditary estate, between self-conscious comfort and habitual luxury. I am not satisfied therefore with the results attained, but my studies disclosed several rules that other writers might follow with profit.

I was confronted for instance with the following opening line of one of Pushkin's most prodigious poems:

Yah pom-new chewed-no-yay mg-no-vain-yay

I have rendered the syllables by the nearest English sounds I could find; their mimetic disguise makes them look rather ugly; but never mind; the "chew" and the "vain" are associated phonetically with other Russian words meaning beautiful and important things, and the melody of the line with the plump, golden-ripe "chewed-no-yay" right in the middle and the "m's" and "n's" balancing each other on both sides, is to the Russian ear most exciting and soothing—a paradoxical combination that any artist will understand.

Now, if you take a dictionary and look up those four words you will obtain the following foolish, flat and familiar statement: "I remember a wonderful moment." What is to be done with this bird you have shot down only to find that it is not a bird of paradise, but an escaped parrot, still screeching its idiotic message as it flaps on the ground? For no stretch of the imagination can persuade an English reader that "I remember a wonderful moment" is the perfect beginning of a perfect poem. The first thing I discovered was that the expression "a literal translation" is more or less nonsense. "Yah pom-new" is a deeper and smoother plunge into the past than "I remember," which falls flat on its belly like an inexperienced diver; "chewed-no-yay" has a lovely Russian "monster" in it, and a whispered "listen," and the dative ending of a "sun-beam," and many other fair relations among Russian words. It belongs phonetically and mentally to a certain series of words, and this Russian series does not correspond to the English series in which "I remember" is found. And inversely, "remember," though it clashes with the corresponding "pom-new" series, is connected with an English series of its own whenever real poets do use it. And the central word in Housman's "What are those blue *remembered* hills?" becomes in Russian "vspom-neev-she-yes-yah," a horrible straggly thing, all humps and horns, which cannot fuse into any inner connection with "blue," as it does so smoothly in English, because the Russian sense of blueness belongs to a different series than the Russian "remember" does.

This interrelation of words and non-correspondence of verbal series in different tongues suggests yet another rule, namely, that the three main words of the line draw one another out, and add something which none of them would have had separately or in any other combination. What makes this exchange of secret values possible is not only the mere contact between the words, but their exact position in regard both to the rhythm of the line and to one another. This must be taken into account by the translator.

Finally, there is the problem of the rhyme. "Mg-no-vain-yay" has over two thousand Jack-in-the-box rhymes popping out at the slightest pressure, whereas I cannot think of one to "moment." The position of "mg-no-vain-yay" at the end of the line is not negligible either, due as it is to Pushkin's more or less consciously knowing that he would not have to hunt for its mate. But the position of "moment" in the English line implies no such security; on the contrary he would be a singularly reckless fellow who placed it there.

Thus I was confronted by that opening line, so full of Pushkin, so individual and harmonious; and after examining it gingerly from the various angles here suggested, I tackled it. The tackling process lasted the worst part of the night. I did translate it at last; but to give my version at this point might lead the reader to doubt that perfection be attainable by merely following a few perfect rules.

L'Envoi

I have led you through the wonderland of one century of literature. That this literature is Russian literature cannot much matter to you since you cannot read Russian—and in the art of literature (I understand it as an art) language is the only reality that divides this universal art into national arts. I have continuously stressed the point in this—and other courses—that literature belongs not to the department of general ideas but to the department of specific words and images.

Tolstoy (1828-1910) and Chekhov (1860-1904) are the last writers we could study in detail. Some of you cannot help noticing that from them to our times—or, less pompously, to *my* time—there is still a space of fifty years left. Some of you may wish to explore those years.

A first difficulty for the American student is that the best artists of the age (1900 to 1950) are so abominably translated. The second difficulty for the American student is that in search for a very few masterpieces, most of them in verse (a few poems by Vladimir Mayakovski and Boris Pasternak), he has to wade through an amorphous and monster mass of mediocre stuff whose only purpose is political.

The period itself falls into two parts, roughly

1900-1917
1920-1957

The first period reveals a definite flourishing of all art forms. The lyrical poems of Aleksandr Blok (1880-1921) and an extraordinary novel by Andrey Bely (1880-1934), *Petersburg* (1916), are its most conspicuous ornaments. These two men are experimenters in form, sometimes difficult to understand even for a Russian intelligent reader, and hopelessly mutilated in English versions. In other words, it would be prodigiously difficult for you to tackle these two without knowing the language.

The second part of the period (1920-1957) I have sketched for you in the beginning of this course. It is the period of increasing governmental pressure, of writers guided by governmental decrees, of poets inspired by the political police, of decline in literature. Dictatorship is always conservative in art—so no wonder that such Russian writers who did not escape from Russia produced a kind of literature that is far more bourgeois than the most bourgeois English or French literature. (Only at the very beginning of the Soviet period was there an attempt on the part of propaganda to make people believe that avant-garde politics were somehow synonymous with avant-garde art.) A great number of artists went into exile, and, as it becomes very clear today, the main wonders of Russian literature of our time have been produced by expatriates. This, however, is a somewhat personal subject, and it is here that I shall stop.

APPENDIX:

Nabokov's notes for an exam on Russian literature.

the ~~main~~ wonders of Russian literature of our time ~~have been~~ produced ~~not~~ by expatriates. This however is a somewhat personal subject and its here that I shall stop - and I turn to the subject of the final examination. This final examinal will consist of twenty questions so devised that none of them will take you more than 10 minutes and most of them around five minutes. You must be careful, however, to write briefly and concisely, abbreviating names (AK for Anna, M for Mousehouse, YY for Yvan Ilich, L for Lipa etc) and avoiding any repetition or padding ~~on~~ the recipe and stick to the question. ~~And~~ And remember those of you who have taken notes and read the books have nothing to fear.

Section I (two min.)

D.   M M   1.

Section II (min)

J.   A K Part One   2.   3.

4   5   6   7

Section III (20 min) Group A Only!

A {   A K   8   9   10   11

Section IV (20 min) Group A only!

A K   12   13   14

Section V (10 min)

J.   J J   15

Section VI (10 min)

Ch.   L D   16

Sect VII (40 min)

J R   17   18   19   20

Section VIII (20 min) Group B only!

B {   J. J J   8   9   10   11

Section IX (20 min) Group B only!

Ch.   12   13   14

6

The twenty questions will be distributed
in the following way
    There will be only one question on
Dostoevski and it will deal with
the Mousehole Memoirs It will
take you ten minutes to answer. This
will be section one. Housecite
    The next section, section two, will
contain seven questions and will
probably take you about half an hour. It
will deal with Part One of Anna
Karenin. These two first sections
must be answered by all students
The class is divided into group A, the
majority, and group B that
have taken my 312 course.
    The next two sections, three and
four will consist of seven questions
in all, and will be answered only
by group A. The questions will deal
with the middle and end of Anna Karenin
and will take another half hour or 40 minutes

Section V , one question on the Death of Ivan's will be answered by everybody — take you ten minutes. The last two sections VI and VII will deal with Chekhov, for everybody — one question from Lady with Little D. and four questions from the Ravine ~~_____~~

The alternate questions (seven questions) for group B only will be ~~for~~ ~~Set~~ Sections VIII and IX , four questions from Ivan 20 min and three from the Duel - 20 min

~~I shall mark~~

8

G = grade for course

M = midterm grade

F = final exam (20 answers marked each from 0 to 5)
[5 = perf]

~~mmmmmmmmmmmmmmmmm~~

$$G = \frac{M + 2F}{3}$$

However (or great improvement)
a bonus for genius ∧ or a loss of marks
for a boner may ~~~~ alter
the final exam mark considerably
& mean this formula $G = \frac{M + 2F}{3}$
is fair

$$G = \frac{60 + 140}{3} = \text{ka } 70$$

$$G = \frac{90 + 0}{3} = 30$$

$$G = \frac{90 + 180}{3} = 90$$